MW01171151

The Wushu Doctor, Year One:

An American at Shanghai University of Sport

Dr. Antonio Graceffo

Webantonio67@gmail.com

The Wushu Doctor, Year One: An American at Shanghai University of Sport
by Antonio Graceffo

First published August 5, 2022
By Mary Labita Press

Copyright © 2021 Antonio Graceffo

ISBN: 978-0-9998305-9-8

Dedication and Acknowledgements

This book is dedicated to the martial arts teachers and English teachers who taught me the skills necessary to live this adventure and to write this book. My first English teacher was my grandmother, Mary Labita, who taught me languages and literature and encouraged me to be a writer.

No part of my martial arts journey would have been possible if not for my first and most important martial arts teacher, H. David Collins. He took me in as a young apprentice at age twelve, taught me to fight, taught me military skills, told me stories about the Shaolin Temple, planted a seed of interest in Asian culture, and sent me off as a journeyman, to learn from as many teachers and in as many countries as I could, before returning to him, decades later, to complete my training.

During the more than forty years of my Martial Arts Odyssey, I have had a number of important teachers who positively influenced me. The ones who stand out the most are: Pra Kru Ba, who allowed me to live in his monastery, teaching me Muay Thai and Thai language; Grand Master San Kim Saen, who promoted me to the rank of black krama in Cambodian Bokator; Paddy Carson, my teacher for boxing and kickboxing, who awarded me my second black belt in bradal serey, Khmer kickboxing; Melvin "Chian Yik" Yeoh, who let me live in his MMA academy for a year, helping me develop a record as a professional MMA fighter; Dai Guobing, my Ph.D. advisor at Shanghai University of Sport, who beat me up and challenged me on academic research on martial arts; and finally, Damdin-bazariin Ganbold Coach who taught me Mongolian Bökh wrestling; as well as Dandar Jamsran Coach, my closest coach in Mongolia.

Special thanks and fond memories go to: Guru Mazlan Man, my teacher for Silat Kalam in Malaysia; Japp Leun, my wrestling coach in Cambodia; and Zheng Tong, my wrestling teammate and best friend in China. I also fondly recall the late Bokator master Kru Ros Serey and the late shuai jiao master Wang Wenyong.

Thank you all for helping me on my journey.

Contents

Prologue

Sports and physical education... on the one hand aim to train physique,
on the other hand they can also implement revolutionary
political education on them.

—Zhen Peng,
"The Task and Work of Youth in the Soviet Region Currently,"
***Lenin's Youth* (Vol. 2, No. 11, 1930)**

In September 2013, I walked onto the campus of Shanghai University of Sport, found the Wu Shu Institute and met with my Ph.D. advisor and the department head, Professor Dai Guobing. When I entered his office, he told me to sit. He gave me a glass full of piping hot water, then sprinkled some herbs into it. The glass burned my fingers. Unsure if it'd be a breach of etiquette to set it on the edge of his desk, I just kept passing it from hand to hand, hoping it'd cool off at some point.

He took a book titled *Shaolin Kung Fu* from the shelf and handed it to me. Calling me by my Chinese name, as he usually did, he said: "Āndōng-ní, do you know what Shaolin Kung Fu is?"

I got excited, thinking I'd nail this one. "Yes, I've studied at Shaolin Temple twice." I responded.

He nodded. "I see. So, you think Shaolin Kung Fu is related to Shaolin Temple?"

I wasn't so sure of myself now. He was still waiting for an answer, so, weakly, I replied "Yes."

He smiled, then asked: "And who lives in temples?"

"Monks," I answered.

"So, Shaolin Kung Fu is something practiced by monks?"

I nodded.

"There are thousands and thousands of monks in China. Do they all practice kung fu?"

I shook my head.

"Is Buddhism practiced by monks?" he asked.

"Yes," I answered.

"So, is kung fu related to Buddhism?"

"Sort of…" I thought, but said nothing. He stood up and did some martial arts movements, then asked me: "Does striking someone with your palm have anything to do with Buddhism?"

"No, it does not," I admitted.

"Who brought Shaolin Kung Fu to Shaolin Temple?" he asked.

"Da Mo," I answered, giving the Chinese name for Bodhidharma.

"Da Mo came from India. Do they have Shaolin Kung Fu in India?"

"No," I answered, wondering if I should jump out the window.

"And India is Hindu. So, how does Shaolin Kung Fu relate to Buddhism, if it's a Hindu art?"

I had no answer.

"So, what is Shaolin Kung Fu?" he repeated. This time, he didn't even wait for me to answer. He explained: "This is the nature of wushu Ph.D. research. We seek to answer such questions as 'What is Shaolin Kung Fu?'"

He then gave me three years to answer that question. And this was the beginning of my very strange life as a martial arts academic.

In June 2016, I became the 15th foreigner and the first American to earn a doctoral degree from Shanghai University of Sport. I was awarded a Ph.D. in wushu after writing and defending my dissertation, *A Cross Cultural Comparison of Chinese and Western Wrestling*, in Chinese.

·•●•·

Between 2001 and 2012, I traveled throughout Asia, successively living, training, and fighting in martial arts schools and temples in Taiwan, China, Thailand, Cambodia, Korea, Burma, Philippines, Laos, and Vietnam. Most of the time, I lived a hand-to-mouth existence, surviving by writing books and magazine articles, or appearing in TV shows and even a few movies. When I found myself in a country I liked, or when I needed cash, I'd stop, dust off my university diplomas, and find a teaching job. I'd teach for anything from a few months to a year, until the call of the road once again overcame me. Then I'd set off to the next martial arts destination.

In 2011, I was in Cambodia and running low on cash when a gym owner called me from Malaysia. He asked me if I was willing to serve as the celebrity guest judge for Malaysia's first ever professional Mixed Martial Arts (MMA) tournament. I thought about it for a few minutes and responded: "No, but would you allow me to fight in it?" I was 44 years old.

With the help of sponsors, I put together the first MMA team in Cambodia's history. It represented the Cambodian martial art of bokator, of which I was one of the first two non-Cambodians to attain black-belt status. Bokator Grand Master San Skim Saen and I led a team of three Cambodian bokator fighters to the tournament in Kuala Lumpur. I fought two fights that day, winning one and losing the other.

After the fight, a friend of my Malaysian martial arts master, Guru Mazlan Man, congratulated me on my win and asked me if I had any plans.

In those days, I never had plans. In fact, I only had enough money in my pocket to pay for one more night in the hotel. Everything I owned was in my backpack.

This man, who turned out to be a *datuk* (a titled bestowed by Malaysia's head of state, similar to "lord"), told me he was planning on doing some business in Cambodia, and also that his doctor had advised him that he was going to die if he didn't start exercising. He invited me to live with his family, construct a home gym for him, and train him each morning. The rest of each day I'd have off, so I could pursue my MMA training. My only other duty would be to periodically fly to Cambodia with him and act as bodyguard and interpreter.

The other offer I received was to join a Wing Chun MMA team, fighting out of Selangor in Malaysia, and begin my career as a full-time professional fighter. Because the *datuk* lived in nearby Kuala Lumpur and had a driver who could take me to daily training sessions in Selangor, I was able to accept both offers. Over the next few months, the coach of the Wing Chun team booked me for several fights. I won all of them.

Wing Chun is a southern Chinese martial art, and the only art that Bruce Lee studied formally. Wing Chun practitioners often cite Lee as an example of how effective their art is. But, in reality, Lee learned and mixed many martial arts styles along the way, formulating a system that used what worked, while throwing away techniques which didn't. Classical Wing Chun is full of the latter. The longer I stayed with the Wing Chun team, the more preposterous it seemed that they were trying to use Wing Chun in MMA fights. Because I kept winning, I was exempted from the Wing Chun training. I just focused on learning jiu-jitsu. The rest of the guys were required to train and use Wing Chun and they kept losing. At one-point, local media published gym statistics, and saw that I accounted for about 70 percent of the gym's victories. Questioning how I could improve in that environment, I began to look for other options.

Meanwhile, things with the *datuk* weren't going well. He refused to train or even follow a diet, and was more and more frequently admitted to hospital or put on bed rest. He was clearly dying, and unwilling to do anything about it. He'd also promised me a chance to manage his businesses in Cambodia, but it looked like those businesses were never going to materialize.

Around this time, I had a short-term job hosting the pilot of an MMA reality TV show about Malaysians competing for a spot on a professional fight team. One of the competitors was Melvin Yeoh, a coach who owned a gym, the Ultimate MMA Academy, in Johor Bahru, Malaysia, right on the Singaporean border. Melvin's gym was becoming famous for hosting their own fight series, called Ultimate Beat Down, and for winning fights all over the country. When Melvin offered me the chance to live in his gym, train full time, and fight regularly, I accepted.

With Melvin as my coach, I improved greatly. I liked the discipline of living in the academy, training two or three times per day, and just eating, recovering, and studying fight videos in between. Melvin worked as a teacher in a Malaysian government high school. One day, he rounded up all of the misbehaving ethnic Chinese boys in his school, brought them to me, and said: "They're your students. Teach them." So I became a coach.

I fought often, and won all of my fights. Eventually, however, injuries began to accumulate. My knees were shot, and I couldn't run anymore. I trained around these problems, and continued fighting. My elbows became too painful to do pushups, so I trained around that, too. I couldn't work the heavy bag anymore, but I kept fighting. On the night I walked into my toughest fight, I couldn't comfortably throw punches or kicks and my back was bothering me, so I also couldn't lift my opponent. I fought terribly, pushing my opponent against the cage, controlling him and scoring points, but not doing much damage. The next morning, I woke up with my trophy, but knew that I had to take a break from training and fighting or I was going to get seriously hurt.

I began looking for jobs and was miraculously offered one at Shanghai University. I say miraculously, but actually, I had a bachelor's degree, as well as a graduate diploma in business and a graduate diploma in Teaching English to Speakers of Other Languages (TESOL). I also spoke Chinese, which wasn't a requirement but was certainly a plus. The issue with my resume, however, was that it'd been several years since I'd taught. It turned out, however, that the dean who'd hired me misunderstood my role at the Ultimate MMA Academy, thinking that it was a type of private high school. That's why he hired me.

The job provided housing and a good salary, but I had to pay my own visa and flight ticket. I'd had been writing for *Black Belt Magazine* for over a decade, and they paid me quarterly. One of my book publishers paid me annually, the other semi-annually. Once a year, all three sources of income would hit in the same month and I'd be rich for a day. Luckily, the cash came together in June, as it usually did, in time for me to get myself sorted to fly to China and start work in July.

The dean who'd hired me at Shanghai University became an important influence in my life, encouraging me to go for my Ph.D. I began applying to programs. After nearly a year of teaching at Shanghai University, I'd achieved financial health, but wanted to get my body back into shape and start fighting again. I discovered that a completely separate university, Shanghai University of Sport, had a wrestling team, and I wondered if they'd let me pay money to go there and train.

I mentioned this on social media, and a long-time Facebook friend who I'd never actually met wrote me saying that his wife knew the person in charge of foreign student admissions at SUS. I got a phone number, called it, and made an appointment. First, I had to meet with the head of foreign student services, Chu Laoshi (Teacher Chu). I explained to him my desire to wrestle and asked if there was a program. He listened intently and answered, "Your Chinese is good. Do you have a master's?" When I told him that I had two graduate diplomas from the UK, he asked: "Would you like a full scholarship for your Ph.D?"

My jaw dropped. I couldn't believe what I was hearing. "Yes! Of course, I would," I blurted out. He had me fill in some forms, then brought me to see Piao Laoshi (Teacher Piao). Piao Laoshi told me they were looking forward to having me as a Ph.D. candidate.

There were many more hoops to jump through, before I'd have the acceptance letter in my hands, but in principle, I knew that I was about to have a dream come true. I'd always dreamed of completing a university degree taught in Chinese. It seemed like an incredible intellectual challenge that would also greatly improve my Chinese fluency. I'd never wrestled in college in the US, but now maybe I could wrestle in college in China. And finally, the department that I'd applied to was the Wu Shu Institute. Beijing Sport University also had an institution conducting research on martial arts, but Shanghai University of Sport was the only place in China (and, to my knowledge, in the world) where you could earn a Ph.D. in martial arts.

Chapter 1
Spider-Man and the Road to the Sport University

"Everybody is to do exercise," physical exercise and education were
systematically promoted in the army, schools, counties, and villages controlled
by the communists.

—**Fan Hong,**
Footbinding, Feminism and Freedom:
The Liberation of Women's Bodies in Modern China

By spring 2013, after nearly a year teaching at Shanghai University, I began to slowly ease myself back into training with a Mixed Martial Arts (MMA) team in Shanghai. An American training at that gym, AJ Richardi, was also studying sanda and Chinese language as a non-degree student at Shanghai University of Sport (SUS). When I first found out about SUS, I planned to work hard for a year, save money, and do what he was doing: pay to study there as a non-degree student. Now it seemed I wouldn't have to. SUS had offered me a full scholarship to do a Ph.D., as well as a monthly stipend. And, of course, I could get free full-time wrestling training.

I applied to the Wu Shu Institute, which conducts scholarly research about martial arts. The university's other institutes include the Olympic Sports Training Department. Although the Wu Shu Institute was the place for martial arts research, it only covered Chinese martial arts. Other martial arts were taught as majors in the Olympic Sports Training Department, including taekwondo, judo, fencing, Greco-Roman wrestling, freestyle wrestling, and boxing. Karate was added later, after it was announced that karate would be an exhibition sport in the 2020 Tokyo Olympics.

Martial arts within the Wu Shu Institute included: Wushu Taolu (kung fu performance forms), martial arts for film, tai chi (moving meditation), qigong (health martial art), sanda (kickboxing), and shuai jiao (Chinese wrestling).

Wushu Taolu, the performance aspect of kung fu forms, was one of the largest majors, and the one most people outside of the martial arts world would be familiar with, as it's the component of martial arts that appears in movies, TV shows, and martial arts demonstrations. Movie-making majors within the institute learned to do stunts for kung fu movies; most of them had a background in Wushu Taolu.

Tai chi, the moving meditation aspect of Chinese martial arts, was also offered as a major. Tai chi is a slow form often practiced by older people in parks in the early morning. Qigong, which combines body movement and postures meant to promote health, was also offered. Some argue that qigong shouldn't be considered a martial art; this is the exact kind of question that researchers in the institute concern themselves with. There was often a blurring of tai chi and qigong in terms of practice, and a tremendous overlap in practitioners of those two arts, as well as of WuShu Taolu. I had the distinct impression that while all of the other martial arts in the institute could be practiced individually, very few people were exclusively practicing qigong. The qigong people tended to be tai chi majors who also practiced qigong to varying degrees.

Sanda is Chinese kickboxing. It's very similar to Muay Thai, except that sanda doesn't allow knee or elbow strikes. However, it allows throws, which are largely based on Chinese wrestling. Sanda differs from MMA in that it doesn't include ground fighting. Most of China's professional MMA fighters do come from a sanda background, however, because it's the only sport within the Wu Shu Institute that has actual fighting and a professional fight component. This always made sanda sort of the odd-man-out within the institute. While sanda was my favorite art, after wrestling, it was clearly the one held in the lowest regard by the old martial arts masters and administrators. Conservatives tended to see sanda as being less traditional and more influenced by Western boxing, kickboxing, and Muay Thai.

My major was shuai jiao wrestling, although I also conducted extensive research and training in sanda. Shuai jiao wrestlers wear uniforms very similar to judo gi. Competitors are permitted to grip the opponent's jacket, as in judo, or his belt or his body or legs, as in wrestling. The goal is to throw the opponent. There's no pin and no ground fighting. A throw or the best three-of-five throws could be a win. The fact that my Ph.D. advisor, Professor Dai, allowed me to have a wrestling major was a huge political issue.

Education, publishing, media, and even sports and martial arts are closely regulated by the Chinese government. Martial arts were once frowned upon by the communist establishment and all but abolished, as they were seen to be too closely tied to the superstitions and religions that predated communism. In the 1990s, after the Jet Li-starring *The Shaolin Temple* became an incredible success, the PRC government saw a chance to use martial arts and the Shaolin name to project the country's soft power. Consequently, martial arts were brought back into prominence. And like everything else that's controlled by the Chinese Communist Party, there had to be "the naming of parts" — for martial arts to exist and serve the state and the people, the proper vocabulary had to be agreed upon.

Many people outside of China are familiar with the term kung fu. This word is downplayed by administrators, because it smacks of traditionalism and has religious ties. It could suggest that practitioners bore allegiance to or believed in something greater than the Communist Party. Instead, the word wushu was adopted. It exists alongside kung fu, but in China wushu tends to mean the government-approved syllabus of martial arts forms, devoid of any significant religious connotations or a larger belief system.

Ahead of the 2008 Olympics, China decided it wanted to become the dominant force in world sports. This meant pumping money and support into the training of Olympic and international sports. It also meant that Chinese sports, largely practiced in China, took a back seat to sports which could win gold medals at international events.

Adherents of the traditional martial arts argued that, since martial arts were part of China's heritage, they deserved political and financial support. The government didn't see it that way, and instead focused on creating a nationwide gold-medal factory.

At SUS, the Chinese shuai jiao wrestling team was part of the Sports Training Department, where students hoped to become PE teachers or coaches. And rather than being wushu practitioners, most of shuai jiao wrestling team members were former Greco-Roman or freestyle wrestlers who'd failed to make the cut for university or national teams. The Wu Shu Institute wanted control of shuai jiao, so when I presented my research topic, *A Cross Cultural Comparison of Chinese and Western Wrestling*, the dean of the Wu Shu Institute was pleased to find that I'd be conducting research on shuai jiao. He saw this as bolstering his argument that shuai jiao should fall under his department.

Most of the 2013 spring semester was taken up by the long, arduous application process for SUS, as well as my teaching job at Shanghai University. These two universities are completely unrelated to one another. Whenever I told people I was going to study at SUS, they always assumed it was the PE department of the university where I was teaching. SUS was a full-on sports university with very few academic majors outside of sport.

Most of the students studying at SUS qualified through sports competition results and entrance exams; the latter had both written and physical elements. At the bachelor's degree level, academic standards in most departments were low. Sports Journalism was the major with the highest academic entrance requirements. Later, I became friends with several Sports Journalism majors, and discovered that many of them had no sports background at all.

The other academic major was English. The PRC government was pushing every university to increase their level of English teaching and encouraged them to offer English degrees. Normally, students have to meet relatively high academic requirements to major in English, but at SUS the requirements were extremely low. Some English majors at SUS had no interest in sport; they were there because they couldn't get into any other school.

·· ● ··

That spring, while struggling to get my body back into shape, my other preoccupation was preparing for the Chinese-language exam, called the HSK.

I found that, even after a year's layoff, I could handle the punches and the sparring, but I was having trouble recovering after wrestling. In MMA sparring, you only get thrown a few times. In wrestling training, by contrast, you get thrown countless times and are physically engaged every second. My style is to press the engagement and force the opponent to carry my weight, slowly wearing him down. I love charging in and using dirty boxing and standup grappling, instead of the kicks and jiu-jitsu preferred by many MMA fighters. Fights last a mere 15 minutes, whereas training goes on for hours. Consequently, wrestling training/sparring is much harder, in many ways, than a real fight.

At the MMA gym in Shanghai, the Muay Thai teacher, who came from Thailand, was happy to find out that I spoke Thai. He thus gave me a lot of personal attention and training. One night, he had us doing footwork, saying, "If a fighter has good footwork, he can move around the ring and it looks beautiful… If you see a fighter, lumbering across the ring, charging like a bull, eating punches, it's very ugly." He didn't say my name, but I know he meant me.

Later, he was holding pads way up above my head, telling me to kick and punch them. When I complained, he asked me how much I weighed. I told him 91 kg (201 lbs). He responded: "There are no 91-kg fighters as short as you." He had a point. But I still felt a little bad about my weight. It made me want to punch something really hard and then overeat.

A contradiction about living and working in Shanghai is that, while everything was interesting and different, everything was just the same as it is everywhere else. I still had to commute to work, do my job, commute home, buy groceries, cook, eat, and live, just as I had in New York. I lived on one of three campuses of Shanghai University, in a serviced apartment, the top floor of which was reserved for foreign teachers. My neighbor was an American guy who I referred to as Dr. Cowboy, because he always wore Tony Lama boots. He was actually a lawyer, but demanded that everyone call him "doctor" because he had a doctor of jurisprudence degree. Apart from his very expensive boots, he was always dressed like he was doing his laundry, even when he was teaching. Even though he'd been in China for six years, he didn't know a word of Chinese. We worked in different departments, on different campuses, so I rarely saw him, but on those occasions that I did, he always seemed to be belittling a new Chinese girlfriend, less than half his age.

At one point, the teachers from Shanghai University had to attend a briefing with the immigration police about how and how not to behave in China. As Dr. Cowboy had attended this meeting six years in a row, they asked him to be a guest speaker. He arrived late, and when he saw the cops sitting up on the stage, waiting for the meeting to begin, he made a big show of greeting them like old friends, to show how acclimated he was. They spoke to him in Mandarin, and as he didn't speak the language, he responded in gibberish. It wasn't that he was attempting to speak Mandarin, but rather, that he was attempting to sound like he was speaking the language, uttering long strings of "Bing bong, ching, chong..." with a healthy smattering of "Har, shh, shh, shar," to approximate a Beijing accent. It was horribly offensive. He also had no grasp of the culture. He was handing bananas to the cops — gifts which, in China, are a horrible insult, because it means you're calling them monkeys.

He then took the microphone, wearing his cowboy boots and crappy T-shirt, and gave the most condescending speech on how we should behave in China. He opened by saying that we all had to learn the culture and not be ugly Americans. I looked around at the teachers from Shanghai University. All of us were wearing business attire, and about a quarter of us were of Chinese descent. The rest, like me, had lived in China before and spoke Chinese. Despite being the least appropriate and the least Chinese person in the room, he was the one that the immigration police trusted. This was a huge lesson about Chinese culture. If they know you, you're an expert. If they don't know you, your credentials don't matter. The Chinese concept of *guānxi* (relationships) is a bit exaggerated in the Western media, but it's very true that personal relationships supersede most other qualities.

After the meeting, we teachers boarded a bus and headed off to a hospital for our health check. We were convinced the doctors randomly assigned diseases and ailments. We kept joking they'd tell a male teacher he was pregnant. When we first arrived at the hospital, they gave us a paper, telling us how to behave:

1. *Please don't make noise in physical exam.* – I always scream when they take blood.

2. *Lady may not wear dress please.* – And man?

3. *If you want to increase any physical exam's items, you may pay the money for yourself* – So, if I don't like the results, I guess I can buy better ones.

4. *You may choose free department in order not to waste your time.* – No idea what this one meant.

5. *For X-ray, without any decorations such as necklace, clothing of cotton.* – Decoration? What am I, a Christmas tree?

In the end, the doctors told all of us that we had fatty livers and were in danger of dying, but then they just let us go home.

Meanwhile, my application process at SUS kept hitting stonewalls and dead-ends. The university would send me lists of requirements which seemed impossible, and they'd go weeks at a time without answering my questions. I often imagined that they'd decided not to accept me, and I began to make alternative plans. Finally — despite my impending death due to a fatty liver — I received my acceptance letter from SUS, and was invited to come take an admissions exam and give a presentation, before a board of professors, about my research proposal.

I was elated for about eight seconds, but I had to use Google Translate to understand the acceptance letter. I thought it might be time to buckle down and improve my Chinese reading skills.

· •●• ·

My Chinese-speaking and listening abilities were reasonably good, but I struggled to read anything. This was because, when I originally learned Chinese in Taiwan, they gave us a choice of learning speaking and listening only or also learning reading and writing. They warned us, however, that if we chose to do all four skills, our progress would be much slower. I chose listening and speaking only; sure enough, six months later, I could function and was beginning to be able to slowly build friendships in Chinese, while other students who'd chosen the reading and writing option were lucky to learn three or four new words per day. Where I was doing a chapter per week, they might need a week to work through a single reading text.

After learning Chinese in Taiwan, I went to live in Shaolin Temple in 2003. There I was fully immersed in spoken Mandarin, so I improved a great deal, but I still couldn't read much more than my own name and a few basic characters.

After Shaolin, I wound up in Bangkok, where I worked on a linguistics research project about a learning methodology called Automatic Language

Growth (ALG). The method was based on a number of older methods, including the silent way and the natural way, and on Dr. Stephen Krashen's comprehensible input hypothesis. The basic concept was that all babies become fluent in their native language, no matter how difficult the rest of us think that language is. Babies achieve this miracle by first listening for about six months before beginning to speak their native tongue. The idea is that input, not output, determines language learning. Therefore, listening to a language for a period of 1,000 to 2,500 hours should result in native-like comprehension and pronunciation.

To this end, since returning to China in the summer of 2012, I'd been collecting Chinese-dubbed American movies and cartoons, to watch and listen to. I tried watching local TV, but I hated most of it and had no context for understanding. The subtleties of Chinese comedy shows are lost on most foreigners. Chinese comedies not only have "bonk" noises. They also have "wonk, wonk" noises and "wha, wha, whaaaaa." The combination of the three, arranged with the precision of a symphony, tells us when the activity on screen is funny, so we'll know when to laugh.

Instead of trying to learn from Chinese TV, I chose Marvel movies and cartoons. Knowing the stories made the Chinese-language audio somewhat comprehensible input. Just listening to radio wouldn't help me learn a language, because there'd be no context for the meanings of foreign words. But with movies and TV shows, you can guess from the visuals. And if you watch stories you're familiar with, it becomes even easier and more useful.

In the little bit of free time I had, I went to various markets in Shanghai, looking for dubbed movies to add to my collection. Finding a boxed set of *Tintin*, the cartoon TV series, was a godsend. When you're trying to accumulate 2,500 hours of listening, you can only watch the same 90-minute movie so many times. The *Tintin* set had 31 episodes, or about 15 hours of listening. If I could sit through it about five times, that would be about 75 hours. The same was true with The Avengers, X-Men, or *Star Trek*. One reason I preferred cartoons, apart from loving them, was that cartoon series ran multiple seasons. The Avengers gave me 52 episodes for a total of 26 hours of listening. If I did that five times, it was 130 hours. The animated *Batman* series ran to 85 episodes...

Eventually, as my Mandarin improved, I did watch some local TV shows, but — like everything else in China — TV is political. The Chinese market and the Chinese people began opening up to more and more American TV shows and movies. Sitcoms like *Friends* and *The Big Bang Theory* were beloved by their Chinese fans. In the US, these were merely considered good shows, but for young Chinese people, they represented dreams and aspirations. Under Xi Jinping, however, the government began moving toward a stricter conservatism, setting quotas on foreign movies and all but banning foreign TV shows.

To get around these restrictions, Chinese TV production companies tried making local versions of American TV shows. One of the most famous was *iPartment* (Àiqíng Gōngyù), which was meant to be the Chinese version of Friends. The first episode, in particular, borrowed (or stole) a lot from its American counterpart. The show became the subject of new legislation, protecting US copyrights of translated materials. The format noticeably changes a few episodes in, but during its five-season run, it maintained a feel very similar to *Friends*, without being an exact copy.

The other Chinese series which I enjoyed and bought as a complete set was *Home With Kids* (Jiā Yǒu Érnǚ), which was similar to the American show *Growing Pains*. These two shows were some of the few sitcoms that survived on Chinese TV, and both ended relatively soon.

Content censorship became so strict that it was nearly impossible to produce shows that told stories. Soap opera-type dreams set in the distant past were popular, but they had to walk a thin line, glorifying China's ancient history without glorifying the concept of monarchy, and without suggesting that China had good times before communism. Shows about how China single-handedly won World War II, easily defeating Japan, were also popular. But again, apart from showing China as the victor and the Japanese as evil, barbaric aggressors, the shows had to avoid any positive message about the government of the Nationalist Republic of China, founded in 1912. Instead, the Chinese Communist Party had to supply the heroes.

Contests, many copied from the US, were popular for a while, but then the government cracked down on those, saying they promoted bad values. In the end, local TV schedules were filled with singing shows and carefully censored dramas. Inevitably, with a few other exceptions, such as *Secret Society of Men* (*Nánrén Bāng*) and a few Taiwan drama series I was able to pick up at the market, the bulk of my 2,500 hours of listening was achieved using American movies and cartoons dubbed into Chinese. I'd put my headphones on and listen to the shows during my commute, while I working out in the gym, or when doing paperwork in the office.

·•●••

It's not uncommon for schools, universities, and other government buildings to have neither heating nor AC. All winter, people wear their coats indoors. The program I taught in at Shanghai University was a joint venture with an Australian university, so we had heating and AC. Oddly, in the dead of winter, it wasn't unusual to walk into a classroom or an office where the heating was on full blast, and find my Chinese colleagues wearing their coats, with the windows wide open. I always joked with them: "You know, if you closed the windows, you wouldn't have to wear your coats." On the first hot day of the year, the AC wouldn't be on yet, but these same co-workers would be sitting in a sweltering office with the windows closed.

One day, I went to the office to ask why nearly two thirds of my students had given me notes, saying that they'd be out for three days. According to rumors, the students were required to donate blood. That night, I received a message from the administration, saying that students shouldn't be marked absent, as they were granted three days bedrest. I didn't understand why they needed three days to recover after donating blood, unless the doctors were taking a few pints or liters from each student. I guess they had a quota to meet.

The MMA gym had scheduled a fight night and offered me a fight. I agreed, but then I twisted my ankle in training and couldn't walk for several days. I sat in my room, watching countless hours of Chinese. The insanity of the fighter's mind is that I wanted to fight so badly, in spite of my injury, that I decided that if I could walk the length of the ring (about five meters or 16 feet), I'd go ahead and fight. I further rationalized this distance down by saying that, while the ring is five meters across, each fighter is standing one meter from the ropes when the fight starts, so actually I'd only need to cross three meters to take my opponent down. On the other hand, I'd never gone into a fight so out of shape or so injured before. But it seemed like a more realistic test of my skills. If I got attacked on the street, I wouldn't ask the mugger: "Can we reschedule this for eight weeks from now, when I'm better prepared?"

I limped down the street for a haircut, clinging to the sides of buildings as I went. Whenever I went for a haircut, I'd listen to the conversations of the people around me. The barbers talked constantly about absolutely nothing. Each time I went, I was amazed that not a single news item found its way into their chatter. The most interesting thing I heard one day was the girl saying that every time she went home to her province, her parents were happy to see her. "You know why?" she asked the guy in the next chair, "Because I bring them money. Last time, I brought them RMB 2,000 RMB [about US$ 320]."

That same day, the TV news was reporting an earthquake that had killed 164 people in southwestern China. The quake never came up in any of these barbershop conversations.

Two seconds after I got back to my room, the cleaning ladies knocked. Japan and Korea are extremely hygienic countries, China less so. The cleaning ladies would take one bucket of clean water to each floor of the building, and clean all of the rooms with it. By the time they got to my room, not only was the water dirty, but it smelled really bad. They never dusted horizontal surfaces and didn't use cleansers or soap of any kind on the floor or in the bathroom. Fortunately, they were also never in the room very long, so the stench of the cleaning water would quickly dissipate. On this day, they were in there for under two minutes — a personal best!

On fight night, I limped to the gym, only to discover that, although the spectators were all there, the opponent gym had canceled. So the evening wouldn't be a total loss, our coach said we should fight each other. The coach had me fight AJ Richardi, the American studying sanda at SUS. He was a good kickboxer but didn't know a great deal of wrestling, so we agreed to wear the larger boxing gloves, rather than the smaller MMA gloves which had free fingers and made it easier for me to grapple. I had to be helped into the ring, because I couldn't stand up very well. I leaned against the ropes, and when the referee said "Fight!" I hobbled quickly across the ring, ate one roundhouse kick to the head, caught AJ in a bearhug, and took him to the ground, landing on top. This was good news, because it took the weight off of my injured leg, but because of the big gloves, AJ was able to squeeze his arms together, trapping my hands, and we were just stalemated, with me on top and neither of us able to do anything. When the referee yelled "Break!" my heart sank. I'd have to stand up and start over.

While I was gripping the rope, standing unsteadily, waiting for the ref to give the signal, I kept expecting AJ's corner to yell "Sweep the leg, Johnny!"

Once again, when the referee shouted "Fight!" I limped over, and caught AJ in a bear hug. He trapped my arms, and we stood in a stalemate. If my leg hadn't been injured, I could easily have lifted him and slammed him from this position, but truth be told, he was actually holding me up and didn't know it. In the end, I think I got the win because of the one takedown and the top control I'd had on the ground. But it was an awful fight. The good news was that AJ and I got to be friends, and that this friendship would be very important to my future in China.

· • ● · ·

The next day, the sports university contacted me, asking that I rewrite my Ph.D. dissertation research proposal. The new proposal was to create the most comprehensive book on Chinese wrestling styles ever written. In the end, my proposal looked like the wish list of a 14-year-old Bruce Lee fan, with training at Shaolin Temple, wrestling in Inner Mongolia, Turkic wrestling in the Taklamakan Desert... and much more. While I was writing my proposal, I realized that no one had ever done this before — but also that I had a very weird skill set, which fit this research almost perfectly.

I put on my headphones, listening to the 1981 *Spider-Man* cartoon series dubbed into Mandarin, and walked to the mall. There I did something stupid. I went into a sports store, thinking I could buy sports equipment. Obviously, they only sold sports fashion. Eventually, I'd discover that the two shops outside the gates of the sports university were the only places to buy sports equipment.

Walking back to my room, I broke 800 hours of listening practice. As a result, my listening ability was head-and-shoulders above most foreigners who'd lived in China for years, but I still couldn't read very effectively. While I was fairly certain I'd be able to sit through lectures at the university, I didn't know how I'd take notes from the blackboard or read my homework. This was a problem I'd struggle with throughout the next 1,700 hours of listening.

Even though my listening was good for a non-Chinese, it was nothing compared to a native speaker. When I watched the news, sometimes I understood an entire report. Sometimes I understood bits and pieces, but couldn't piece the overall picture together. Other times I was completely lost. Sometimes, however, Jupiter aligned with Mars and the comprehension came effortlessly. On my best days, I'd have the TV news running in the bedroom while I was shaving in the bathroom, and without even seeing the screen, and only half listening, I'd understand the whole report.

I saw a documentary about the education of deaf students in Chinese elementary schools. In addition to using sign language, the teachers talked constantly in Chinese. They knew the students wouldn't understand most of what they said, but even if the students understood a little, it was a help in communicating. This led me to wonder why so many Chinese, when talking to foreigners, refused to speak? They used hand gestures and I generally had no idea what they were trying to convey. The other thing many people did was ignore my Chinese and try to use school English to communicate, although they couldn't express themselves and had zero English listening ability.

Once I entered a bank and told the security guard, in Mandarin, that I wanted to change money. He started doing a pantomime, dancing, pointing at a chair, pointing at his watch, pointing at a counter... All through it, I kept interrupting him, saying: "I speak Chinese. Can you please just tell me in Chinese?" He ignored that, and kept pointing at things. At some point he blurted out in English, "You..." And as much as that helped, I still wasn't sure what he was on about, so I walked over to a counter, and asked the employee about changing money. She explained, in Mandarin, that the money changer would reopen at 1:30 p.m., so I should come back then. I asked her why the security guard hadn't told me that, and she said, "He didn't know you spoke Chinese." But I pointed out, "Then how did he understand my question?"

There's a YouTube video titled "But We're Speaking Japanese," in which foreigners living in Japan try to order at a restaurant, but the waitress keeps saying, in Japanese, "Sorry, I do not speak English." I faced the same problem as them: Having a foreign face meant that local people assumed they couldn't understand you, so they tuned out your Japanese or Mandarin and then tried to use broken English or hand gestures.

At the bus stop, I'd ask someone if the 9 a.m. bus had already left, and they'd give me a bunch of hand gestures and possibly blurt out some random English words like, "Morning, traffic, margarine..." From that, I was meant to understand that the bus had already left, so I'd need to take the 9:30 a.m. bus. If they'd just spoken Chinese, we could have communicated much better.

After I began my Ph.D. studies, I figured out that this was a major reason why Asian-Americans or students from Vietnam often learned Chinese faster. It wasn't innate ability, linguistic similarities, or genetics, but the locals' greater willingness to speak Mandarin to a foreigner with an Asian face, regardless of whether that person understood or not.

A Chinese-American professor at Shanghai University didn't speak a word of Chinese. When I'd take her grocery shopping or help her at the bank, the workers would ignore me, then speak to her in Chinese, which she didn't understand. Then I'd translate for her. She'd tell me in English what she wanted, and I'd tell the workers, who would ignore me…

Apart from martial arts, linguistics is my other lifelong interest. Before being accepted to the Ph.D. program at SUS, I applied to linguistics Ph.D. programs at a number of universities in Asia, finally being accepted by one in Thailand and another in Malaysia. My research proposal consisted of tracing the origin of the Cham language, which is still spoken in unique communities scattered around Southeast Asia. Both universities offered me a scholarship if I'd change my research topic to ESL (English as a second language), so I declined. But the dream was still in my mind.

While I wouldn't be studying linguistics at SUS, getting into a Ph.D. program in China, taught entirely in Chinese, and having the opportunity to attend classes with Chinese students, is a linguist's second-biggest dream come true. The biggest dream of most linguists is to be dropped in the middle of the Amazon somewhere, surrounded by some tribe most people had never heard of, with vague instructions to "Learn their language. Invent an alphabet. Write a dictionary. Translate some books. And we'll be back to pick you up in 30 years."

Toward the end of April, I was called to a panel interview at SUS, chaired by my advisor, the dean of the Wu Shu Institute, Professor Dai Guobing. All of the other doctoral candidates were Chinese and most worked as kung fu subject instructors at other Chinese universities or schools. The interview was actually called a "test" in Chinese. We were given questions in advance, then we all sat nervously in a room, preparing our answers, while waiting to be called. When your name came up, you went into a large lecture hall, where a panel of professors listened to your answers, then cross-examined you. Obviously, the whole thing was in Chinese.

The interviews took at least ten minutes per person, and I was number nine of nine. While the others were preparing their answers, I was wondering what the questions said. I was able to read a lot of the paper, but not all of it. At one point, a secretary came in and asked if we'd filled in a stack of forms that we needed for the interview. The coordinator of student enrollment had sent me all of the forms by email, so I'd used my computer and translation software to fill them in and print them. This was one of my coping strategies for functioning in a language where my literacy was at an incredibly low level.

I handed her the forms. To my horror, she said, "Here's one more." She gave me a new form and my heart sunk. I was actually able to read all of the questions, but didn't know how to write the answers in Chinese. Coping mechanism no. 2 for functioning in Chinese academia is, whenever I need to write something, I'd look through other documents, search for the words I need, then copy them. I spread my documents out on the table, rifling through them, painfully copying characters one at a time, to answer the questions. My Chinese writing looked like a third grader's, with huge, disjointed letters. Finally, the secretary offered to fill in the form for me.

While we were waiting to be called, one of the other candidates told me that his research area was the martial arts of the Miao ethnic minority (also called H'Mong in English). I thought that was a cool area to specialize in. It also overlapped with my research area of all forms of grappling practiced in China, including the wrestling forms of ethnic minorities such as Uyghurs, Mongolians, the Yi people, and the PRC's ethnic Korean population, as well as the Han majority.

One doctoral candidate nervously said, "*Wǒ wàngle dài jiàn.*" I clearly understood what he said: "I forgot to bring a sword." But you almost never hear people saying that, so I decided he must have said, "*Wŏ wàngle dài qián*" (I forgot to bring money) — much more normal and it sounded almost the same. Just as I was opening my wallet, another candidate handed him a sword, and said "You can use mine."

This is a perfect example of why Chinese people often don't understand foreigners when we speak Mandarin. Research has shown you only listen to one in five words in your own language. The rest of communication is a combination of non-verbal cues and expectation. Non-Chinese often say things which, for Chinese people, are so unexpected that they've no way of knowing what we're saying. In this case, I'd clearly heard him right, but I second-guessed myself because of past experience. More people have forgotten to bring money, in my experience, than have forgotten swords.

When the second-to-last person was in the meeting with the professors, a young teacher came to me and said in Chinese, "I'm your translator." He meant he'd read the questions to me in Chinese and explain them in Chinese if I needed help. And I did need it. Also, let me add, this was the most actual help anyone has ever given me since coming to Asia. Usually, they want to translate it into English, which generally doesn't help, because their English is poor. Also, next time, I wouldn't know how to read it. Because he read the questions to me in Chinese, rather than translating them, I was able to recognize the same questions later, during the interview. Consequently, I was able to answer them. Had he translated, I wouldn't have been able to answer the questions and would have failed.

This way, I learned something, got real help I needed for the interview, and — most importantly — felt like he'd treated me as an adult, instead of an idiot child.

When I was called into the room, the professors had me present my new research proposal in Chinese, then asked me a number of questions about the intent and feasibility of the research I wanted to conduct. Here I had to do a little bit of a balancing act. I tried to affirm my credibility as a field researcher by telling them about my book *The Monk from Brooklyn*, and how I'd lived in Shaolin Temple in order to write it. But I didn't want them to become so interested in the book that they'd go read it and find out how critical I'd been of China. They also asked a great deal about my past experience in martial arts, my professional fights, TV shows, and publishing. They showed a lot of interest in hearing about the years I'd spent living in monasteries and gyms and fight centers around Asia, writing and publishing about martial arts. In the end, they seemed to be enjoying the conversation, rather than trying to shoot holes in my research proposal.

Every Ph.D. candidate had to go through the same grilling, but whereas the professors were relatively easy on me, and excited to have a foreign student who could speak Chinese, they were absolutely brutal toward my would-be classmates. Sitting in the waiting room, I watched them walk into the interview room young, nervous, and hopeful, only to emerge, a half hour later, defeated and old.

The next part of the admissions selections was the physical test. We were instructed to change into our martial arts clothing and "perform" for the professors. My classmates all had beautiful, traditional silken uniforms and each performed an elegant Wushu Taolu or tai chi form. In the second round of performances, they changed clothes again and did a weapons form. I don't know how most people picture a Ph.D. program, but I'd imagine one doesn't normally expect his classmates to be adept with long spears, a long sword, two short swords, or a fighting staff. While I was nervous about passing the test, inside I was so excited and happy. This was a childhood fantasy coming to life.

Aside from being the only foreigner, I felt so out of place with my martial art, compared to everyone else's. Where my classmates were all dressed like the inheritors of an ancient art, handed down for centuries, I wore my MMA gear, including gloves. I envied their dedication to traditional arts like tai chi, but tai chi never appealed to me. It wasn't angry enough.

Later, at one of the first meetings I'd have with my professor, he'd tell me that one of the greatest differences between Chinese and Western martial arts is that Western martial arts have no performance component. And this was a real problem for me that day. I'd have been happy to fight if they could have put me on the mat with an opponent, but this was meant to be a one-person demo. One of the candidates represented sanda (Chinese kickboxing). I thought maybe we could fight, as our demo. But he'd prepared a demo already and wouldn't want to risk getting injured or influencing the judges by fighting me.

The professors said they wanted to see me do one round of MMA shadow boxing and one round of shadow wrestling. I moved around, fighting an imaginary opponent, kicking, punching, throwing knees and elbows. In the second round, after my teammates had finished showing off their weapons skills, I wrestled an imaginary opponent. I circled, faked, shot, took a single leg or double leg take down, lifted my opponent over my head, slammed him into the canvas, then pinned him. I did a fireman's carry, running double leg, ankle pick, back control, and hip throw.

The judges appeared to be happy. But I'm not going to lie to you. I'm not as young as I used to be, and my imaginary opponent almost pinned me, twice. Later, I found out he was on steroids.

Many of the students who'd crowded in to watch the performances came over and congratulated me and wanted to take photos with me. Maybe they were being polite, but maybe seeing MMA and wrestling in the Wu Shu Institute was a brand-new experience for them. It's amazing how they have these beautiful, ancient martial traditions — and yet a pair of MMA gloves and some ground-and-pound looks exotic to them.

That night, I was picking up some extra money, working as a color commentator for a professional fight event in Shanghai. When I arrived, I saw a bunch of young, slim guys with bald heads hanging around out front. While the organizer of the event and I were nailing down the details of how I was to do the Chinese commentary, a long-haired, unsavory looking guy, with tattoos and fighting scars, who was with the bald kids, said "Āndōng-ní, nǐ zěnme yang?" Antonio, how are you? It turned out he was a Shaolin monk I'd known at Shaolin Temple in Bangkok several years before. I was so happy to see him. A group of former Shaolin monks would be performing at the beginning of the show and he was helping them travel around. One of the performers came over and I immediately recognized him as having appeared in the Shaolin Bangkok episode of *Martial Arts Odyssey*, my web series. The one who was performing looked pretty much the same as I remembered, but the unsavory-looking one had changed for the worse. He used to be a lean, muscular Shaolin athlete.

Seeing them reminded me of my time at the real Shaolin Temple in Henan, China, where they'd grown up and where I'd studied, before we finally met in Bangkok. They made me nostalgic for the temple, and a new crazy idea was born. SUS had informed me that I'd have to pass the Chinese proficiency exam, HSK Level-4, before the first week of August, in order to submit the results by September 7, the day classes started. I needed to prepare for the exam and get my body into shape before the beginning of the semester, so I began wondering if I should go live in the temple for the summer, immerse myself in Chinese, and dedicate my time to training and preparing for the exam.

Whenever I mention Shaolin Temple to New Yorkers, most of them think I'm talking about a synagogue.

·•●·•

Leading up to the 2008 Beijing Olympics, a lot of international media ran stories about the Chinese sports school system (known in the PRC as *tǐ xiào*), and how kids are selected at a young age, separated from their parents, and put through rigorous training. According to these reports, if they didn't make the Olympic cut, they were tossed out on the street, uneducated, often physically broken, and having no job skills. While there was definitely some truth in these reports, this is a subject I'd revisit again and again over the next three years, revising my understanding of the system, and flip-flopping on whether or not I approved of it.

Most foreign media never wrote about the sports university system, which was one more destination for those who failed to make it to the Olympics. The few who got into sports universities could still get some education, while qualifying for a good job in the police, army, security, as a PE teacher in a government school, or cash in on China's growing urban affluence, by working as a personal trainer in a commercial gym.

Parallel to the sports school system was the *wǔ xiào* system of martial arts boarding schools. Shaolin Temple is the best known one among people outside China, but there are hundreds of these live-in martial arts schools across the country. At SUS, I'd discover that many of the students majoring in wushu had grown up in Shaolin Temple or in a *wǔ xiào* somewhere in China. The *tǐ xiào* schools also offered wushu and other martial arts, in addition to Olympic sports. This meant that competition for slots in the wushu departments of the sports universities was fierce; there were thousands of wushu programs across China, but only a handful of sports universities, as well as a few other universities with significant sport or wushu departments.

I referred to my two Shaolin friends as "former monks," but technically they were never monks. They were boys who grew up in the *wǔ xiào* system, and had the benefit of having lived in a *wǔ xiào* at the actual Shaolin Temple. Trainees at all of the temple schools shave their heads and wear uniforms, but they're not actually monks. If they're good enough to be chosen for the performance teams, they'll wear monk's clothes, but they never actually take vows. Most will graduate and leave, returning to a secular life. In the schools surrounding Shaolin Temple there were an estimated 60,000 students, while the temple only had about 60 monks.

The boy who was on the performance team was lucky because he could continue to train and perform kung fu while earning a living, but the cost was that he had to remain in tip-top condition or he'd be cut from the team. The acrobatic form of martial arts performed in the traveling Shaolin shows could best be done by teenagers. Their ability would peak somewhere between the ages of 16 and 18. Many could continue into their early twenties, but for the most part, by 22, it was very unlikely they'd be able to perform well enough to remain on the team.

The other boy, the one with the long hair and scars, was obviously not performing. Now fat, and looking much the worse for wear, he told me that he'd been off the team for several years. He was basically a cautionary tale of what the future held for the bulk of young kung fu trainees. I asked what he was doing in Shanghai and it seemed he had no job. He was just hanging around, doing this and that. I suspected this and that wasn't legal. A lot of these boys wound up working as muscle for low-level gangsters.

We talked a bit about what we were doing with our lives, and how we'd been since our training together in Bangkok. There really wasn't much we could say. We were following very different paths, now. As the conversation ran out, I was called to the commentator's table for my soundcheck.

The organizers brought the referees, judges, and myself to the center of the ring to introduce us to the crowd. I started cracking up, realizing it was the first time I'd ever worn shoes in a boxing ring.

The fight card that night had Muay Thai, sanda, and MMA fights, as well as demos by the Shaolin team, a Wing Chun team, and a few others. Sanda is my favorite fighting art, after MMA and wrestling. The best sanda fighters come out of *wǔ xiào* or *tǐ xiào* programs where they first learn wushu for two or more years, and later learn to fight. This gives them tremendous flexibility, high kicks, and great balance. Once they start fighting, they work on power, strength, boxing, and wrestling. Of all the Chinese sports, this is the one that I wish would take off around the world. It's extremely exciting, with lots of movement, strikes, kicks, and throws, but without the ground fighting which some people find boring when they watch MMA. Apart from the throws, the other thing that makes sanda more interesting to watch than Muay Thai is the variety of kicks used. Although Muay Thai actually has a number of different kicks, the two you will see most of the time are the roundhouse and the front push kick. Sanda, on the other hand, includes the full range of kicks one learns in two years of Wushu Taolu training. They do you use the roundhouse a lot, but they also use a very powerful side kick and spinning back kick and other kung fu kicks which are hard for uninitiated opponents to block and counter.

When I lived in Shaolin Temple in 2003, I tried to focus on learning sanda, but most of the schools focused on Wushu Taolu and we only had a little bit of sanda training each week. When we had sparring, just by using my Western boxing skills I could beat most of the students and hold my own with all but the best coaches. At that time, I had a relatively negative feeling about sanda. I didn't understand that what I was seeing at the temple was part-time sanda, which is very different from the guys who grow up in a sanda school or as sanda majors in a *wǔ xiào* and then go on to become professional fighters.

The guys fighting that night in Shanghai were seasoned professionals, displaying a far superior level of skill. Many of the bouts were Muay Thai vs. sanda and you could see how much more well-rounded sanda was, how many more techniques they used, and how many more ranges they could fight from.

It reminded me of an event I'd watched when I was training and fighting in Malaysia. I'd been invited to a fight event called China Conquers the World, which pitted sanda fighters from China against Muay Thai fighters from Malaysia. Every Muay Thai fighter opened by kicking incredibly hard with a right roundhouse kick, off of their back leg. Muay Thai fighters can kick very hard, and you could see that the blows stunned — but didn't stop — the Chinese fighters. When the Muay Thai guys realized their strategy of kicking really hard with the right leg didn't work, they had nothing else. I could see them thinking, "I gotta change it up. I know: I'll kick even harder with my right leg." The sanda guys, by contrast, had boxing, throwing, straight kicks... a huge arsenal. Also, I was amazed at the aggressive wrestling in sanda. In both Muay Thai and sanda, you can throw the opponent from the clinch or when you catch his kicks, but sanda fighters will often attack with a throw, including lifts and slams. I even saw one suplex.

In the middle of the fights, there was a demo by a nunchaku (nunchucks) team who wore yellow track suits, like Bruce Lee in *The Game of Death*. I was thinking, instead of kung fu vs. Muay Thai, they should do nunchucks vs. MMA. That'd be a fight I'd pay to watch.

Doing commentary in a foreign language, I was feeling very nervous. I always tell my students, "If seeing the audience makes you nervous, take off your glasses."

To make matters worse, this was my first time working as a fight commentator, and I couldn't always think of smart things to say. One of the brilliant comments I made was "This is Brazilian Jiu-Jitsu. It originated in Japan, where it was called Japanese Jiu-Jitsu." Not only is that stupid, it's not even right. When the art existed only in Japan, they didn't need to call it Japanese Jiu-Jitsu. Like the old joke: "Do they have Chinese restaurants in China?" And the answer, "Yes, but they just call them restaurants."

While I was announcing the fights, I kept forgetting I wasn't teaching school. I asked the audience to take their seats. Ten minutes later, when they were still milling about, I almost said, "I distinctly remember telling you people to sit down. Well, I can wait as long as you can."

During the fights, I sat next to a judge. Occasionally, it was really hard to speak into the mic because he was shouting instructions to his fighters. In China, fairness has different standards than in the West. No one said to him, "Maybe you shouldn't be a judge, if your fighters are fighting." Or, at least, "You can be a judge, but you can't shout instructions to your fighters." To be fair, when I saw a few of my friends loosing, I was tempted to shout instructions over the mic as well.

China is famous for bad judging. I have to say, however, that all of the fights involving foreigners were judged fairly. Not to criticize anyone, but when you know the judges aren't the best, you need to win decisively. This is something foreign fighters always said: "Don't leave it in the hands of the judges." If you win by KO, you win. But if you let the fight go to a judges' decision, you never know what'll happen. Only a few of the Chinese fights were completely misjudged. A few others were judged differently than I'd have judged, but it depends how much you count throws vs. strikes. Those fights could have gone either way.

In professional fights, one corner is the blue corner and one is the red corner, and the judges fill out score cards, designating blue or red as the winner. The score cards are given to the head judge, who holds up a blue or red paddle, signifying who won. In one of the fights, for some moronic reason, the organizers put a guy with blue shorts in the red corner. He clearly won the fight, but several of the judges marked the winner as blue, because of the color of his shorts, giving the win to his opponent.

In another fight I saw in China, the blue corner clearly won, but the head judge held up the red paddle, signifying that red had won. I asked the judge I was sitting with, and he said, "I think we all chose blue, but the head judge picked up the wrong paddle by accident." When the award was given to red, the head judge began to protest, till he realized he was holding the wrong paddle. Obviously, he'd have lost face if he'd admitted making a mistake. So the wrong fighter went home with a payday and a trophy.

The next morning, I went to the HSK office to pay for my Chinese-language exam, pick up my study books, and lock in the final details. I stopped off at the market on the way home, and was excited to finally obtain five of the *Star Trek* movies, plus the 2009 *Star Trek* movie, all dubbed into Chinese. That was about another nine hours of listening. And when I'd done it five times, I'd be 45 hours closer to my goal.

The semester was coming to an end at Shanghai University. On my final performance review, I scored well on student approval. Interestingly, in the comment box, most students wrote, "Teacher is very funny," or "Teacher is very strict." Or both.

It's always sad when the academic year ends, but exciting, too. This year was even more exciting because I had the sports university to look forward to, as well as a couple of other adventures in between. I bought a plane ticket to Shaolin Temple, where I'd arranged to study sanda and Chinese for the next two months. This would be the ten-year anniversary of when I first studied there, an experience which resulted in my first book, *The Monk from Brooklyn*. I wondered if the sequel book should be called *The Monk from Brooklyn II*.

Chapter 2
Return to Shaolin Temple

There is kung fu in everything. The way you teach at the university is kung fu. The way you translate is also kung fu. The way you carry buckets of water or stones up and down the hill each day. It is all kung fu.

—Du Shifu

An Italian Shaolin monk I knew through Facebook had connected me with Jacky, the business director of a Shaolin Temple school. Over the past few weeks, we'd been setting up my stay, including accommodation, training, and Chinese lessons. When I arrived at the airport at Zhengzhou, the capital of Henan province, Jacky picked me up for the long drive to Dengfeng, where Shaolin Temple is located.

While China is one of the fastest developing countries in the world, it's amazing how undeveloped most of the country still is. It was about a two-hour drive to Dengfeng, and in between there was absolutely nothing but open fields and some very small, rundown looking houses. It all looked pretty much as I remembered from ten years earlier. The government had expanded the administrative zone of Zhengzhou so it now included Dengfeng. On paper, the population had increased considerably, but that was misleading. When we finally arrived in Dengfeng, I saw that, in terms of development, it still looked the same: communist-style housing blocks that looked very poor, and a complete absence of foreign chains or convenience stores.

The agreement I'd made with Jacky was that, in my martial arts training, I only wanted to learn sanda. He'd also agreed to arrange a teacher to give me two hours of Chinese classes each day, to help me prepare for the HSK Chinese test. During the drive, he told me he'd be my Chinese teacher, which made me a bit apprehensive. Next, he was trying to talk me into studying Wushu Taolu, rather than sanda. "Wushu is the basis of sanda. One cannot study sanda without wushu," he declared.

"I can," I answered. Then I added, "You agreed to make that happen. And I'm confident you will."

Obviously, he wanted me to do Wushu Taolu because that was what they were already teaching at the school and it'd be easier for him. Reluctantly, he finally agreed to make good on the contract we'd already signed. There's a joke in China: "The negotiations begin after the contract is signed."

Apart from the fact that I felt that Jacky was trying to pull a fast one on me by trying to back out of our agreement, I really enjoyed talking to him. He liked talking about politics, history, and sociology. He also explained the sports university system to me and how the *wŭ xiào* system fit in. Of course, this was all in Mandarin, which really helped my Chinese level.

One of the things he said to me was that Chinese people respect the words of Mao Zedong. "He's very much like your George Washington, Americans learn to recite the words of George Washington, and you'd never criticize George Washington. This is why Chinese people get so angry when foreign media criticize Mao Zedong." That single statement revealed so much about how Jacky, and many other Chinese, saw the world.

When someone says they are going to study at Shaolin Temple, they usually mean studying in one of the sixty or so schools that surround the actual temple. The school I was headed to was Shaolin Temple Kung Fu

Culture Institute. Most of the schools used some similar permutation of these six words in their names, to add legitimacy, like: Culture Institute of Shaolin Temple Kung Fu, or Kung Fu and Cultural Institute of Shaolin Temple. A few years later, I'd read that the Shaolin name had been protected by the government. Today, it's possible these schools no longer include the name Shaolin in their title.

Our school, like the majority of these schools, consisted of a house, where students lived, and a large backyard, where we trained outdoors.

Jacky took me inside and gave me a full set of training gear, which of course I had to pay for. As he handed me the Feiyue brand Shaolin sneakers, I started laughing, because those were the same shoes I'd worn ten years earlier. He gave me several sanda uniforms, and they were identical to the ones from before. I also requested some tai chi pants, so I'd have something warm to wear at night. The gear included a pair of very cheap, low-quality Chinese-made boxing gloves and — to my surprise — a pair of cheap MMA gloves. Ten years earlier, no one at Shaolin Temple had heard of MMA, but MMA gloves were now standard issue. There'd clearly been some development in the training. Of course, I never saw anyone actually use the gloves, but every students had to pay for them, so there was progress.

The first significant difference I noticed from my earlier stint at the temple was that the average age of the students had dropped. Jacky told me that because the country was so much richer now, as soon as students reached the age of 18, they generally left the temple to take jobs in the cities. Consequently, he said it'd been difficult to find sparring partners for me. "But we have a big, strong boy who you can fight with," he explained.

When he introduced me to my training partner, I wanted to ask, "So I guess he'll be my partner till that big strong boy gets here?" Actually, by Shaolin standards, he was pretty big, weighing over 60 kg (132 lbs) and a head taller than me. Right away, I could see that he lacked the grace and flexibility of the smaller boys. He was more like a lumbering but powerful giant compared to the sprightly, flexible Shaolin kids. He'd been put in the sanda program because he was physically unsuited for Wushu Taolu. This meant that he'd probably never qualify for the traveling shows. And, growing up in a school where he was the biggest guy and where he had no real competition in sanda, it was unlikely he'd be able to turn professional. This made me wonder about the goals of these kids' parents. To what end had they shipped their kids off to Shaolin Temple, rather than having them graduate high school?

The trainees generally took new names when they entered the temple, and this boy had chosen the name Yi Long, which he'd copied from a famous (albeit fake) Shaolin monk who was making a name for himself as a novelty attraction on the international kickboxing circuit.

There were about ten Chinese trainees living in two rooms in the house. I had a huge room to myself, but was told that when other foreigners came, they'd be living with me. Two other foreigners were already living there: Hugo from Mexico and Jaka, a New York-raised US citizen who'd been born in Slovenia. They had a room down the hall. This was quite different from my first experience in Shaolin, where I was the first foreigner almost everyone there had ever met. Also, the house was so much nicer than the one I'd lived in in 2003. We had a kitchen, microwave, toilets, showers, AC, and WiFi.

Most of the Shaolin schools were associated with a monk who'd partnered with a guy like Jacky. Jacky ran the business while the monk lent his name and his photo to the school, and also oversaw training. Our monk was named Du Shifu. He and Jacky had rooms on the second floor of the house.

Morning training, which ran from 6 a.m. to 7 a.m., largely consisted of running and man carries. We then ate cold fried rice the cook had prepared the previous night for breakfast. Training resumed from 8:30 a.m. to 10:30 a.m., and consisted of Wushu Taolu for the others but sanda for Yi Long and I. We all did strength training, and it was a lot of fun, like something right out of a kung fu movie.

Du Shifu had us stand on posts, sometimes on one leg, holding heavy buckets full of stones. He made us do squats with logs. We also did weight-lifting, using stones for dumbbells. He had us run down to the river, collect one huge stone or two medium ones, and then run back up to the house, again and again. He then used the stones to construct paths, to separate the yard into practice areas and fighting areas. He built a fence around the training area. He even used stones to make a desk for himself so he could use his laptop to play music during training or show us videos of techniques he wanted us to learn. The coolest thing he built was a *Flint-stones*-style exercise machine, where we had to lift stones using a wooden frame and pullies. This was all so different than Shaolin 2003, when most of the kids were barely aware that the internet existed.

Some days we'd do hours of Shaolin power stretches. A lot of martial arts schools hold each stretch for ten or twenty seconds. At Shaolin, stretches are held for two and even three minutes, often with someone pulling or pushing on you. Flexibility has always been one of my problems. I hoped Shaolin could help me.

On that first day, Du Shifu had me do several minutes of shadow fighting, so he could see what I already knew. Afterward, he told me that speed was my biggest problem and flexibility was next. And, of course, my kicks were poor and my wrestling was awkward. If I could learn the proper techniques, I'd be able to take guys down faster and more beautifully.

He taught Yi Long and I a very short, front side kick which he said was the power kick of sanda. Next, he had us stand against the wall and throw the kick slowly, with him counting the movements. It took a count of four to raise the knee above your waist, twist your hips, flex your back and buttocks, and extend the leg. Then we had to hold the kick out, till he told us to take it back, slowly, with another four-count. We had to do 100 with each leg.

The power of Shaolin kicks comes not from weightlifting or from the heavy bag, but throwing thousands of long, slow kicks per day, hitting only air. If you train like this, your technique will be better and you won't have injuries. My technique, of course, was terrible. And I've always had injuries.

For the next exercise, I lay on my side, with my leg up in the air, as if I were throwing a side kick. Yi Long put a kick pad on his chest and leaned all of his weight on the bottom of my foot. And I had to kick slowly, from the ground, lifting his body, 100 times on each side. When we switched places, I really pitied him, having to lift my much heavier body. For me, this was like the legend of Milo, who trained by carrying a calf every day from its birth until it became an adult ox. Learning the technique while only lifting a 60 kg opponent was good for me, in that I didn't struggle with the weight so much, so I could concentrate on the technique. Eventually, when I trained with someone my own size, hopefully I'd have good technique, and the weight wouldn't matter.

We did 100 squats with an opponent sitting on our shoulders. Once again, Yi Long almost died. We did all kinds of crazy sit-ups, followed by shoot and lift, for a sanda double-leg take down. The mechanics were similar to what I'd learned in MMA, but we were taught to trap the opponent's legs between our forearms, rather than grabbing or laying hands on them, because the boxing gloves would interfere with our grip. Once again, we did 100 lifts. In sanda, you wear boxing gloves, whereas in MMA we wear fingerless gloves, which make it easier to grip the opponent. Consequently, many sanda grappling techniques utilize the forearms or the entire hand to trap the opponent's leg or body, rather than to truly grip it, as you would in MMA or wrestling.

In the final exercise, we each wore one Thai pad (a small, square pad used as a kicking target). We circled like in a real fight. Yi Long side kicked my Thai pad, then I side kicked his. We did this for five minutes.

After morning training, we had a rest, followed by lunch, then a sleep. At 1 p.m., my Chinese class began. The Chinese lessons weren't great, but they were better than nothing. Jacky wasn't the worst teacher, but in true Chinese form, he kept chastising me for trying to learn the language, rather than concentrating on passing the exam. A lot of Chinese teachers pride themselves on being able to teach you how to pass the HSK, even if your Chinese is terrible, but they couldn't necessarily teach you the language. After my two-hour lesson, the other students did calligraphy for an hour and a half. During that time, I did my Chinese homework.

Afternoon training was more kicking and kick catching with Yi Long. After dinner, there was one more training session, running with river stones and doing man carries. At 8:10 p.m., Du Shifu ordered us to break a sweat, any way we could. If we broke a sweat, we could stop for the day. If not, we had to keep going. It usually took me until about 8:40 p.m. to sweat enough for him to let me stop.

In addition to this great physical training, I spoke more Mandarin in a typical day at Shaolin than I did in an entire month living in Shanghai. Du Shifu always asked me to translate for him, and since I spent almost every training minute with Yi Long, I was speaking and listening to Chinese constantly.

Another difference between this experience and my previous one was that our house had showers. When I first lived in the temple, we'd go weeks at a time without bathing. Here, I took a shower at noon and again at the end of the training day. Then I slept soundly, thanks to the AC.

I believed this was going to be a good experience. I'd improve my Chinese and get healthy and strong. The only issue was the lack of good sparring opportunities. Coming back a third time at some point in the future probably wouldn't make sense. But, for this moment in my life, it was the best choice.

In my first Shaolin experience, while I was the only foreigner and immersed in a Chinese-speaking environment, my Chinese wasn't at the level it was now. Immersion is only helpful if you're already at a level where you can have deep conversations and actually engage constantly with people, rather than tuning out because you don't understand. In my first stint, I wouldn't have wanted another foreign student there, because having no one else to talk to, I had to speak and listen Mandarin all day. But this time, I was happy there were some other foreigners. Firstly, I could translate for them, which was good mental exercise. Secondly, it was fun to have other foreigners to share ideas with all day, during this very unique experience.

I told Jaka that the food we had at lunch tasted good. "Yeah, because of all the MSG," he said, telling me, "Last week, I went to a noodle restaurant and there was so much MSG in the food that, about halfway through the meal, I felt like I'd just eaten a large bag of Doritos. There was a carnival going on in my mouth, just all of these pointless tastes."

The amount of strength training Du Shifu had us do was amazing. It was like he'd read my mind and knew what would appeal to me. After fetching rocks from the river, we had to toss them back and forth to each other like medicine balls for thirty minutes. Sometimes I wished we'd had the styrofoam fake rocks they use when making movies. After Du Shifu trained Yi Long and I how to do sanda throws for an hour, he made us go running, carrying heavy bags on our shoulders.

The food at Shaolin was so much better than before, but meat was still a rarity. Jaka, Hugo, and I snuck off to Dengfeng fairly regularly, to eat goat meat and beef and ice cream. We also went to a grocery store and bought chicken, to bring back to the school, so I could add a little to my soup at meal times. The store also had a huge adult-diaper section. I was wondering if there was something in the water in Dengfeng I should worry about.

Leaving the store, we passed a police station that said, in both English and Chinese, "Criminal Policeman." And I thought, they shouldn't let criminals become policemen.

A gaggle of children were running up and down the street in Dengfeng, harmlessly pranking the shop owners, and laughing the whole time. This reminded me of my friends and I, on the streets of New York, when we were kids. An American friend of mine who's married and raising a child in Shanghai told me that he never saw Chinese kids playing together. Due to the PRC's one-child policy, most families only had one child. And that child, more often than not, was being cared for by retired grandparents who had nothing to do but spoil him or her. And, according to my friend, it wasn't common for children to visit each other's houses. "They don't have play dates." He told me. "The grandparents don't let the children out of close proximity. The parents or grandparents take the kids to the park and only let them play within arm's reach. You see an adult with a child here, and one there, but they never let the kids play together."

Once kids started school, they'd do almost nothing apart from studying. Childhood in China's urban areas seemed to be characterized by several years of lonely play, overseen by grandparents, followed by 12 years of intense academic pressure.

In general, Dengfeng was noticeably less developed, less prosperous, and less expensive than Shanghai. The adults were also noticeably less attractive than their counterparts in Shanghai. But one nice thing in Dengfeng was that I always saw loads of children playing together, skinning their knees, trying and failing and trying again, interacting with other kids, and basically experiencing something other than school, like normal kids.

As undeveloped as Dengfeng was, it was still good to get away from the temple. One day, we followed up on an internet rumor that there was a steak-and-pizza café in the town. We were ecstatic to find out that it was true. We ate the lowest quality steak and the worst pizza ever, but we loved it.

Some mornings, the other foreign students would get up at 4 a.m. and go to Shaolin Temple with Jacky to chant. Instead, I chose to get up at 5:30 a.m. to carry river rocks with the Chinese students, as I did every day. When I first got to Asia, I was martial arts crazy, wanting to do and see everything. Now, after 12 years, I'd been there and done that. I could separate out and concentrate on what I wanted and needed from my experiences. In this case, I needed to pass my HSK, lose weight, learn sanda, and carry river rocks. Besides, if I didn't carry river rocks, who would?

Chinese steamed buns (*mántou*) are a dietary staple at Shaolin. When I was first there, I believed they'd be good with jam and coffee. Now I had proof. Every morning after the 6 a.m. training session, I made coffee, got the jam from my room, then sat down with the other trainees and ate my *mántou* with jam. That was really a nice start to the day.

We had sanda sparring once a week. All of the kids had to fight, even though they were learning Wushu Taolu rather than sanda. But every trainee opened with so much aggression. It was really exciting, if not a little comical, to see how many punches and kicks they threw per round.

I felt bad for Yi Long, because he was so much smaller than me. Du Shifu told me not to take Yi Long down, but to just work on punches and kicks. I was planning to go really easy on him, because of the size and age difference.

When Du Shifu told us to start, Yi Long came at me, crazily kicking and punching. I'd get one or two good, controlled boxing punches in, then Yi Long would be right inside, banging me furiously with all kind of behind-the-supermarket punches. Normally, the way I neutralize chaos is to clinch. So I clinched, which wasn't quite fair because of my size advantage. Then Du Shifu would break us and the exact same pathology would be repeated.

He kept reminding me that I was there to learn to fight sanda by sanda rules, and to practice sanda, not something else. He said, "You need to learn sanda techniques, practice sanda techniques. If this were a competition, you'd win. But that's not why you're here. You're here to learn this." He was so right. In his mind, I wasn't learning sanda to add to my MMA arsenal. Instead, he was training me as if I wanted to go fight in sanda contests. That meant following all the rules. For example, I didn't know if you were allowed to dirty box in sanda, but that's one of my best techniques, holding the head and punching it with the other hand.

The next day, Du Shifu worked with Yi Long and I on sanda throws. Once, a traditional wrestling master back in Shanghai had asked to see a video of my fights to see how I threw people. After watching it, he said, "You don't throw anyone. You just make them fall down. There's a difference." Here, working with the sanda teacher, I saw the difference. When I catch an opponent's kick in MMA, all I care about is tripping him or dragging him to the ground, to gain control and to ground and pound. But in sanda, Du Shifu used that leg the same way a judo master would use an arm. He could throw the guy — *kerthwack!* — rather than just getting him to the ground. It made a lot of sense to throw the opponent properly, possibly injuring him with a hard throw, and then diving on top of him. My experience with sanda now was truly about unlearning, rather than learning.

I didn't want to get all mystical and emotional, but in the evenings, when we were in the middle of our final training session for the day, I'd look across and, beneath a setting sun, I could see the actual Shaolin Temple, nestled in the mountains below the statue of Bodhidharma (Da Mo), the founder of Shaolin Kung Fu. And I'd think: "Wow! What an incredible place to be training."

One day, Yi Long's father came to visit. Apparently, he was a truck driver. Jacky told me he'd earn about RMB 350 (US$ 55) per day, but fuel and the police took a chunk out of that. He also told me that some of the kids were orphans and studied for free. Other kids had parents working in Shanghai or Shenzhen, so they were being looked after by grandparents and had been misbehaving. At our school, in addition to martial arts, they attended classes in the three mandatory academic courses, English, Math, and Culture. With those three they could sit an exam to enter a sports university without having to pass China's famous National College Entrance Examination (*gāokǎo*). So, at least in theory, they might have a future.

The Shaolin schools take their holidays in turn, so Dengfeng doesn't get inundated with wushu trainees on any given day. When it was our school's turn for a holiday, Jacky took the foreign students to Dengfeng for dinner. On the way, he told me we were going to a famous vegetarian restaurant and I actually got angry. It turned out it was actually a goat meat place, and I was in heaven.

An American colleague of mine, who was married to a local girl in Shanghai and who spoke Mandarin incredibly well, told me: "Most foreigners who really hate it here or constantly complain about China or about their local marriage don't speak Chinese well. Being able to communicate makes all the difference." I totally agreed with him. And on this Shaolin trip I really saw a difference. I didn't feel a fraction of the frustration I'd felt the first time I was there. A lot of that was because this was a much better Shaolin school, with a friendlier environment. But some of it was also because of my language skills and because I was more used to Chinese culture now.

The following morning, Yi Long and I had to go to the river and each carry back two buckets of water. Then we learned how to lift Chinese kettle bells. While we did that, the rest of the team had to fetch large rocks from the river and carry them to the training area. Du Shifu told me that, when he was young and still living inside the temple walls, in the morning they had to wake up, go to the river, fetch a large stone and place it in a field far away. The next morning, they had to go to the field, and fetch the stone back to the river. If it were me, I'd have written my name on my stone, so I could get the same one every day. Or, like the US Marines do with their rifles, you could give your stone a girl's name.

After we got back with our buckets of water, the young trainees and foreign students jogged to Shaolin Temple. I rode in the van with the master. Looking out the window, everything I remembered from ten years ago was gone.

Spending one-on-one time with Du Shifu was great. He was very funny, and he talked constantly, sharing stories about his life. He'd lived in the temple for six years. "It was harder then. The kids were afraid of the shifus then, because they beat us," he said. It was rare to meet someone who'd grown up under such conditions yet who could now create such a positive environment for his own students. The kids in our house seemed happy. Du Shifu took good care of them, making them laugh and teaching them well.

The master had opinions on everything, which was extremely entertaining. He told me, "Foreigners and Chinese are different. Your body is covered in hair, because you eat so much meat." Next: "There are only three things Chinese people cannot do. We cannot fly, swim, or climb trees." This turned out to be an old saying which I'd hear again, many times, during my three years at SUS. While it's true that most Chinese cannot swim, and none can fly, surely they could climb a tree if they so desired.

Du Shifu explained that one reason why Chinese people speed when they're driving is because, if you drive slowly, some tricksters will throw themselves in front of your car to collect money from you. "They usually ask for about RMB 300 [US$ 48], he explained. "They do it once in the morning and then again in the evening, and they get RMB 600 [US$ 95] a day. That's a great salary." But, he pointed out, if you drive fast, they don't dare, because the impact might kill them.

Villages near the temple had been relocated and huge roads built. The whole area had become a UNESCO World Heritage Site, like a theme park or a tourist attraction. I used to be able to walk out of the temple and stroll through the village, meet people, and buy food. At that time anyone could walk right up to the temple's walls. Now the park was surrounded by a wall. From the gates of the park to the wall of the temple was a reasonably long run. Also, you needed to buy a ticket or have a pass to even be admitted.

The entire ride was full of ghosts for Du Shifu. He stopped the car and pointed at the dry riverbed that ran parallel to the road. "That's where we used to wash our clothes. In winter, we had to break the ice first."

The village that used to surround the temple had contained several martial arts schools. They were mostly gone. One of the few schools still permitted to remain inside the park was the massive Tagou, the largest Shaolin Temple school.

According to Du Shifu, Tagou had nearly 30,000 students. From the van, we could see an ocean of students, in brightly colored uniforms, training wushu, weapons, and sanda, in massive military-style formations. About the sanda training, he said. "They do the same things we do, but it just costs more. And because there are so many students, you get no personalized training."

For foreigners, it was even more extreme. They lived and trained separately from Chinese students. "If you're going to train with other foreigners all the time, why even come to China," Du Shifu said.

The master's points about the quality of training at Tagou were well-taken, but the school still had a reputation for being one of the best places in the world to study sanda. I knew I was too old for such dreams, but it would have been incredible for me to remain there and study sanda for several months.

Tourists from across China flock to Shaolin Temple for an authentic glimpse into traditional culture. Just inside the temple's entrance, which is now a four-lane road, there's a convenience store. There's also a cable car which takes tourists to a holy place, atop the mountain, although I suspect that the store and the cable car may not be the original cable car and convenience store that were here when Bodhidharma (Da Mo) came sometime in the fifth or sixth century.

We parked the van, met the other students, and hiked up the mountain to a sacred pool. There, Du Shifu taught the boys some meditation and qigong. Jaka started stripping down to swim in the water, but the students and Du Shifu admonished him. It was exactly like that scene in *Kung Fu Panda:* "We do not wash our pits in the pool of wisdom."

I felt that Du Shifu really understood me. He asked once, sheepishly, if I'd also do the qigong, but he knew I wouldn't. I was as respectful as I could be. But I knew why I was there, and what I needed to focus on. I'm a fighter. And until my knees and ankles give out for the last time, I will be a fighter. This is what I study, and this is what I focus on. Du Shifu seemed to be OK with that. Inside the van he said, "I know you don't believe in a lot of this because you're Catholic."

We drove back to the house and had the rest of the day off. Hugo had a Colombian friend, Sebastiano, who was training at one of the few schools left inside the temple grounds. He invited Jaka and me to return to the temple with him for dinner.

Once again, we walked the several kilometers to the temple, showed our passes and entered the grounds. But now, rather than taking the road to the foot of the mountain as we had that morning, we followed a path to the heart of the complex. We walked, seemingly forever, passing the government wushu school. That's when it hit me how much the place had changed. The four-lane road we now walked on had been a narrow and mainly dirt road, and before there were houses and shops all of the way up to and beyond the government wushu school. In fact, I think the main entrance to the temple parking lot had been directly in front of the temple. Now, the main entrance led into this massive park which included hotels, shops, and restaurants. When they expanded the grounds of the temple, they also built a synthetic Shaolin village, with a number of kung fu schools, restaurants, and shops. It looked like the set of *Kung Fu Panda*, but it was really nice.

I was so jealous of the foreigners who got to live and train there. Not because of training, but because of access to food. Where we lived, we had to go all the way to Dengfeng to get meat. But Sebastiano had a few shops and some excellent yet cheap restaurants right next to his school. Also, he got to live in the temple grounds. The downside, though, is that there were no Chinese students in his school, and the training was conducted entirely in English.

On the way back to our house, we passed by Tagou, which was having a movie night. A thousand or two Tagou students sat on the training ground watching a kung fu movie on a huge jumbotron screen. It was surreal.

Technology in general played a much larger role at the temple than it had in 2003. It was funny to see Shaolin kids learning sword forms from the internet. They also watched fights as well as instructional videos and demos. They all asked me about UFC champion Anderson Silva. Everyone had access to much more information than before, and everything was modernizing. Du Shifu used the Chinese word for core strength. The development of sports and technology was reaching even into this remote part of China. With it came — for me, at least — proof that modern science and modern ways of training are superior. Give me a fighter who's never watched videos of professional fights, and I'll show you a guy who can only go so far.

Another change in Shaolin life was that they were aware of and willing to admit that there were people elsewhere who knew how to fight. When I lived in Shaolin before, they were very fond of telling me that no Shaolin-trained fighter had ever lost a fight to an outsider. That was a complete fabrication. This time around, Du Shifu had me teach boxing to Yi Long in the evenings. In Yi Long, I was witnessing with my own eyes the transformation of a mediocre kung fu guy into a fighter. And it wasn't an easy transformation to make. Kung fu has rules and forms and positions which must be maintained. Everything is dictated to you by the unseen generations of long-dead masters. In boxing, or fighting, you have to be creative, thinking of unique strategies, combinations, and movements.

The next day was back to full training, with four sessions. Between training sessions, I'd try to eat protein-rich snacks, like compressed meat scrapings mixed with some kind of pork product, mango pudding cups, mini-Snickers bars, and water mixed with Sprite. I was truly living the monk's life, a Brooklyn monk's life.

The final training session of every day came right after dinner and lasted an hour and a half. Naturally, I never wanted to do anything at that time, but I pushed myself. Du Shifu always had me review my sanda takedowns and kicks. Then we did power stretching. Finally, I'd do a complete body-strength workout, 300 pushups, 600 abs, a full set of bodybuilding exercises with bricks, squats, and curls with a heavy wooden fence post, takedown and lift practice with the wooden post… By the end, when the sun would be just setting behind the mountains, I'd always look out across the valley and shout "D-R-A-G-O!"

How quickly we adjust to comforts. After morning training, I found myself complaining that my Shaolin house had 18 people, but only two bathrooms. My old Shaolin house had 40 people and no bathrooms. But I felt I had a legitimate gripe about the filth. When I complained to Jacky about how dirty the house was, and the fact there was no soap in the bathroom for the kids to wash their hands, he told me: "You don't understand Chinese culture. Maybe, after you've lived here for five years, you won't wash your hands either." There you have it, straight from the horse's mouth: Uncleanliness is a part of the culture.

When I wrote about this on Facebook, people in the West called me a racist and said I didn't understand foreign culture and that I should go back to Brooklyn. I was half inclined to agree, fly home, wash my hands, and come back.

After lunch, I slept and then had Chinese class. Each time we finished Chinese class, I had to laugh at myself and at the differences in culture. I always said that 90 percent of the problems we have with communication and with language aren't linguistic, but rather cultural. If we compare exams, for example, the English exams (IELTS and TOEFL) require a tremendous background of allegedly general knowledge. There are paragraphs and stories about the migration of whales, inventions, and biographies of famous people. The Chinese HSK exam, on the other hand, contained a lot of general philosophical statements, such as "Protecting the environment is everyone's responsibility," or "In raising children, it's important to praise their success, without chastising their failures." So much of passing the exam is dependent on understanding not only the language, but also the way Chinese people think, what they would consider fair test questions and appropriate answers. One of the sentences in today's lesson was, "If you only look at people's weak points, you'll miss many opportunities to make friends."

Jaka told me that he gave up his career in New York to live in China, practice wushu and learn Chinese. I connected him with Chu Laoshi at Shanghai University of Sport, and Jacky wrote him a recommendation letter. He eventually got a full scholarship to do a master's degree in wushu. The difference between his acceptance and mine, however, was that because he couldn't pass the HSK, he'd be provisionally admitted to study Chinese for a year first. If, at the end of the year, he could pass the HSK, he'd be admitted to the full degree program. Because of the language requirement, the master's would take him four years.

Two new Chinese students joined our house. Sheepishly, once they understood I spoke Mandarin, one of them asked me: "Do you know Kobe Bryant?" I said that I'd heard of him. The new student asked if I'd ever met him. When I told him that I hadn't, he looked disappointed. Then his friend sort of slapped him and said, "He's from New York. Kobe Bryant lives in California. It's far away." Yes, that's the reason I never met Koe Bryant.

I'd been watching Yi Long transition from kung fu to sanda, and now I got to watch these two Chinese kids start wushu from scratch. Your logical brain tells you that everyone has to start at zero, but somehow, when you see the Shaolin guys perform, you just assume they were born with those skills. But watching the two new guys, they didn't seem to have been born with any skills at all. Worse, they were from well-off families. In addition to never having played sports, they'd also never had to work.

The Shaolin students were incredibly skinny. But the two new arrivals were even skinnier, just skin and bones. After they got their heads shaved, they looked like cancer patients. It amazed me that the parents wouldn't take one look at their kids and start force feeding them lasagna.

During sanda takedown training, Du Shifu kept telling me not to use my wrestling takedowns which often involved long clinches, and in-fighting, followed by a lift. He warned me that I'd get tired. It took me a while to figure this out, but the reason he was so careful about not wanting me to get worn out throwing people is because, in an MMA fight, you may only throw your opponent once, and keep him there the rest of the fight. In sanda, however, you have to be ready to throw the guy five times in a single round. The master was right: You could get tired.

After sanda training, I was weightlifting with rocks, when one of the young trainees asked, "Do your muscles burn when you do that?" I told him they did. He thought about it a minute, and asked, "But then you continue doing it?" I told him that was right. Finally, he said, "That's why I'll never be big and strong. I stop when it hurts."

For several days, Jaka, Hugo, and I had been looking forward to the arrival of two new Italian students. We'd been joking about Italian stereotypes and how the Italians would be friendly, happy, loud, and generally more fun than a circus. Even the Chinese kids knew that Italians were loud and funny, and completely unable to adapt. One Italian had left just before I arrived. He'd been there six months and still complained about the kitchen closing between meals and other annoyances that the rest of us had simply resigned ourselves to. Jacky told me that the Italian used to go into Dengfeng every day to eat burgers and buy cigarettes. He met a Chinese girlfriend online and stayed busy with a bunch of new friends. His mother even came and stayed for a few weeks. Somewhere in that busy schedule, he managed to do some kung fu. I wish I'd known him. He sounded like a hero.

He'd left his mark on the house, as all the Chinese kids were running around Shaolin Temple saying, "Veloce, ciao bella, and culo." Isn't globalization wonderful? If it wasn't for all of the Italian students, the kids wouldn't have known these useful words and phrases.

The two Italians arrived and they were the most boring people I'd ever met. They didn't want to speak to me in Italian because my Italian wasn't great, and they needed to learn Chinese and English. But they didn't speak English or Chinese well enough, so they only talked to each other in Italian, ignoring the rest of us. Fortunately, a few days later, several more Italians arrived who were more friendly and more fun. They always engaged me in conversation and asked me to translate for them. This became one more of the many surreal things about living in Shaolin: I got to speak Italian every day, and translate Italian into and out of Chinese.

If it rained overnight, 6 a.m. training was usually cancelled. There was one kid who'd memorized the phrase, "no training" in English. He'd go around, knocking on everyone's door, saying "no training." If you understood him, he'd smile proudly. This morning, he knocked on my door and told me "no training." Then he switched to Chinese and said, "Tell your roommate." My Italian roommate was fast asleep, and I told the boy that. He answered, "You have to tell him!" So I woke Stefano up, and told him there was no training. He looked confused, but then went back to sleep, and the Chinese boy was happy.

In Shaolin Temple, outstanding trainees, generally when they're about sixteen years old, will be tapped by the master to become *jiàoliàn* (coaches). In many schools, the *jiàoliàn* run most training sessions, and the monks only stop in once in a while, to see if everything is going smoothly. In my old school, the monk might run one session per day, or might go days without even attending a session. In this school, Du Shifu was much more engaged, and we had lessons with him every single day, which was a great experience. Still, he selected two young *jiàoliàn* to run physical training and lead the others on runs and during sessions when Du Shifu might be called away on pressing business.

At sanda training, Yi Long, Hugo, the two *jiàoliàn* and I learned about how to referee a competitions. The rules and steps to setting up a contest were fascinating. Afterward, our test was having to referee the weekly sanda fights between the younger kids.

It was a great experience. I felt like when I was back at the Ultimate MMA Academy (UMA) in Malaysia, where I lived when I was a pro fighter. My coach had basically forced me to learn to be a teacher as the next phase in my development as a martial artist. And here I was in China, helping these young kids learn to fight.

One difference between MMA and sanda is that in MMA there's no eight-count. If a fighter gets hit so hard that he's nearly knocked out, in MMA the fight just continues. In boxing or sanda, the referee stops the fight, counts to eight, and if the fighter's head has sufficiently cleared, the fight continues. Another difference in the rules, at least for these competitions, was that if there was any blood at all, the referee stopped the fight. In MMA you usually only stop a fight to check a wound if there's profuse bleeding over the eyes. But profuse bleeding anywhere else would generally not be cause for a stoppage.

Several times I stopped a fight for unanswered blows. In amateur boxing, this means that a fighter got hit, say ten or more times in a row, without striking back, or he turned his head and hid in the corner. In amateur boxing, especially for kids, we'd stop the fight, separate the fighters and do an eight-count, even though the kid wasn't hurt, just because he didn't fight back. If that happens three times, that kid loses. But in sanda, they told me to just let them keep fighting, even if one kid was all balled up in the corner and not fighting back.

The first time I watched the kids fight, when I first arrived, I noticed that none of them had mouthguards. I told Jacky to buy mouthguards for them, which he did. But during these fights, I saw that a lot of the kids choked on their mouthguards or spit them out. It turned out that no one had ever taught them how to boil the mouthguard and form-fit it to their mouths. After the fights, therefore, I showed the *jiàoliàn* and a couple of the kids how to do their mouthguards. The results excited them; they were all saying, "Wow! That's better!" The *jiàoliàn* were both very smart kids, and they instantly asked me: "Can I boil it again, and again, and keep fitting it, till it's perfect?"

Cool! They got it. And once I'd taught the *jiàoliàn*, I knew they'd teach the other kids and it would hopefully become part of the culture of the house.

Two of the trainees were brothers who had no parents. Their tuition was supported by their older sister, who was also poor and had two children of her own. When I arrived, one of the brothers was wearing old eyeglasses held together with string. When the glasses finally fell apart, I took the two brothers to Dengfeng and bought glasses for the older brother. Then the three of us ate huge plates of meat in a restaurant. We got some ice cream and headed back to the temple, where I organized a movie night. We set up a TV and watched *Kung Fu Panda* in Chinese, with all of the students. Everyone was happy and laughing together. It'd been a great day.

The next morning, Jaka and I were going to go to Dengfeng to buy food, but when we walked out the front door, we found a mob of angry farmers, armed with hoes and other farm implements. Jacky was nowhere to be found, so I sent him a text telling him that the villagers had come with torches and pitchforks. He responded: "OK, no problem. Can you please stay?" Jacky apparently needed backup.

The crowd grew to 14 people with a lot of loud talk. Du Shifu came down, saying nothing. He just stood in the corner, limbering up and watching everyone. Finally, Jacky came home, and it turned out that the leader of the farm association was angry that Jacky had put up a sign for the school on land which didn't belong to the school. It also seemed they were angry that our school was using water from the river, as they needed it to irrigate their crops.

After a lot of posturing and screaming, Jacky invited them into the house. He then went around, handing them each a cigarette and lighting it for them. As each of them shouted their complaints, Jacky just smiled and nodded, agreeing. This is how negotiations are done in China. One side acts very aggressively and emotionally, to show how concerned they are about the problem. The other side says nothing, just smiles and agrees.

In the West, we put a lot of value on words and would have been coun-
terarguing, every step of the way: "No, that sign is on our property," or "I
have a water permit from the provincial government," and so forth. But in
Chinese culture, words aren't terribly important. In a very practical sense,
do you really care what your opponent is saying? All you really care about is
if you have to pay damages and how much. And again, in China, if a large
group of neighbors claims for damages like this, there's no way you could
pay nothing, no matter what papers you had, or what you said.

In the West, we'd examine the facts to see if the neighbors had a legitimate claim or not. Then we'd determine guilt, assess the guilt, and calculate
the amount of damages to be paid. In China, it was more a matter of assessing how angry the farmers were, letting them vent, and then negotiating a
cash settlement. Jacky wasn't going to get away with paying nothing, but he
also wouldn't have to pay the large sums the farmers had demanded when
they first arrived. Instead, this theater would play out, running its historical
and cultural course, with each actor playing his part. The reason the crowd
grew was probably because the original group of farmers were the ones with
the most legitimate claim, whereas the latecomers were like rubberneckers
who hoped to cash in.

People like Jacky are cunning masters of strategy. They have to be, in
order to thrive in a country like China. In the West, we'd have told the
latecomers they had no legitimate claim, and to get lost. But, by doing that,
you'd be legitimizing the claims of the others. Instead, by allowing those
with no claim to have equal talking time, Jacky was actually reducing the
legitimacy of all of the claims. In the end, Jacky agreed to pay the farmers
RMB 100 (US$ 16) each and cover the sign for two weeks.

The irony of this cash payment is that each of the foreign students had
paid Jacky close to US$ 1,000 for a month of training, food, and lodging.
What Jacky paid to the farmers only amounted to about a quarter of the
money paid by a single foreign student in a single month. Maybe six of the
claimants had no legitimate grievance at all, but so what? The money was

minimal and now Jacky had built goodwill with the community. It was in their interest to ensure that his business survived, because then they'd get additional payments next summer. When they broke out the bottles of *báijiǔ* ("white liquor"), I knew the negotiations had finished. Jacky signaled that I was free to leave.

Sanda sparring day was coming up and I wanted to have a good, strong opponent, to really test my skills. I contacted AJ in Shanghai and Greg, a freelance journalist, and asked if they'd come to Shaolin Temple. As a life-long martial arts fanatic, AJ jumped at the chance. Greg said he'd do photos and write a story about the trip.

The first time I was in the temple, just being there was weird and surreal. This second time, having WiFi and being alongside other foreigners, not to mention speaking Italian every day, made the experience even weirder. And now I'd have my American friends from Shanghai join the cast of characters.

In China, rooms almost never have shelves. Even in larger apartments, you may only have one wardrobe and no closets. In Shaolin, my room had neither a wardrobe nor a closet, so I'd been storing my gear on the two empty beds. Now that my friends were occupying the beds, there was no place to store anything. To quote the movie *Step Brothers*, I wished we'd bunk beds, because then we'd have so much more room for activities.

AJ was about 8 kg (18 lbs) lighter than me, extremely fit and an excellent kickboxer. Greg had heard of martial arts before coming, but had no specific interest. But as a journalist, he fascinated by every aspect of Chinese history and culture, so this trip suited him. Sharing the Shaolin experience with the two of them was priceless. AJ joined Yi Long and me as we did our morning runs, carrying the heavy bag, lifting rocks, standing on posts — and Greg took pictures. Documenting this experience was a team effort, yet it seemed Greg had the easier job.

Du Shifu had AJ, the trainees, and me carry stones and buckets of water up and down the mountain. It looked like forced labor, but it was just training. Even so, AJ and I joked that if we saw the master mixing cement or measuring and cutting lumber, we'd know we were just doing free construction work.

On fight day, the students gathered in the practice field, where we fought on filthy old mattresses. Two older boys were serving as *jiàoliàn*, and Du Shifu had them referee our competition. I'd been working with Yi Long on his boxing every day since coming to the temple, and when he got in the ring with one of the Italian guys — despite looking a bit nervous — he absolutely destroyed the guy. His punches had become nice, long, disciplined, and powerful. Add to this his natural gift of long legs and arms, and the incredible power in his thighs, from years of living in the temple, and he'd become a double threat. He could now punch and kick very effectively. He still needed a lot more sparring and experience and needed to learn strategy if he wanted to be a fighter, but against most part-time martial artists in a sanda fight, he'd win.

My mind was too focused on MMA and I very much regret how I fought that day. Because I knew AJ was the better kicker and I was the better grappler, every time the referee said "Fight!" I'd rush out, punch him once or twice, and then clinch and try to toss him out of the ring for some points. I should have just boxed with him and allowed him to throw more punches and kicks, so the fight would have been more interesting. Instead, I kept going for the cheap, boring win. Du Shifu was not happy, telling me, "This isn't sumo, it's sanda."

The other criticism the master made of both AJ and me was that when we caught the opponent's kick, we'd punch him in the face, instead of taking him down. In sanda, takedowns are a lot of points — but in my opinion, free shots to the face are nice, too.

AJ and Greg had both been studying Chinese in Shanghai. Of course, they saw the value of a stay in Shaolin as an opportunities for actual immersion. Many language-learners overestimate the value of just living in another country, mistakenly believing they're immersed in the language. The vast majority of foreigners in China aren't immersed; in fact, they've very limited exposure to the Chinese language. Most people sleep eight hours at night, and get no Chinese language input while sleeping. The rest of the time, most of them work in jobs where they have to speak English or they work with colleagues who speak English. Their friends are other foreigners or English-speaking Chinese; and, of course, they watch English-language TV shows and movies.

If they do attend Chinese classes, their classmates are all foreigners. I often confronted people who claimed to be immersed, asking them: "Exactly which part of your day do you mistakenly feel qualifies as immersion?" Or, using the Automatic Language Growth (ALG) concept of counting hours, "How many hours are you truly exposed to Chinese language each day?" Shaolin Temple was one of the few experiences I had in China where a foreigner could be truly immersed in the Chinese language. Shanghai University of Sport was a completely different kind of immersion, with advantages and disadvantages — but going to China and taking a Ph.D. taught in Chinese isn't an option open to everyone, whereas anyone could just fly to Dengfeng, pay money and live in a Shaolin Temple school. The only issue with this option is that, in most Shaolin schools, foreigners are kept separate from the Chinese students and thus have very limited exposure to the language.

My two friends were interested in touring around and comparing the various Shaolin schools to see if AJ might want to live and train in one and if Greg might find a program that interested him. We thought there might be a school where the monks were teaching Buddhism, history, culture, or calligraphy in Chinese, and Greg could arrange his immersion, while also adding to his knowledge about China.

We hired a taxi and visited several of the larger schools. All of them were cheaper than where we lived. I was paying about RMB 6,000 (US$ 952) a month, but the cheapest schools we found cost about RMB 4,000 (US$ 635). And all of them had nicer accommodation than ours. Tagao and the bigger schools cost about RMB 5,000 to RMB 6,000 every month, but you lived in hotel-style accommodation. They all professed to serve meat three times a day. On the downside, all of the schools we visited had Chinese and foreigners separated, except in the sanda programs which were mostly Chinese and a few foreigners. Since AJ and I both wanted sanda, that aspect of the schools appealed to us, but then there was the size issue. Most of the Shaolin trainees were under eighteen. Training four times a day and eating almost no meat, they were generally too small for AJ and me to spar with.

The PRC wants to be a world-class tourism and study destination, but in general, the country is clueless about marketing, or how to listen to customers' needs and wants and then fulfill them. Jacky's attempts to talk me into doing Wushu Taolu instead of sanda, after I'd bought my plane ticket and paid my money, was a classic example. It was almost as if they thought they could fool you or convince you that you wanted something other than what you'd asked for. And there seemed no concern on their part that I'd go on the internet and tell people not to go to this or that Shaolin school because they'll rip you off.

Another example of cluelessness was a lack of customer service, or even willingness to interact with prospective customers. We walked into one of the Shaolin schools and an administrator asked aggressively, if not suspiciously, "What do you want?" I told him that we were looking for a place to study for several months. The administrator answered "OK," and that was it. We just stood there in awkward silence, so I asked if he could show us around or tell us about the place. He thought it over, as if it were a strange request, but reluctantly agreed. He led us around the school, which was like a concrete prison with thousands of students, and the foreigners kept completely separate.

At another huge school, they did the same thing, only reluctantly agreeing to show us around or talk to us. We were so turned off that we started heading for the exit, but the guy ran after us, asking for our passports so they could start the visa process and get us moved in.

After touring a number of schools, it seemed that not only did foreigners live separately, but all of the big schools even had separate cafeterias for the foreigners. The biggest ones, like Tagou, were like villages, complete with ATM machines and shops.

In most of the schools — despite AJ and I saying we only wanted to learn sanda — they tried to convince us that we wanted to learn tai chi, qigong, or Wushu Taolu, because that was what they had the most of. They all assured us that we'd get sanda training, but when we pressed about the hours, it inevitably turned out that sanda would only be a few times per week.

The best sanda program, by far, was at Tagou. Aside from having students who actually specialized in sanda, Tagou had indoor training, which was cooler in summer and where, ostensibly, one could continue training in winter. Also, there were so few foreigners in the sanda section that Chinese and foreign students trained together. But when we visited, the sanda team was taking an exam, so there weren't many people training. We saw one fat kid who weighed the same as AJ or me. This was another problem I faced when training in Asia: In addition to not finding enough sparring partners at my weight, when I did find guys who weighed as much as me, they were generally fat and shouldn't have weighed as much as me. At the sports university, of course, I did find strong heavyweights who were in shape and could destroy me in a fight — but they were a small minority, selected from across a very large country.

Back at our house, the foreign students had all been asking me to translate all sorts of intellectual and cultural kung fu questions for Du Shifu. Finally, I suggested to Du Shifu, that we should have a class in the classroom; everyone should bring their notebooks, and they could ask whatever they wanted to know.

We spent two hours in the classroom, with me translating the questions and answers. Occasionally, it was difficult because I didn't really do wushu. I didn't always know the proper names for the forms and things they were talking about. But that was a small problem. The big problem was that the foreign students kept asking things that no Asian person would ever ask, or be prepared to answer. Sometimes I felt I didn't blend so well in Asia. But at times like this, I realized just how ingrained Asian culture had become. I'd sometimes shudder at the questions they wanted me to translate, thinking: "Wow! That's a huge insult."

One example was that Du Shifu was writing on the board in the sort of lazy script which people use in their daily lives in China. One student kept asking me to tell the master to write in the more formal school script, so they could copy the Chinese words more easily. I simply refused. Asking him that might insult him, as if you were saying he didn't write well. Face is huge issue for Chinese people. It was also possible that he didn't know how to write school script, because he'd lived in Shaolin Temple from age of 11.

Another student asked how many forms Du Shifu knew, which is an example of a question that a foreigner might ask, but which the master would find revealing. He was constantly saying it's better to practice the basics for years before learning even one form. And similarly, it was better to master one form than learn two. He'd told us numerous times about a foreign shifu who'd come to Shaolin claiming to know eighty forms, but they were all terrible.

Other questions were reasonable from a Western perspective, but strange from an Asian one. One guy said that he loved kung fu so much he'd quit his well-paying job to come study at Shaolin. He explained that Shaolin had brought so many good things to his life. He asked me to ask Du Shifu what kung fu had brought to his life. I completely understood why he wanted to ask this. However, from an Asian perspective, things often are as they are, and simply that. In other words, Du Shifu had lived in the temple for twenty years. That was his reality. He didn't think or wonder about other realities, just this one. He couldn't say if it was better or worse, because he had nothing to compare it to.

Other students asked the names and meanings of various forms and movements. Often the explanations were incredibly long and touched on elements of ancient Chinese culture, religion, or history. Many of the names were plays on words in Chinese, where the same name could be interpreted two ways. A Westerner might think the two meanings were a million years apart, but from Chinese perspective they were next-door neighbors.

The very meaning of kung fu (*gōngfu*), the most basic term, which defines everything we were learning, is one of these multi-layered, dual-meaning, culturally-tied words. The *gōng* can mean work; it can also mean a kind of skill or a kind of endurance, developed over time. Du Shifu said, for example, when the kids fight sanda on Tuesdays, sometimes they cry or they quit when they get punched. Seasoned fighters get hit ten times as hard, but don't quit. They have developed a resistance to pain over a period of years. In his words, "There's kung fu in everything. The way you teach at the university is kung fu. The way you translate is also kung fu. The way you carry buckets of water or stones up and down the hill each day. It's all kung fu."

Looked at from that perspective, I guessed I did do kung fu. My fighting and my studying were kung fu.

As the class went on, I realized why there were no classes like this in the Shaolin curriculum. All of these facts would have or should be learned naturally, over a period of years and years of practicing with a shifu.

When I wrote *The Monk from Brooklyn*, I was extremely critical, partly because of the inhuman living conditions in my old Shaolin school, but also because I'd come there hoping to find some sort of magic, a transformation, or ancient secret fighting skills that would help me develop as a fighter. After I got here, I realized that Shaolin Kung Fu had almost nothing to do with fighting. A lot of the anger and frustration that I expressed in that book was a reaction to a general public perception that Shaolin students were phenomenal fighters, or a belief that if they went into the cage, they'd kill their opponents. And that was simply not the case.

After I left Shaolin in 2003, I more or less wrote off Chinese martial arts as not being viable for fighting. Even sanda, I thought, was useless because I'd only seen amateur sanda, and it didn't stand up to the Muay Thai in Thailand or MMA anywhere. Fast forward to 2011, I was in Kuala Lumpur, watching the China vs. The World kickboxing tournament. The Chinese fighters were all professional sanda fighters and they all won their bouts. That's when I made several realizations. First, pro sanda is a completely different world from amateur sanda. Next, sanda is much more adaptable than Muay Thai. And of course, with the striking, combined with aggressive takedowns, sanda only lacked ground fighting, to be MMA.

And so, my interest in sanda was renewed.

Now it was July 2013, and I was sitting in my room at Shaolin, writing about the things I'd seen. The dedication that it took for these boys to master their forms, the number of years of living in the temple, enduring hardship to become a shifu... I now had a huge amount of respect for what they did. Interestingly, they seemed to know that what they did wasn't fighting and had nothing to do with fighting. They practiced the art, for the art's sake, for discipline and tradition, but not for fighting.

In all the Shaolin schools I'd visited, the sanda training was completely separate from the kung fu. So I didn't understand why Westerners on the internet would argue with me about how the Shaolin students were great fighters and how they'd kill people in the cage and on and on, when the Shaolin guys themselves would never think that for a minute. I understood that now, with the steps involved in transforming Yi Long from Shaolin to sanda. Going from performance to fighting wasn't a natural progression.

How was it, then, that I was constantly coming under attack on the internet, and forced to defend my opinions, which were supported by obvious facts and experience? Now I'd lived in the temple twice and visited many schools, and all of this experience had reinforced my conclusions about the relationship between fighting and Shaolin. On the internet, I seemed to always be arguing against people who'd neither had fights nor trained in a place like this. In my case, I could also compare my Shaolin experienced to the year I spent living in an MMA academy in Malaysia and fighting as a full-time professional. I was arriving at my conclusions based on comparing two known quantities. The people who disagreed with me on the internet had generally done neither of these things. They were arriving at a conclusion by comparing two unknown quantities.

When I look at the year I spent in the MMA academy and compare it to Shaolin, MMA is fighting. Shaolin isn't, but it's incredible. The students were gymnastics/ballet/kung fu experts. Through years of training and sacrifice, they achieved an inhuman level of physical skill.

The schizophrenia of this experience was periodically experiencing kung-fuey moments of deep appreciation, followed by losing my mind at how very basic, human activities were unnecessarily complicated in Shaolin or in China in general.

Once time I was doing my laundry when Jacky told me that school rules forbade washing socks or underwear in the machine, because everyone uses it and that would be dirty. Where to begin? These are the same people who have never cleaned the refrigerator or the microwave and who leave food out uncovered, who have never cleaned the kitchen, who have used the same pair of filthy disposable gloves to prepare all of our meals, who don't use disinfectant in the two bathrooms that serve 25 students and teachers, and who don't wash their hands after using the toilet.

"In China, people think it's dirty to wash clothes in a public laundry," explained Jacky.

"But isn't the washing machine self-cleaning?" I protested.

When it became clear that I wasn't going to acquiesce, Jacky walked away. That way he could pretend he didn't know I'd disobeyed him.

Later that evening, in spite of the laundry rebellion, Jacky invited me to have tea with a veteran monk from the temple who'd spent his entire life hardening his body. His head was shaped like some type of Viking helmet and could break steel bars. I was so tempted to ask if I could use it to crack walnuts. His hands were hard as stone, even the muscles that control the thumb were solid. He was famous for stabbing trees with his fingers. When I was invited to feel his fingers, they felt like steel rods.

The iron-body master said that, thirty years ago, he stood in front of the temple gate, waiting to be given permission to enter. He stood there for seven days, till they allowed him to come work in the kitchen. He worked in the kitchen for three years before they allowed him to begin studying kung fu.

It was such a classic and awesome story, and probably true, but it sounded like a movie plot. Today, anyone willing to pay tuition can join. Maybe the martial arts have lost something through the rapid development of China's economy.

The master told me that kung fu is in everything. "You cannot separate kung fu," he said. "Wudang, Shaolin, tai chi… are all one, and you can't separate them." Wudang is another large, famous martial arts temple, located in Hubei Province. "By the same token, you cannot separate your mind and body, if you wish to learn kung fu." From his viewpoint, even when working in the kitchen, he was learning kung fu. His mind was focused. And both his body and his spirit were inside Shaolin Temple, nowhere else. When he began studying kung fu, he didn't begin at level zero. In his own words, he began at level two or three.

The next day, the iron-body master returned to do a demo for us. He not only did pushups on two fingers and broke bricks with two fingers, but when he broke the bricks, they were supported, not suspended or bridged, and he didn't shatter them, he shaved off big chucks, like an expert chef chopping a block of chocolate. Afterward, he hung stones from his groin. That part was very disturbing. I saw this demo with my own eyes, and yet couldn't fully believe it.

The master said that nowadays, very few young people wanted to learn iron body, because the conditioning was so painful. And most didn't want to suspend heavy objects from their groins. He was in his forties, had never married or had children, and still hadn't found a young apprentice who wished to follow him and take his place after he passed on. He predicted that iron body might die out.

Du Shifu then had me teach a grappling class for the Italians. When I taught boxing to Yi Long, obviously I had to use Mandarin to teach. When I taught at the MMA academy in Malaysia, I often had to teach in Chinese. Teaching grappling to those foreign students was the first time I ever taught a martial arts class using Italian.

When I teach MMA grappling, it's a mix of boxing and wrestling, rather than Brazilian Jiu-Jitsu (BJJ) and Muay Thai. Boxing and wrestling suit my personality — I'm aggressive, I like to fight, to mix it up. BJJ is a different mindset. There are certain people who don't even like martial arts but they love BJJ. In fact, a lot of BJJ people are doctors and lawyers, educated people who don't even like fighting, but are brilliant at BJJ. I've never trained in Brazil, but hope to go there some day.

After our grappling class, a set of parents came to enroll their son in the school. The question when they come to the Shaolin area isn't if they'll leave their child in a temple school for years, but which one. They drive around, visiting several schools and somehow arrive at a decision. It's really amazing that this type of culture still exists in China. The only places remotely similar are the Muay Thai boxing camps in Thailand. But kids usually go to those out of economic necessity, not because their middle-class parents chose it for them.

That night, Du Shifu gave me my final exam in sanda and chin na (Chinese grappling, *qínná*). Yi Long and I had to run through all of the kick defenses, kick catches, and takedowns we'd learned, as well as the chin na grappling. It felt pretty amazing to be able to pass an exam, taught in Chinese, and know that I'd be getting a sanda certificate from Shaolin Temple (or, more accurately, the Shaolin Temple Kung Fu and Culture Institute). It probably didn't mean anything to anyone else, but to me it meant a lot. It also gave me hope that I'd be able to pass my Ph.D.

The next day was my last. Yi Long had red, leaky eyes. Obviously I'd miss him the most, but I also felt the worst for him. All of the others would get over my leaving in a day or so, but Yi Long and I had been principal training partners, several times a day for the past two months. His life was now going to dramatically change for the worse. Not only would he no longer be getting boxing training, but he'd be training alone. There'd been one day where I had to miss training because I went to see a doctor about my ankle. When I got back, Jaka said, "Yi Long looked so sad and lonely, standing under a tree, punching the bag, all by himself." Now, unfortunately, he'd be doing that every day, as he had before I came.

The whole school turned out, wearing their uniforms, and Du Shifu and Jacky gave me my certificate. Guess who started crying when he was making his farewell speech to his friends at Shaolin Temple?

I made a speech in Chinese, right from the heart. If you've read *The Monk from Brooklyn*, you'll know that I left on horrible terms the first time. Locked inside the school, I grabbed a halberd off the wall and began pounding on the gate, demanding to be let out. But this time around, I'd only good experiences and good memories, not all of which are in this book. Those experiences gave me a lot of joy, and also encouragement on the days when I struggled to run one more mile or carry one more stone.

Being the Brooklyn Monk, I get to go places and see things that most people don't. But there's an emotional cost. No matter where I am or how happy or how miserable I feel, it's only temporary, as I'll be moving on.

I don't remember much of the drive back to Zhengzhou or the flight to Shanghai. I think I was just quiet and emotional. And the luckiest man in the world. I knew that I had two huge adventures coming up. After taking the HSK exam, I'd be going to a traditional wrestling school in Beijing. And, of course, I was about to start my Ph.D. at Shanghai University of Sport, an adventure that would last for three years.

Chapter 3
Concussion and HSK

The Red Sports Movement, established by the Communist Party and the Red Army between 1929 and 1934, consisted of a mass movement of formal physical exercise for workers and peasants, guided by the ideology of anti-imperialism.

Back in Shanghai, an American friend who'd gone back to Chicago for a few months said I could use his apartment. Just like when you finish boot camp or some other arduous chapter in your life, I was dying for a proper shower and about ten hot meals, all of which I had the first day back. A proper bed felt amazing and I slept like the dead. But when I woke up for 6 a.m. training, and there was none, I felt sad and empty.

I had a lot of hoops to jump through, before school started in September, so that kept me mentally busy. I spent the whole of the first day running around, trying to sort out my student visa for the Ph.D. program. At 10 a.m. I was turned away by the visa office because I needed four documents. By that evening, I had three of them, and a promise that the fourth would be delivered the next day.

It was hectic, but several random people helped me that day: An old colleague who I dumped soup on; security guards at the building where I was staying; a pretty policewoman who helped me fill in one of my forms because I still couldn't write Chinese properly. One person who went above and beyond was a university administrator whose paperwork had been rejected by the visa office. While never admitting that he'd screwed up my papers in the first place, he straightened them out for me.

The visa office explained that I'd be granted a three-year multiple entry visa, which meant that I wouldn't have to worry about renewing it during my studies. Once all of these papers were done, I wouldn't need to do anything visa-wise until I graduated in 2016.

I had to meet Professor Dai, my Ph.D. advisor, who told me I'd scored 85 percent on my dissertation research proposal and committee interview. He said that was considered a very high score, especially because of the language issue. That was very encouraging.

That night, surfing the internet, I stumbled across something that broke my heart. I discovered that I'd wasted my time doing all that training at the temple. There's an easier way — an online Shaolin course, where you can get a Shaolin diploma by distance learning. But as far as I knew, it wasn't in any sense legitimate.

The friend who'd loaned me the apartment connected me with a Chinese teacher, surnamed Li, who could prepare me for the HSK Chinese proficiency exam, which I'd be sitting in about three weeks. After giving me some practice tests covering all four skills — reading, writing, listening, and speaking — she developed a strategy for me.

She told me I'd need to score as high as possible in the listening and reading sections, to compensate for a low grade in the writing part. You only need an overall score of 60 percent to pass, and on the practice exams, I was generally scoring 75 to 100 percent on listening and 50 to 70 percent on reading. One of the tricks she taught me for passing the writing was getting your reading scores way up, so you can clearly understand the writing questions and have a good idea of how to answer them. She also recommended answering the questions using characters copied out of other questions.

We made a schedule of classes, two hours per day, seven days a week until the exam. After class, I'd hit the gym. Every night, I studied on my own, working through listening exercises on the computer.

Taking a break from studying, I went to a coffee shop, and instantly remembered that I should have brought a book, because in China, they never have English newspapers or magazines. The only English-language newspaper readily available in the PRC is *China Daily*, a Communist Party mouthpiece. It has very little real content. I like to think of it as the *Seinfeld* of newspapers. It's literally a newspaper about nothing. But Chinese people I've spoken with largely support censorship. From their point of view, the government helps you by blocking controversial stories which you may find confusing.

Once, I had a political argument with a PRC citizen who'd graduated from Peking University, one of China's top universities. He was defending North Korea, saying: "The North Korean government is doing a good job and the US shouldn't get involved."

In China, people will often believe conflicting propaganda. In a separate conversation, I asked the Peking University graduate if he'd like to live in North Korea. He answered, "Of course not! They don't have any food."

I then asked him if China or North Korea had more freedoms. He answered, "China is much freer than North Korea. North Korea is like living in a prison." But when I asked if the US claim that North Korea has few freedoms, awful human rights, and a low standard of living, was accurate, he replied: "No, that's an invention of the US media."

He then hit me with his winning argument: "Luckily, you're in China now. You'll have access to much better information and you can form your own opinion."

My jaw dropped. I said nothing, but was thinking: "Better access to information? You mean other than *The New York Times* and any other media critical of China?"

The list of media blocked in China includes, BBC, Bloomberg, *The Washington Post*, *The Wall Street Journal*, *Time*, ABC (Australian Broadcasting Corporation), *The Guardian*, *The Economist*, NBC, and Al Jazeera — not to mention social media like YouTube, Facebook, and Twitter. Even if he believed that Chinese state media presented better information than all foreign media combined, then I'd still gain nothing by being in China, rather than outside, because no Chinese state media are blocked in the US. In the US, everyone has access to Western media and Chinese-state media. In China, he could only access Chinese-state media.

This was the typical type of argument that would continue all during my degree. Foreign students generally used a virtual private network (VPN), a subscription service which allowed us to bypass the Great Fire Wall of China, and access sites and information banned by the PRC government. Many professors and research students were also secretly using VPNs, but they'd publicly praise the government and the Communist Party for providing them with reliable, state-sanctioned information, while protecting them from "bad" information.

When I was a translation student in Germany in the 1990s, even though very little information was banned in Germany, German academics were scrambling to learn English because the lag time between the publication date of an English-language research paper and the German-language version of it was often a whole year. Also, of course, the majority of papers published in English are never translated into German or other languages. This put German academics at a severe disadvantage. Those who could read English were able to access the newest information in real time.

In the PRC, there were two issues: the lag time until the Chinese-language version was ready for publication; and government censorship. Consequently, the quantity of up-to-date and accurate information available to Chinese academics is a fraction of what's available to scholars in other countries.

To counter any criticism, China decided to become the no. 1 publisher of academic papers. To do this, they made blanket requirements that all masters and Ph.D. students had to publish X number of papers before graduation. And X times the nearly three million graduate students in China would make the country no. 1 in academic publishing, in terms of sheer volume. As the world catches up, China simply increases the number of papers required for graduation. There is, however, no metric for the quality of these papers. The bulk of them rehash papers published by their advisors, which are themselves often rehashed versions of papers published in the West, but with a lag of several years, to allow for translation and censorship.

After the coffee shop, I had to stop by a police station to register my address. In China, the government is supposed to know where everyone is, every day. If you check into a hotel, they have you fill in a police notification form which goes to the local authorities. The same is true of rental contracts. If you stay at someone else's house overnight, you're supposed to go to the local police station, register, and tell them the number of nights you'll be staying. The fine for not doing so is RMB 500 to 2,000 (US$ 80 to 318) for both you and your host.

A lot of foreigners see this as an invasion of privacy and a draconian attempt to control the public, which it is, but you still have to do it. If you don't, there could be tremendous consequences. Some foreigners brag about never having registered, then one day, they go for their new visa or for a tax declaration, and the authorities need to see the pink slips (registration receipts) for every night they've spent in China, without a single omission. In my case, I'd lived in the teacher's hotel for a year, for which I had a pink slip. For the time I lived in Shaolin, I also had a pink slip. Now, I had to inform the police that I was staying at my friend's apartment. In the end, the registration took about two seconds and the police were extremely nice.

As a foreigner, when you go in a government office, take a number and wait in line, if you speak Mandarin, it's extremely likely they'll just jump you to the front of the line. You'll be processed and released, ahead of locals who've been waiting, sometimes for hours. Whenever this happened, I'd see a wave of relief wash over the government worker's face when they realized I could speak Chinese. They genuinely wanted to help, or maybe just wanted to get rid of you, but maybe they couldn't speak English, which made them nervous that they might lose face. Once they found out that I could speak Chinese, they were always extremely helpful.

For Chinese citizens, household registration is a bit of a nightmare. As well as having to register their address, they need to get a permit to move house. To live in Shanghai, they need something like an internal visa. They need a separate document, similar to a passport, to visit Hong Kong, a separate one for Macao, and a separate one for Taiwan. Generally, only people from the wealthiest and most developed cities were allowed to visit those places. As an American, I could of course go to Hong Kong, Macao, or Taiwan without a visa.

My next stop was the visa office, where I had to submit the papers to convert my work permit to a three-year student visa. While I was waiting to be called to the service window, I saw a middle-aged French guy come in wearing some kind of monk's skirt and monk's slippers. His head was shaved and he had a huge, dangling earring. His T-Shirt looked like it'd smell if I got too near him. My first thought was: Why would they give this genie-looking weirdo a visa? Then it hit me, because genies get three wishes.

My number was called, and when I handed in my papers, they told me to go to an office marked "Overstay." It turned out that, although my work visa in my passport said it was good until August 12, it'd actually been terminated when I left my job in June. I didn't realize this, but as they were explaining it to me, it hit me that one of the papers I had to turn in for my new visa was a dated release letter from my employer. That release also marked the termination of my work visa. Technically, I'd been in China illegally for about sixty days, would could cost me a per-day fine of around US$ 75. If you overstay for a long period, you could get permanently banned from ever returning to the country. Ironically, over the past several months, I'd shown the work visa to housing police in Shanghai and Shaolin, and used it at the immigration kiosk at the airport, with no issues, because of the expiration date written on the visa in my passport. I was lucky no one had double-checked it, because I could have been instantly detained and possibly expelled from the PRC.

Obviously, this was all a huge misunderstanding and I'd come in, on my own, to register and legally remain in China. I wasn't hiding anything. The immigration officer essentially needed me to admit that I was wrong, which I did. After that, he gave me a verbal warning, and then passed me on to the next step in obtaining my student visa. Once again, if I'd not been able to speak Mandarin, I don't think I'd have been treated so well.

After I was let me off the hook, I had to stop at several more counters, and obtain various stamps and papers. At the final counter, I had to submit all the papers and leave my passport with them. They told me to return on August 20 to collect my passport and student visa. They gave me a passport receipt which I could show to the police or use for travel within China, but, as far as I knew, I needed my passport to sit the HSK exam. I'd also been considering leaving China until school started, but now that was off the table. I couldn't travel internationally until I got my passport back.

On the way back to the apartment, I noticed a restaurant that had plastic food on display. It looked pretty good, but I never ate there, because I really don't like plastic food. Any time I was with friends, walking past a shop with plastic food in the window, I always loved making that corny joke, or: "If the plastic burgers aren't for sale, why do they put them in the window?"

People told me that the smelly toilets, sweaty days and nights, dirty food and other unpleasantness I endured in Shaolin would make me appreciate civilization. I could have skipped that step: I've always been a huge fan of civilization.

Getting on the Shanghai subway, to go the HSK center, however, one has to ask the definition of civilization. Yes, the subway is hyper-modern, but the people are not. On the platforms, unlike in New York, they didn't walk quickly, but nor did they seem to want to let you get around them. Often, they were looking at their phone, while slowly shuffling through the station. During rush hour, this slowed everything down. Sometimes, they didn't even realize that they were standing at the top of the escalator, and it was their turn to get on. So there'd be a long line of people, standing behind someone who was focused on trying to reach the next level in a game on their phone.

On the subway, people ate full meals, hawked and spit, clipped their nails or talked unbelievably loudly on their cellphones. Once, a guy got on the subway with a bag full of live chickens. Often, I'd see families, clearly coming from the countryside, carrying impossible volumes of baggage and burlap sacks and possibly farm implements.

Whenever a subway train (or an elevator) arrived, people would attempt to crowd in, rather than let the people out first. Once, I happened to be at the front of a large crowd waiting for an elevator, pretty much guaranteed a place. But when it opened, it turned out to be full of huge machinery, some kind of industrial ventilators, that two workers were taking to an upper floor. I saw that and deduced there'd be no room, so I didn't budge, thinking everyone would just wait and take the next elevator. Instead, people pushed me out of the way and tried to squeeze into the elevator. Seeing that, I thought, "This is why so many people die in lifeboat tragedies."

Packed like sardines on Shanghai's subway, I was thinking back to the subway math I'd learned in New York. One skinny person got off, and two fat people got on. It just didn't seem fair. I was now even more crushed than before, simply because some guy had no willpower at the buffet table.

I don't know if it's because of the massive population, the one-child policy, or the totalitarian system, but young and old alike seemed to have zero situational awareness. People got on carrying huge sacks or hoes. They'd accidentally bang you with it, then, two minutes later, accidentally bang you again. You'd move, but they'd manage to bang you again. At the airport, the person in line behind you always bumped your legs with their luggage cart. And there was never an apology or even an acknowledgment that maybe it wasn't nice to bang people with the cart.

Compared to China, Taiwan is *The Jetsons*. In the two-plus years I lived in Taiwan, I never saw an outhouse. Even when I camped in the mountains, the toilets were clean. Taiwanese people take showers. They wash their clothes, and they never spit. But on the plane back to Shanghai from Shaolin Temple, I heard people hawking and spitting in the seats behind me.

·· • ··

At the HSK center, they told me that my temporary passport would be an acceptable identity document. Then they asked me if I had my exam admission ticket. I'd received an email from them, saying I had to download the ticket, but as there was no attachment, I thought I just needed to take a screenshot of the admission information, with my ID number and exam number. It turned out that the admissions ticket was not meant to be attached to the email. Rather, you had to go back to the HSK website, login, enter your numbers, download it, and print it. Luckily, the people at the center were super helpful, and they did this for me. Had I not stopped by and had they not told me this, I wouldn't have been allowed to sit the exam. On the day of the test, I saw several people being turned away. Some of them were shouting: "What exam ticket? There was nothing attached to the email!"

That night, at the MMA gym, I did grappling training with a high-level BJJ guy from Saitama near Tokyo. He was also the Japanese equivalent of a collegiate wrestler. Every time I get around Japanese people, I wonder if they later complain to their friends about me the way I do about China. The Japanese athletes we trained with were always incredibly clean. On this occasional, I was very embarrassed when he asked me, in the middle of the workout, if I'd please change my shirt, because I was all sweaty.

Training in Japan must be very disciplined and systematic, because this was another aspect of these athletes that I really liked. I was amazed at how incredible his takedowns and techniques were. But also, how slowly, and with how little effort he could complete a takedown. He told me that he'd trained in sports BJJ for years, from the bottom up, drilling the basics over and over again.

Training with someone like that makes you question everything you're doing. I hated the way we learned in MMA. It seemed careless and unsystematic. When people asked me if I knew jiu-jitsu or wrestling, I always said: "No." They'd then ask: "But you must have learned it for MMA." So I'd answer, "Yes, I learned a little for MMA." I was tired of that answer, and I was hoping to learn wrestling — really learn it, step by step, drilling with well-trained partners and opponents — at the sports university in September.

Training and studying, on top of worrying about the HSK, was taxing, but AC made all the difference in the world. You can't imagine how much more comfortable I was, not constantly dripping sweat and not having flies crawling all over me, like at the temple. The stomach cramps I'd been suffering due to dirty food disappeared. Living at the temple, it occurred to me, had a lot in common with the symptoms of heroin withdrawal.

By 7 a.m., it was already 31 degrees Celsius (88 degrees Fahrenheit). I suspected it'd be another hot one. At 8 a.m., on my way to Chinese class, I saw a workman about to take the elevator. Before getting in, he threw his still-lit half-finished cigarette on the floor in the hallway.

Each time I took the elevator, I got a kick out of seeing which numbers were missing. In the West, the unlucky number is 13. Here in China, the death number is 4. In Shanghai, they cover both bases. My apartment building had no floor 4, floor 13, 14 or any number ending in 4. As I ran through the building's courtyard, I passed the groundskeepers. They were just finishing huge bottles of beer.

I was meeting my Chinese teacher at a coffee shop. Approaching, and reading its name for the millionth time, I realized I'd been an idiot. The shop's name was Caffè Bene. (It's a Korean-owned chain.) For more than a year, I'd believed was a takeoff on The Coffee Bean. That day it finally hit me that "bene" wasn't a misspelling of the English word "bean," but the correct spelling of the Italian word "bene," which means "well." But, to keep myself from feeling too stupid, I could now make fun of the poor grammar. In Italian, "bene" should modify a verb, not a noun. Man, those guys are dumb!

My Chinese teacher told me that she was from Yanbian Korean Autonomous Prefecture, a place in northeastern China I'd fantasized about for years. It's home to Yanbian University, China's only bilingual university, which teaches in both Korean and Chinese. I'd dreamed of going to study there and to learn Korean wrestling. I even built it into my preliminary research proposal for my Ph.D., but it seemed an impossibly far off dream.

At the moment, all I could think about was getting through the HSK. Before I started my exam prep, I knew fewer than 200 Chinese characters, although I could pass the listening and speaking exams. My teacher was going to try and teach me to write the characters, but that's so time consuming. We'd only be able to do about sixty or so characters by exam day, which wouldn't be a help. So, our strategy was for me to learn to read as many characters as possible, but then to just write them, however I could, as poorly and as horribly as need be, copying characters out of exam questions, just, somehow, fail the written with a high enough score, that I could have a passing average on the exam overall.

That night, I wrote in my diary: "Can't wait to get this bloody exam out of the way and stop speaking Chinese."

At MMA that night, we did hard sparring. One of the guys I sparred with was a French guy with a good BJJ level. He was an OK guy but sometimes I felt he was a little bit of a bully with his superior BJJ skills, even picking on new guys. Generally, when we rolled (did BJJ sparring) he could take me down sometimes, but I could often defend his takedowns or get a reversal. Our BJJ rolls were a true example of MMA vs. BJJ because he definitely had the BJJ skill and could often submit me on the ground, but I could often completely neutralize him and get top position.

Tonight was different, however, because we were doing MMA hard sparring together. It was the first time we'd ever done MMA together, and this was meant to be like a fight with about 70-percent power. One criticism I make of some BJJ guys is that, although BJJ is a crucial component of MMA, BJJ isn't MMA. I think he thought he'd just roll over me with his BJJ. When the signal went for us to start, I came out boxing, and he immediately went for the take down. Working from inside of the clinch I pounded him. I don't normally hit anyone that hard in sparring, but I just wanted to take him down a few notches. I hit him a few times so hard that he winced or shouted. When he went again for the takedown, he clearly forgot that this was MMA, not BJJ. He left himself wide open to being repeatedly punched. I got the reversal and crushed his body when I landed on him. I immediately jumped back to my feet and I could see he'd have preferred if I'd remained on the floor with him. Reluctantly, he stood up, and again he kept trying to clinch and take me down, and I kept hitting him from inside. I nearly knocked him out from inside the clinch. He went for yet another takedown and I landed on top of him and pounded him. There was still a glimmer of hope in his eyes as he got guard. But working within the guard is my specialty. I hit him so hard from inside of his guard he finally tapped.

Afterward he looked shocked, like everything he'd ever known about fighting or MMA went out the window. He quietly collected his gear and left. I respect all martial arts. I think taekwondo is wonderful for children, karate is good for anyone who loves it, tai chi is good for health, and BJJ is amazing for grappling competitions. But everyone needs to remember what they're learning and where their world is. BJJ people can become phenomenal MMA fighters, but they have to learn MMA. You can't get in an MMA ring and do pure BJJ or boxing or Muay Thai and hope to have the same success you do in your own sport, under that sport's rules.

Later, I sparred with a huge Russian kickboxer, which was good practice for both of us. I was teaching him how to do some takedowns, when his head collided with my eye. I was ducking, he was raising, and the impact was incredible. There was a flash of lightning behind my eye, a buzzing sound in my ears, and a lot of pain. Then I did some more sparring, which I thought was good training for when I get hurt in a fight and have to cover it up really well.

By the time I got home, my eye was swollen shut. I glanced in the mirror, and it looked like a large, alien lifeform had attached itself to my face, to suck out my brains. It was so huge and full of blood, I was tempted to yell, "Cut me, Mick!" and open it with a razor blade. I seriously wished I could treat it with leeches.

The next morning, it'd gone from pink to bright red, and as impossible as it seems, it was even larger. I was still feeling slightly confused and uneasy on my feet, which led me to believe that I had a slight concussion, but I heard from *Archer* cartoons that you get like six freebies.

My head pounded during Chinese class and I had trouble reading Chinese characters with only one eye. By the time I got home, the eye had turned dark blue. By lunch, it was a greenish blue. All I wanted to do was sleep, but I wondered if the old urban myth was true, that if you go to sleep with a concussion, you don't wake up. Or was that, if you get a concussion in a dream, you don't wake up. Either way, I took a nap, and when I woke up, my head still hurt, and the wound had changed color again.

Originally, I'd thought that after the HSK, I'd go to Cambodia for training, to get a break from China before school started. But now, because

I couldn't leave China till my student visa was ready, I decided to stay in the country and go to a training camp. Sadly, so many businesses in China simply don't have websites, or if they do, there's no one checking and replying to email. I was trying to go to Beijing Sports Institute to train in wrestling, but I had to go through an agent. This usually means paying huge fees, but even the agent didn't respond. In the end, I got lucky. Doing a Google search, I located a Chinese wrestling master in Beijing, Wang Wenyong of the Beijing Wang Wenyong Wrestling & Kung Fu Club. I called him and introduced myself. The next morning, my teacher helped me call him again. He said I was welcome to come train for free, I'd just need to pay for my room and board.

After finishing my final Chinese class, the morning before the exam, rather than studying more at home, I decided to stay in the house, sleep, and ice my eye, bringing down the swelling so I could see properly.

The next morning, on the way to the HSK, I saw a girl on the subway, carrying a fashion bag which said "One after another nice claup." I knew this was a sign.

I arrived in the testing room a bit early, so I asked the monitor, in Mandarin, if it was OK to enter the testing room and study until test time. She stared at me amazed and asked in Chinese, "You can speak Chinese?" My first instinct was to get angry at how clueless a lot of Chinese seemed to be about language learning… but then I thought, maybe in her experience the bulk of foreigners sitting the exam couldn't communicate verbally in Chinese. So, luckily, I could still be angry, just not at Chinese people.

Originally, I thought the exam would be on a computer, so I wouldn't have to write by hand, but it turned out that it was on paper. When I finished, I thought it highly likely that I'd failed the writing section. I ran out of time on the reading, so the last five questions I just marked "C." But, on the whole, the reading and listening had been relatively easy and I was fairly certain I'd scored high, perhaps a combined 150 or 160 points. This meant I only needed 20 or 30 points on the writing section to get a combined 180 passing mark. I thought I'd answered enough writing questions correctly to get the points I needed, but only if they overlooked my horrible handwriting. Even so, in retrospect, a mild concussion had probably been the wrong thing to bring to the exam.

My eye injury kept changing shape and color, making each day a new adventure. I couldn't wait to arrive at wrestling school on Monday. I imagined some young wrestler would say, "Look at his face, he must be tough." To which, the master would respond, "No, the man who gave him that face must be tough."

Chapter 4
Beijing Wrestling Academy

Sports and physical education train the physique, on the other hand they
can also implement revolutionary political education.

— **James Riordan,**
"Marx, Lenin and Physical Culture,"
***Journal of Sport History* (Vol. 3, No. 2, Summer 1976)**

One of the first things I noticed on arriving in Beijing was how bad the pollution was. My joke was that Beijing was OK if you didn't like breathing. It felt like someone forcing a pillow down on your face.

The trip to Beijing was my first time on China's high-speed rail network. It was more comfortable than an airplane, with lots of leg room. The distance was 1,318 km (819 miles), but only took between four and a half and six and a half hours. As high tech as that leg of the journey was, I still had to take an old-style taxi to the wrestling school, and got stuck in rush hour traffic.

On the phone, the master had told me that his name was Wang, but after I met him, he told me his name was actually Meng Shifu. Like many disciples, he'd taken the last name of his master, Wang Wenyong. Meng

Shifu was the 63-year-old student of 83-year-old Master Wang Wenyong. Meng Shifu started training with the master when he was nine years old. The two of them had seen a lot of history together.

Meng Shifu owned a fancy restaurant and had converted a room upstairs into a wrestling room. That's where we trained, twice a day. To give you an idea of how fancy the restaurant was, most Chinese restaurants have a menu item called "Five Delicious" in English. His had a dish called "Eight Delicious." That's a net gain of three delicious.

We'd tried to find somewhere for me to stay, but in the PRC, hotels have to be specifically licensed to accept foreign guests, and all of the ones with that license were incredibly expensive. In the end, the restaurant manager agreed to rent me the spare office/bedroom down the hall from the wrestling room. It had TV, internet, a pull-out bed, private bathroom, and AC. I asked her if there was somewhere I could do laundry." When she answered, "Yes, you can use my basin. It's under the sink," it was obvious we were coming from two very different places.

She made a meal schedule for me. The restaurant agreed to make three hot, nutritious meals for me every day, planned around my wrestling schedule. True to his word, Meng Shifu didn't charge me for training, but my room plus food was RMB 230 (US$ 36) per day. This was RMB 30 more than I'd paid to live in squalor and eat dirty food in Shaolin Temple, so I was quite happy.

On the first day of training, Meng Shifu said to me, "Your body is perfect for wrestling." It was nice to finally hear that. Growing up, I'd boxed, not wrestled, and my boxing coaches always said I looked more like a wrestler than a boxer. We were in the wrestling room, which was basically a banquet room with mats on the floor. If the restaurant got very busy, they would roll up the mats and fill the room with tables. The team consisted of about four or five smallish guys who worked as waiters at the restaurant, and a couple of heavyweights who worked elsewhere, but came in for training. The oldest student was Lu Yansan, Meng Shifu's driver. He was in his forties, about a year older than me.

In Chinese shuai jiao wrestling, you try to throw the opponent to the floor. If you throw him and remain standing, you get two points. If you throw him and land on him, you get one point. Each fight has five rounds, and the winner is the one with the most points at the end. The wrestlers wear thick, kimono-style jackets and much of the style is based on the basic techniques of grabbing and pulling the jacket. The throws were largely not done by using upper body strength, but by employing very unique sweeping techniques. Modifying the grip from jacket to head, shoulder or triceps, many of the throws could be used in MMA.

Technically, any grip on the jackets or belts was legal, but there were about seven standard grips which we had to learn and practice. It was legal to grab the legs, but not so common. It also seemed to be uncommon to lift the opponent off the ground and throw him.

The strength and flexibility for the throws came from doing a series of exercises, called *jībĕngōng*, countless thousands of times, each day. During my preliminary research, I'd noticed hat some of these exercises were the same as top judo athletes used.

The first training session included strength training, lifting rocks and concrete blocks. It made me wonder: What is it with traditional martial arts and lifting rocks and odd bits of concrete? Didn't they have health spas 2,000 years ago when these martial arts were invented?

The bulk of the strength training for Chinese traditional wrestling is on your legs, not your arms. I really felt like an ape out there with big biceps and my hairy body. I tried to wrestle my opponents using my upper body strength. The Chinese wrestlers, however, used very unusual sweeping techniques, leg-based throws to take me down. It was as much a clash of cultures as a clash of wrestling styles.

Before coming, I'd watched several of Grand Master Wang Wenyong's *jībĕngōng* videos online. These exercises mimic the specific strength, flexibility, and movement of shuai jiao throws, moving through the specific muscular pathways. In theory, if you learned these exercises and did them correctly 10,000 times, you could throw anyone. I'd later learn that the culture of the old men who'd kept the tradition alive in Beijing was that they'd done *jīběngōng* alone in the park, every day of their lives, since childhood, but only wrestled opponents on Sundays, when they'd all gather in the park.

Just a few of the exercises dealt with upper body strength. Most dealt with turning, dropping, squatting, raising up, and twisting. Interestingly, there were also kicking and punching drills, even though the fighting system doesn't include punches and kicks. The kicks are designed to develop the muscles and speed necessary to do the sweeps. The punches are to teach you to quickly shoot your hand out, grab the opponent's jacket, and pull him in or throw him.

The master said that a beginning student would normally learn two exercises, and practice them for a week before learning the next one. It would thus take close to two months to learn the basics. I wished I could do the whole program, but time didn't allow.

The spirit of traditional martial arts training differs from MMA training. The latter is much more intense, and all about increasing your heart rate and pushing your muscles to collapse. Traditional masters have a different rhythm. As soon as you start sweating, they say, "You're sweating. You must be tired. *Xiūxí yīhuǐ'er, hē hē chá.*" (Rest a while, drink tea.). When I got back from Shaolin, I found that a two-hour MMA workout left me more tired than a whole day of Shaolin training.

The old shifus, the training brothers of Meng Shifu, would come and watch the training. Most were too unhealthy to get on the mat, but they enjoyed watching training, while drinking alcohol, smoking cigarettes, and shouting at the wrestlers.

To be fair, the wrestlers also smoked between training sessions. Also, they offered me alcohol at lunch. I think these guys got good at their art because they did it for years and years, but the intensity was missing. I didn't think they could teach someone to get good quickly.

The smoke in the training room was killing me, and the culture of smoking had a definite impact on my training mates. They had no cardio. For all I knew, they each ran a full marathon every morning, but still wheezed during sparring, like I was fighting my grandfather.

Meng Shifu wanted to see my MMA highlight reel. Afterward, he said it was too violent. The other shifus also said they didn't like MMA because of the violence. Whenever I was sparring, the guys kept joking with me, reminding me "No kicking, no punching." After I was thrown, I instinctively did a reversal or started going for control on the ground, and they would come running over screaming "Stop!" Every time a student asked who I was or if I'd had other training, the students who already knew me would point at my face and say, "You see his black eye? He does MMA."

One of the heavyweights I trained with was called Jao. He was taller than me and looked a lot bigger, but in fact was probably a bit lighter than me, because his legs were smaller. His skills and strength were good for shuai jiao. During strength and conditioning training, I saw that he tired out much faster than me. When I sparred him, I did almost nothing, just counter-wrestling, waiting for him to run low on energy.

The shuai jiao uniform is like a judo uniform, thick and very strong for gripping. When I first started, I only wanted to grab the body, rather than the jacket, because that's what I was used to and what I'd have to go back to after I left. Of course, by doing that, I wasn't really learning shuai jiao. This was the same complaint Du Shifu had back in Shaolin Temple, and it was the reason why I wound up my video series, *Martial Arts Odyssey*.

The original intent of *Martial Arts Odyssey* was to travel to different places, train, and experience their martial arts. But once I started fighting pro again, the goal shifted to picking up techniques I could add to my MMA arsenal. And while that goal is also fine, it's not consistent with the goal of actually learning other styles. Over the next ten years, I'd continue to travel and train and fight, but *Martial Arts Odyssey*, as it was originally intended, ended as soon as I stepped into a professional MMA cage for the first time in 2011.

The shuai jiao clothing gave me a lot of problems in sparring. I'd try to rush in and grab the body or legs, but my opponent would get control of my jacket and throw me. Another issue was the fact that you can't let your knee or back touch the ground or you lose. Finally, if you went down with the opponent, your throw was only worth one point, rather than two. I did win a few rounds, but my points were always low, because I went down with my opponent and covered him. When they'd throw me, I'd want to just continue and take them with me, but you weren't allowed to do that.

When I called home, I complained to my family: "In the only rounds of sparring I won, I got disqualified. No kicking, no punching, and no choking. How can they even call that wrestling?"

In shuai jiao, you wear wrestling shoes which give you good traction, and also protect your ankles from injury. In MMA, we're barefoot. The guys were all fascinated by the fact that I wore a mouthguard. None of them wore a mouthguard or a groin-guard, and some of them got their groins smashed. In fact, I never saw so many injuries in such a short period of time as I did in Beijing. I got back-elbowed in my injured eye, which was a special feeling. Fingers in eyes were common, not because they were dirty fighters, but because they all practiced throwing with open hands, to try and grab the opponent's jacket. If you ducked, you might catch a finger in the eye. There were also injuries to wrists and fingers from gripping the opponent's clothing and throwing him. Falling wrong, usually by the thrower, and getting punched or elbowed by accident, were also common injuries. I never saw them practicing breakfalls or shoulder rolls. When new people started, they learned *jīběngōng*, but never seemed to learn how to fall. There were a lot of black eyes, but none as cool as mine.

As for shuai jiao techniques, I was extremely impressed by the simplicity of the throwing skills. People always ask me if the people I train with in these various places could be retrained to fight MMA or to do Olympic wrestling. The answer is: Probably, but we could also retrain dentists or soccer players. Practitioners of traditional martial arts absolutely don't want to be retrained for MMA or Olympic wrestling. They love their art, and that's what they want to do.

The pace of Chinese wrestling is much more frantic than MMA. Because of the jackets, the second each round starts, they grab you and get a really solid hold. In MMA, to get that kind of control you'd need to get double under hooks or a strong Thai clinch, both of which require a lot of fighting to achieve. But in Chinese wrestling, once they grab your jacket, they just start jerking you, and pulling and pushing you around the circle, looking for an opening. I felt like a baby seal being attacked by a killer whale. My goal was always to reduce the chaos, by getting control first of their hands then their head or body, but it probably made me very predictable, and of course I needed to learn proper shuai jiao techniques, of grabbing the clothing and defending when my clothing was grabbed. So I was a beginner once again.

The eternal student, the new guy in the gym yet again. Because of *Martial Arts Odyssey*, I was always the new guy, and usually the only foreigner or the first foreigner. Every time, I experienced the same pressure, everyone watching you, everyone wanting to spar you. And always those negative thoughts at the back of my mind. Is this the time someone will hurt you on purpose? Will I be able to beat them? If I fight well, but fail to win, will I still win their respect? Will they be offended if I beat them? Will they write me off if the first guy I spar mops the floor with me? Luckily, however, 90 percent of the time, after sparring, everyone becomes friends and we all respect each other. I didn't even know these guys names yet, but I already liked them, because we'd sparred.

That night, a couple of wrestlers came in my room to get some of the equipment stored there. I was watching the *The Ultimate Fighter*, the UFC reality show, and they stayed and watched for a few minutes with me.

When one of them commented, "How can they wrestle with no jacket? They're too sweaty and it's hard to grab," I could only agree. Afterward Meng Shifu asked them what I was watching, and they said *bójí* which is simply "fighting." Most people in China, including athletes, didn't have a word for MMA yet.

Where my MMA friends were all interested in exploring different kinds of martial arts, the traditional martial artists often weren't. I asked one of my shuai jiao training brothers, Li Yuan, if he had ever tried fighting a judo guy; he said simply "no," like he wasn't even interested. Matching Chinese wrestling guys against judo or Mongolian wrestling just seemed like an obvious and interesting experience to me. But once again, we were coming from different places. These guys were practicing Chinese wrestling, to get good at Chinese wrestling. And to do that, they didn't need to match with judo guys or Mongolian wrestlers.

The next day, Meng Shifu introduced me to a wrestling master, Professor Li Mingyuan (no relation to Li Yuan, my training brother.) Professor Li was famous for having been a national champion multiple times. Now retired, he'd once been head wrestling coach at Beijing Sport Institute, China's premier training facility. He was 67 years old and told me about the harsh days of his youth. In Chinese, when you want to make it clear that you've suffered, you say, "I ate bitter." He actually said to me: "I ate bitter. And other than bitter, we had nothing to eat." That's hardcore. He went on to say, "We had bitter and we had suffering, our training was suffering, but there was no prize at the end. There was nothing to win. We just trained." This is something that wrestlers the world over can relate to. All wrestling is hardship and sacrifice. In very few countries is there any chance of financial rewards at the end.

Professor Li said that, as a teenager, he'd had to pay RMB 0.2 (a few US cents) to enter his first national championship. It was the only money he had, so he didn't eat that day. Before the match, Wang Wenyong had noticed that Li looked distressed, and asked him why. Li told him he was terribly hungry, so Wang Wenyong bought him dinner. Professor Li had never forgotten that act of kindness, and adored Grand Master Wang Wenyong.

He, like many of the older sifus, complained that the character of Chinese wrestling changed after the Cultural Revolution, and that the art became heavily influenced by Western wrestling. Many modern shuai jiao practitioners are wrestling students from Chinese sports high schools or sports universities. They cross-train in freestyle or Greco-Roman wrestling, and they carry those foreign techniques into their Chinese wrestling bouts. For example, while Chinese wrestling doesn't typically feature a lot of leg-grabbing techniques, they're not forbidden. Accordingly, students of modern wrestling styles will often use a modified high, single-leg take down to throw their opponent. Similarly, although the Chinese techniques are meant to be based on grabbing the opponent's jacket, cross-trained athletes will often throw the opponent from a body lock or a bear-hug position borrowed from modern wrestling.

Professor Li told me about the role *jīběngōng* had played in his training: "Much of the wrestling training is based on students completing the basic exercises 10,000 times. Traditionally, students had to do only these exercises for up to a year before learning any wrestling moves." Consequently, training consisted of the master teaching the students a single exercise, then sending them home to practice on their own. They'd only meet with the master once a week, so the master could check the progress of their exercises.

He told me that when he was a young boy, first learning wrestling, his teacher asked him, "When and where do you practice?" Professor Li told the master the time and place, and the master said, "If I ever come to that place at that time, and you're not practicing, I will disown you." Professor Li said he was so afraid of his teacher that he went to that place at that time every day and practiced. As a result, his basics became perfect and for many years he was undefeated.

"The student has to have fear and respect for the teacher," said Professor Li. "The student can't say, 'I want to practice this. I want to practice that.' The master has to say, 'You must practice this. You must practice that...'"

And, of course, he complained that young people today don't know bitterness, so they can never learn to wrestle.

During afternoon sparring, each person sparred one complete fight, then rested, while everyone else wrestled, then they wrestled again. When my turn came, I wrestled the two biggest guys and got killed, but I stayed in the ring and wrestled three more opponents, all of whom were smaller than me, but with skills. Finally, I wrestled Jao, the big guy, again. That was the most consecutive wrestling any of them had done. This was another example of the different intensities of MMA and traditional martial arts. I didn't think these guys could even imagine a 17-minute fight or a 45-minute sparring session, both of which are normal for MMA. The flip side is, if you did what they were doing, every day, twice a day, for years, you'd probably not have injuries and you'd steadily, albeit slowly, improve.

I usually ate breakfast alone, but almost always ate lunch with Meng Sifu. By the end of the meal, more often than not the old shifus would join us, start drinking, and be about half drunk by the time afternoon training started. It was a great opportunity to hear their theories on life and martial arts.

Meng Shifu told me that when he was a kid all they had to eat was pressed corn cakes and they were never full. Interestingly, scientists have said that the diet Chinese people ate before they became prosperous enough to eat polished rice was much healthier than it is now. They ate a lot of grains then, but because they were poor, portions were small and people were hungry. Meng Shifu was now rich, and he didn't even charge any of the boys who trained with him. I guess he wanted to put his memories of poverty behind him. He told me: "If you don't eat lots of meat and drink lots of alcohol every day, what's the sense of living?"

"You know that Outer Mongolia belongs to China," he said, switching gears. In Chinese, the independent country of Mongolia is called Outer

Mongolia, to distinguish it from Inner Mongolia, which is an "autonomous region" of the PRC. This is a large bone of contention with Mongolians, who don't like any implication that their independent republic is part of China.

In Chinese wrestling circles, Mongolia is talked about a lot, because Chinese shuai jiao is very similar to Mongolian national Bökh wrestling. And, of course, the Chinese claim that the Mongolian national sport was stolen from China. Later, in my Ph.D. research, I'd find countless dissertations and research papers done by academics, including Chinese academics, showing that shuai jiao, as it exists today, is an amalgam, developed over centuries, with influences from numerous, older ethnic wrestling styles, including Mongolian.

Meng Shifu continued explaining to me that the independent nation of Mongolia still belongs to China. "That's why until today, Taiwan still hasn't granted independence to Outer Mongolia." On the one hand, he was way off, because Mongolia declared independence from the Qing Dynasty in 1911. On the other, there was a grain of truth in what he said about Taiwan-Mongolia relations.

When the Nationalist Republic of China was formed, in 1911, they made a map of their country. It included Tibet, Outer Mongolia, Hong Kong, and Macao (but not Taiwan). In 2002, Taiwan (officially the Republic of China) granted independence to Mongolia, hoping to receive mutual recognition. Mongolia officially thanked Taiwan for a generous cash award, but regretfully refused to recognize Taiwan, for fear of hurting their relationship with the People's Republic of China. Of course, I said none of his to Meng Shifu.

In the mornings, I had private or semi-private training, which was just the basic exercises. In the afternoons, we did sparring. We started working on one throw, but I almost didn't want to learn it till I had better basics. At sparring, I began to notice that many of the guys had bad basics, in other words, they hadn't done the exercises enough times, although they'd learned to throw people. They hated doing the exercises so, after their initial trainee period, they didn't continue. Shifu told me that, if I stayed six months and did the exercises every morning, I'd be better than all of them. I believed him, but it was true that if anyone stayed and did those exercises, they'd quickly surpass the competition.

The basic exercises were the good part of Chinese coaching. The bad part was that one of the old, drunken shifus, generally with a cigarette hanging out of his mouth, would laugh at me when I made a mistake. In the West, that would be considered bad coaching. It didn't make me want to improve. It made me want to kick him in the head. The other thing they tried to do, several times, was to take away my water bottle, telling me I could only sip tinny cups of scalding hot tea during training. I wanted to say to them: "You see those liters of sweat all over the gym floor after I train? Well, those used to be inside my body. Now, we need to replace them. And it's going to take more than dainty cups of hot tea."

I couldn't take down any of the heavyweights. Not only were they bigger and stronger, but they'd been with the master since they were children, so their skills were good. Two of them had been at sports school, one for boxing and one for freestyle wrestling. They had no stamina, though, so I wondered if, next time we sparred, I could sacrifice myself the first four rounds and get a single throw in on the final round when they were coughing up cigarettes.

None of the heavyweights showed up that day, so I was wrestling with the smaller guys. Against the smaller opponents, with a more even skill set, I was able to get some take downs, but my points were low, and I wasn't sure if everything I did was legal. At one point, I accidentally tapped out my opponent. I got him in a standing front headlock, and while I was looking for the throw, he panicked and tapped because he mistakenly believed he couldn't breathe. I got one actual Chinese sweep or something like a Chinese sweep, just from watching the other guys. I also had two or three throws where I managed to get back-control, because my opponent was going for a hip throw, and I reversed, lifted him off the ground, and slammed him. But I wasn't sure if that was legal. I also grabbed the opponent's shirt for the first time.

One of the many issues about transitioning from MMA to Chinese wrestling was that these guys spent almost 100 percent of their training time on takedowns. In MMA, we practiced, boxing, Muay Thai, jiu-jitsu, wrestling, strength and conditioning, and takedowns. For us, takedowns are a small part of what we know, whereas these guys are specialists. Another issue is that I couldn't distract them with punches or kicks and then go for a takedown. As soon as the round started, the opponent knew I was looking for the takedown. It's much harder to attack someone who knows exactly what you want to do, and who's a specialist at defending against that one thing.

Later, I sparred with the teacher who'd laughed at me. I accidentally fell on him — a lot.

After training, I showered and went down to the restaurant where my dinner was waiting. This may sound like a weird complaint, but I was on meat overload. I couldn't possibly eat the huge portions they put in front of me three times a day. I asked for a single chicken leg at breakfast each day, but they gave me a huge dinosaur leg, I wasn't even sure what animal it came from, but I hoped I'd never run into one. Lunch was almost always a ludicrously decadent multi-course meal eaten with the shifus. And dinner was another huge serving of meat and vegetables which I rarely finished. In the mornings, I actually woke up bloated from the previous day's food and still had to face that pterodactyl leg which dwarfed my boiled eggs and manto.

· • ● · ·

One morning, Meng Shifu told me that the next day we'd be go and see the grandmaster, Wang Wenyong, at his house. Later, one of the wrestlers told me how lucky I was to be meeting him. He said: "Our grand master is so strong and healthy because of a lifetime of wrestling. He's 81, but he can still drink and smoke every day!"

Meng Shifu told me we'd leave at 8:30 a.m., so I'd have to get up earlier than usual to do morning training. Doing some quick math, I figured I'd have to finish training by about 7:30 a.m. in order to shower and eat breakfast. Finishing at 7:30 a.m. would mean starting at 6 a.m. Also, leaving immediately after training would mean not taking a nap and I couldn't imagine what I'd feel like by evening training. So I told him: "No thanks, we'll just skip morning training then."

I had no idea that this was going to turn into a huge fight. "When I tell you to train, you train," he shouted. I respectfully told him that I'd been training for about 30 years, and I knew my body and how to train, and it made more sense to skip this one session.

The next morning, my training brother, Li Yuan, picked me up an hour late. Had I known he was going to be late, I could have put in a breakfast order the night before. But now I was starving, so Li Yuan took me for breakfast.

As we drove, Li Yuan told me that China is the cleanest country in the world. Of course, he'd never been to another country, so I wasn't sure what he was comparing it to. But in my experience, China was the world's dirtiest country given its level of economic development. When I moved into my room in the wrestling school, the shower was covered in thick green slime which obviously had taken years of careful farming to cultivate. The toilet was encrusted in sludge. I refused to move in until the maid had cleaned the room. After she'd finished, the slime and the sludge were still there. The refrigerator in my room smelled like rotten meat. It was so bad that I didn't keep food in it. I was trying to at least keep my sports drinks in there, but the smell permeated the plastic bottles. In fact, if you opened the refrigerator for even a second, the smell filled the room, and it had an incredible hang time. But at least they didn't use public laundry mats, because that would be dirty.

Apart from the fact that he espoused government propaganda, I liked Li Yuan and appreciated him training with me and coming to pick me up.

Where the majority of the boys on the wrestling team were uneducated provincial kids working as busboys in the restaurant, Li Yuan was from Beijing. He was big, tall, good looking, and fashionably dressed. He spoke some English, and drove a Mercedes. The car, he explained, actually belonged to his boss, who hired him as a driver and bodyguard. By the standards of non-degreed people, Li Yuan had it all. And yet, when we were around the grand master, he was humble and polite. That's the absolute mark of a great master. When you see students, who have other options in life and seemingly everything going for them, willing to prostrate themselves before the master, you know the master is someone special.

When we arrived, Grand Maser Wang Wenyong and several old shifus were waiting for us. Li Yuan immediately poured tea for them. While I talked with the shifus, he sat on a backless stool, off to the side, so that, in traditional fashion, it was clear that he wasn't part of the discussion, but he was close enough to serve the shifus when they needed anything. Without even having to ask him, he was constantly popping off the stool to refill their cups of tea or liquor, or to hand them cigarettes. When it was time for lunch, he served the food, but didn't eat.

Wang Wenyong still had a full head of hair, albeit white. I'd seen pictures of him wrestling into his seventies. Even now, he still did some coaching. He told me that he's famous in France. The shifus made Li Yuan bring me a signature bottle of wine to prove it. In France, when they name a wine after you, you know you've really made it.

Having these lunches with the old shifus was a priceless experience. It was excellent training for my Chinese language, but it was exhausting. I originally learned Chinese in Taiwan, and it'd taken me a year to get used to Shanghai Mandarin, which is fairly standard. Beijing dialect, however, was different again. Beijingers have a special accent, with a lot of "har" sounds added to words, and it took some getting used to.

Young people were easier to communicate with, because they talked like the TV shows and movies that I'd learned from. The kids on the wrestling team were uneducated and came from multiple locations, each with its own dialect, and yet I understood all of them perfectly well in Mandarin, and they understood me.

The PRC government had really pushed, in the past ten years or so, to get everyone to speak standard Mandarin. But the shifus were all 60 and over. Part of the problem was that they were harder of hearing, and another is that they were part of the generation that almost never attended school. China was poor when they were born, so only a small percentage of the population received an education. For years during the Cultural Revolution, which began in 1966, nearly all schools and universities were closed. Although China has worked admirably to catch up, during the period when I was doing my Ph.D., the number of years of formal education of the average Chinese adult was still only about five years. Compound partial deafness with a lack of education and a thick Beijing accent, and the fact they were drunk much of the time, communicating with the shifus made me feel I was at Level 0 in Chinese.

With older people, like the shifus, not only did I have trouble understanding them, but they didn't understand me. So usually I just listened. Often, I couldn't even ask questions that they'd understand, unless there was a young kid around, to translate my Mandarin into their Mandarin.

Lu Yansan, Meng Shifu's assistant and driver, often decided not to understand me. Sometimes, when he needed to tell me simple things, he'd just point and use hand gestures, because he thought I wouldn't understand. But then, when he had to tell me something complicated, he spoke Chinese, because he couldn't figure out how to do it with sign language. After a month together, he hadn't figured out the irony of believing my Chinese was so bad that I could only understand the most complicated things.

Once, he showed me a photo of Wang Wenyong exercising with a huge metal pole with concrete at both ends. It looked incredibly heavy, but he was holding it effortlessly, using it to practice his throws and sweeps.

The grand master was clearly already old in the photo, and I was going to ask his age and then act amazed at how strong he was, whatever age Lu Yansan told me. So I said, "Wow! How old is he in that picture?"

Lu Yansan's answer was: "This is our grand master."

"Yes, I know. He's very strong. How old is he in this picture?" I asked again.

"He's lifting a heavy weight," explained Lu Yansan.

"Yes, he is," I agreed, giving up. To avoid frustration, most of the time, I just sat and listened, like a good little boy.

In people's homes or in the office, I often saw the AC on but the windows or doors open. The grand master's house was like that: AC on, yet doors and windows open on a sweltering day. Ironically, they all kept complaining that the AC wasn't strong enough, as if it were a great mystery why the room was still hot. In the training room, in spite of the heat, I appreciated having the door open — even though the AC was on — because it let out the cigarette smoke.

The shifus gave me a long talk about how I had to be obedient and respectful if I wanted to become an official student. And if I chose to become an official student, then everything was free; training, room, and board.

Meng Shifu got really drunk. When it was time to leave, Li Yuan had to help him to the car. Meng Shifu kept talking to me in the car on the way back, asking me the same questions over and over. At times, I thought maybe I hadn't understood, because I'd just answered that question two seconds earlier. Yet when he repeated, I was pretty certain it was the same question.

He told me that when we got back to the wrestling school, we'd do evening training at 6 p.m. Then he told me again that I had to have discipline and respect to be a good wrestler. Then he changed evening training to 7 p.m. Then he told me again about obedience and dedication. Then he changed the training time to 7.45 p.m. He again explained the relevance of traditional culture to becoming a great wrestler, and changed the time of evening training to 6.30 p.m.

He went on and on about how I had to do this or that for my health, and it was all based on preposterous folk beliefs. Chinese people are always so worried about health: Don't sit so close to the AC or you'll get sick. Don't drink cold things. You have to drink this tea, with those herbs, or eat that soup, or do this or that, because it's medicine. Then two seconds later they hold out a pack of cigarettes and ask if you'd like one? Or they insist that you drink some liquor after you told them eight times you don't drink alcohol. And at least these guys were exercising, but I'd say that 90 percent of the people in China trying to give me health advice never exercised and had no muscle tone.

Meng Shifu had actually said to me, on numerous occasions, "You have to learn to drink alcohol." To which I always replied, "No, I don't."

A few days later, Lu Yansan took me sightseeing at Tiananmen Square and the Forbidden City. It was interesting seeing the square and walking around this image I'd seen on TV so many times, but on the other hand, this had been the site of a massacre of pro-democracy demonstrators, even though official propaganda said it hadn't happened. Families and children were walking around, carefree and laughing, on a site which, for me, represented most of what was wrong with China. As for the Forbidden City, everything I'd read said that the artifacts had all been looted during the Cultural Revolution. Consequently, I wasn't terribly motivated to go inside.

I'm just no good at visiting tourist attractions. I like having real experiences, like living in Shaolin Temple or the wrestling school in Beijing, speaking Mandarin and getting to know Chinese people. This is how I learn about China and Chinese culture, but tourist attractions have never interested me. Also, there's a Starbucks in the Forbidden City. This detracts from its authenticity, because it's not the original Starbucks, constructed during the Ming Dynasty.

I asked if we should go in and Lu Yansan was quick to tell me that it cost money. Chinese people generally don't tell you anything directly, but they also never tell you anything for no reason. The message is often coded and has very little to with the actual words being said. So I asked him: "Are you saying you don't want to go inside?"

He replied, "It costs money. I've seen it many times, but if you want to go in, we can."

I wasn't sure what he was trying to tell me, but it really seemed like he didn't want to go in. I asked again, "Are you saying we shouldn't go in?" He gave me some sort of cryptic answer, and I became frustrated. It was an incredibly hot day. I was tired from training and from Chinese overload. And I was too weary to decipher yet one more mystery, so I said: "That's fine. We can just go."

After the palace, we met Meng Shifu at his other business, a Japanese restaurant. When Lu Yansan told him that we hadn't gone inside the palace, the master became angry and told me I'd wasted an opportunity. Writing this several years later, I'm still fine with my decision.

Meng Shifu handed me the menu and said that I could order whatever I wanted. I went nuts ordering sushi and sashimi. I've always loved Japanese food and after eating so many questionable dishes in China, it was nice to have a change. Meng Shifu was actually concerned that I didn't eat enough, which is hilarious, because I always felt I ate a lot. Then I weighed about 91 kg (200 lbs), although I was less than 173 cm (5' 8"). He probably arrived at that conclusion based on the amount of food I wasted at his restaurant. They prepared so much food for me at each meal that I usually only ate one third of it. On the other hand, at the meals I had feasting with the masters, I couldn't believe how much they ate.

The Chinese trainers seemed to have no concept of nutrition. The guys ate three meals a day, whereas I ate five or six meals. My breakfast was relatively large and consisted of meat, fruit, and eggs. The Chinese athletes tended to eat a small breakfast, completely bereft of nutrition, usually *mántou* (steamed bread), or *yóutiáo* (fried dough sticks) and warm soymilk. They ate a massive lunch, but most of the calories came from rice. They ate a pretty large dinner, but again it was mostly rice.

When I ate with them, I usually ate a modest serving of rice, about a fifth of what the smaller guys ate. Then I ate meat and vegetables, and when I was full, I stopped eating. When the Chinese wrestlers ate with the shifus, no matter how much food there was, and no matter how much food they'd eaten, they were expected to eat until all the food was gone from the table. I simply refused. When I'd eaten enough, I stopped. I didn't understand why they couldn't just put it in the fridge and eat it later. When they saw me eat so little, they always commented on it, concerned. I told them I planned to eat again in two hours, but they simply didn't get it. They ate massive lunches like this and then went straight into the training room. Of course, they did stop for a cigarette break first.

Either way, on that day in the Japanese restaurant, no one had to worry about me eating enough. I gorged myself on delicious Japanese food. The master looked pleased to hear me ordering so much, and he bragged to the other masters: "Because he lived in Taiwan, Antonio knows about Japanese food."

My other sightseeing foray was to the Great Wall. Lu Yansan put me on the bus to Badaling, telling me that a training younger brother (called a *shī dì*) would pick me up at the other end and take me to the Great Wall. To be sure I'd make it to the right place, I asked Lu Yansan to tell the bus driver where I needed to get off.

About twenty minutes later, the bus driver told me that we'd reached Badaling. He then told me that there were multiple bus stops, and asked which one I wanted. I therefore asked him where Lu Yansan had told him to drop me. He said that Lu Yansan had only told him Badaling, but not the specific stop. I called Lu Yansan twice, and both times he assured me that *shī dì* would meet me. I said, "Yes, I'm sure he'll meet me, but only if he knows where I am. So where do I need to get off the bus?" I tried several times to get him to give me the information I needed, but he kept repeating, "And you will see the Great Wall… Chinese history and culture."

In the end, I just got off at one of the stops. Eventually, *shī dì* somehow found me.

I was grateful that the master had taken so much trouble to ensure that I got to see the sites. Unfortunately, I'm just not terribly excited about this type of tourist destinations. Besides, the Great Wall looked exactly like it did in *Mulan*, except that it was covered with tourists, instead of barbarian invaders. It was an absolute sea of humans, including foreign and Chinese tour groups, all having the adventure of a lifetime. One of the funny things about visiting these places is that you want to take photos, but the best photos are the ones you find online. There was no way for me to take a photo of the wall by itself, rather than the wall with thousands of tourists. And there's no way to capture the enormity of the wall when you're there. The best photos are aerial images which show how it goes on for thousands of miles.

In China, people carry huge bags of food on the subway. At airports, they also have tremendous carry-ons, full of snacks to eat while waiting for the plane. When I was touring the Great Wall, I saw families lugging sacks of food, like villagers fleeing a Mongol invasion.

People criticize me because I hate doing tourist destinations and visiting things on someone else's bucket list. Millions of tourists come to China, visit the Great Wall, the Forbidden Palace, and the Starbucks in the Forbidden City — but I'd been a student in Shaolin Temple, twice!

There was a coffee shop across from the wall and I suggested we just go have a coffee and watch the tourists from a safe distance. The coffee shop owner knew my training brother and asked who I was. When he explained that I was an MMA fighter, the guy's face lit up and he said in broken English "*Martial Arts Odyssey.*" We hung out, drank coffee, and talked about martial arts. It was a great day.

I took the bus back. Along the way, I called Lu Yansan and asked, "Where do you want to meet?" His reply was: "I will be there in ten minutes." The bus pulled into a huge station, and I called again. "Great, where do you want to meet?"

"Ten minutes," he confirmed. Rather than fight, I just sat down in front of the KFC inside the station, waiting for him to tell me which of the four exits to go out.

When he arrived, he called me and I asked, "Where do you want to meet?" To which he replied, "Where are you?" The way I saw it, where I was wasn't relevant because the station was huge and he probably couldn't drive around to a different exit once he was committed to one. It'd be more constructive for him to tell me where he was and I could go there. Instead, he insisted I tell him my location. So, I said "KFC".

"Come outside."

"Which exit?"

"Yes, I'm waiting for you."

"Where?"

"Where I dropped you off. Do you remember?"

"No, I don't remember." I'd only been to the station once, and didn't remember which exit he'd dropped me at, and I certainly wouldn't know how to get back to it if I had. Reading the exit signs, I asked him, "North, South, East, or West."

"Where I dropped you last time. Do you understand?"

"Yes, I understand, but I don't know where that is. North, South, East, or West?"

He started giving me directions like, "Turn left, then walk twenty meters, and turn right…" But I protested: "You don't know where I am or what direction I'm facing. How could these directions help?" And he responded, "Ten meters further on, turn left…" I gave in, followed the directions, and wound up in an underground parking lot. I gave my phone to a kindly attendant, who told Lu Yansan in to pick me up there. He even said he'd give Lu Yansan a pass, so he could get in and out for free.

I yelled a lot over the phone that day. So it was no surprise that, when I told Lu Yansan my final departure day and time, he said, "I'm busy that day."

·•●··

I got on really well with all of the young guys, but that counts for nothing in traditional martial arts cultures. You have to get on with the older ones, because they hold all of the cards and all of the power. But I had nothing in common with them. Also, they couldn't understand me and I couldn't understand them.

Having lunch at Meng Shifu's Japanese restaurant, none of the Chinese would eat any of the sushi or sashimi. Instead, they ordered a ton of Chinese food, most of which I'd have found inedible.

The meal lasted hours. The shifus got very drunk, but along the way, they kept telling me little pearls of wisdom. In the end it was a productive day, although I was exhausted and couldn't wait for it to be over.

At one point they asked me to clarify again exactly what my dissertation would focus on. I explained that it wasn't going to be about techniques or how to wrestle. I wanted to focus on the culture of wrestling, the people. The masters were between 60 and 83 years old, and had lived through some of the toughest times in Chinese history. Also, Jin Bao San, a famed, almost mythical wrestler, had been the teacher of our grand master, Wang Wenyong. All of these men had fascinating stories. I also wanted to write about the boys who came from the provinces and worked in the restaurant 12 hours a day, so they could train in wrestling. The story, for me, was the people, their lives, and their experiences. I went on to tell them that I'd write it twice, once in Chinese and once in English. That way, I could not only share Chinese wrestling culture with the West, but also with the young people who were born in an affluent China after 1980. This would help preserve ancient cultural heritage among a younger generation more concerned with material comforts than martial arts. The masters said they were happier than ever to help me.

Traditional martial arts masters, my traditional wrestling teacher included, always listed numerous benefits of practicing their art. But 90 percent of those benefits would be true of any sport at all. Meng Shifu told me that if you practice shuai jiao, "You'll have more energy, lose weight, sleep well, be more manly…" I've heard the same spiel, followed by anecdotal evidence of students who practiced everything from silat to tennis and then made miraculous life changes. It's wonderful if a martial arts teacher or sports coach can positively impact people's lives, but I think we need to recognize that all sports and all martial arts can do that. I once knew a recovering drug addict and convict who told me how learning to cook had changed his life. Any discipline that we love can have these benefits.

The wrestling school had a very traditional culture and we were all called training brothers, *shī gē* for older brother and *shī dì* for younger. The older shifus were called training grandfathers, *shī yé*. And the grand master was called "the big, old one," or "grand uncle," *dà yé*. At dinner one night, there was a heated discussion, between the students and Meng Shifu, about what to call me. One boy suggested I be called "older foreign brother." But the master said they shouldn't make a distinction on account of me being foreign. He said I was one of them, regardless of nationality. Technically, I was the second oldest, so I should be called "second older brother." But one of the younger guys, Hao Liqiang said, "But he just started wrestling, so he's the lowest brother." I thought this was reasonable. Meng Shifu replied, "Really? Who at this table can take him down?" The heavyweights weren't there, and the master had watched me beat everyone else at the table. He laughed. Hao Liqiang, who I liked a lot, vowed: "I will beat him," so Meng Shifu said: "OK, on Tuesday, you can fight Antonio for the name." Everyone laughed. Then I jumped in and added, "Let's fight with no jackets." Then they all laughed even harder, knowing Hao Liqiang would be at an even bigger disadvantage. The master agreed: "Good idea. Āndōngní vs. Hao Liqiang, with no jackets."

In a separate conversation Meng Shifu told me again "You need to learn to drink alcohol." They worried about me because I didn't drink alcohol and didn't overeat. Also, in addition to wrestling training twice a day, I kept up with my own training, weights and abs. They thought that this, combined with my going to bed early, were all bad habits that needed to be broken.

Going to bed early became an issue because the room I was renting was also used as an office. At around 9 p.m., I'd lock the door and refuse to open it. It was so incredibly hard to listen to and speak Mandarin all day. That, plus all of the new experiences and sights, meant that my brain was on overload. Add to that the physical fatigue of training, and I just needed quiet, alone time in the evening, to decompress. I couldn't tolerate people walking in and out of the room, talking or making noise. Meng Shifu actually said to me, "You can't go to bed at 9 p.m. You need to start thinking like a businessman." I wasn't sure why I needed to think like a businessman, but I was determined to prove to him that I could go to bed at 9 p.m. All through my experiences, Shaolin Temple, wrestling school in Beijing, and later at the sports university, I'd experience frustrations and would criticize China and the people around me. At the same time, I'd often feel grateful for the opportunities they were affording me and the pleasant experiences I had. After the publication of *The Monk from Brooklyn*, I was attacked online for having been too critical and for complaining too much about China. At the time, I felt I was just being honest. In fact, that book was almost a word-for-word copy of my diary. This time around, I was much more balanced. I'd changed. And China had changed. And we were coming closer together. But I still had to be honest about things I saw and experienced. They weren't all good and didn't all make sense.

Even after having improved my language skills and my cultural understanding, I stand by my original opinion, which is: Any Westerner who tells me how mystical the East is has never lived here.

The next afternoon, both heavyweights turned up for training and worked with me on Chinese wrestling moves that were similar enough to Western wrestling that I'd feel comfortable with them. Later, one of the old shifus came to teach me the hand positions for grabbing the wrestling jacket. Afterward, when we sparred, I actually did grab the clothes sometimes, but I also reverted to grabbing the head, like I do in wrestling. I used a Chinese sweep once and was very excited about that. Unfortunately, the opponent was really good and strong and while he was on the way to the ground, he reversed the throw and got the points.

One shifu told me that my breathing was wrong, and in a fight I'd get tired. This is something even Western coaches had talked to me about. I needed to relax my shoulders and stop holding my breath.

Apart from the wrestlers, the restaurant had a large staff of young people from the poorer parts of China. Meng Shifu brought them to Beijing, gave them free room and board, and paid them wages even lower than those he'd have to pay a Beijing native. The equivalent in the US would be a restaurant owner in New York bringing staff in from Alabama, and giving them free room and board, but paying them less than the normal restaurant wage. The prevailing restaurant wage for a low-level worker in New York is about US$ 15 per hour, which is already less than what it costs for room and board in New York. If the restaurant owner wanted to pay these workers US$ 8 an hour, plus room and board, it'd cost him double or triple the cost of hiring locally. And I bet a lot of people would snap up that deal.

Not only does this demonstrate how vastly different the two economies are, but it also raises the question of whether or not it's fair to say that low-level workers here in China are much worse off than low-level workers in the USA. At least Chinese workers could come to the city, get a job like this, and send some money home. In New York, the same workers wouldn't even be able to live, much less support a family back in Alabama.

The flip side is that China lives on the myth of being a developed country. The workers all told me they'd only completed junior high school, which was probably more schooling than their parents had had. How can a country claim to be developed when a third of the population are still uneducated peasants, willing to uproot and see their families only once a year, for a job, that's 12 hours per day, 28 days a month, for a monthly wage of just US$ 250?

Training in a restaurant, wrestling in a private dining room, I kept thinking about the fight scene in *Dragon: the Bruce Lee Story*, where Lee is working in a restaurant in Seattle, and he gets in a fight with the cook which leads to a massive battle with all of the waiters coming after him with meat cleavers.

In wrestling practice, we got slammed on the mats a lot. When you get rocked like that on your back, it effects your breathing for a second or two. It just pops all the air out of your lungs. When my training brothers got slammed, you could hear tar or nicotine and phlegm rattling around in their chest like gravel in a clothes dryer. Immediately afterward, they usually had violent coughing fits. These guys were all between 18 and 28 years old. What would their lungs be like when they were 38 or 48?

Meng Shifu told us that, on Sunday, we'd have to attend a wrestling association lunch, and he gave us brand-new white shirts to wear. We drove to another and much larger restaurant, where we remained from 10:30 a.m. until almost 5 p.m., meeting with shifus from other places. I knew it was a fancy affair when I saw the quality of the poultry heads they were serving. On the other hand, I heard people hawking and spitting on the floor, so it couldn't have been too fancy. I guess it was semi-formal.

Listening to Mandarin for that many hours was exhausting. Plus, they all smoked. Chinese people don't seem to need alone time, reflection, creativity, or quiet. Their whole life is consumed by doing their job and fulfilling their social-cultural obligations. For most of the young wrestlers who worked in the restaurant, Sunday was their only day off, and they spent it in meetings and lunch with the shifus all day.

The whole event was consumed by long and tedious speeches. Important people in Asia never get tired of hearing themselves talk. I thought we were done at 2 p.m., but no, we had to wait 25 minutes for the next shifu to speak. Then I thought we were done, but there was another one-hour speech. Li Yuan tried to escape, but Meng Shifu wouldn't let him. An hour later, he tried again, and finally begged off with a good-enough excuse. I wish I'd heard what that excuse was, because I would have claimed to have had the same problem.

Even between speeches, it was impossible to talk to people and get to know them, because every five seconds someone would come over and interrupt the conversation, wanting to *gānbēi* (toast one another and down an entire glass of white liquor). They tried to toast me a few times, but inside I was like, "Don't ever interrupt an Italian man when he's eating."

The shifus, and older Chinese in general, often speak in *chéngyǔ*, idiomatic expressions each composed of four Chinese characters. These represent complex meanings which have to be explained, often at length. The explanations themselves are like parables, and they followed a similar pattern.

First, Meng Shifu would say the four characters, such as *wén jī qǐ wǔ*. Chinese characters compose words, but may not be complete words on their own. So, after saying the four characters, he had to explain which word each of the characters represented: *Wén*, in modern Chinese, means to smell; in this case, however, he was using an older definition, which was to listen. This was another aspect of *chéngyǔ* that made them very difficult to comprehend. Many of the meanings of the characters aren't commonly used nowadays. The next character was *jī*, as in *gōngjī* (rooster). The third character was *qǐ* as in *qǐchuáng* (to get out of bed). Finally, *wǔ* as in *wǔjiàn*, to do the sword dance or sword practice.

The final step was to reveal what the idiom actually meant. In this case, it meant "Practice the sword, when the rooster crows." Then, he'd go on to explain the relevance: You should get up early in the morning and begin training at the break of dawn.

It seemed that the older and wiser a shifu was, the more *chéngyǔ* he used. Consequently, speeches and discussions often became nothing more than a long series of idioms, followed by explanations, followed by more *chéngyǔ*...

It was so hard for me to deal with regular Mandarin, hour after hour, but listening to *chéngyǔ* was the language training equivalent of sparring. My head was splitting.

Professor Li Mingyuan came to talk to me, which I appreciated, but being an educated man and a shifu, his speech was about 90 percent *chéngyǔ*. And he wouldn't just talk, he'd constantly ask: "Did you understand?" Before I could say anything, he'd answer, "No? OK, I'll explain." But I was so tired, I was like, "Please don't."

Later, at the sports university, I found my Ph.D. advisor also spoke like this. Moreover, I discovered that the question, "Did you understand?" immediately followed by "No? I'll explain," was actually part of the standard pattern of discourse. Originally, I thought people like Professor Li Mingyuan were asking me if I understood because of my flawed Chinese. But at SUS, I saw my advisor do this with all of the Chinese students as well. It was just a cultural norm.

In a way, it was similar to how, in the West, it's normal to ask people how they feel. And the standard pattern is to say, "I'm fine," even if your whole family recently died in a fire. It's just a normal social rhythm that we follow. It also reminded me of how the Puritans or Rabbinical scholars would argue with one another, quoting scripture. And the most learned person was the one who could most cleverly think of and recite scripture that supported his opinion.

Isaac: Should I buy my wife whatever she wants?

Rabbi: The Good Book says a man must care for his wife.

Anatole: But does the Good Book not also say, "If a man buys his wife two shoes, she will run away?"

I'm not sure if this exact dialogue is in the Bible, but this is how I explain *chéngyǔ* to my students at the university.

•• ● •·

A guy wanted to show off his English, so he came up to me and asked in English, "Can you speak Chinese." I answered in Mandarin that I could, hoping he'd change languages. Instead, he continued in English: "But you don't speak a lot, right?" I repeated in Chinese that I spoke Chinese well, and that he should talk to me in Chinese. Still in English, he said, "But when you hear people talk, you don't know what they're saying, right?" I shoved my chair away from the table and stood up. "Is there something I can help you with?" I asked in very forceful Chinese.

"No." he said, sheepishly.

"OK, I'll go over to that other table then." I concluded and walked away.

I hate someone using me to show off their English skills. A friend of mine, who wrote a book about Taiwan, referred to these people as English attackers. They pounce on you to practice their English or to show off how clever they are. They're effectively using you, without your permission. Also, from a purely linguistic standpoint, if he truly wanted to evaluate my Chinese level, wouldn't it make more sense to speak to me in Mandarin, and see how I reacted, rather than asking me insulting and leading questions in English? Later, of course, I found out he was really important in the association and that he lived in Shanghai and that I could have trained with him after I went back to Shanghai.

I went and sat with Qi Han, a former student of Meng Shifu who'd just finished his studies in the US. He told me that he couldn't practice wrestling anymore because of health problems which he attributed to having had a Mexican roommate in the US who made him eat spicy food. He told me that he'd experienced sleeplessness and dysphoria. I had no idea how respond, so I just nodded and mumbled something like, "Yeah, I love Mexican food."

This lunch meeting consisted of about 15 old guys making speeches, about how the shuai jiao tradition had to be preserved, and only eight young wrestlers, counting me, not listening. No one seemed worried about this ratio. Was it possible the sport was dying? I asked Qi Han if he'd practiced martial arts in America. He said, "I did boxing for a while and BJJ for a while." Then he said, "In America, martial arts are very popular, but not in China."

Sitting in that meeting with the wrestling masters, it also occurred to me: Once you notice someone has a comb over, it's really hard to stop staring at it.

During the meeting, everyone was falling asleep. First, it was the young guys, but eventually even the shifus were nodding off. I wondered why they found it preferable to have a seven-hour event, where no one listened and everyone passed out, rather than a three-hour event, and then go home when they were tired.

When we got back that evening, I saw that I'd got some stains on my new white shirt, so I wanted to wash it out. I took off the shirt and was about to put it in the sink, when I noticed the sink was so dirty, it would have make the shirt worse. I wanted to clean the sink first, but there was nowhere to lay the shirt. Chinese rooms often have no horizontal spaces at all. No shelves, closets, wardrobe, dresser... if they do, of course, they're filthy. For a second, I thought of laying the shirt on the floor, but it hadn't been cleaned since the Nationalist republic had been declared in 1911. Eventually, I had to walk to my bedroom, lay the dirty shirt on my bed, then go back and clean the bathroom floor, so I had a place to stand while cleaning the sink. Once I was done cleaning the sink, I was finally ready to wash my shirt. When it was done, of course, there was no place to hang it.

The next day, the heavyweights turned up to train with me. Whenever you meet a truly huge wrestler, people always joke: "He should go into sumo." Out of curiosity, I looked up weight divisions for amateur sumo competitions. For women, heavyweight is over 80 kg (176 lbs). For men, lightweight is under 85 kg (187 lbs). So, in amateur Sumo, if I were a woman, I'd be at the small end of heavyweight. And as a man, I'm barely a lightweight. I like that sport. It makes me feel skinny.

It's important in sparring to try new moves and new techniques, to not care if you win or lose, or else you'll never learn and grow. If you only think about winning, you'll always go with the safe and sure, which is what you already know. But the culture in this Chinese wrestling school was that they always wrestled to win. All of the old shifus always came to watch us spar. Sometimes there were more shifus than wrestlers. They applauded when you won and often shouted at us when we lost. Sparring always became like a tournament fight, rather than a practice, which discouraged the trying out of new techniques.

We were stretching out and one of the old drunken shifus came over to me and said, "Put your head on the floor like that boy."

I told him, "I'm trying, but I can't do it."

He just ignored me, saying, "I mean like that boy. Put your head on the floor."

"Yes, I understand the concept, but I can't do it," I explained.

The old shifu repeated himself about three more times, insisting: "No, all the way."

"I can't." I explained again. He kept pushing me to do the full stretch. Finally, I asked him. "Can you speak French?" He said he couldn't, so I responded, "I can, but I can't do that stretch. You see, we all have things we're good at and things we aren't."

"All the way to the floor, like that boy." He repeated.

Finally, I shouted. "I can't do it. He's 22 years old. He has no body fat. He's been training for years. I'm doing my best. I can't do it." All the shifus and the grand master looked at me, and I knew I shouldn't have shown so much emotion, but on the other hand, why didn't this guy just take "no" for an answer?

The old shifu backed off, shocked. Then Qi Han, the one who'd studied in the US, told me in English: "You don't have to achieve this level today. The grand master said you can learn it at your own pace." I should have thanked him. Instead, I said in English, "Yes, I know. I was planning on learning at my own pace." When the grand master asked what I had said. Qi Han answered, "He said that he knows."

I felt bad for the rest of the day. Then, in the first wrestling sparring, I wasn't wearing my mouthguard, and I bit through my tongue. I wondered if God had punished me.

On Sundays, old men often gather in the park in Beijing and wrestle. Meng Shifu told me that we'd all go watch them and then eat together. It was a million degrees out and we were going to be outdoors in a park, so I wore shorts. Shifu scolded me, saying that it was against Chinese culture to wear shorts. The rest of team showed up and Meng Shifu was the only one not wearing shorts.

Park wrestling is an entire culture unto itself. Many people turn out to watch, and essentially anyone could jump in and wrestle. People didn't necessarily bring their own wrestling jackets, so they'd just borrow one from the wrestlers in the previous round. The master told me not to wrestle, and I think there were several reasons why he did so. First, the park wrestlers really only wanted to see Chinese shuai jiao techniques, not some hodgepodge of MMA and freestyle wrestling, mixed with Cambodian bokator.

Next, the people there didn't know me and probably had never wrestled a foreigner before. I think Meng Shifu was worried that someone might intentionally injure me. Finally, given that he'd seen me lose my temper a few times when I felt someone had insulted me, I think he was worried that if someone tried to hurt me, I'd retaliate with extreme violence, and we'd have an incident on our hands. So I was relegated to watching and taking photos.

Some of the wrestlers were old men who used perfect, traditional techniques and no strength. They easily defeated my teammates and a lot of younger men. Next, a huge young guy put on the jacket and defeated all comers. One by one, my teammates stepped into the circle, to challenge him, but they all got creamed.

It reminded me of when I was learning competitive tui shou ("pushing hands," tai chi wrestling) in Taiwan. When I watched a big competition, it looked like there were two types of competitors; old people who'd perfected their skills and techniques over a period of decades, and young people who had some technique, but short-circuited the process by lifting weights and possibly taking steroids. In the end, the winners seemed to be split fifty-fifty between the old-style and new-style. Unfortunately, there were very few young people following the old path. This means that in twenty years, maybe all of the competitors would be following the new way.

After the park, we had another, long, smoke-filled lunch with the old shifus. The next morning, I had strength, conditioning, and wrestling basics. In the afternoon, we had team training and sparring for about three hours. I wrestled about 15 rounds, against five different opponents and I won about 11 or so rounds. The next day, I woke up very tired, and dragged myself through two hours of morning training. We had just one hour of training in the afternoon.

·•●•·

I needed to run back to Shanghai to do some paperwork for my studies. While I was there, I continued doing my *jībĕngōng* every day. When I got back to Beijing, my training went so much easier than before. At first, I attributed this to the magic of *jībĕngōng*, but then I realized that it was the first time, in three months, that I'd had two consecutive days off. Amazing what a little rest can do.

Sparring that afternoon, Meng Shifu was pleased with how well I was able to defend and get reversals. But when I threw my opponents, aggressively, I often reverted to Western techniques or half and half. For example, I took a leg (Western), but then used an inside hook trip (Chinese). Once, I took my opponent's back and body slammed him. I think you could say that was 100-percent Southern, as in WWE.

After practice, Meng Shifu told me that I'd been accepted as an official student of Grand Master Wang Wenyong, and would now be a disciple of him and his style of Chinese wrestling, under the tutelage of Meng Shifu. The following, after training, they held a big ceremony for my induction. It consisted of an hour of talking, three hours of eating and drinking, followed immediately by nearly three hours of wrestling. It was a very long day.

At lunch, they served the best food. It was like they went through the restaurant receipts from all of the meals I'd ordered since coming there and served my favorites. They had deep fried lamb, shrimp and vegetables, lots of beef dishes… It was all so good.

I had to read a special pledge aloud, but I couldn't read the ornate Chinese script in the fancy book, so my training brother, Zhao Zhiming, wrote cheat notes for me in hanyu pinyin (Chinese written in a Latin phonetic script).

With everyone watching, I stood before the grand master. He said he had a question for me. I thought, please God, let me understand his question. He asked: "Tibet is part of which country?" Without a second's hesitation, I said, "China." He laughed loudly, patted me on the shoulder and said, "Good answer, good answer." Then he went over to his table and recounted to all the other shifus what we had said. They were all pleased. He probably told the story five times that day, each time finished by saying: "A lot of foreigners are confused about that."

Later, one of the shifus gave us a lecture on how great Chinese culture is. Apparently, it's the oldest, and thus best, culture in the world.

My induction ceremony and acceptance into the wrestling association was a lot like when Tommy got made in *Goodfellas*. I kept expecting to get whacked. Instead, Meng Shifu came to me and said, "I am your father now."

During my induction luncheon, one of the old shifus got very drunk and was sort of bullying me wrestling. He took off his shirt, and threw me down, on the hard wooden floor. I did a breakfall, stood up, and he threw me down again. Of course, I didn't resist. He threw me down again, and I could have resisted, but I knew the polite thing to do was to fall down and say "Thank you." Which I did. But then, he suggested that he wanted me to fight back. I then grabbed his head and snapped it down. I reached across, and grabbed his bicep, pulling him into me by the bicep and head, then dropped my weight on his neck.

I thought he'd wanted to challenge himself or that he was going to show me how he could escape from a complete control position. I was curious to see what was coming next, but he just froze. Then Li Yuan, the oldest of the young guys, told me to release the old shifu, making an excuse about him having a bad shoulder. I let him go, but couldn't understand what his motivation had been or what outcome he'd hoped for.

Apart from possibly being guilty of bullying a bully, that day I did the best in wrestling I'd done so far. I wrestled Lu Yansan for the first time. He'd been with Meng Shifu for countless years and was a year older than me, so I had to pay him respect. In the first round, when he swept me, I felt the incredible strength of his legs from years of doing the basic exercises.

In the second round, however, I leaned on him, held him, mauled him, and wore him down. The smoking, drinking, and lack of running and cross training meant that he had no cardio, and also that he only had strength for the exact movements they'd practiced. Also, I was the only one who trained twice a day everyday. I wore him down, then swept him. He hit the canvass hard and didn't get up for a long time.

The shuai jiao techniques are so wonderful. I wanted to learn them. In the meantime, I didn't understand why these guys refused to be healthy and strong, or why that wouldn't be a benefit for them.

After that, they put in young guy after young guy, round after round. Eventually, I was too tired to even defend myself anymore. But it was a good experience.

My only loss was to Li Yuan. After that, I stood up and — determined not to lose to him again — grabbed a leg. I couldn't get him down, so I grabbed the other leg too, lifted him, and did a slam. In another match, one guy tried to take me over his shoulder, but I hooked under his bottom and he went down first. I also did a body lock takedown once or twice. Meng Shifu was really excited and said, jokingly, that I was a *shuāi fù* ("master of throws").

The old master who'd bullied me at my party came over and was chewing out the kids, saying how easy it was to stuff my takedowns. He had the kids grab his leg, as I'd done, and he did a defense and threw them.

The defense was wrapping his leg around my leg, then doing an underarm pry as a reversal. But the kids argued back, saying I was too heavy and too strong. "Nonsense" he said, "Watch, it works on Āndōngní." He had me grab his leg and he did the technique two or three times and I dutifully allowed my takedown to be stuffed, while allowing him to easily throw me to the ground.

He told me to try again, "And this time, really try to fight back." It was a good technique he was teaching, but in the real world, when your takedown fails, the match isn't over. You should just transition to another technique. And that's what I did. I took his leg. He stuffed my takedown with his technique, wrapping his leg around mine. Then, I stepped over his leg and although he was pushing down on my head, I simply drove into his leg and took him down.

Pandemonium ensued. Apparently, you were never supposed to take down the old guys. No matter what they said or did, you were just supposed to say: "Yes, thank you, grandfather. I'll try harder next time."

Li Yuan ran over to try and catch the master before he hit the ground, but he was too late. He helped the shifu up and out of the room on unsteady legs. As they left, Li Yuan shot me a look that suggested I'd broken the rules. This master was really big and strong, and had good technique, but also a fat belly. He was probably in his fifties, not very old, but he was strong enough and good enough at wresting that I prayed I'd be that good in my fifties. I respected him. I just didn't like being bullied. I felt horrible after this incident.

Meng Shifu didn't seem angry. In fact, his face just looked blank. That night, he came in my room and showed me a bunch of techniques that involved lifting and slamming the opponent. He said they were techniques suitable for my body type and experience. "We'll learn the *jīběngōng* for these lifts, when you come back."

The master was very kind to me and taught me a lot. I felt sad about the times I'd lost my cool, but I wondered if either I was just too old to follow a shifu now, or if the issue was that our cultures were just too different for me to try and live with them and become one of them.

I was fairly certain that Meng Shifu wanted me to be friends with Lu Yansan, because he was only a year older than me. However, we had nothing in common. I was still training in new martial arts to improve my overall game, whereas the only martial art Lu Yansan had any experience with was Chinese wrestling. I was still fit and still hoping to fight again. Lu

Yansan drank and smoked and often collapsed after ten minutes of exercise, and was definitely not planning to fight professionally.

They swept the wrestling floor during practice the next day, for the first time. But it hadn't been mopped or disinfected since I'd started over a month earlier. The whole restaurant, including my room, was carpeted, but I never heard the cleaning staff using a vacuum cleaner.

My departure was nearing and when I went down for lunch the restaurant manager asked me about how I wanted to do my bill. This was a bit of a shock, because I understood the terms of my being a student of Meng Shifu were that I got free food and lodging. This was stated in the contract I'd signed, and it was explained to me about four times by Meng Shifu and Li Yuan. The manager kept insisting that I had to pay. It suddenly occurred to me that I actually had no idea what was stated in the contract I'd signed, because I couldn't read it. The only thing I had was my recollection that the master had said I'd have free food, lodging, and training.

My last day of sparring before going back to Shanghai was also the day before my 46th birthday. It would be one of the longest and best days of wrestling sparring I had. I probably wrestled about 17 or 18 rounds (Wrestling rounds are short; they end when someone gets thrown.)

Against the younger guys, I won most of the time. I'd never beaten Li Yuan, and he usually won the standard five quick rounds with little resistance. This time I was determined to dig my heels in and not make it easy for him. It was both the longest match I'd ever had and the longest I'd ever seen in this club. It was the first time I was able to grab his jacket. Not only did I manage to grab it, but in two places, with both hands. Next, I stuffed takedown after takedown, with him winning only two throws. Finally, the shifus told us to stop because we were both exhausted. I really felt like it was a victory. Although I still hadn't got him down, I held out against him and he couldn't complete the customary five takedowns. I really felt like this was my birthday present, to do so well against the best guy. After a rest, I wrestled one of the younger guys for a couple of rounds. Then they threw

Li Yuan back in with me. Sadly, I didn't film this second set of rounds, but I finally managed to drive in, through his defense, and grab a leg.

Li Yuan was probably as heavy or heavier than me, but much taller. In freestyle wrestling or MMA, I'd simply take his legs out from under him with my arms. Being that tall might even make it easier. The problem with doing this type of technique in Chinese wrestling, however, is the jacket. Normally, when we sparred, as soon as the round started, he grabbed my jacket in two positions and could either use it to pull me or to push me off. The few times I'd tried to go for a leg, he was able to push me so far away as to make it impossible. On this day, when I was wrestling the younger guys, I realized that most of the time when I was able to take their leg it was because they pulled me in close for a hip throw; then I didn't have to fight through their grip. I was already close up on them. I could take their leg easily, and take them down.

When Li Yuan went for a throw, I did the same technique, I dropped and grabbed his leg, solidly with my whole arm and lifted it off the ground. The problem was, however, that he was still holding my jacket in two good positions and was able to push me down, like he was going to just drive my face into the floor. In freestyle or MMA, I'd simply drop on one knee and take him down, but in Chinese wrestling, I'd have lost if I allowed my knee to touch the ground. Seeing no other option, and with his entire weight pushing down on my neck, I used a sanda throw which is similar to a judo hip throw, except that instead of throwing the opponent by his arm, you throw him by his leg.

I flung Li Yuan with all my might, and I went with him. In all fairness, I probably hit the ground first, so he got the point, but it was the first time I'd ever taken him down. He flew over my body and landed with a thud. Luckily, his leg was unhurt. He won the next round easily and that was the end of our bout.

It was a great way to end my fourth week of traditional Chinese wrestling training and a good prelude to my birthday.

After practice, the other restaurant manager asked me again about my bill. Now I was beginning to worry. I found Meng Shifu and asked him about not paying for food and lodging, as it said in the contract, but he said "No, you don't pay for training, but you have to pay for food and lodging, just like the other students." The rest of the students worked and lived in the restaurant. If he was charging them for food and lodging, it'd be more than their salary. Also, before becoming his official student, he'd promised me free training. So what exactly had been the advantage of signing that document?

Not only was I still paying for food, but the restaurant manager told me that from the time I became an official student, until now, they were charging me the à la carte menu price for everything I ate, instead of the fixed room-and-board cost which had applied beforehand. That meant my food, which had cost RMB 70 (US$ 11) a day before was now RMB 100 (US$ 16) per meal. When I confronted Meng Shifu about this, he said, "This way you don't have to waste money. You only pay for what you eat."

When someone tells you, "I'm your father," you expect free room and board, especially if he suggests, "We'll rule the galaxy together as father and son."

My train back to Shanghai was booked for 9 a.m. the next day. The master told Guo Ze, one of the restaurant workers, to take me to the train station. I asked Guo Ze how he'd get me there, since he didn't have a car. He was very elusive and sort of said, "7:30 a.m."

I asked again how we'd get there. And he said, "I'll meet you at 7:30 a.m."

The whole time I was thinking that, if he doesn't have a car, I'll just take a taxi in front of the restaurant.

The next morning he met me in my room and took me out on the street, where I saw a long line of taxis. I motioned, as if to get in a taxi, but he told me to follow him. We walked past the taxis, and walked and walked. I asked where we were going, and he said, "The train station."

I stopped, and said: "Yes, that's the end destination. But where are you taking me right now? We can't walk to the train station, it's too far." My train was at 9 a.m. We could make it if we left at 7:30 a.m. and were in a vehicle, but not if we were walking somewhere first. I kept asking where he was leading me, but he just wouldn't give me a straight answer.

Finally, I stopped walking and demanded, "Where are you taking me? Time is running out!" He used a term I didn't quite recognize. Because there are several different words for bus, I then asked if it was a bus.

When he said "Yes," I thought that an express bus would be cheaper than a taxi and just as fast. I then asked him how far we'd have to walk to get to the bus. He pretended not to understand, so I asked how many minutes it'd take. Again, no answer.

We walked about a kilometer with me carrying all my gear, and I was really losing my cool as time was short. Now it was almost 8 a.m., and I just didn't see how I could make my train. I told him angrily, "Next time, I'll take a taxi."

He said, "Yes, that's what I'm doing now. I'm finding a taxi for you." And he stood in the street to wave down a taxi. I exploded. "Why did you waste so much of my time and make me walk this far? There were taxis in front of the restaurant."

He darted into traffic to avoid me. When I finally waved down a taxi, the driver didn't want to commit to taking me to the station, because traffic was particularly bad and it could take hours. I was fuming and trying to get the taxi driver to stop talking and just drive, when I realized that he was trying to help me. When I'd calmed down enough to listen, he said: "There's no way you'll make a 9 a.m. train in a taxi. But there's a subway stop ahead. If I drop you there, you can take the subway. It takes less than thirty minutes."

I thanked him, and he was absolutely right. The subway to the train station was painless and I arrived with 15 minutes to spare.

There was also a subway station right behind the restaurant. Why didn't Guo Ze take me there? I think it was a bunch of cultural issues. He probably didn't know the answers to my questions. And he'd probably never taken the express bus before. Maybe Meng Shifu had told him about it. Since the subway was nearby, that was probably how he got to the station when he went home to visit his family. He probably intended to put me on the bus, but when he saw how angry I was, and how late it was, he tried to get me a taxi.

Once again, my temper flareup had broken a possible friendship. On the other hand, with Meng Shifu now charging me such a price to visit him, I doubted I'd ever be coming back.

My next adventure was about to start in Shanghai.

Fighting professional MMA in Johor Bahru, Malaysia, Spring 2012

San da training Shaolin

Fighting professional MMA in Johor
Bahru, Malaysia, Spring 2012

With the young trainees, at Shaolin Temple
carrying water buckets for morning exercise
Summer, 2013

A guardian statue at the Shaolin Temple

Wu Shu wrestling statue, one of the only elements of wrestling at the Shaolin Temple

The entrance to the Shaolin Temple

The master looks like a movie character.

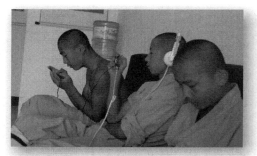

Shaolin trainees are teenagers, just like anywhere else.

Wu shu training

Da Mo, Bodhidharma, Indian monk credited with developing Shaolin kung fu

Trainees all learn weapons forms

San da training with Du Shifu

Du Shifu meditating

Strength training, like the Flinstones

Technically, Shaolin kids had to take three hours of school per
day, but they would generally fall asleep during homework.

Shuaijiao wrestling in Beijing   Shuaijiao jacket grab

My training mates and shifus at the shuaijiao school in Beijing

Sunday wrestling in the park, in Beijing

Chapter 5
School Begins

Sport was a central part of Chinese nationalism during the Republican period (1912-1927), when military citizenship was the guiding philosophy of the educational system.

— **Tony Hwang & Grant Jarvie,**
"Sport, Nationalism and the Early Chinese Republic 1912–1927,"
The Sports Historian **(Vol. 21, No. 2, November 2001)**

Back in Shanghai, I made a mad dash for McDonalds and discovered a potential wrestler name. In Chinese, a Big Mac is called Ju Wu Ba. It means huge and mighty, and was the name of a famous giant during the Qin Dynasty. I think it'd be a perfect moniker for a bad guy wrestler.

I went to the visa office and picked up my passport with my three-year student visa. It felt great to know I had one less thing to worry about. My next stop was at Shanghai University of Sport (SUS), to see about my dorm room. It was a fifth-floor walkup in a concrete block building. The stairwell had never been cleaned, and the hallways were full of broken furniture and rubbish. At first, I thought maybe they were doing the summer renovations, replacing furniture, and setting old furniture in the hallways for trash pickup. But it turned out that the old furniture and rubbish would still be there, three years later, when I graduated. Even so, the room itself was great by Chinese standards. We foreign students had our own bathrooms, showers, heating, and AC.

The Chinese student dorms, by contrast, lacked showers. Also, there were none in the training halls. Local students had to walk to a shower house, where they were allowed to shower once a day after dinner. Their dorms had neither AC nor heating. In winter, they'd often take hot water bottles to bed.

At Shanghai University, my students had to practice writing a letter of complaint, and about half of them chose to complain about their dorm rooms. They all complained that the rooms had no refrigerator, no TV, no shower, no toilet, and no heating or AC. They also complained about the smell of the bathrooms. One girl said that, any time she stepped out of her room, she could smell it. One surprising complaint was that they only had one roommate, but wanted more. I'd heard from my Chinese classmates how bad the dorms were and I wondered how anyone could live like that. But then, at the end, the girl said: "For RMB 3,000 [US$ 476] per year, we expect more." In the United States, the dorms were US$ 500 per semester, 25 years ago when I was a student. On the one hand, I thought it was awful to make students live in poor conditions, and I complained about the lack of gyms and amenities on Shanghai University's campus, yet university is so much cheaper in China than in the US. Graduate tuition in China was only about US$ 4,000 per year.

I knew my Chinese classmates lived in Dickensian conditions, but I was fine with my accommodation. The two best aspects of my room were the price and the location. It was free as part of my scholarship. And it was located about 100 meters (330 ft) from the front gate of SUS.

The registration lady gave me a form to take to the Agricultural Bank of China, so I could open an account and start receiving my monthly stipend.

Next, I walked to the Wu Shu Institute and met with Professor Dai, who was both my Ph.D. advisor and head of the department. When I entered his office, he gave me a cup of tea and asked me to sit. Handing a book about kung fu to me, he asked: "Do you know what Shaolin Kung Fu is?"

So began the exchange described in this book's prologue.

·•●•·

Every year in China, the fall semester gets off to a very slow start, because of the numerous holidays. I moved into the dorm, went to the registration office to turn in some papers, and I was done for the week. The following week we only had a day of orientation, then Moon Festival. That was the second week of the semester done.

We were told that classes would probably start in earnest in the third week of September. I say probably, because the authorities the university often announce holidays at the last minute. Also, no one was able to tell me which, if any, classes I needed to take. At this point, I was still unclear if my program was all research or if classes were also involved.

One of my American friends from Shaolin Temple, Jaka, was there, waiting to start an master's degree in wushu. He moved into the dorm, then went over to the university to train. He came back ten minutes later, telling me that all of the training halls were locked. He said that he'd asked the foreign student advisor, Chu Laoshi, where he could train these two or three weeks until school got started. Chu told him: "For training, you'll need to contact the Wu Shu Institute and pay separate fees. But we recommend you not train during your four years here."

Sorry — did he just recommend that we not train during our training at the sports university? Twelve years in Asia had taught me to be patient, and things would generally work themselves out, to some diminished degree of satisfaction. In the interim, I continued training at the MMA gym downtown.

The police were checking IDs at the train station. I showed them my expired Tennessee driver's license and they let me board the train. You gotta love China. Of course, it would have been cooler if they'd let me drive the train.

In a shopping mall, I tried to buy an electronic dictionary which I thought I'd need for my studies. However, the saleswoman kept talking about all these features I didn't need, like Cantonese and Spanish and a basic Chinese course. I kept saying: "No, all I need is the ability to write characters on the screen and get pinyin [phonetic spellings] or a translation." But she kept talking about other applications. I couldn't shut her down or get her to answer my actual questions. Finally, I just asked how much it cost, because I'd have paid anything to end the madness.

In sales training in the US, they tell you, "How much is it?" is a buying signal. She apparently had never had any sales training. She kept talking and trying to show me more features. I finally walked away. In sales parlance, we call this "talking past the sale." I had to go all the way back to town the next day, so as to buy the same device from someone else. Although I paid less than I would have from the features-lady, it was still very expensive. And when I got it home, I had no idea how to use it, because the instruction manual was in Chinese. What irony.

Looking for Chinese movies to watch, I wound up buying the absolute coolest thing. It was a Chinese language-learning book and DVD, based on a Chinese TV show I enjoyed watching called, *Home With Kids*. This was a series I'd watched to improve my Mandarin listening. Now I had a textbook with reading and writing and listening exercises based on the episodes. This was perfect, contextualized learning and real-world TV language.

Using my down time to study Chinese, I was watching a Chinese movie with Chinese subtitles. One of the characters in it had a stutter, but I realized there's no way in Chinese to write a stutter. In fact, you can't even write regional accents. Very few Chinese dialects have their own writing system. Chinese dialects, plus Japanese and old Vietnamese and Korean, were written in largely identical traditional Chinese script, but pronounced in the local dialect or the local language. Today, Hong Kong uses traditional Chinese characters, whereas the Chinese mainland uses simplified script. When Hong Kongers read characters, they pronounce them in Cantonese. There's actually nothing about the characters themselves that dictates how they should be pronounced. If a mainland Chinese person reads a Hong Kong newspaper, he'll just pronounce the words in Mandarin. In Taiwan, traditional characters are read in Mandarin, whereas a Latin script is used for the Taiwanese language.

The language attitude of Chinese learning English is very different to the attitude of foreigners learning Chinese. Many times, I saw Jaka using a phrase book when trying to communicate with locals. Meanwhile, in the 100-percent English-language Australian university program I taught in at Shanghai University, a significant number of students refused to speak in class. A Chinese administrator told me, "They're shy to speak English to foreigners."

"Maybe they should have chosen a different program." I retorted. Also, the purpose of the program was to prepare those students for education in Australia. But the joke was on me, because they wouldn't be seeing any foreigners there either — they'd be in a special dorm and take all of their classes with other students from the PRC. So maybe it was me who was wrong about the purpose and nature of language learning.

The university organized a welcome mixer for international students. The email promised water, beer, and crackers. I went to that meeting, but there were no crackers. That's how they get you: Lure you in with the promise of free crackers, then rip your heart out of your chest. Also, you had to choose between one beer or one water, both of which were at room temperature, and it was bloody hot outside. Among the students was a huge Mongolian, named Bata, who was easily 120 kg (265 lbs). He was also majoring in wrestling. I went over and told him, "You may not understand this now, but you're meeting your best friend." I was so excited about having a Mongolian to train with, and I hoped my wrestling research would take me to Inner Mongolia or independent Mongolia. My dream was to one day wrestle in Naadam, the traditional summer festival. What a wonderful stroke of luck, meeting my first Mongolian wrestling friend. It almost made up for the hundreds of dollars I'd lost by buying an electronic dictionary I didn't know how to use.

An American student called Michael had told me earlier that Chu Laoshi had informed him that he'd have a Viennese roommate. We were joking about how his Viennese roommate would always be making great coffee, eating chocolate, and composing classical music. But when I saw Michael at the party, he was with an Asian guy. Michael laughed, saying: "Apparently, Chu Laoshi meant Vietnamese."

SUS had about 7,000 students in total, with about 300 foreign students Most of the foreign students were Asian, with Koreans and Vietnamese being in the majority. China had been courting Africa and countries involved in the Belt and Road Initiative (a massive collection of projects in which Beijing loans money to developing countries, so they can pay Chinese companies to build infrastructure, so China can make money). China also offered scholarships, so there were thirty or so African students. In addition, SUS had about six Mongolians, six Russians, nine Americans, no Brits, and one Belgian.

We only had one Arab student. When Michael told me she was from Syria, I just said "Wow!" I had nothing else to add. What could I say? "I hear it's lovely" or "Syria? Oh yeah, my country is about to bomb you."

The Koreans mostly lived off campus and never came to class or events. They had no interest in talking to the rest of us, so we tended not to know them. I actually met some Koreans who were getting ready to graduate and they couldn't speak Chinese well enough to have a basic conversation. People say, "It takes time to learn Chinese." If that were true, then every person on the planet, over a certain age, would speak it. But they don't. So it must take something more than just the passage of time. It begins with a desire to speak the language and is followed by a long period of hard work.

The Vietnamese were all nice, but they tended to stick together, helping one another. Many of them were of Chinese descent, so they already spoke Chinese when they arrived. The ones who weren't took a very long time to speak Mandarin well enough to make friends with.

In general, while one may believe that having this or that language as a base is an advantage in learning some other language, my experience has been that, in most cases, English speakers have a huge advantage learning other languages. This is because most textbooks are written in English and, if the teachers speak a foreign language, it's usually English. We had Chinese teachers who spoke Japanese and Korean, as well as materials for speakers of Japanese and Korean, so those students had their own, separate Chinese classes. But the Vietnamese students really struggled, having to rely on a system of veteran students helping newer students. Could you imagine being in class and not being able to ask a single question? It must have been terrifying. Consequently, they learned much slower.

China is one of the largest foreign-student destinations in the world. But, most students are there to learn the language, rather than to take a degree. One generally found that students from undeveloped countries were seeking degrees in China, while those from wealthy countries would stay for a summer, or six months or a year, to do a language course. In the sports university, there were two American master's degree students who were a year ahead of me, and one who was just starting. I was the first American Ph.D. candidate at SUS. All the other Americans were just doing language courses. Three of them were doing language and martial arts. In the end, four of us would graduate and for the next several years, there'd be no new American students.

Chu Laoshi, the foreign student advisor, passed out a declaration form which we had to sign, swearing we had no diseases. The form had a place for a signature, but not for printing your name. After we turned them in, I guessed they had no way of knowing whose form was whose.

The following day, my advisor Professor Dai summoned me to his office, where he told me that my speaking and listening were the highest of all the foreign students and he was excited to have me there. He was hoping I could help them translate and publish in English. Sadly, my Chinese reading level was still so low it was embarrassing. There was no way I could help them translate and publish. But I just smiled and nodded.

He also told me to concentrate my research on a comparison of Chinese wrestling and Olympic wrestling.

Professor Dai asked me where I was working. We weren't allowed to work if we were on scholarship, but it was obvious I'd need to, because the scholarship wasn't enough to live on. I told him I wasn't working at the moment. I didn't go into details, but I hadn't renewed my contract at Shanghai University because I wanted to take a semester to get settled into the Ph.D. program before making any decisions about how much and where I could work.

He got really upset. "Working is very important, if you want to be a Chinese academic!" he told me. "Our salaries are so small, we all have other jobs or other businesses. One of the professors sells watermelons, for example." I hoped he meant the teacher had a watermelon farm, and not that he stood on the side of the road selling fruit from a cart, because that wouldn't have been very motivating.

My American economist friend Chase, who was teaching in the Business Department at Shanghai University, told me that just about every Chinese teacher had an outside job. Seniority usually meant more time and more accommodation to do your outside job. Low-level assistant professors were expected to live on their university wage, plus some tutoring, while running errands and freeing up important people so they could work their outside hustles.

I told him I was planning to wait and see how hard my class schedule was, but once I was settled in, I'd like to start teaching again. He said that was good and that he'd like me to come teach. However, he immediately warned me that the salary wasn't great. He went on to say that they were forming some type of foreign joint-venture department and that teaching there would pay well. So maybe I could do that later. He also said that they needed a foreign professor who could be the liaison for foreign exchanges with US universities.

I'd have loved the opportunities he was describing, but the surest option would be to just go get myself a job, as soon as I was ready. Then, if the university called me, even if the salary was say 40 percent lower than what I had outside, I'd probably take it.

Next, Professor Dai discussed my dissertation research. There are several types of analysis that can be done in a Ph.D. dissertation. In the US, they usually want you to prove something new. Originally, I wanted to write a massive book, documenting and exploring the culture and history of wrestling styles, but of course this wouldn't be a proof or an analysis. In China, one of the accepted analyses was a comparison. Consequently, Professor Dai told me that he wanted me to narrow the focus of my research down to comparing Chinese traditional wrestling with modern wrestling. This was slightly different than what he'd said before, about Olympic wrestling, but I liked the idea of modern, rather than Olympic, because it was less restricting.

After talking about my research, I asked him about my courses. I wanted to know whether or not I had any, and if there was a schedule. He didn't seem very interested in that subject, so he called his assistant, Han Hongyu, a senior Ph.D. candidate. Han Hongyu walked in and Professor Dai told him to help me register for classes.

Han Hongyu instantly said, "Impossible!" Professor Dai wanted to know why. "He's a foreigner. How can he take classes?" asked Han Hongyu.

"He speaks Chinese." replied Professor Dai.

"Yes, but not well," countered Han Hongyu, who I'd never met and who'd never heard me speak Mandarin. Professor Dai told him that I could understand everything they were saying.

Listening to them argue about me, talking past me like this, was pretty dehumanizing. I almost wanted to remind them that I was in the room.

When Professor Dai told Han Hongyu that I could be useful, helping them get published in English, Han Hongyu asked: "How do we know he can write English well?"

"I'm a published author," I blurted out. "I've written seven books."

"Have you published papers?" asked Han Hongyu. I said I had, so he asked me which field.

"Linguistics." I answered. They both stared at me, and I explained about my linguistics background.

Han Hongyu threw up his hands. "What are you even doing here?" He seemed genuinely angry that I'd been admitted to the university.

I was speechless.

"Can he read Chinese?" asked Han Hongyu.

Now I started to sweat. So many times, during my studies, I was reminded of an adult literacy campaign on the radio in Tennessee when I was a kid. It began with an old man's voice, sadly saying, "For thirty long years, I lived with a lonely secret. I could not read." I never knew that was going to be me one day.

"Of course he can," said Professor Dai. He looked at me and said, "Āndōngní, open that book to any page and read for us."

In Chinese academic circles, I always feel like the illiterate adult who's invented all sorts of self-defense mechanisms to prevent people from discovering he can't read. But now my worst fears had been realized. I simply had to tell them.

"I can't read or write Chinese," I admitted.

Professor Dai looked like I'd seriously let him down, while Han Hongyu looked vindicated. "How could that be?" asked the professor, flabbergasted. "Didn't you take the HSK exam?"

I wanted to explain that passing a reading exam and reading real academic materials are two very different things. But I suspected they wouldn't understand and possibly wouldn't even believe me. Instead, I just sort of shrugged. "I want to take reading classes here," I whispered, feeling like a fraud who'd just been exposed to the public.

Professor Dai immediately turned to Han Hongyu, saying, "He needs wrestling and Chinese reading."

"Impossible!" shouted Han Hongyu. Then they sort of lapsed into a kind of dialect, or more accurately, relaxed colloquial speech which I couldn't quite follow. Apparently, my advisor wanted Han Hongyu to bring me to someone, but I was unclear whom, maybe the wrestling coach, but Han Hongyu was saying the guy wouldn't meet me. So Professor Dai asked, "Does he smoke? Bring him some cigarettes."

The two laughed and the mood in the room lightened. They continued talking, more casually. Later, I heard the professor ask, "What kind of alcohol does he drink? Bring him a bottle."

Eventually Han Hongyu and I left, ostensibly to straighten out my classes. Outside, I could see he really didn't like me, well not me exactly, but the idea of me. He asked, "You didn't even have to test to get into this program, did you?"

I answered "No" because I knew that's what he wanted to hear. But actually I'd had to come to the university for the entrance exam, along with all of the Chinese Ph.D. candidates, present my research proposal in Chinese, and field questions from a panel of professors, as well as pass a martial arts exam, the same as everyone else.

But Han Hongyu wanted to believe that I'd been handed something for free, possibly at the exclusion of a deserving Chinese student, so he could hate me. I gave him that gift… so that he'd like me.

To be fair, Han Hongyu and other Chinese students probably did have to jump through a lot more hoops and did have it a lot harder than me. Also, Han Hongyu and others seemed frustrated by the fact that I had degrees in teaching and business and had studied linguistics, but now I was in a wushu program. In China, all Ph.D. programs require a master's degree, and all master's degrees require a bachelor's degree, and all three degrees are usually in the same subject. Although they weren't fond of being reminded of this fact, they all knew that the academic level of a sports university was far below that of teaching, linguistics, or business programs elsewhere. So some people either felt I didn't belong there, or that I'd taken the easy way out. Or maybe they thought I was a screw-up who couldn't get into one of those other academic programs and this was my university of last resort. I certainly found that to be the case among the journalism and English majors at SUS. They were academic students who couldn't get in anywhere else, so they settled for a sports university.

This was another issue of culture. I tried many times, over the next three years, to explain to people that studying at SUS was a dream of mine, something I aspired to, not something I fell into. It'd always been my dream to complete a degree, taught in a foreign language, and to complete a full study of martial arts, in China. I tried to make them understand that I'd given up my position as a university lecturer, for which I'd earned double or triple what top professors earned at SUS. But this was inconceivable to them. Those who did understand on some level were offended on another level. They'd worked their whole lives to get here. They'd started out in small villages in impoverished regions of the PRC. Most said they'd never even heard of their sport before being selected to leave home, at age seven, to live, train, and suffer through a sports school or *wǔ xiào* (martial arts school) for twelve years. Then they had to compete in order to win admission to the sports university. They were generally the first in their family to finish high school, let alone a university or a Ph.D. program. And here I was, waltzing in and doing this program just because it interested me.

Over the next three years, I'd only have a few negative interactions of this nature with graduate students or professors. But my closest friends would be the wrestlers and sanda fighters and athletes I trained with, because they only judged me on how hard I trained and how respectful I was of their training and their lives. Eventually, many came to me for advice about their studies and their careers. But I didn't know that at the time. At this point, Professor Dai and Han Hongyu were the only people I knew from the Wu Shu Institute and one of them hated me. That was fifty percent.

And, of course, I couldn't read. I knew that, and now they knew it, too. And I already doubted myself. Getting through three years of classes, and writing a thesis in Chinese, seemed like an impossible goal at that moment.

Han Hongyu took me to the registration office, downstairs from Professor Dai's office. They asked me for my student number. I told them I didn't have one. Han Hongyu got really angry, saying: "Why don't you have a student number? You cannot register for classes without a student number."

The registration people told me to see Chu Laoshi and get a number. Han Hongyu disappeared. I ran back to Chu's office, and he gave me my number. I wondered why they hadn't given each of us a welcome package containing that type of information at orientation. I called Han Hongyu, expecting we'd meet, so he could help me with whatever it was he was supposed to help me with. But instead he just asked for my number over the phone. And we were done.

It was Wednesday, and I still wasn't registered for any of the classes that would be starting on Monday.

I was supposed to have a Vietnamese roommate, but he didn't show up. Then late one night, a Vietnamese guy knocked on the door and said he was my roommate, but that he was living downstairs with the other Vietnamese. This was typical: The Vietnamese students seemed very nice, but also very cliquish. They cooked and ate and lived together. Apparently the Vietnamese guy he was living with was supposed to have a Japanese roommate who was coming in a few days, and he asked if I could live with the Japanese student and let the Vietnamese stay together. I said it'd be no problem. I figured that, although I get on really well with Vietnamese people, I'd prefer a roommate whose friends wouldn't constantly be in and out of the room. And, if stereotypes are to be believed, it'd be really cool if my Japanese roommate built a robot. Of course, living with him would probably make me feel like an impolite, dirty barbarian.

The next day was orientation. Foreign students who were already in a degree program had to attend two separate orientations, one where they were majoring, and another specially for foreigners. The hilarious thing about the latter was that it was done in Mandarin, which about 80 percent of the students couldn't speak. There was an English translation for part of it, which 75 percent of students couldn't understand.

Orientation day was my first experience of using Chinese as a lingua franca, in other words, using it to communicate with non-Chinese students. The Americans and some of the Africans spoke English together. But with the Vietnamese, Koreans, Japanese, Russians, and others, we spoke Chinese. It was really kind of fun. The third most common lingua franca, after English and Chinese, was Russian. The students from Central Asia and the former Soviet republics all spoke Russian.

The orientation was one boring speech after another. I couldn't imagine being one of these dignitaries, just sitting there, reading from a paper, droning on, not caring if anyone was listening. One of my African friends commented, "Not only do the students not want to listen, but the professors talk like they don't want to talk."

All over campus, in shopping malls, and on the subway, I saw young people taking an insane number of photos and selfies, and I wondered what they did with all of these images. During orientation, students actually used their phones to take photos of the three boring professors sitting on the stage, reading their mind-numbing speeches.

Next was the orientation for wushu majors. One guy droned on and on, not making any attempt to be interesting, funny, or engaging, and the entire audience either slept or played with their phones. It seemed like a very inefficient way to communicate. A doctoral candidate blew his nose on the auditorium floor.

Quite a bit of time was devoted to what people would do after graduation. Because teacher salaries are so low in China, it was almost expected that the majority of students would graduate and never do anything with sports or teaching again. Even my advisor, after discussing my life's work that I wanted to write about wrestling, asked me what my plan was for a job after graduation. I felt the Chinese understood vocation, but not evocation. If I succeeded in writing a work which was recognized as adding to the body of knowledge, that would have meaning for me. But Chinese people didn't understand that. Their goal was to make money.

I'd hoped that my new classmates would be training and that we could train together. But after meeting them, I found out that most of the doctoral candidates in the Wu Shu Institute didn't exercise on a regular basis. Even the ones who'd been working as kung fu instructors in government schools, before being accepted, said they only trained two or three times a week.

I had to wonder how I and so many Chinese people could all arrive at the same place, but with completely different motivations and completely different goals? None of them were planning on competing again, not even the sanda guys. In fact, most stopped competing in their very early twenties, before they'd graduated from their bachelor's degree programs. Most smoked and drank, and all of them eventually got fat bellies and pencil arms.

People like my heroes — Mas Oyama, Masahiko Kimura, and Miyamoto Musashi, in Asia, or Rilio Gracie, Judo Gene LaBelle, and Dan Inosanto in the West — were anomalies, I guess. They trained and fought right up to the end of their lives, and dedicated every waking minute to training and improving. None of these guys I studied with, at age 46 or even 26, would consider starting over as a wrestler or a judoka.

One of the doctoral candidates from the Wu Shu Institute came to up me all excited, and shook my hand. "I heard you're writing about wrestling. American wrestling is the best. My favorite wrestler is John Cena."

I was about to say, "Not that kind of wrestling." But then I thought, What the hell? If it makes him happy to think I'm writing my doctoral dissertation about WWE, who am I to burst his bubble and tell him it's not real? I told him my favorite is Randy the Ram, "And I'm learning his patented move, the Ram Jam."

Professor Dai assigned a second-year Ph.D. student named Duan Limae to help me with my course registration. She'd wind up being the one who dragged me the whole way through my studies. Without her, and without so many other friends helping, I'd never have made it. She brought me over to the Wu Shu Institute; now that we had my student number, registration took about thirty seconds. All first-year Ph.D. students had to take the same classes, so they just printed out a schedule and handed it to me.

I was shocked to discover that I had 26 credits of mandatory academic classes over the three years. Six of them were Chinese-languages class, but the other 20 were regular academic courses taught in Chinese. Among the mandatory classes were English, Political Thought, and two units of Marxism. Wrestling was conspicuously absent from the list. I assumed that I was allowed to chose some electives, but had no idea how I'd cram those into the schedule. As doctoral students, we also had tutorials for about four hours per week with Professor Dai.

Duan Limae and I went to see Professor Dai to ask if I could be excused from English, Political Thought, and Marxism, but he said: "No, you should go along with your Chinese classmates, get to know them, and see how those courses are taught. It'll be interesting for you."

I really didn't want to have to do that, so I went over to the Foreign Students Office to see if they could help. They said foreign students could be exempted from Political Thought classes, and they grudgingly exempted me from English, but demanded that I take an equal number of Chinese classes. In China, you often get what you want, but not always for the reasons you think. Anyway, I was really happy because I wanted to take Advanced Chinese Reading and now there'd be time in my schedule. But, of course, there was a cost: Now I wouldn't know how to think politically or in a Marxist manner.

I was also pleased to find out from Duan Limae that one of my research courses consisted of regularly meeting one-on-one with Professor Dai. He'd assign me articles to read and discuss and also I'd do two papers for him. Those would be the first scholarly papers I wrote in Chinese, and they were quite bad.

The training halls finally opened. I stopped by the wrestling room and watched the Greco-Roman team training for a bit. I was so incredibly impressed by the wrestlers. They were all immensely strong, yet athletic and flexible. Forget about sweeps, throws, and takedowns, Greco is the art of lifting your opponent off the ground and slamming him. Where some of the freestyle wrestlers had a little fat on them, the Greco guys looked like Greek statues. I couldn't wait to start training with them the following week. Of course, I was worried I wouldn't make the cut the way I did in Beijing with my wrestling team there.

Would a wrestling singlet make me look fat? I wondered. What about Chips Ahoy! cookies? I so desperately wanted to fit in with the other kids on the team.

I introduced myself to the coach and explained that I was a foreign Ph.D. student writing my dissertation on wrestling, and asked him if I could train. He said he didn't have the authority to allow me to do that and I had to get the administration involved.

Leaving the training hall, I tried to get out of the elevator, but I was surrounded by the fattest group of Chinese people I had ever seen in my life. It seemed an odd coincidence to see so many people of that size on the campus of an elite sports university, on the same day, at the same time. I wondered if my school had participated in *The Biggest Loser: China*.

I stopped in a small shop to buy a cold soda, but the cans were all out on the shelves, at room temperature. I asked if they had cold ones and the owner pointed to the refrigerator. I reached in, grabbed one, and realized it was probably one degree cooler than room temperature. In fact, I wasn't even sure if the refrigerator was on. And I thought, if the drink isn't cold, why store it in the refrigerator? That's somewhere between a cargo cult mentality and false advertising.

·· ● ··

At a mandatory meeting of the wushu Ph.D. students, I discovered there were seven of us in all, and I was the only foreigner. After that meeting, I went to straighten out my Chinese classes at the Chinese Language Department. They told me that, since I needed help with my writing, I'd have to attend first semester Chinese classes with foreign students who didn't know a single word of Chinese. I'd also attend much higher-level reading classes, as well as research methodology and other courses taught exclusively in Chinese, and where I expected to be the only foreign student.

It was going to be crazy, switching on a daily basis between the world of graduate-level Chinese students, beginning-level foreign students, and sport classes taught in Mandarin.

I asked Professor Dai if he could help me start training in wrestling and maybe also in judo. He made a couple of phone calls, but said I had to go get permission from the Foreign Students Department. When I got there and asked about wrestling and martial arts training, both Chu Laoshi and Piao Laoshi said that foreign students were discouraged from sports training during their stay at the sports university. They said this with a straight face, making me wonder if they had any sense of irony at all. I knew for a fact that AJ and Jaka had come here exclusively because of the martial arts training, and now they were telling us we couldn't train.

I'd done what I thought was a clever thing. I'd written into my official study plan that I'd be attending wrestling, sanda, and judo classes as part of my research. This plan had been submitted in triplicate to the university and signed off by my advisor and the Foreign Students Department. But Piao Laoshi said, "You have to pay money for sports training."

"But it's part of my research," I protested.

"No, sports training is extra," she said.

"But you signed off on my research plan. And my scholarship covers all classes. So that makes sanda and wrestling official classes that I need for my studies."

"No, sports are extra," she insisted. "For example, if a student wanted to learn to dance, that would cost extra."

"It's part of my research," I repeated, realizing she wasn't going to budge.

"Then you can go there with a notebook and watch. But if you change clothes and train, you'll have to pay," she concluded.

At nearly every meeting the foreign students were forced to attend, we were told, very proudly, that SUS is the only university in the world where you can do a Ph.D. in martial arts. In every advert or poster for the university, they show pictures of foreigners studying martial arts at the university. In all fairness, no one claimed that the classes were free or covered by our scholarship. On a parallel note, the Marxism course is free, but wouldn't it be ironic if it wasn't?

In the end, I agreed to pay. But the price was insane. They actually wanted me to pay a per session fee, assessed and paid for the whole semester in advance, which came to thousands of US dollars. The other option they gave me was unlimited training for US$ 3,000. Finally, I convinced Piao Laoshi to drop the price to US$ 1,500 for only wrestling team and two sanda classes per week. She agreed, but when I went to the Greco-Roman wrestling coach, he emphatically rebuffed me. The wrestling team was an official A-team, representing the university, so no foreigners were allowed.

I looked at the university's website, to try and find a list of sports courses with their dates and times, so I could choose my sanda and wrestling courses, but there didn't seem to be one. In China, it was often difficult to get lists of information like that, particularly schedules. They were often drawn up at the last minute, and they were frequently wrong. In the university where I'd been teaching, schedules often weren't finalized until the second week of the semester; even then, they might be wrong, because the government and the university had discretion to declare or ignore certain holidays and makeup days.

I went back to the Foreign Students Department and asked for a list of all of the sports classes. Chu Laoshi said I could find it online. I told him I'd been all over the website, but it didn't seem to be there. Then he said, "Ask your Ph.D. advisor." I told him I had, but that he didn't have one. Finally, he conceded, "I'll send it to you."

Not only was information hard to come by, but administrators either didn't want to admit that they didn't know, or didn't want to admit that they didn't have the information, or didn't want to admit that the information was unavailable. I guess this was all part of national defense. If China was ever invaded, the enemy wouldn't know what time badminton was. Three days later, Chu Laoshi still hadn't sent it, so I went and asked for it. Once again Chu Laoshi said he'd send it. The list finally arrived in my inbox, several days after the third time I'd reminded him.

I went through the list, chose a sanda class, copied the class info from the list, and emailed it back to him, asking him to sign me up. He replied that I was good to go. The first day, I went to that class, but there was no one there. I came back and told him, "The list you sent me was wrong. There's no class at that time."

"Yes, you must have read it wrong," he surmised.

"But I copied the list you sent me, exactly, sent it back to you, and you approved it. So, the problem can't be that I misread it?"

Chu Laoshi instantly changed the subject. "Blue looks good on you. It goes well with your eyes." He then told me that he'd send the class details to me that night. Two days later, I had to ask for it again. Over a period of a week, I had his promise several times that he'd send me the schedule. Each time, it failed to appear. Finally, about the fifth time, I walked into his office and refused to leave without a schedule. When he saw that I wasn't budging, he made a phone call, then another and another, trying to find out who had such a list. Eventually, he got someone to send him a correct list, and I rounded out my training schedule. Easy as pie!

The other foreign students I talked to, who'd been on campus for a few years, told me that once I'd established relationships with the teachers, I'd be permitted to train for free. Robert, one of the Americans, said it'd taken him two years, but he eventually became an official disciple of his professor and traveled and trained with her without paying. A Czech student, Kat, told me a similar story. One African guy somehow turned up on campus and a week later was training with the sanda team. AJ was paying his coach directly. One of the more ironic stories concerned a foreign student who'd been turned away by the wushu teachers on campus so many times that — although he was doing his masters at SUS — he'd paid for a wushu class at Fudan University (a top academic university in Shanghai), because he'd somehow been introduced to a wushu teacher there who was willing to convince the school to take his money. So now he was living at the no. 2 training facility in China, studying at the world's only Ph.D.-level Wu Shu Institute, but he was taking wushu as part of a club, with a bunch of smart, non-athletic kids, at a different university a few miles away.

The following day I received great news. I'd passed the HSK-4 Chinese proficiency exam. Now my registration at the university was complete and official. I was ready to start school. Ironically, this news came on September 11, which is usually a hard day for me. This year, it was like a gift. Passing the HSK requires a minimum score of 180 points. I'd scored 197. I missed reading by one point (scoring 59 out of 100) and writing by five (scoring 55). Both of those were much better than I'd expected. My listening (83 of out 100) had saved me. At that point I'd logged over 1,000 hours of listening — and it'd paid off.

Now I'd be the first person in history to pass HSK-4, and then take Introductory Chinese Writing class and taught-in-Chinese Ph.D.-level courses at the same time.

•●•·

On the way back to my room, I noticed a horrible smell coming from a Vietnamese room, where a bunch of students were cooking. I wanted to shout, "The racks in the hallway are for drying laundry, not fish!"

Speaking of laundry, the laundry situation at SUS was simply untenable. First off, there were no changing or shower facilities on campus. You had to wear your training clothes to your training sessions, and if you had class after, you wore the same sweaty disgusting clothes to class. Then you could go back to your room and do laundry by hand. There was a laundry service on the other side of campus, but they only washed clothes and didn't dry them. You were supposed to drop off your clothes, clearly labeled, in a bucket, along with your detergent. Then, you went back later, picked up your bucket of clean but wet clothes, carried them back to your room, and hung them. That just seemed like a lot of work.

The other laundry option comprised two broken washing machines and zero driers in the downstairs of our building, which housed 130 people. I looked for a drop-off laundry service, but of course I couldn't find one, because Chinese people think it's dirty for everyone's clothes to be washed together. I tried explaining to people who weren't from Brooklyn the irony of there being no laundromats in China. But they didn't get it.

Before I moved out of the Shanghai University teachers' accommodation, my coworker had given me a gift of several large, plastic, watertight clothes containers. I bet that when she gave them to me, she never guessed I'd be using them to do laundry. Every time I came back from training, I got in the shower, with one of those tubs, filled it with water and detergent, and then stood in it and walked on my clothes, the way my ancestors did with grapes when they made wine, or coffee beans when they made espresso. Afterward, I hung the clothes to dry in the room. It wasn't ideal, but it was the lesser of three evils.

I went to visit a Vietnamese neighbor and on his bookshelf was Matthew Polly's book, *American Shaolin*. Matthew and I had been in contact for years, because my Shaolin book, *The Monk from Brooklyn*, came out around the same time as his. He and I had recently been chatting on Facebook about my return to Shaolin. As far as I knew, he'd read *The Monk from Brooklyn* and even defended me on some martial arts forums. My book had been with a no-name publisher, while his was with Gotham books, and I think it became a bestseller. He also did the first interview with Jet Li when he came to the US, for *Playboy*.

I was honored when *Kung Fu* magazine asked me to write a story for the 40th anniversary of Bruce Lee's death. But someone paid Matthew to write a whole book about Bruce Lee, the first major biography to come out in ages.

Because Matthew's book was much more successful than mine, he could afford to buy other books. I never had the heart to tell him I couldn't afford to buy his book. But now my Vietnamese friend had given it to me. I asked him where he'd got it, and he said that he'd found it in his first dorm room in China, six years earlier, and had had it ever since. But since he couldn't read English, he didn't even know what it was or what it was about. That was such a strange piece of serendipity. I couldn't believe people were complaining about him drying fish on the laundry rack.

Actually, it turned out the smell wasn't from drying fish on the laundry rack, but was from imported fish sauce, made from decaying fish, that someone else had dried on a laundry rack in Vietnam.

That night, my Japanese roommate arrived. He had about 200 words of English and spoke no Chinese at all. Somehow, with a mix of electronics and English, I discovered that his name was Natsuki and that he was an Olympic hopeful in the 400-meter hurdles.

I felt like Tom Cruise, in *The Last Samurai*: "I have introduced myself. You have introduced yourself. This has been a good conversation." But we were able to go a bit further, in the introducing-ourselves department.

Natsuki said he'd chosen SUS because the coach here had produced a famous world champion hurdler. He believed he could get good training and also become a champion. Another reason he chose China was that, in Japan, he was ranked in the top eight, and all eight were slotted to train at Japan's premier sports university. He didn't want to train with the guys he'd be competing against. By coming here, maybe he'd have an edge.

I hated to be the one to break the news to him, but foreign students were generally not permitted to train at this university, unless we paid separately for training. Also, I'd already had teachers from both the sports and Chinese departments try to sell me private lessons.

Nonetheless, Natsuki was a perfect roommate. Because of the language barrier, he wasn't always talking my head off. He was an Olympic hopeful, so he trained every day like me. He didn't keep late hours, didn't drink or smoke, and didn't have many guests.

The next morning, I walked over to campus to do my strength training, but found all the facilities locked. There were multiple weight-rooms on campus, but some of them were off limits to foreign students. Some were only for athletes, but two should have been open for anyone to use, according to the schedule. But time and time again, we'd go there at the scheduled time and the rooms would be locked. When we complained to the administration, they urged us to "Read the schedule carefully."

Even if the weight rooms actually kept to their schedule, they were never opened on Saturdays, Sundays, or holidays. Even worse, they closed each time there were sports competitions or exams on campus.

The obstacles preventing us from training regularly were causing me to lose my mind. Apparently, you can take the monk out of Brooklyn, but not the Brooklyn out of the monk.

Suddenly, I had an epiphany, like that moment when Steven Seagal realized he was a deity. I'd pay money and join a fitness gym in the mall near our campus.

The gym, located on the third floor of the mall, wasn't great, but it wasn't terrible. When I signed my contract, they gave me a free watermelon shake. It had no sugar, so it wasn't sweet at all. It was made from low-quality Chinese watermelons, mixed with water. It had no flavor. And best of all, it was served at room temperature. Although it looked nice, there was no reason anyone would have taken a second sip. I sometimes suspected that China was modeling their new society after photos of the developed world.

Now I was paying for training both on and off campus. I felt like my life finally had balance.

Food was a huge problem at SUS. I'd assumed the cafeteria would serve scientifically planned meals, possibly even based on which sport people played. But actually it was the same, incredibly low-cost, completely inedible food that they served in university cafeterias across China. The first few days, I tried. I bought a plate full of what I thought was meat, but it was fried dough. I got vegetables a couple of times, but they were oily, overcooked, and bereft of nutrition. The next time I went, they had no vegetables at all. At other meals, they served mayonnaise-laden potato salad as a vegetable. A few times, I found cold, fried eggs in the morning, but not on other days. It was inconceivable to me that the athletes were eating fried bread and rice, very little meat, almost no healthy vegetables, and absolutely no fruit at all, three times per day.

A shop nearby sold tiny hamburgers and fried chicken legs, so I tried using that for my protein, but there was so much filler (cereal, bread, and oil) involved that I eventually gave up. But finding no better option, I went back again… then gave up, and went back, over and over, during the three years.

I found a street market right around the corner from the university. It was only open at night, and not very often, and it was often raided by the police. When it was open, however, I was able to get fried rice for RMB 5 (US\$ 0.80) and mysterious meats on a stick for RMB 23 (US\$ 3.70). There was no ice, and uncooked meat sat out for hours in the late summer heat, until someone bought it. I ate the meat, then looked at my watch. It was 6:45 p.m. I decided that if, by 9:45 p.m., I hadn't become violently ill, I'd eat there again the next day. And since I hadn't found a better meat option, even if I did get sick I'd probably eat there again.

The university's supermarket had some food items, but no meat, vegetables, or fruit. I had to go to the mall to buy coffee, but I managed to find a small bag of sugar in the university shop. It was labeled "High Candy" in English, like something you shouldn't try to take through customs.

Monday morning finally came, and my first class was a three-hour-long Ph.D.-level sanda ge do class on the third floor of the training hall. The sanda room was huge, with the entire floor covered with mats. There was a row of about ten heavy bags. And there were two sanda competition platforms (like boxing rings, but without the ropes). You could get points for throwing your opponent out of the platform, and if you threw him out twice, he automatically lost. Often that rule wasn't needed, because the platform was about a meter high. If you got thrown out twice, you were usually incapable of continuing the fight. The rest of the room was open space, where as many as three classes or two tournaments might be going on at the same time.

Sanda is Chinese kickboxing, and it includes wrestling takedowns. Sanda ge do means "all ways," so it included knees, elbows, and forearm strikes. There was also some chin na, joint manipulations, and — at last theoretically — there was ground fighting. Sanda ge do is often taught to military and police personnel, or advanced students, but it's rare to see any sparring at all in sanda ge do classes or in professional competition. When they sparred or fought professionally, they tended not to include the joint locks, knees, elbows, or ground fighting.

This course was covered by my scholarship because it was mandatory for all wushu Ph.D. students. My classmates were the people who'd gone through the intake exam with me. Two of them were relatively young, master's students who were majoring in sanda. The rest were older Ph.D. students majoring in wushu, tai chi, or qigong. The former were a bit fitter and could have been good partners for me in class, but they were already partnered with each other, and everyone was hesitant to train with me. Not to brag, but on that first day, if we'd had to fight for grades, I'd have bet all my money on me. But that was all hypothetical: As a monk, of course, I'm not allowed to bet.

The teacher was Jiang Laoshi, who immediately took a liking to me. I was impressed with his knowledge and experience. Although he wasn't young, he was one of the few coaches I'd met in China who looked fit. He really understood fighting and asked a lot about MMA. He invited me to his other sanda classes, which I wouldn't have to pay for, and this really rounded out my training. He'd wind up becoming an important friend and ally for the rest of my studies.

After sanda ge do class, I attended my first set of lectures. We sat in the classroom, waiting for the teacher, with the lights out. I wondered if we should spring out and yell, "Surprise!" But this was common in China. Classes were during the day, so of course the lights weren't turned on. There were thirty or more of us in the class, as it was a class required for both master's and Ph.D. students. Some students dressed a bit better, because it was the first day of school. A few were dressed as typical college students, rather sloppily. The bulk of us, myself included, were wearing track suits, because we'd just come from or were on our way to a training class.

When the teacher walked in, the class leader called us to attention, we shouted in unison, "*Lǎoshī hǎo*," ("Good day, teacher") to greet the lecturer. We did a wushu salute, left hand draped over the right fist, and then sat when the teacher told us to. At the end of class, we did the same thing, but then shouted, "*Lǎoshī, zàijiàn!*" ("See you again, teacher").

This class had been on the history and culture of martial arts. Afterward, we had a ten-minute break, followed by another three-hour lecture on the development of sport. Neither course had a textbook.

Chinese college classes are about a teacher droning on and students pretending to listen. Usually, there's no discussion, questions, interactions, or exchanges of ideas. In the classes I attended, I had to be very careful about what I did, because my situation was so special. I was the oldest, so even if I made a cultural mistake maybe no one would tell me. And I was a foreigner, so sometimes I got away with murder. Having said that, sometimes I might make what I saw as a small mistake, but it'd cause someone to hate me forever. Also, I didn't know all of the rules yet, so I didn't want to start breaking them. Just the way I walked into the classroom or the way I sat, or the way I held my pen, might already be considered wrong. Just by admitting me to the program, they were already tolerating me. I didn't want to push it, so I couldn't initiate discussions or ask questions. I just sat and listened. But I did participate whenever a discussion broke out.

One student was chosen to clean the blackboard. Another student had to refill the teacher's tea thermos. There was a class leader and a *lǎo dà* ("older brother" or informal class leader). It was all so traditional and cool.

The second class, development of sport, was only for doctoral students. It started out the same way, with students being called to attention, greeting the teacher in unison, and then sitting and listening (or not) to a boring lecture. But then the teacher actually initiated, perhaps by accident, a discussion. One significant point about that second class was that the student who launched the conversation, my Ph.D. classmate Yan Shan, was an instructor at the university and our class *lǎo dà*. I was grateful he was there, because he was senior enough to start a discussion; this made it much more tolerable than a conventional three-hour lecture. Yan Shan and I got to be friends because he'd been at my dissertation proposal, and I'd noticed him watching very intently during my MMA demo. It turned out that he taught the Movie Kung Fu classes and was studying with us, so he could complete his Ph.D. and become a full professor.

During break, the Ph.D. classmates and I discussed what to call me. I was the oldest, but I didn't need to be the *lǎo dà*. I told them to call me *shī gē* ("older study brother").

That night was the first paid-for sanda class. I walked in and showed my receipt to the teacher, Zhou Laoshi, but she just refused to understand my Chinese. Luckily, one of the students was a master's degree wushu student who knew me, so he came over and translated my Mandarin into Zhou Laoshi's Mandarin. Even though she now understood that I'd be attending her class, and that I'd paid, she still said "No." I had to call Professor Dai, Piao Laoshi, and my new friend and ally, the sanda ge do teacher Jiang Laoshi, and put her on the phone with them. Eventually, she grudgingly let me join the class.

Sanda was probably the single largest subject on campus, other than English, which every student had to take. Sanda majors obviously had to take sanda, but all wushu students also had to take sanda. Additionally, among the 40 percent or so of students on campus who weren't majoring in wushu, many selected sanda as a sports elective for their degree requirements. Consequently, SUS had at least four sanda teachers, teaching several times per day, every day.

The popularity of sanda meant that the class was an odd mix of students and abilities. There were wushu students who didn't know how to fight, but who were incredibly flexible and could kick high and fast. There were tai chi students who couldn't fight, but who also had the flexibility and experience to be able to mimic the kicks. However, they had a lot of problems punching and grappling. There were two graduate-level sanda students. The others came from various sports, and possibly one or two were journalism or English major with no athletic background. While some of the students had kicks or athleticism, none had the wrestling skills necessary for sanda, apart from the two sanda majors.

Zhou Laoshi told us to find a partner and do practice drills. No one wanted to partner with me, so I just observed for the first few minutes. A huge guy, muscular but fat, was bullying all of the other students, until they actually complained to the teacher. So I went over and partnered with him. He was a head taller than me and weighed 90 kg (198 lbs). He was a swimmer with no fight experience. I let him hit me hard a couple of times, then I took him down. He stood up, hit me again, and I took him down. When he stood up, I took him down. I did that, three more times, until he didn't want to stand up again. He was sitting on the ground, with me standing over him, saying, "Come on, let's drill properly. We still have over an hour to go." The kids all started laughing. Then, like an eight-year-old, he called to Zhou Laoshi, "Can I have a different partner?" The whole room erupted in laughter. Even Zhou Laoshi, who I never succeeded in getting close to, had to laugh. She knew exactly what was going on, and that this guy had got a taste of his own medicine.

She said, "Why don't you rest a bit and Āndōngní can train with Ma Pei and Jiang Huaying." She was referring to the two professional sanda fighters. I was so glad she said it. I would have trained with them, but because we were doing partner drills, I thought I'd be in their way.

The two guys were nice, if a little wary of me at first. They asked about my sanda experience and I said I only had a little bit, from Shaolin Temple, but when they saw I was willing to fight and throw, they warmed to me immediately, and began teaching me. Jiang Hauying was very small, only 60 kg (132 lbs), but an excellent fighter and very fast. Ma Pei was a lot closer to my size. And they were both very fit, all muscle with no fat. Ma Pei and I liked sparring each other because we were the same size. And I really liked sparring Jiang Huaying because his speed posed really interesting challenges for me. It turned out that their advisor was Jiang Laoshi, my sanda ge do teacher, and so we became close friends, and remained so for the rest of our studies. We'd see each other not only at training, but also at wushu events and meetings, and we graduated together. In fact, I was at Jiang Huaying's thesis defense. After meeting these two, the sanda community opened up for me, and they helped me learn so much.

Each sanda class was an hour and a half. During the final twenty-minute cool down, I noticed two muscular guys play fighting in the back of the room. Of course, when people fight, I have to go say "Hello." They both had cauliflower ears that looked like alien life forms. They told me they were from the university's Greco-Roman wrestling team and were interested in MMA. We sparred around a bit. Of course, their wrestling skills were amazing, and their strength was incredible. They were attending this sanda class as a degree requirement, but they couldn't be bothered to participate. So most days they either skipped, or came late and just wrestled each other in the back of the room.

The smaller one, Zheng Xiaoliang, said he was 22 and had been living in sports schools since age of eight. He started with wushu as a child, switched to sanda, because he liked to fight, but later changed to freestyle wrestling, which he loved. He won admission to SUS, but because there was no men's freestyle wrestling, he'd had to learn Greco-Roman wrestling. Walking with me back to the dorms, he said: "The last 14 years of my life, all I've done is learn to fight."

The other guy, Zheng Tong, was my size and about 20 years old. He was one of the strongest people I'd ever wrestled. He told me that he'd been living in a sports school, doing Greco-Roman wrestling since nine years old.

The next morning was my first day of shuai jiao. I had nearly the same fight with the shuai jiao coach I'd had with Zhou Laoshi the night before, with him not wanting to allow me to join. I called the same teachers I'd called before, but he said the wushu department had no authority over him. This was the issue Professor Dai had with shuai jiao. He felt that shuai jiao should be within the Wu Shu Institute. Instead, it was part of the modern sports training majors and almost everyone associated with it came from a wrestling background, rather than a martial arts background. Eventually, Piao Laoshi called someone who called the shuai jiao coach and we got it sorted. Skeptically, the coach said, "OK, you can train. Go over there with the team."

We were in the wrestling hall on the fourth floor of the training building. The massive space had a mat-covered floor, except for a narrow passage way from the door to the coach's desk. This way, the coach and other visitors could leave their street shoes on. In traditional wrestling, wrestlers wore special Chinese wrestling shoes. The shifus and coaches usually wore street shoes on the mat. but it didn't matter, because they never cleaned the mats anyway.

The room was split down the middle, with the judo team training on the other side. The judo side was noticeably cleaner. It seemed everywhere I traveled and trained, judo coaches were heavily influenced by Japan, requiring more discipline and cleanliness in the training halls, and doing their training systematically. On the third floor was the sanda room; it stunk to high heaven, because thousands of students trained there each day, barefoot, and it was never cleaned. On the first floor were the weight rooms. This building is where I'd spend most of my time over the next three years, and I saw it as a kind of immune-system strength training. After two years in China, I bet I could drink tap water in India and not get sick.

The team had all stopped training the minute I walked in, and they were staring at me silently. I was always the new guy, but this was different, more intimidating. These kids had been wrestling their whole lives. Some of them had been friends since they'd left their home as children. None of them spoke English; most of them had never seen a foreigner before; and none had ever trained with a foreigner. Also, I was in my mid-forties, and they were all 18 to 22 years old. Their staring was justified. I'd never felt so foreign.

I must have frozen, because the coach shouted impatiently, "Go over to the team and start training."

Just then, a voice among the wrestlers shouted excitedly: "That's my friend!" The wrestlers parted to let him through. He shouted at least twice, "He's my friend." It was Zheng Tong, the larger of the two wrestlers I'd met the night before in Zhou Laoshi's sanda class. He hugged me, took me by the arm, and led me over to the team. Immediately, the atmosphere went from intimidating to welcoming. Everyone came over to greet me. They kept asking Zheng Tong questions about me, but he kept answering: "He speaks Chinese. You can ask him."

And that was all it took. Having one friend changed everything about my experience at SUS. Not only would Zheng Tong become my closest friend during my years of study, but two years after I graduated, he was instrumental in me taking the best-paying job I had in China. He'd also wind up coaching me through my MMA comeback, years later, traveling with me to fight in Malaysia, and we'd both wrestle before a crowd of 40,000 people in India. And it all started with him yelling, "That's my friend."

People sometimes ask me how *Martial Arts Odyssey* got started. I always joke, "I never intended to drop out of modern American life. I just left the office for ten minutes to get really fresh Chinese food… and 12 years later, I was wrestling in China."

The coach had us do a warmup, which, like many days, was a game of tag. We had a big fat guy on the team, and tag always turned into a game of "Pick on the fat kid." He was the easiest one to catch and tag, other than me, because I couldn't run at all on my bad knees.

After the warmup, the coach ordered everyone to put on their wrestling jackets. While I was clearly putting mine on, in front of everyone the coach told the students: "Āndōngní is a foreigner and doesn't have a wrestling jacket." I was standing right in front of him, and yet, like the Emperor's New Clothes, no one pointed out his mistake. Finally, one brave girl spoke up. "Look, he's wearing a wrestling jacket." So the teacher asked me where I'd got my jacket.

My jacket carried the name of my master, Wang Wenyong, and my wrestling club in Beijing. I was going to point that out, but instead I said: "From my wrestling teacher in Beijing."

The coach repeated the question slowly and patiently, so I replied, equally slowly and clearly, "Beijing." The teacher looked lost, like he wanted someone to translate. "I guess he doesn't understand the question," he concluded.

"I got it in Beijing," I almost yelled. Under my breath I added, "I told you twice already." Then I tried a different tact. I said, "My shifu gave it to me, in Beijing." He didn't look convinced that I was wearing a wrestling jacket, but he decided to go ahead with the training and said that we'd see if we could order one for me in the morning.

Before and after training each day, we had to stand at attention, like in the military, "Eyes right, front, parade rest, attention, cover, recover…" Then we had to count off. After that, the teacher put us at parade rest and talked to us for a few minutes. During his talk, he asked me, in front of everyone, if I was married. I said I wasn't. He repeated the question, so I repeated my answer. He then told the group: "He doesn't understand the question."

In linguistics training, I'd learned that most of what you understand, in your native tongue, is based on expectations. In China, it's expected that everyone my age would be married. So even though I said that I wasn't married, the teacher expected me to say that I was. Consequently, he assumed that either he'd heard me wrong or I'd misunderstood the question.

I therefore spoke up: "I was married, but now I'm divorced." I really think it's no one's business, but I wanted to be clear that I'd both heard and understood him. And, from that point on, every time someone asked me if I was married, that was my answer. And they generally only made me say it two to three times before accepting it.

After wrestling practice, I went back to my room for a shower and a rest. Then I had some academic classes. The first was Chinese reading class. It was terribly boring and low level, but it was my own fault, because I needed to learn to read and write. It seemed so pointless, though, to sit in a class with people who spoke no Chinese at all, learning two to three characters per day. You need around 1,500 characters to read a newspaper — so the good news was that I'd need only about 500 more days of class.

After the Chinese class, I went and sat through a Ph.D. lecture with my Chinese classmates. A doctoral candidate arrived late, so the teacher made him do pushups. Afterward, I went to my off-campus gym to lift weights. When I told the gym trainers that the university was charging me for wrestling, they told me they had a wrestling teacher — an Asian Games medalist — who could give me private lessons. It turned out she was female. I honestly wouldn't have a problem being trained by a female coach, but lifting and wrestling with someone so much smaller wouldn't help me develop strength. Also, as a monk, wrestling a girl alone, and giving her money, just seemed a bit… improper. Bad jokes aside, it also turned out that she wanted US$ 50 per lesson, which I thought was madness. How could anyone afford to pay that five times a week?

She was trying to dissuade me from wrestling at SUS, saying "If you wrestle at the university, it's very difficult and you'll get tired. But if you hire me as private coach, we could take it easy." Even if I'd been interested, she just lost the sale. Obviously, if I wanted to take it easy, I wouldn't be wrestling.

Back at school, it was getting harder for me to keep up my Chinese listening practice. Before coming to the university, I had very little contact with Chinese people and little real-world exposure to the language. So I watched TV and logged my listening hours. Now I had a lot more exposure and interaction, but I wasn't sure that it replaced what I'd been doing before. The problem now was that when I got back to my room, I just wanted to escape, watching UFC and American TV shows, in English. I wasn't convinced that attending lectures where I tuned out, Chinese classes where I learned three characters per day, and training sessions where I talked to wrestlers and fighters, was going to raise my academic Chinese level sufficiently. I was considering hiring a tutor. And if I did, then I'd be paying for wrestling at the university, my gym, and my Chinese classes. This free scholarship was about to get really expensive.

I talked to foreign students who'd already passed the HSK-5 or HSK-6, the most difficult levels, and they all said they'd quit Chinese classes straight away and just studied on their own.

My friend AJ had given up on trying to arrange sports classes and instead hired a private sanda trainer on campus. He was paying about US$30 a lesson, twice a week, which worked out to a little less than what I was paying for my semester of training, but he missed out on the experience of the group classes, which I enjoyed and gave me a chance to make friends.

Some people like AJ and me were paying money. Some foreigners, through their own personality and intellect, managed to arrange training. But most just quit. It was an extremely common discussion among foreign students: "I used to play [insert name of sport] at world level, but after I came here, there was no training, so I stopped." AJ and I were both working. In fact, anyone with a European face found it easy to find work, off campus, teaching English. We therefore had more money than other students, who were living on their scholarships. Ph.D. students received about US$ 500 per month. Bachelor's students only received about US$ 300 a month, which was really just enough to survive, if they ate all their meals in the horrible cafeteria, and they'd always run out by the end of the month. There was no way they could pay for Chinese lessons or sport training.

Also, as bachelors' students, it was unlikely their professors would know them or take an interest in them and help them find training. Consequently, they generally gave up on sport training. If they survived in Chinese, it was because they just locked themselves in their rooms, studying Chinese on their own, day and night, until they were at a sufficiently high level. It was one more irony of this program that the people who achieved the highest academic level in Chinese were the ones who stopped going to class.

I think this was the plan all along. The university made everything so impossible that one by one, students opted to stay in their rooms and study for the exams on their own, and the teachers could take some time off, or sell some private lessons.

A Chinese student needed to ask a question in one of our doctoral lectures, but first apologized, then asked permission to ask questions in class.

Most classes were incredibly boring. The teacher would just talk endlessly. Looking around, I noticed that no one was taking notes. What a horrible way to live. During one lecture, the teacher's phone rang and, as he answered it, we all breathed a sigh of relief, because we'd get a few seconds break. I looked over at my classmate and pitied him. For me, this was a temporary difficulty I had to survive. But for him, his entire education had been like this.

After class, I rushed outside, like a little kid. As I ran past the outdoor swimming pool, it hit me that I'd never seen the swim team, nor heard of anyone using this pool. In Shanghai, it's too cold to swim outdoors most of the year, and campus was closed in summer. I don't know what that pool cost, but they could have spent the money better on almost anything else. And just like the martial arts lessons, that pool was in a lot of the university's advertisements. Then again, to be fair, the ads didn't actually say you could use the pool, only that it existed.

Other than my dissertation class, Basic Writing was the only Chinese class I was required to attend. The class was absolutely preposterous. The teacher kept talking to me in English, although I talked to him in Chinese. Finally, I just demanded he speak to me in Chinese, so he did. He explained that he was speaking English because many students couldn't speak Chinese. Looking around the room, I saw a sea of Vietnamese, Mongolians, Japanese, Russians, and people from other countries who didn't speak English. Some of the Asian students were in the same boat as me: They could speak Chinese well or had been there for a year or two already, but they needed help with writing. It appeared that speaking English or Chinese the teacher was going to reach about the same number of students. The difference, of course, is that if he spoke Chinese, he'd be helping all of the students learn Chinese, which was the point of the program. He handed out a matching exercise, with all of the answers written in English. And once again, the bulk of the students couldn't read English. It dawned on me just how screwed up the teaching of Chinese to foreigners was and how hard it must have been for non-English speakers.

Since coming to China, I'd met a lot of people who'd try to tell me simple things in English, but difficult things in Chinese. I just find it insulting and often confusing when they suddenly blurt out English words like "One, two, three" or "Your teacher," with no context and no verbs. If they'd just speak Mandarin, normally and in complete sentences, I'd be able to follow. But saying nothing other than "this" or "twice times" doesn't really explain anything to me. One day, in the Wu Shu Institute, I actually had two teacher/administrators tell me: "You don't always understand Chinese, so I'll tell you simple things in English and complicated things in Chinese." Yes, that's sure to clear up all the misunderstandings. Also, the best way to learn Mandarin and improve your communication skills for next time is if everyone speaks to you in really bad English. I think I read that in a teaching manual.

More than once, I encountered people who'd talk to you in Chinese for an hour, then suddenly, in English, say "Thrivety-thirty o'clock" because, although you spoke Chinese well, they assumed you didn't know numbers.

But since "Thrivety-thirty o'clock" doesn't exist, I found it hard to meet people at that time.

Once in Taiwan, I met an old man in a restaurant. We talked for about 45 minutes in Mandarin. He was very nice and told me interesting stories about his life and Taiwan's history. When he finished, I began eating, and he said, "You're very intelligent." I thought he was going to compliment me for my Chinese, and I was prepared to say, "You're too kind. I'm not that good." Instead he said, "You're very intelligent. You can eat with chopsticks. Most foreigners can't." I had to laugh because, first off, in major cities like New York, most Westerners can eat with chopsticks, and new arrivals tended to learn eating with chopsticks quite quickly. By contrast, it takes years to achieve enough knowledge of Chinese to have an intelligent conversation with a native speaker for 45 minutes.

Taiwan has always had a special place in my heart, because it was the first Asian country I lived in and the place where I learned Chinese. It was also in Taiwan that I'd been given my Chinese name, Āndōngní, which I always wrote in the traditional characters used in Taiwan, rather than the simplified characters used on the mainland. We had to sign the register at the beginning of each class and I finally gave in and started writing my name in simplified characters. It only affects the middle character, *dōng*, but still my name was part of my identity. I'd written it that way for 11 years already. Changing it meant admitting that I'd become Beijingified. Maybe soon I'd begin adding "ar" to the ends of words, like in Beijing dialect.

I kept trying to force myself to write Chinese. After a few days of class, I took a few lecture notes in Chinese for the first time. Not a lot, just a few key points about our research assignment, but it marked my first usage of written Chinese in the classroom. I thought it'd slowly become a habit and I'd get better at it. But I'll save you some reading: I didn't. I never learned to write Chinese by hand, but I did eventually learn to type Chinese pretty fast on my phone or my computer.

For homework, the teacher asked us to find a dissertation online about sports performance and do an evaluation of it, all in Chinese. Baby steps. From that first homework assignment, I determined that every homework assignment I did would be related to wrestling, so I could include it in my dissertation. I opened a folder in my computer called "Literature Review" to list every article or paper I used for a homework assignment, along with quotes related to my topic. For the first assignment, I chose an article on sports performance in wrestling, and added it to my annotated bibliography. When I finally sat down to write my dissertation, three years later, my literature review file had nearly 2,000 entries.

Later, when I became a professor, I told all of my advisees to do the same. And I still have my Ph.D. students doing that today. Rather than scrambling to have enough sources, my students need to pare down and throw out sources which they've read and documented. This means they can truly claim to be experts in their field, because they'll have read a significant volume of the existing literature.

My class schedule was set by the university and the department. Now it looked like I had my training schedule sorted out as well. My week included five three-hour sessions of wrestling and sanda, augmented with private lessons, plus my strength and conditioning work.

In our sanda ge do class, we learned some basic chin na (*qínná*) grappling, similar to what I'd learned at the Shaolin Temple. For my next homework assignment, I skewed the topic toward chin na, so I could make it part of my dissertation research. After all, it was a form of Chinese grappling, so it made sense to include it.

In between training, studying, and research, I was trying to squeeze in my Chinese TV viewing, but, I just wanted to watch English TV and veg out. *Seinfeld* is so much better than the best Chinese drama. But I had to find a way to keep watching Chinese, or I was afraid that a year later, I still wouldn't know what was going on.

Ph.D. dissertation defenses are held each June, but Ph.D. students don't graduate until the fall. As his graduating students were in town, each fall, Professor Dai called all of his graduate advisees and alumni together for a dinner. This was a formal meal in two private rooms in a restaurant, with our own servers. The dishes were all ordered in advance, by the professor, and placed on a lazy Susan in the center. The students were meant to buy alcohol for the dinner, including red wine, white liquor, and beer. To my dismay, each student would drink all three.

Even though I'd studied Chinese for a long time, I still found that I didn't always understand all of the conversations. I also didn't know all of the cultural rules. For example, although Chinese people are often late for appointments, you had to be on time for a dinner like this, because everyone had to sit down at the same time. And where you sat was a big deal. Two of the older students actually went into the room first, surveyed the layout, then had a heated discussion about who should sit where, depending on some combination of factors, including age, time in the program, and closeness to Professor Dai. And no matter how well-thought-out the arrangements were, when the host arrived, he'd change them.

Once we were seated, there were strict rules about which foods to take first, which part of the lazy Susan to take food from, how to eat it, and so forth. In Chinese culture, it's assumed that everyone at the table likes every dish. It's not acceptable to let a dish slip by, saying "I don't like this one, but I'm waiting for that one, over there." Of course, this is what I did. And one of the reasons I was so adamant about controlling the types and quantity of food that entered my body was because I saw that, by the end of these meetings, the students were all extremely uncomfortable from having been forced, by social pressure, to eat and drink impossible quantities of things they didn't want to. The first few times I'd been to a dinner like this, I felt so bloated that I couldn't sleep, and I suffered from a food hangover the next day. After that, I just refused to eat anything I didn't like or didn't want to.

One trick I learned was to leave your plate full. If you ate everything, people would put more food in your plate, regardless of how many times you said, "No." But if your plate was full, there was no place to put the food. So I'd just eat the things I liked, and when I'd had enough, I would leave my plate completely full and just stop eating.

Alcohol was a huge problem for me. I don't drink at all, but there's a strict culture of toasting at these dinners. Every event was a huge battle with me saying, "Sorry, I don't drink alcohol."

"Just a little," they'd insist.

"No, even a little is alcohol. And I don't drink alcohol."

"Just white liquor."

"No, white liquor is still alcohol." This didn't happen just once, at the beginning of the night. The conversation was repeated over and over, all evening. These dinners could be very uncomfortable experiences for me.

Also, I just couldn't imagine that anyone actually enjoyed drinking beer, red wine, and white liquor (which smelled like paint thinner) at room temperature, on the same evening. From the looks on their faces, most of them hated it. I kept waiting for the day when someone would have an "Aha!" moment and say: "We don't have to keep doing this." And, one by one, they'd stop. Well, maybe in my next life. At the end of my seven years in China, they were still doing it.

Once we got past the alcohol issue, I still had to participate in the toasts. I'd do it with Sprite or water, but the etiquette was still complicated. The younger students had to toast me. We all had to toast the teacher. The teacher toasted us. We had to toast the older students…

Sometimes, you remained seated while toasting. At others, you stood in place. For some toasts, you had to walk over and stand beside the person you were toasting. For certain toasts, you held the glass normally. For others, your hand had to be lower than the hand of the person you were toasting. Some toasts required your hand to be on the bottom of the glass.

Sometimes, you only needed to take a sip. At other times, you needed to empty the whole glass. I never actually learned the rules, and just did what my classmates told me to do. At some point, they would inevitably whisper to me, "You have to toast the teacher now."

When my professor introduced me at the dinner, he said, "This is Āndōngní, he has a BA in English." English was my minor, but that wasn't on any of my Chinese records, because in China there are no minors. So I wondered how he came up with this. Then it hit me: In our very first meeting, he'd asked me what my bachelor's degree was in, and I'd said, "Foreign Languages." In Western countries, if you say you major in "Foreign Languages," people will ask you which languages you studied. But in China, "Foreign Languages" always meant English.

· · ● · ·

The following evening was an open fighting day at the MMA gym. Fighters from different disciplines came to spar together and exchange techniques: boxing, wrestling, Muay Thai, BJJ, sanda, and so on. I organized 12 SUS international students (Mongolians, Vietnamese, Japanese, Kazakhs, a Ghanaian, and an American, plus one Chinese classmate) to attend. For several of them, it was their first time on Shanghai's subway. It's amazing how easy it is to get a seat on the subway when you're traveling with a 120 kg (264 lbs) Mongolian wrestler.

When we got to the gym, the first thing I wanted to do was wrestle Bata, my huge Mongolian friend. In every photo I'm smiling, because I was so happy to finally be wrestling a Mongolian and holding my own. Because of the tremendous size difference — about 30 kg (66 lbs) — I started getting a bit aggressive, grabbing his head. I wasn't sure if they knew Thai clinch in Mongolia or if he'd get offended. By controlling his head, I was actually able to defend his take downs. My strategy against a bigger, better-trained opponent was to simply defend, and make him work and hopefully open up an opportunity when he got tired. He took me down twice, but that's pretty good, given how long we wrestled and how much bigger and more experienced he was.

The other two Mongolians, Zolar and Baida, also wrestled me. They were badminton majors, but being Mongolian, they still knew how to wrestle. They were at a disadvantage without their wrestling jackets, and I just needed to wear them down. They each got one throw on me, but after several minutes of carrying my weight on their neck and head, they got tired and I took them down

Some of the international students wrestled each other, others had a box-off in the ring. Most of them had never worn boxing gloves or fought before. There was a lot of laughing and running away.

I'd just recovered from the worst blackeye ever, about two weeks earlier, and that night I sustained a fresh injury. A 110 kg (242 lbs) American wrestler hit me with his elbow. It occurred to me that I should probably find a new line of work. I never got cut that badly when I was a linguist.

Dana, the American wrestler, had pro MMA fighting experience, as well as wrestling. We were doing standup wrestling and he accidentally finger-poked my eye so badly it affected my vision frighteningly. I could see out of either eye, but not both, and I felt mildly concussed. I rested. When we continued, he inadvertently hit me in the eye with his elbow and I got cut pretty badly. Afterward, in ground sparing, he smashed my face with a huge elbow. He said he was sorry, but how did this happen three times? It was wrestling, not MMA. No strikes!

I told my friends that the injury must have happened because I'd skipped my prefight ritual of drinking a half liter of warm yogurt. (This wasn't really my prefight ritual, but I always told people it was, in the hope it'd take off).

I decided I'd never train with Dana again. Meanwhile, we found a first-aid kit. Using some Vaseline and bandages, I managed to stop the bleeding long enough to teach a little MMA wrestling to my friends from the university.

One reason why people with no MMA training believe they can beat MMA fighters is that, for some reason, it's widely believed that the low-single and low-double leg takedown on the knees are the only takedowns. I've talked to people coming from arts as diverse as street fighting, taekwondo, Wing Chun, and watching TV who believed that because they learned how to throw a knee or how to sprawl (quickly dropping your center of gravity to avoid being taken down, when your opponent catches one or both of your legs) they could avoid 100 percent of takedowns, and thereby beat an MMA fighter. In reality, however, there are hundreds of other takedowns. And, if you defend the first attempt, the wrestler will just transition to the next, and the next, and the next, until he gets you down. If knowing the sprawl meant that you could always defend the takedown, then all wrestling matches would end in a stalemate.

Afterward, the SUS students and I went to eat low-quality steak and pizza together. Everywhere we went, people asked us if we were *liú xuéshēng*, and even the university referred to us as *liú xuéshēng*. But that name always bothered me, because it literally means "travel student," which to me sounds like an exchange student or someone who's doing a language course for the summer. It conjures of images of Brits and Americans, slacking off, hanging around Paris or Prague, studying the language and lounging in cafes, having the time of their lives, rather than graduate students struggling to do the near impossible.

The students were taking loads of photos, which was fine, but once the food came, I just wanted to eat and be left alone. When someone said, "Look at the camera." I just grunted, "No!" and kept eating. These international students were so much fun and this was a totally new experience for them. Also, I was one of the few who had Chinese classmates, because I was already in my major study, while most of them were still learning Chinese. So it was a good chance for Chinese and international students to get to know each other. It really was a great day.

Back at the university, I went to four pharmacies trying to get some aspirin and some sort of antibiotic ointment for the huge gash on my face.

All four assured me that you couldn't buy aspirin or any kind of pain medicine without a prescription. When I asked for something for my eye, they handed me a bottle of alcohol and cotton swabs. In the West, we haven't put alcohol on cuts in probably thirty years. Also, I didn't want to get alcohol anywhere near my eye. What I wanted was some sort of antibiotic gel that would seal the wound and moisturize it, so it wouldn't scar. In the end, I bought nothing and prayed it wouldn't get infected.

I had two Russian neighbors. One spoke really good English and they both spoke Chinese. It turned out that the one who only spoke Chinese was also doing his Ph.D. in wrestling. I talked to the English-speaking one first, and he gave me a lot of interesting information. Then I started talking to the other one, in Chinese, and he kept dominating the conversation, talking over me, and not answering my questions. This behavior is a defensive mechanism of language learners. By dominating, they know the conversation will never go somewhere where they feel lost. They want to prevent you from saying something that they don't understand.

Both of these men were speaking a foreign language, but the one who spoke English didn't display this behavior so much, and I had a theory as to why. Perhaps people who learn English learn to adopt English conversation culture: Interaction, back and forth, real listening, and the exchange of ideas. In fact, arguably, the other guy had adopted Chinese conversation culture: you talk and talk, and if the other person stopped listening, walked away, or burst into flames, you just ignored them and plowed on through whatever it was you were saying.

An alternative theory is that English is so dominant in the world that, no matter how long and how well they study Chinese, there are still areas where people would feel more comfortable with English because they've heard it their whole lives.

I told Jaka that I was happy to have a Japanese roommate because he didn't know English and didn't talk to me too much. "That way, we don't get sick of each other." He then complained: "My Italian roommate keeps trying to talk to me." I was cracking up, picturing a quiet introvert trying to live with my loud, Italian family. It'd drive someone like Jaka to distraction.

Jun Yinbiao, one of the *jiàoliàn* (young coaches) from Shaolin Temple, called me to see how I was doing. He sounded so happy and grown up on the phone. Yi Long texted me a few times, as well, to tell me he liked our pictures together and we were still brothers. They were just the sweetest kids ever. When I was at the temple, I'd had a dispute with Jacky over money. After that, many of the kids, particularly Jun Yinbiao, told me they hated Jacky and were leaving once their tuition expired. True to his word, Jun Yinbiao said he was leaving the next day. He planned to go home for a while, then look for a new temple school.

A few weeks later, the Italian monk who'd sent me to Jacky called. He said that Du Shifu and Jacky had had a falling out, and that Du Shifu had gone back to his village and opened his own school, and that all of the kids I'd known had followed him. Also, the Italian monk would now send his students to Du Shifu, rather than to Jacky. I really liked Du Shifu, and suspected that the kids did too. This was all good news.

I went downstairs to tell Jaka. Then we went to the bank together. One of the annoying things about waiting at the bank or at the airport or for a train in China is that, if you aren't physically touching the person in line in front of you, someone will try to squeeze between you. And if you're touching, they still may jump to the front of the line.

Jaka said to me, "Chinese people are nice but strange." I told him, "They feel the same way about you, what with your toothbrushing and appointment-keeping behavior."

Until Jaka learned to speak Chinese, I always had to translate for him. Whenever we went to eat, after I gave his order to the waitress, he'd always say, "Can you ask her to make it without MSG?" Or, "Tell her to only lightly fry it." Or, "Can I substitute this for that?" To which I always replied in the negative. China is a no-substitution culture. They generally make food a certain way and you can't ask them to modify it or customize it. If the order comes a little wrong, or even very wrong, you just eat it.

One time, he wanted me to order him a small coffee, but he wanted it in a large cup. They absolutely couldn't do that. For one thing, the bosses counted the cups and if a large cup was missing, the price of a large cup of coffee should be in the register. In this case, I actually did try and translate for him, but the request was so unusual that they confirmed, "You want a large coffee."

"No, a small coffee in a large cup."

"A large coffee."

"No, a small coffee in a large cup."

"Two large coffees?"

"OK," I finally said. I paid for both coffees. When Jaka protested about the order being wrong, I said, "It's OK, you can give me half of yours." I was always winning a little extra food like that when Jaka was around.

We went to get one of those big fried sandwiches I loved. I ordered mine with lots of extra meat and vegetables. Jaka ordered his without meat. The lady knew me, and always put three kinds of sauce on my sandwich. When Jaka's sandwich was done, she put the three sauces on his as well.

"I didn't want sauce." he said in English.

"Oh, sorry, we should have told her." I said, making it our problem, so he'd feel better. She was still cooking mine and hadn't added meat yet, so he asked me, "Could you give her this sandwich back and tell her to put meat on it, and let it be yours. Then the one that's on the grill right now, that doesn't have meat on it yet, could be mine?"

To that I replied, "No." It was way too complicated, and you simply didn't do that in China. Also, there's a special way they cook it and fold it, and the order in which the ingredients go in... It'd be impossible for them to convert a perfectly cooked meat sandwich into an already cooked vegetable sandwich. The sandwich with no meat is just RMB 3 (less than US$ 0.50). If you don't like it, don't eat it. Order a new one and you're out fifty cents.

Jaka got really angry and asked me several more times to translate for him, but I refused. Finally, he ordered a new one. Then he handed me his old one and said, "Well, I guess you just got a free sandwich, because I'm not going to eat this."

Victory was mine!

Because the students were so young (18 to 22), and because training sessions were so long, at both Chinese wrestling training and at sanda, warmup was usually some kind of a game, variations of tag, keep away, or handball. After that, training started with tumbling and gymnastics. They made me do shoulder rolls, break falls, cartwheels, and a lot of stuff that I hated and wasn't good at. My body wasn't designed for that, but it amazed me that every wrestler and fighter could do handsprings, one armed cartwheels, backflips... I guess if things didn't work out with the Ph.D., I could always try clown college.

At sanda ge do, as always, Jiang Laoshi scolded me for my kicks being too slow and too low. How was it, that after more than thirty years of martial arts, I still didn't kick well? I wondered if there was a connection between my bad kicks and my inability to do gymnastics.

Sanda and wrestling classes, conditioning, strength training, getting smacked around and bruised every day... training twice a day and still having to keep up with my academic classes... How does anyone get through a Ph.D. program?

Taking all of my classes in Chinese was incredibly hard. At times, I got really down. In Chinese, if you hear a word you don't know, it's very difficult to look it up by sound. If you read a word you don't know, it's very hard to look up by appearance. I asked a Chinese graduate student who'd studied in the US how she got through her classes. She said she just did a lot of supplemental reading in English and got people to translate her papers for her. I'd have liked to have researched my courses in English, but I didn't know what they were about.

Because I couldn't understand the lecture, I couldn't take notes, which always made me jealous of my Chinese classmates. Having said that, I noticed that most of them never took notes either. They generally wrote less than one paragraph for a three-hour lecture. In fact, they didn't even listen. So I wasn't sure how much of a disadvantage I really had.

Since I couldn't understand what was being said, I thought maybe I could at least copy the characters off the board and look them up in the dictionary, but most of the teachers wrote on the board in Chinese cursive, which I found absolutely illegible.

My electronic dictionary was called BESTA, and when you turned it on, it sang "B-E-S-T-A." I usually left it open during class, but then it'd go into suspend mode. When I'd wake it up, it'd sing the song again. About five times per class, I had everyone staring at me.

Most of my Ph.D. classmates were school teachers, teaching wushu at public schools or universities. One of the rare interesting lectures we had was about teaching wushu to children; many students stood up and shared their experiences and how to motivate kids to learn wushu.

I often wondered how Asian martial arts teachers, who were used to teaching 12 -year-olds who trained 12 hours per day, could transition into teaching adults in the West. Here in Asia, US students worked as hard as local students, but we were older and lacked flexibility, and lacked a willingness to get injured for no reason. And those limitations caused problems. But translate that attitude back to the US, where people have jobs and lives and only train twice a week... I always wondered how that worked. I guess successful Asian teachers are the ones who completely change their style and expectations after opening a martial arts school in the US.

A friend once said: "Chinese are great students but terrible teachers." And this was so true. One example; we were playing some crazy tag game in wrestling training. No one explained it to me, and I simply couldn't figure out what the rules were. It was like one of those insane Japanese game shows they parody on *Saturday Night Live*, where you had to run, then do math problems, then the monkey drove the go kart and someone threw knives… Anyway, in this tag game, I always seemed to be standing in the wrong place, finally one girl said to me, in English, "You stand there." Wow! Thanks. It's all so clear now. If she'd said that in Chinese, I'd also have understood, but been no less confused. After that, in my mind, that game was called "You Stand There." And every time we played, I stood there and refused to move. Anyone who tried to move me, I just referred them to that girl.

After warmup, morning training was obnoxiously hard: weightlifting, wrestling exercises, kicks, bag work… Evening training was a beginners sanda class, way too easy, but still good for me to learn step by step and — most importantly — to learn how to teach sanda. Also, it helped me learn the Chinese vocabulary for sanda and for training in general. When we were doing drills, kicking and punching each other, I didn't always understand the instructions, so sometimes someone had an accident. It reminded me of the documentary *The Hammer*, about Matt "The Hammer" Hamill, a deaf MMA fighter. In training, he couldn't hear the coach yell "Start," so he sometimes got creamed. In real fights, he couldn't hear the ref shout "Stop!!!" so he kept punching people beyond the bell.

In sanda classes, we did a lot of drilling. I think this is what was missing in a lot of the MMA and boxing training I'd had. A lot of our training was lining up, crossing the training floor, and throwing a particular combination the teacher had given us, like left right punch, kick, or sometimes a more involved combo, like sidekick, back kick, punch, punch. Other times, we did similar drills with a partner, where one guy kicked and one guy blocked or countered. We did takedown drills like this, with one guy moving backward and one guy shooting and lifting. We also did drills where we locked up in a clinch and either pushed or dragged our opponent across the training floor. These are the kinds of drills I saw students doing at Tagou Shaolin and other sports academies, which I thought would be extremely useful.

I went with some students to eat at a Korean bulgogi restaurant, where you were served a bunch of raw meat which you had to cook yourself. Don't get me started on the irony of paying money to cook my own dinner. If I'd wanted to cook, I'd have stayed home. They brought me a plate of cold octopus in hot sauce, which I assumed was like a snack to eat while your meat was cooking. I popped a huge handful in my mouth before I realized it wasn't cooked. I'll eat sashimi with the best of them; in Japan, I'd probably even eat raw octopus. But that stuff was intended to be eaten raw. My rule is: Never eat anything raw that was meant to be cooked, especially in China, where baby formula kills.

I wanted to spit the octopus out, but being China, there were no napkins on the table. I ran for the bathroom, but it was on the second floor, through the upstairs dining room, down a hall, through a door way, past the kitchen… It was the longest I'd ever run with food in my mouth. When I finally got there and spit it out, I felt like a mother bird, returning to the nest to feed her young.

The next morning, I had wrestling practice. Wrestling equipment check list: mask, tights, knee-high boots, folding metal chair…

The coach had Zheng Tong and me partner up, because we were friends and about the same size. Not only did Zheng Tong love Greco-Roman wrestling, but he told me he hated shuai jiao. So although we were supposed to be doing shuai jiao, we bent, if not broke, the rules in most of our bouts. He shot on his knees a few times, and I choked him out once or twice.

One of the things that I liked about our wrestling class was that we drilled. We actually learned a couple of throws per day, then drilled them. We also did different kinds of sparring, for example, grabbing sparring, which the teacher called *qiāng shŏu* ("gunfighter"). We had to circle each other, like in a fight, but the goal was not to complete the takedown, but rather, to shoot your hands out, as fast as possible, and get a two-handed grip on your opponent. In Beijing we never trained like this. Another difference between training at SUS and training in Beijing is that at the university, no one smoked or drank while we were training.

As much as I missed MMA training, one thing I liked better about wrestling was that, when I failed to get the takedown, no one hit me in the head with an elbow or kicked me in the face.

One of my wrestling teammates said that he'd lived in sports schools and trained full time since he was eight. Only training twice a day at university was the most freedom he'd ever had. He liked it, but now that he was only training six or seven hours a day, I was worried he'd get fat.

Another of my teammates told me he liked to be called "Tiger." And I thought, you know what China needs? One more martial artist or fighter who takes the nickname *Lǎohŭ* ("tiger") or *Lóng* ("dragon"). Surely there must have been other cool animals in China. It wasn't like all Russian fighters are called "Bear" or all American fighters are called "Mountain Lion." There are other scary animals in China. I later told AJ about it and he laughed, saying, "They also need one more foreigner called *Báilóng* ['white dragon']." This was true, too — so many white guys were proud of their nickname, they'd tell me "The Chinese respect me so much, they call me 'the white dragon.'" And I'd respond, "The Chinese respect me so much, they call me by my name."

After wrestling practice, I barely had enough time to shower and run to my class. I didn't worry too much about eating, because I thought the class was only an hour and a half. But it turned out the class was three hours. By the end of it, I was worried I'd need to be carried out. I dragged myself over to an eatery for a chicken leg, two small hamburgers, four lamb shish kebab, a *zhēnzhū năichá* (sweet bubble tea with milk), a huge cup of coffee, and some chocolate chip cookies. I figured that would hold me until dinner, two hours later.

Walking around campus, I saw a lot more students playing pickup sports and engaging in activities like skating than I had when I was teaching at Shanghai University. There were also a lot of girls and guys that were preposterously developed, almost like caricatures of well- conditioned athletes. Up ahead, I saw a sanda fighter with bulging muscles, and then realized she was a girl.

The other thing that really struck me when we lined up for wrestling was how many of the guys at this university were taller than me. The average male height in China is just under 168 cm (5' 6"), or a little shorter than me. And the average male weight is 66.5 kg (146 lbs), 30 percent lighter than me. So, if we were lining up by height anywhere else in China, I'd be toward the taller end of the line. But at SUS, I was somewhere in the middle, slightly closer to the shorter end of the line. If we lined up by weight, at 92 kg (202 lbs), I'd still be one of the heavier guys, between light heavyweight and heavyweight. However, in China and elsewhere in Asia, I found out that when I fought in the heavyweight division, it was filled by monster outliers who were freakishly large.

The average American is larger than the average Chinese person. And although we had such big guys on our team in China, the absolute largest guys were still larger in the US. The heaviest weight class in US high school wrestling is 285 lbs (129 kg). In China, almost no adults weigh that much.

When you think of the number of sports where height is perceived as an advantage, I'd have to believe the average height at SUS was greater than at a non-sports university. In taekwondo, for example, I heard — but wasn't able to verify — that when a call went out for the national taekwondo team, which is composed of 49 members, thousands turned up for the selection process. According to one of my martial arts teachers, an announcement was made over the loudspeaker: "Everyone under 180 cm (5'11"), please go home." That was the first stage, to reduce the pool of athletes to a reasonable number, after which further tests and assessments were held.

Other friends told me that, when scouts came to their village, in addition to giving all sorts of athletic tests to the children, they also weighed them, and measured, not only their height, but also the length of their arms and legs, and the size of their hands and feet. They also looked at the parents, to determine how large they thought the child would grow, before assigning him or her to a sport.

This early selection process is the most likely explanation for the average sports student being much larger than the average person. Additionally, you tend to date and marry the people you know, so athletes often marry other athletes, producing babies who also go on to become exceptional athletes. Chinese basketball star Yao Ming, for example stands 229 cm (7'6"), while his father was 201 cm (6' 7") and his mother was 191 cm (6'3"). Both of them were basketball players. Many SUS students told me their parents were sports champions or famous trainers.

For the majority of the foreign students, the sports university was their only experience in China. They'll probably go home and tell their families, "Everyone in China is really tall, and they have muscular legs that look like highly-polished stone."

In my Coaching Science class, the teacher told us that there was a textbook, but only one copy existed in China. The teacher told us to get organized and have someone make copies. This was an example of institutional copyright infringement which I'd see again and again in both of the Ph.D. programs I attended in China. An American economics professor working in China told me, "I believe the sum total of what some of my Chinese colleges know about economics is the single book which they've been teaching from, since they started, twenty years ago." He said that each year, the books were reviewed and the younger teachers wanted to replace the outdated ones, but the veteran professors refused, because they'd have to learn new things. They also liked the old books, because they had all of their courses, lectures, and assessments already designed, and they needed do nothing apart from show up and read the same lecture they'd been reading for the past twenty years.

A Chinese Ph.D. candidate came up to me during the break. In nervous, stuttering Chinese, he asked, "Could we sometimes hang out when you have free time?" He followed this with, "Because I want to improve my English."

"That sounds fun, and not the least bit creepy." I thought, but then murmured some sort of a noncommittal, "Maybe."

The teacher wrote some characters on the board and asked me to read them. Luckily, I knew they said "sport science." He then asked me, "What is sport science?" I wanted to say it included nutrition and recovery, as well as training, but I didn't know the right words for nutrition and recovery. So I said, "You have to eat good things and sleep well." The whole class laughed. Then my teacher said, "You probably don't know anything about sport science because your graduate degree is in teaching." He then asked a Chinese student who rattled off the five elements of sport science, which the students had been forced to memorize during their masters degree. Of course, that list was the only correct answer to that particular question.

The course made me think a lot about MMA training. MMA is unique when it comes to training. In my mind, sports are divided into three major groups: performance (running and swimming), strength (weightlifting), and skill (shooting and archery). Obviously, many sports, such as tennis or basketball, combine performance and skill. Some sports even combine elements of all of three, most notably rugby or American football. But no sport requires the variety of skills that MMA does. American football players are all specialists, playing offense or defense, or playing a particular position. Rugby players are probably more versatile, but they still only play rugby. The skill set in MMA includes boxing, wrestling, Muay Thai, jiu-jitsu, and on and on. The only sport that might be similar in terms of skill would be a multi-discipline sport, such as decathlon or modern pentathlon, which requires participants to run, swim, shoot, fence, and ride horses. But to be more like MMA, they'd need to carry, not ride, those horses across the finish line.

Skill is a mystery to me. And I think it's somehow less of a quantified science than is either performance or strength.

Obviously, there were martial artists who ran or lifted weights before MMA, but martial arts generally didn't incorporate fitness and strength training as an absolute integral component of the training. As a kid, when we had karate or taekwondo lessons, there was maybe a twenty-minute warmup, some exercises, running in circles, and some pushups and stretches. When I used to box, we did a lot of cardio fitness, but it was all skipping rope and running. We almost never cross-trained or did strength. In fact, I remember reading articles in martial arts magazines in the 1970s and 1980s asking if it was possible to lift weights and still be good at martial arts.

No martial art and almost no sport (apart from wrestling) had all of the crazy, completely exhausting MMA running, jumping, and carrying drills. MMA is possibly the only sport where fighters were expected to lift so much weight, but were still expected to have explosive speed, and to be able to last for 15 minutes.

Wrestling, almost an orphan sport that no one gave respect to or even thought about before MMA, became the training model for MMA. Dan Gable, arguably the greatest American wrestling coach of all time, was famous for inventing, as he put it, "New ways to make my guys tired." His wrestlers trained twice a day on stamina, strength, explosiveness... They ran up and down stadium stairs and climbed ropes up to the ceiling. A lot of MMA training, and the obsession with fitness and strength training, came from wrestling.

My Coaching Science class was the only Ph.D. course I had where I wasn't the only foreigner. Eight of the thirty students were foreign. The teacher handed out articles written in English, which we'd then discuss and write about in Chinese. The articles were easy for me to read, but I was the only English native speaker. The class also had Russian and Vietnamese students who didn't speak any English. Also, most of the Chinese students couldn't really read in English. The teacher asked if the foreign students had any problems to discuss. The oldest Vietnamese student stood up and told the teacher, "Most of us can't read English." I felt bad for them. This program was hard enough, dealing with one language. Arguably, it would be no less random to have had articles written in French or German. The Chinese students all smirked and the teacher said something dismissive like, "Well, you should have thought of that before coming to a Ph.D. program in China."

On those occasions when the teacher asked the students to give their opinions, the foreign students were either too shy or not confident enough in Chinese to speak out. But even the Chinese students would generally sit there in silence, saying nothing. I guess that was why the teachers just talked endlessly.

In Coaching Science, we learned the secrets of China's recent Olympic success. One day, we had a two-hour workshop on choosing and implementing rods and whips. I noticed there was no talk of carrots, just punishments or other punishments. We needed to write a paper, exploring two coaching techniques. I kept joking that I chose threats and intimidation.

At wrestling practice, the coach asked me if I'd compete in the upcoming tournament. Of course I said, "Yes." Hilariously, after checking our weight, he asked me to cut 1 kg (2 lbs), so I could be at the top of the next smaller weight class. Basically, all I had to do was not eat dinner and lunch the day before and skip breakfast the day of weigh-in, and I was golden. I was teasing all of my fighter friends, many of whom had to cut 5 to 7 kg (11 to 15 lbs): "I don't know why you guys complain so much about cutting weight. It's a snap."

One of the exercises the wrestlers did, which I could not, was that they would bridge and then spin on their heads and do walkovers and rotate around in a circle, without their head leaving the mat. I told them that when I was in high school, that was considered breakdancing.

After the exercises, we did freestyle wrestling sparring. It was interesting to do freestyle with those guys because they were all members of the traditional wrestling team, and many were also former Greco-Roman team members. A lot of them had come from sports high schools where they'd specialized in modern freestyle, but they hadn't done it in years, because the university didn't have men's freestyle. As a result, when we did freestyle, they used a unique mix of techniques. It was also cool to see what they'd learned since coming to the university, suddenly using a traditional Chinese trip.

We also did takedown sparring, which is so different to what we do in MMA. In MMA you'd rather not be taken down, but it's not the end of the world if you are, because you just keep fighting on the ground or you go for the reversal. But in takedown sparring or competition, as soon as you hit the mat, you lose. To be good at traditional wrestling, you needed to develop that killer instinct to absolutely not get taken down at any cost.

On most days, we did shuai jiao wrestling, which ends with the takedown. But eventually, I found that on those days when we did freestyle and wrestled for the pin, I was losing some of my edge. Also, I was so used to seeing my teammates doing shuai jiao that I'd forgotten how well a collegiate wrestler can control on the ground and avoid getting dominated. I body slammed one of my partners, took back control, and next thing I knew, he had me tied up in a pretzel, although I outweighed him by about 20 kg (44 lbs).

After practice, I bumped into an international student I was friends with. A Chinese American guy who'd played basketball for NYU, he'd moved from Shanghai when he was about eight and then lived in Brooklyn. His accent was hilarious. In spite of being a graduate of a great school, he spoke like the New York melting pot, a mix of Italian, black, and Puerto Rican. He'd say things like, "He's a freakin' shyster, that mouli don't be representin'. I gonna cut him up so bad, dios mio, but good. Oy Vey! Mensch! What'a you gonna do about it?" He had some problem with his scholarship because he'd entered the PRC on his Chinese passport, wanted the scholarship that some Americans got, while also getting the visa and working rights that Chinese citizens enjoyed. He'd left the program, disappointed. He told me that, immediately after, he'd found a dream job working with the Chinese Basketball Association. He was on campus to offer internships to some foreign students who might be interested.

My roommate, Natsuki, an Olympic hopeful in the 400-meters hurdles who wasn't permitted to join the track team, eventually obtained permission to train full-time with the team. Every time I came limping back from the training hall, often dripping blood, he claimed to have just finished training, but I was a bit suspicious. While he looked sweaty and tired, his face didn't look all busted up. How was that called training? He had no cuts and didn't even have cauliflower ears!

There was a holiday coming up, so the university declared we'd have to do a makeup day. This was pretty common in China. We had a random Friday off, but then had to attend a Friday schedule on a Sunday. On Friday, all training was canceled, because it was a holiday, so I did research in my room while Natsuki watched *Fast and Furious 6*.

My assignment was to prepare a report and a presentation, in Chinese, about sport as a component of national identity. The funny thing about the United States, is that — other than the Olympics — our biggest sports are played in few other countries. The rest of the world is very concerned about who wins the soccer World Cup, but the biggest sporting events in the US are the Super Bowl, the NBA playoffs, and the World Series, which contrary to the name, is really only America vs America (I believe a Canadian team has won once or twice). With Americans only playing against other Americans, you'd assume that there was no nationalism, but actually, there's a great deal of patriotism tied to American sports. Games start with the national anthem and there's always a prominent American flag in the stadium.

For my report, I was going to talk about the 1970s breakfast cereal boxes with Bruce Jenner and Mark Spitz on them, but instead, I decided that American sports nationalism was best defined by three events: Joe Louis vs. Max Schmeling in 1936 (when an African-American boxer defeated Hitler's Aryan champion); "The Miracle on Ice" of 1980, when a US hockey team composed of amateurs and college students beat the Russians, who'd won nearly every Olympic and world title since 1954 (*Sports Illustrated* called it "the Top Sports Moment of the 20th Century"); and finally, the victory in 1985 of Rocky Balboa over Ivan Drago, in *Rocky IV*, proving that capitalism was superior to communism.

I spent the rest of the weekend thinking about Professor Dai's question: What is the meaning of Shaolin Kung Fu? I wondered if the meaning of Shaolin Kung Fu would be revealed to me if I could read Chinese better. Or, being more kung-fuey about it, I wondered if the pursuit of better Chinese reading would already be the answer.

Chapter 6
The Wrestling Tournament

State-sponsored sport serves to train a fit, obedient and disciplined workforce.

— **Fu Yu,**
"Tapping the Potential of Sports:
Incentives in China's Reformation of the Sports Industry,"
Claremont McKenna College Senior Thesis (2017)

The wrestling coach told me that, to get me into the wrestling tournament, he'd had to lie about my age. Apparently, my registration form said I was 22 years old. Which is true: I was 22 years old, once.

For the tournament, I needed to weigh in at at no more than 90 kg (198 lbs). That week's training must have been especially hard, as I'd lost 1 kg (2 lbs) without knowing it. When the coach weighed me, instead of my usual 91.5 kg (202 lbs), I was only 90.5 kg. I skipped breakfast and lunch, and rode a bike for an hour. That got me down to 89.4 kg (197 lbs). I just needed to keep my water down and avoid food until after the official weigh-in the next day. I was able to eat a small dinner of some chicken and a banana, because you lose about half a kilogram overnight. After the weigh-in, I planned to eat two pizzas.

Someone contacted me from the MMA club and asked about the tournament. I told them it was a shuai jiao tournament, but they sent me the official flyer, which said BJJ Open Tournament. Asking around campus, the judo team told me they were going too, and that they'd been working on their submissions. I certainly hoped that meant that there were two different events, with different rules going on, or my teammates, with their grab-by-jackets and no submission training would be at a distinct disadvantage.

The next morning, the whole team boarded a bus and rode to the event hall for the weigh-in. Our wrestling coach wasn't with us, so we had a huddle inside the prep area, where our assistant coach told us that he was in charge. But he was also serving as an official in the event, so the assistant's assistant told us that he'd be looking after us. I raised my hand and joked: "The assistant coach is like our father. I guess that makes you our mother." The whole team laughed.

An official sitting at the table next to us didn't laugh. She asked my teammates: "What did he say? I don't speak English." Obviously, I had been speaking Chinese. Luckily, my teammates laughed again. Then one of them said, "I'll translate for you. He said..." After the joke was retold by a Chinese person, she laughed. Then she said to my teammates, none of whom spoke English, "Wow! It must be so hard for you guys to have to speak English with him all the time."

We lined up by weight and when it came my turn to weigh-in, an official jumped between me and the scales, shouting, "Foreigner tomorrow."

He then told my teammates that all of the foreigners for the BJJ tournament had to weigh in the next day. I protested that I was part of the shuai jiao tournament, and a member of the Shanghai University of Sport team. He just nodded, ignored what I said, and repeated, "Tomorrow."

I pushed past him, and stood on the scale. Then he became emphatic: "No! You, tomorrow."

"No! Me, today!" I protested.

He reached for my arm, to pull me down from the scale, and, as if on cue, the entire team surged forward, separating us and crowding the official who looked shocked. The assistant coach pushed through our wrestlers and explained to the coach that I was part of the team and that the team was scheduled to weigh in now, and that I should be allowed to weigh in with the team.

The official then said, "Oh, I thought he was part of the BJJ tournament." The fact that we were wearing our uniforms, that we all matched and that I was with the team and that I'd told him I was with the team… none of that mattered. He believed that all foreigners were doing BJJ, and thus he felt he should exclude me. If he hadn't let me weigh in, I wouldn't have been permitted to compete. Fortunately, my teammates and the assistant coach had saved me. I felt very moved.

I made weight easily, then got to participate in the opening ceremony. There were foreign and Chinese BJJ teams. There was also a shuai jiao wrestling team from France. There were countless shuai jiao teams from sports high schools. There was a girls' junior high shuai jiao team who didn't compete, but they did a demo, which was the cutest thing ever. Then there was our team. I noticed that the foreign BJJ teams and even the foreign shuai jiao team included both Asians and Westerners, whereas I was the only Westerner on a Chinese team.

My good friend Yang Wenbin — who wanted to be called Tiger, was 185 cm (6'1") tall, and weighed 100 kg (220 lbs) — and I looked around, joking who our opponents might be. Usually when I fight in Asia, my teammates and I know that my opponent will be the biggest, hugest guy in the crowd. On the wrestling team, however, I was only in the top third in terms of size and weight. At this tournament, we didn't see anyone even close to our weight. In fact, other than the French team, there were no adults. Unless they were going to make us wrestle fat high school kids, we assumed we'd probably be wrestling the Europeans, the largest of whom looked like he was only 70 kg (154 lbs). The joke would certainly be on us if the Shanghai team had other wrestlers who weren't there that day, because they were bench-pressing cars.

I met a Canadian wrestler, named Kirk, who was there to compete in BJJ, but he hated BJJ. "I just want to wrestle." He told me. "I don't want to get all tied up like a pretzel." He made a convincing point.

He asked if there was any way he could train with us at the university, and told me he was a nationally ranked wrestler in his country. There are over 260,000 wrestlers in the US, and the US is better known for wrestling than Canada, but a nationally ranked Canadian would certainly beat me up. So I brought up Dave "Dangerous" Beneteau, the first Canadian national wrestler to fight in the UFC. Kirk liked that, and then he mentioned Georges St-Pierre, a Canadian who many consider to be the greatest UFC fighter of all time. Now that we'd found common ground, we could be friends. Kirk and I exchanged contact information and he'd wind up being one of my training partners through the entirety of my studies.

A massively fat guy on our wrestling team weighed at least 120 kg (265 lbs). The coach was always yelling at him, and never let him actually practice with us. He just had to keep running laps while the rest of us trained. Occasionally the coach would say things to him like: "You're moving like you're waiting for something. What are you waiting for, dinner?" I always felt bad for that guy, and reckoned that, if someone encouraged him, maybe he could lose weight and gain self-confidence.

The day before the tournament, I asked him if he was competing. He said, "Yes" in a way that suggested I was a moron. He followed this up with: "Everyone knows the tournament is this weekend." I thought to say, but didn't, "They do, but that doesn't mean you're in it."

He didn't appear at the weigh-in, but I guessed he may have been excused because he was already in the open weight division. He didn't show up at the actual tournament until late in the afternoon. He walked in wearing street clothes, so I asked him: "Why aren't you competing?" He replied, "Because I was out drinking too late last night."

When I hear answers like that, I feel a knife going through my heart. What kind of priorities are those? He went on to tell me he'd been drinking whisky. It was like he was trying to suck me in and get me to say something like, "Yeah, we've all been there." But I just walked away. Later, he tried to talk to me again about what he'd done the previous night. I told him straight up, that if he wanted to learn or train, I'd help him, and be his friend. But if he wanted to make stupid life choices, he could tell someone else about it.

In the tournament, I saw a young kid win his division. He was probably 17 years old and 65 to 70 kg (143 to 154 lbs) of solid muscle. I was particularly impressed by his use of actual Chinese techniques and not freestyle or Greco like my teammates and myself. When I mentioned this to my best friend Zheng Tong, he told me: "We all did that when we weighed the same as him. But when we got up into the 80 kg [176 lbs] plus, we started to use a lot more strength techniques."

I wrestled the best I'd ever wrestled that morning during the warm up. Afterward, I felt great, extremely positive about the tournament, but then we sat there till noon, and my turn to wrestle never came up. The gym was pretty cold and my muscles were stiffening up. Just before lunch, we did a wrestling warm up again and I got slammed on my bad shoulder. It was immensely painful and I'd later find out that the arm was knocked slightly out of socket. After lunch I fell asleep on a bench in the stadium. At some point, my teammates woke me up and said, "You're up." My injured shoulder refused to work, so my teammates had to help me put on my wrestling jacket.

It turned out that although they'd spent tens of thousands of dollars to attend, the French shuai jiao team wasn't permitted to compete in the tournament. For some arbitrary reason, it was restricted to Chinese teams. As a result, there weren't enough adult competitors and not enough heavier weights, so I had to wrestle my teammate who was really good. He took me in the first two throws very quickly and easily. But then I sort of woke up and started fighting like mad. I got at least one takedown and I think two reversals. I lost the match, fairly, but I also lost points at least twice for stalling. There seemed to be a rule that you have to keep your opponent's feet moving by pushing and pulling him, but I was effectively holding him in one spot, controlling him, as I do in MMA. All in all, the match was OK, but not great. During the fight, I could feel my injured leg and my injured shoulder and arm failing me repeatedly.

Winning or wrestling a little better would have been icing on the cake. I was satisfied just to have had one of those crazy, incredible experiences that very few foreigners in China get to have. At the end, there was an Olympic-style medal ceremony. I won the silver medal, because there were only three of us in my division; they put the three names in a hat, and I got an automatic walk (a bye) to the finals. My teammate had to beat a high school kid, in order to advance to the finals, where, he had to wrestle me. It didn't bother me that I didn't exactly win it, I was ecstatic, and looked at it as a reward for all I'd gone through just to get to the tournament.

I bit into my medal, but it turned out it wasn't really silver. A cheap Chinese copy! But I didn't care. I wore it for the next seven days straight.

Afterward, the shifu from the French Shuai Jiao team asked me to go over and talk to the team. His name was Yuan Zumou, and he was a 1963 graduate of what was then Shanghai Institute of Sport, and which was now my university. The funny thing about seeing all of those Caucasian faces in a sea of Chinese is that we thought, and probably all the Chinese thought, that we'd be able to communicate with each other. But my French is quite weak. In the end, I spoke Chinese to Master Yuan Zumou and he translated into French for the others. That had to be one of the strangest meetings I ever had.

After I got back to the university and checked my photos from the tournament, I saw that one of the kids on the medal podium with me was wearing a T-shirt that read, "Check your justice off!" Never has a truer or more confusing slogan been uttered.

That night, when I got back to the dorm, I related to some foreign students about how the foreigners had been barred from competing in the tournament. They all told me horror stories of their own attempts to compete in sports in China. "Sports competitions in China are never fair. And the Chinese team can't lose." said one. "Last year, the foreign girls formed a basketball team, which beat a Chinese girls' team. When the Chinese girls team came back for a rematch, they had a bunch of guys on the team. The foreign girls complained to the referee, that there were boys on the other team. But, he said, 'No, those are girls.'"

The best story of all was about a foreign girl who attended a *tuīshǒu* ("pushing hands," a kind of tai chi wrestling) competition. The organizers matched her with a 120 kg (265 lbs) male opponent.

My arm was completely useless. Natsuki had to help me get my shirt off so I could shower. After a painful, sleepless night, I went to the on-campus clinic. The terms of our student insurance were that we had to first go to the so-called "doctor" on campus, and then he could refer us to a real hospital, where we'd pay a heavily subsidized rate.

Living in a rapidly developing part of China, it was easy to forget how things had been ten years earlier. The university hospital was a trip back in time to the days of real communism and cholera plagues. A concrete block with unpainted walls and bare 20-watt lightbulbs, it was small, dirty, and dimly lit. Even though I was the only patient, I had to wait at three successive windows to explain my ailment, pay my fee, get a receipt for paying my fee, turn in the receipt, and get it stamped. At the final window, the woman took my stamped receipt, handed me an admission ticket and said, "Go upstairs and give this to the doctor."

The fee was only RMB 1 (about 16 US cents), but I still felt it wasn't worth it.

The stairs were dark and uneven, and there was no railing, so you could easily have fallen. On the way up, I passed a nurse carrying a huge load of dirty bedding, scrunched up against her chest and face. Some of the bedding was splattered with blood. It wasn't in a bag, and she wasn't wearing a mask or gloves. I tried my best to get past her and not get infected, but I also had to be careful not to bump her off the stairs.

The walls were old and the paint was peeling. The hallways were dusty, and the floor tiles were crumbling. The old wooden doors were full of cracks and crevices, the kind in which bacteria like to take up residence. One door was slightly ajar. I glanced in and, although the lights were out, I made out the gray silhouette of a man in a white coat. He was sitting alone at a desk. I asked if he was a doctor. He nodded, and motioned for me to enter.

The examination room was dark and the floor was bare concrete. There were several beds, so I imagined either patients or staff slept in there. The sink was filthy and the three towels hanging above looked as though they'd never been washed. The doctor's desk was one of those heavy metal tanks we used in the army. Other than the desk, the only medical equipment in the room was a rack of glass cups used for moxibustion. They were charred black and filthy.

Over the years, there have been a number of TV shows about attractive, young doctors, living movie-star lifestyles and dating hot women. I suspect that none of these shows were based on this guy, who looked like a misshapen gnome who'd crawled out from under something that dripped smelly water. His hands, which were folded on the table, looked like claws, with yellow nails that would infect and slowly poison his prey.

The "doctor" — assuming he was a doctor — examined my shoulder and said that probably nothing was broken. He then informed me that they didn't have an X-ray machine. He wrote a script for two kinds of medicine and sent me back downstairs. The hospital pharmacy was out of one of the medicines, so the pharmacist apologized and asked if I could come back in thirty days. She interpreted my laugher as a "No," and sent me back to the doctor to get a different prescription. When I told him what had happened, he said: "Don't worry. Just use the one medicine they have and that should be fine."

Once again, I had to get a receipt, go to another window, pay the receipt, get it stamped, go to another window... all the while, the clock was edging dangerously close to 11:45 a.m., when I knew they would roll down metal grates and close the windows until about 1:30 p.m. I was thinking how ironic it would be if I had to come back again later, to get my final stamp and have my medicine dispensed. In the end, though, they got everything done by the moment the clock struck 11:45 a.m. I managed to snatch my medicine up, just as the metal grate was coming down.

The one prescription they filled was for medical strips that attach to your skin and smell like ginger. These completely cleared my sinuses, but did nothing to move my shoulder back into its socket.

On the plus side, the entire cost, including medicine, was RMB 3.50 (US$ 0.55).

One of the most obvious things to do after an impact injury is to take aspirin and an anti-inflammatory, but both times I was injured in China, I found out they either didn't sell those medicines, didn't use them, or didn't know about them.

The following morning, I couldn't even lift my arm high enough to brush my teeth, so I had to do it left-handed. I couldn't put on a sweatshirt, so I had to wear a jacket. I always joked that I was glad to no longer be boxing, because I used to get tired of walking around with facial bruises and a cloudy perception of reality. But at least with boxing the injuries were predictable. Your face and brain took the brunt of it. In wrestling, however, you can get twisted into insane shapes, and any portion of your body can get torqued, crushed, broken, sprained, cauliflowered, or just fall off. I decided to stop training for the rest of the week.

I wore my silver wrestling medal to school every day that week. I posted a message on Facebook, for the foreign students to see: "In case you didn't get to see my wrestling silver medal that I wore to all my classes today, you can see it tomorrow when I wear it again."

Back in class, I couldn't take notes, because I couldn't move my right arm, and also because I couldn't write Chinese. But now, I had an excuse. That week we received our first group project assignment and I'd come to understand the rhythm of a Chinese university. You sit in classes, where no one, not even local students, takes notes or cares what's being said. Then, a couple of times per semester, you do a group project. If you're popular, the group pulls you through. A disadvantage for most foreign students, however, is that their groups are often composed of other foreign students. In my case, my work group was Chinese. Once again, being able to speak Chinese and being an athlete was paying off.

High school in China is a high-pressure nightmare, but the university is relatively easy for local students. Many Westerners falsely believe that education is better in Asia, but you can just go online and find a great deal of research that supports my position. People have written doctoral dissertations on the cheating, copying, and lack of original thought that goes on in Asian universities. In US universities, you always have to produce new ideas and new research. In Asia, you just copy. In the US, to pay for your studies, you often have to work part- or full-time, or do military duty to get military funding for college. If you get a sports scholarship, you have to train.

Asian students do nothing but go to classes and cheat. And cheating is considered 100-percent normal. Everyone copies and cheats and copies from online libraries. As a teacher, my colleagues and I used Turnitin, an online plagiarism checking service. Of course, the bulk of students were guilty of copying. At Shanghai University, I got angry about all of the cheating and plagiarism. At SUS, I wasn't sure if the students could do any better. For one thing, most students at a sports university had never passed the *gāokǎo*. Instead, they'd passed a watered-down sports-related exam.

After class, walking slowly so as not to jar my shoulder, I was on a quest for food, particularly meat. I actually considered eating hotdogs from a convenience store. Hotdogs are readily available in China, but not — for some reason — mustard.

Passing on the hotdogs, I headed to the grocery store. Whether it's New York or China, grocery shopping in the middle of a weekday is always a gamble. There are fewer shoppers, but the ones who get ahead of you are in no hurry, because they've nothing else to do.

The grocery store had hawkers who shouted into microphones, over and over, the whole time you were shopping. It was like psychological torture, designed to wear you down. If I wasn't planning to buy a particular product, a hawker would shout through a faulty loudspeaker that crackled and screeched. People out in the street could hear the sales pitch. My eyes zombified and my only thought was: "Must buy other products."

Every grocery store in China seemed to stock exactly one type of cold cut. There were about five brands of this low-quality ham product, each with marginally different packaging, but they all contained an identical product. There were several identical brands of horrible processed yellow cheese, as well as three brands of soft tasteless cheese that I used for a sandwich spread. There were various brands of sliced white bread, all exactly the same, but no brown bread or wholewheat. China had bakeries, but with the exception of a few foreign chains, they all offered the same products, and never came up with new items or rotating specialties. They mainly sold soft semi-sweet breads which often contained marzipan paste and pork floss. They were too sweet for meat or tuna sandwiches and too gross for peanut butter and jelly.

I'd been dying for a huge hunk of plain roasted meat with a bit of salt and pepper, but everything in Shanghai came dripping with sauce, usually a sweet sauce. Finally, I made a ham sandwich with the only ingredients available. The ham was sweet, the bread was sweet, and the mayonnaise was sweet. I felt I should have stuck a candle in it and sang, "Happy Birthday."

The great irony of Chinese food is that, while chicken often tastes like birthday cake, desserts aren't sweet. The pastries never had any kind of icing on them. Cakes were always filled with cream and covered with cream, but almost never icing. During my seven years in China, none of this changed.

I often ate in Muslim goat meat restaurants, because they were a cheap source of protein. I normally ordered a bowl of goat meat with noodles, added eggs, and asked for an additional plate of goat meat.

One of my wrestling teammates stopped by my room to pick up some photos from the tournament. We watched my old MMA highlight reel and the two of us were shocked at how bad my wrestling had been while I was fighting MMA. Thank goodness, I'd improved a lot since coming to the sports university. But obviously I still had a very long way to go.

On Tuesdays, I had eight hours of academic classes and no physical training. It started in the morning with a three-hour class on sports development, taught by my advisor. Unfortunately, in that class I understood literally nothing. Even the Chinese students complained about his Jiangsu accent. Then I had a two-hour HSK 5 class, in which I understood everything. The final class of the day was a three-hour class on sports development. It was taught by a different professor each week, giving us an overview of various disciplines and types of research. My understanding varied dramatically from one week to the next.

One of the more interesting lectures was by a professor who'd done her dissertation on the health benefits of tai chi. After a two-year paid research fellowship in the US and Japan, her conclusion was that the health benefits of tai chi included flexibility, bone density, strength, movement, increased circulation, and balance. I don't doubt that doing tai chi is healthy, but would a list of the health benefits of wrestling, tennis, or ballroom dancing be much different?

Whether the lectures were interesting or not and whether I understood them or not depended on who the instructor was that week. One I understood and really enjoyed was a professor who'd spent a year as a visiting scholar at Indiana State University. Her presentation was about the American sports education system in schools. It was good to hear concepts I was familiar with expressed in Chinese. That helped me learn useful vocabulary. I was even able to comment and add to what she was saying. I wish I'd understood all of my lessons that well.

One interesting point she made was this: All sorts of associations oversee physical education in American schools, but they're all associations, not part of the government. In the PRC, the government does that. Also, in China every sports trainer at a school is a full-time employee. In the US, the gym teacher is normally a full-time teacher, but sports coaches are often employed on a part-time basis.

She also noted that the US has the best and cheapest sports gear (cost relative to quality). This equipment was all made in China, but it wasn't available in China. Apparently, China produces two grades of equipment: terrible but cheap gear for the domestic market, and decent yet inexpensive equipment for export. Every time I went home to the US, professors would ask me to pick up some gear for them. Sure enough, most of it was made in China, but it was much better than anything we could buy locally.

The text for our modern coaching class was in English, although the lectures, discussions, assignments, and assessments were all in Chinese. The teacher assigned about twenty pages of reading homework each week, and at the start of each class, students took turns to go to the front of the room and cover the material. Because the professor had made it clear that he didn't want a discussion or summary, but rather a word-for-word translation of the text, during the three-hour class, we'd get through about a page and a half of text.

My Chinese students and my colleagues at Shanghai University, as well as my professors and my classmates at SUS, were just too tied to the original words, which, when translated, had no meaning. Instead, I wished they'd accept that a translation is about meaning, not words.

An example I always use to illustrate this point for my students is the German expression: "vom Tellerwäscher zum Millionär" which literally means "from dishwasher to millionaire." But, a more correct translation would be "from rags to riches." In this case, the correct translation contains none of the same words as the literal translation.

The coaching science texts contained so much specialized and colloquial language that I just didn't see how my Chinese classmates could understand them. Although they'd all passed an English exam, the level was extremely low; none of them could speak English, let alone understand a technical text. To put their language skills in perspective, none of my classmates at SUS would have qualified to be incoming freshmen in the program I taught at Shanghai University.

The class leader kept track of whose turn it was to translate, and gave us a week to prepare. When it was my turn, I read the text at home, jotted down some notes, and wrote a very short summary of each page. When I got to the front, I did what I normally do when I'm teaching. I put my notes on the podium and I walked around, talking to the audience, teaching. Just after I started talking, the teacher said, "only do the first two pages." I looked, and my notes for those two pages were only about three sentences. So, I went through, reading each paragraph and explaining it in Chinese. Obviously, I have problems translating English to Chinese. Sometimes I had trouble explaining it. Sometimes my vocabulary was inadequate, but I explained my way around it as best I could.

After a bit, the teacher told me to sit down. I thought I'd done OK. It was far from perfect, but honestly, none of the other foreign students could have done as well. And I was funnier than the Chinese students. I had the whole class laughing. Later, the teacher caught me in the hallway and in very slow, tortured English, he said: "You… have… difficulty…. translating into Chinese."

I looked at the teacher, and in English said, "Of course."

His expression definitely conveyed that he didn't feel I'd answered his question. So I repeated, "Of course." And I walked away.

Because Chinese people seldom admit their own failings, they seemed to not get it when I said, "I can't do it" or "Yeah, of course I can't translate high level English into Chinese." But it's like this with everything, even sports training. On the wrestling team they told me to do a cartwheel, then a handstand, then a forward roll, then a forward roll into a split.

"I can't do that last one." I said.

"No, I mean forward roll into a split," the trainer explained.

"Yes, I understand what you want, but I can't do it." He demonstrated, then waited for me to copy him.

"I can't do it," I repeated.

It went on and on with him simply restating and reexplaining. "I mean do a forward roll, but when you land, land in a split." When he finally threw his hands up in the air in resignation, he told the onlookers, "I guess he doesn't understand what I want him to do."

They didn't seem to be able to accept it when I said I couldn't do something. By the same token, I wondered if they couldn't see it when they couldn't do something, like using that English textbook in coaching science class. What could they possibly have gotten out of those texts? Since we were only able to cover about two pages per session, this meant they were investing an entire week of class, plus God-only-knows how many hours of translation, into reading two pages of a text. Americans studying coaching science would, I assume, read a twenty-page text for homework, then discuss it in class, then move on to the next text, covering, discussing and understanding about ten times as much material per course.

Along with a refusal to search for meaning rather than direct translation, another issue is that language affects how we think. There's actually a Chinese term, *chăngshĭ*, which means "factory history." That says a lot about the culture and the economy. Another useful term I found in the dictionary was the Chinese character, "zhu" which means "to save." But the example sentence wasn't relevant to most people I knew, "To layup 50,000 catties of forage grass." This further supported my theory that relying on a dictionary for translation could be useless. If an American read the translation of "zhu" and it said "to save" we might picture a lifeguard rescuing someone. We'd probably not picture laying up 50,000 catties of forage grass. But the latter may have been the intended meaning in the Chinese text.

During my Ph.D. program, I often wondered if psycholinguistics explained some of the behavior that I found unusual. Experts have said that Chinese people are better at math because of the way they say numbers. In Chinese, one to ten are all single-syllable words, which makes them faster to say and makes it easier to remember a series of numbers, such as a telephone number. Next, conceptually, in Chinese, at least on the mainland, 110 is pronounced "one hundred and one ten". This means they are recognizing mathematical place, and filling it with a single digit, single-syllable word. Chinese continues with this conceptual unit system by having a unit for 100 (*yībǎi*), 1,000 (*yīqiān*), and 10,000 (*yīwàn*). And a million is 100 x 10,000 (*yībǎi wàn*).

Another psycholinguistic aspect of Chinese culture is that words cannot be spelled, so they have to be memorized. Imagine memorizing every single word you know and only knowing words you've memorized. This constant memorization means Chinese students are good at memorization, but not good at thinking, creating, or guessing. They also tend to believe there's exactly one way to do or say anything, which comes from the writing system, where there's one correct way to write a character. When they face a problem, they search for some memorized solution which can be applied. If they don't find a match, they're at a loss.

I always joked, thanks to a Chinese education, I can rattle-off all 25 advantages of rote memorization.

When Chinese students learn English, they memorize one translation for each English word and struggle with the concept of a word having very different meanings based on context. An example is the first dictionary definition of the English word "policy," *zhèngcè* (meaning a type of rule).

But when my business students met the word insurance policy, it was hard to convince them that policy meant a contract. Students asked me: "Are you saying that the dictionary is wrong?" I said, "No, the dictionary is right in one context, but in another context, it means a contract." I often believed that overcoming this single obstacle was probably the difference between those who succeeded overseas and those who didn't.

In China, a more intelligent person knows more Chinese characters. In English, we have 26 letters. And Shakespeare was a better writer than me, not because he knew more letters than me, but because he knew better how to combine them.

Relating this back to martial arts. Chinese martial artists memorize patterns. The more patterns they know and the more beautifully they can execute them, the better they are. From a fighting perspective, the idea was that if you were attacked, you'd execute the appropriate pattern. The more patterns you knew, the more situations you could deal with. In Western boxing, by contrast, we only have about six basic punches. Muhammad Ali was The Greatest of All Time not because he knew more punches than others. Rather, it was because he said he was The Greatest of All Time — and also because he could skillfully and creatively combine and recombine those six punches better than anyone else.

Whereas the Western alphabet and Western martial arts lend themselves to students finding their own, unique, and creative voice, China's language and martial arts are about students repeating the words and patterns of the masters. I once asked a class what their opinion of the homework reading was, but they didn't answer. Later, a foreign teacher told me, "That's a trick question. You hadn't told them their opinion yet." But once I told them, they'd all remember it and accurately spit it out during the exam. According to the opinion I gave them, *Curious George Gets a Tattoo* is the greatest book of the 20th century, an intellectual foray into the primitive, darker side of the human soul, just one step removed from the dirty stinking apes."

This dutiful repetition of the master's words and thoughts also explained a lot of the plagiarism I encountered. When I called students out for plagiarism, their defense was often either, "But I thought the writer was an expert," or, "I thought the writer knew more about this topic than me."

I loved wrestling because it has a creativity similar to boxing. No one was expected to memorize the exact pattern to use in every situation that could arise in wrestling. The same was true for sanda. It was a form of fighting based on free flow, self-expression and creativity. And that's one of the reasons why sanda was always the orphan sport within the Wu Shu Institute, and regarded as more of a fight sport than a traditional martial art. Similarly, Chinese wrestling — in my mind at least — lay somewhere between a traditional martial art and a combat sport. The *jībēngōng*, in many ways, made shuai jiao seem like a traditional martial art, while the competition aspect made it more like a fight sport. I often wondered if this second aspect was the reason that shuai jiao had been grouped with modern sports training, rather than in the Wu Shu Institute.

Training in sanda class, we learned two takedowns. One was a kind of suplex, a variation on other suplexes I'd learned. But the second one was a throw for when your opponent has an underhook. This throw fascinated me, because it required zero energy and was identical to a number of shuai jiao throws where you use one hand to brace your opponent's knee, then use a quick jerking motion to make him fall.

One guy in my sanda class outweighed me by a lot, and he was a bit of a bully. I planned to counter-bully him until I found out he was from the ping pong team. My reaction was: "Are you joking me? 120 kg (265 lbs) and on the ping pong team?" Life had already picked on him enough. In the end, I resolved to only bully him if he got in my way, or if I got really bored, or if I was having a bad day.

My shoulder was still painful and didn't work right, so I went back to the on-campus clinic. The doctor ignored the fact that I'd been injured in a wrestling tournament, instead telling me that my problem was caused by using too much AC and drinking cold drinks. I asked if he could give me a referral to the big hospital off campus, and he grudgingly wrote it out for me.

At the big hospital, they made me wait in line, fill in a form, and describe my symptoms to someone who'd never been to medical school. The whole ground floor was a circus, with thousands of people milling about, shouting at the top of their lungs, hawking and spitting, jumping line, fighting, and arguing. Before I'd even finished telling the women behind the counter my symptoms, she wrote something on a piece of paper. Handing it to me, she ordered me to wait in another line, and outline my symptoms to yet another non-medic. This time, I had to shout through bulletproof glass, and God only knows what she was or wasn't able to understand. I paid, got a receipt, and was sent to the department she felt would deal with my problem. When I got there, I saw another line and a cashier, so I just walked out.

A month later, my unlicensed chiropractor in Cambodia (who also worked on animals) told me my shoulder was partially out of socket. He put it back in and it felt much better.

Giving up on the hospital, I went in search of food. At the place where I always bought my fried Chinese sandwiches, when they asked what I wanted on the sandwich, I always said, "meat" to which, they replied, "Chicken leg?" The first time I heard this, I responded, "If that's the only meat you have," and waited — but there was no response or reaction from the cook. Finally, remembering I was in the land of conditioned response, I answered, "Yes." And the cook happily made me a sandwich.

After that, every time I went there, when they asked, "Chicken leg?" I always answered, "Yes." One day, I went there and ordered fried noodles with pork. The woman didn't even acknowledge that I'd asked for pork. Neither did she say that she didn't have pork. She just asked, "Chicken leg?" Going from "meat" to "chicken leg" sort of makes sense. But going from "pork" to "chicken leg" is quite a jump. It's not even the same number of syllables. But, of course, I said, "Yes."

In China, when you buy products, there are no options. Chinese manufacturers and retailers compete on price alone, so there's generally no customization, no service, and no variation, just the lowest-priced, lowest-quality products. Rooms in houses in China often have only one electrical outlet, so everyone has multiplugs extension cords for their various lamps and appliances. My father had been a master electrician, he'd told me to never use a multiplug, because they often caused fires. He always followed this advice with: "If you absolutely have to use on, buy the most expensive one they have."

I went to the grocery store and asked for a four-plug multiplug. They showed me one made of flimsy plastic. It looked like it could burst into flames without even being plugged in, but the price was only RMB 20 (US$ 3.20). When I asked if they had one that cost RMB 60 (US$ 9.50), they showed me a 12-plug device. It was of identical quality, just more dangerous. In spite of my Pop's advice, I bought the cheaper one.

I went to buy boxing gloves at the sports gear store next to the university. They showed me a pair costing RMB 80 (US$ 12.70). Honestly, considering the price, they weren't bad for most students. However, I'm used to having professional equipment, so I asked if they had a RMB 200 (US$ 32) pair. The shopkeeper said she'd be happy to sell me this pair for RMB 200.

On the way to HSK class, I passed my advisor's office, and suddenly remembered that in the first week of school he'd told me he really wanted to help me improve my Chinese, so I should keep a diary and stop in once a week and show it to him. He also told a random student who happened to be in the office that it was her duty to teach me three new words per day. Obviously, I didn't have time for either of those activities, and neither did the other student. In fact, I was pretty certain that if I'd started showing up at my advisor's office, asking him to read my diary, he'd think I was nuts. But when he made those recommendations, my response was: "Yes, thank you for helping me learn Chinese."

That had been over a month ago. The diary had never been mentioned again, although I'd seen my advisor countless times since then. And in spite of seeing that student in class on a regular basis, she'd never taught me three Chinese words. But the important thing is that he made an effort, thereby creating the illusion of helping me.

The HSK teacher drew a map of China, to show us how China looks like a hen, sitting on its eggs. "Here is the hen's back, in Mongolia," she said, tracing on the map, "and here are the eggs, Taiwan and the Diaoyu Islands."

This was pure propaganda. Mongolia hadn't been part of China for over a hundred years. Taiwan considers itself independent. And no one had ever heard of or cared about the Diaoyu Islands — which the Japanese call the Senkaku Islands — until the recent territorial dispute with Japan erupted.

Next, in our dissertation writing class, the teacher asked several of us from different countries to come up to the front and tell the class how we did internet research as undergraduates. When it came my turn, I had to tell him, "When I was an undergraduate, the people who invented the internet hadn't yet been born."

After that, I had research methodology, where the teacher kept using a lot of English words like criteria, methodology, introduction, and references. I didn't think this was for my benefit, as I was the only foreigner in the room. I have to believe it was because they learned their research methodology from the West.

In general, I tuned out a lot in lectures, because it was so much work to understand. When I tuned back in, the lectures were so boring, I was actually grateful I didn't understand everything. Sitting in class, completely zoned out, not listening to a word the teacher was saying, it'd often suddenly occur to me that there was going to be an exam at some point. Then I'd try to listen, but that put me in a lonely category, as even my Chinese classmates weren't paying attention.

A friend told me that the Chinese register for official speech is different to that for conversational speech. In fact, grammar, vocabulary and cadence all change when you make a speech. Interestingly, the Chinese population is conditioned to tune out when they hear someone making a speech. Apparently, rather than communication, speeches are a symbolic occasion of power or showing how important you are.

That night, we had our first sparring session in Zhou Laoshi's sanda class. I was slipping on my groin guard, mouth guard, and hand wraps, when one of the students asked Zhou Laoshi what I was doing. Zhou Laoshi answered, "He's professional." I just didn't understand why students at SUS didn't use mouthguards and groin guards when sparring.

Once they started fighting, few of my classmates showed much stamina. I hadn't trained with the Greco-Roman team, but they looked like supermen. The same was probably true of the professional sanda team. But the guys on my traditional wrestling team wore out easily, and the people in the sanda class were even worse, slowing down to a snail's pace after thirty or forty frantic seconds of sparring.

The other students in Zhou Laoshi's sanda class were a little too easy for me to work with. Zheng Tong was in that class, so together we usually did some wrestling or some boxing plus wrestling, but as a rule, the intensity of the class was quite low because the students just sort of wanted to enjoy themselves. They weren't fighters. It was interesting to listen to them talk about their ping pong and tennis competitions. They were also excused if they were away competing in other sports.

One good point about training at SUS was that, with the exception of the low-level sanda class, I had about 90 training partners aged 18 to 22, and most of them were reasonably fit. They came in all shapes and sizes, so I also had a good number of heavyweights to train with. On other teams, like the one in Beijing, the heavyweights were the older guys who tended to be a bit out of shape. But, at the sports university, some of them were all muscle and downright scary looking.

The other pleasant thing about training at SUS was that my wrestling and sanda classmates were so great to be around. They were young, energetic, happy, and optimistic. I laughed a lot when I trained with them. I think one reason they were all so happy is because they weren't yet middle aged, shattered, or divorced.

In many of my classes, it was time to give presentations. At Shanghai University, when I saw my students fail to give good presentations in English, I attributed it to linguistic issues. But now, watching Chinese students give presentations in their native language, it seemed they were nearly as bad. Whether they were speaking English or Mandarin, they'd always just read in a monotone, rather than talk, often holding the paper right in front of their face. There was no eye contact, no body language, no movement, and no interaction.

I attended a Korean Ph.D. candidate's mock dissertation defense. He was the only other foreigner in my program, and the defense really scared me. After he presented, senior classmates asked him all manner of highly technical questions which neither he, nor I, could understand or answer.

His dissertation compared Bul Moo Do (a Korean Buddhist martial art) to Shaolin Kung Fu, and he was presenting to a room full of people with Ph.D. degrees in wushu or in the process of getting them. Straightaway I realized how hard that was. They were calling him out, left and right. I'd have one huge advantage, however, in that I was writing about wrestling, which hardly anyone knew much about.

Yet there was still the language issue. The poor Korean student may well have known the answers, but neither he nor I could understand the questions the panel were firing at him. He just stood at the podium, squirming. My first mock dissertation defense was still two years off, but I realized I needed to get my Chinese to a much higher level.

I staggered out of the defense, feeling exhausted and a bit dejected. It'd been a long day. Oftentimes, when I made that final trek back to my room, and had to climb five flights of stairs, I was so tired that nothing around me seemed real. It was like watching a faraway TV, through a rice paper screen.

School was really tough, but my options were either: Survive the next three years of school, get my Ph.D., and teach at universities; or quit now and go back to teaching English to children in Taiwan for the next twenty years. When I looked at it that way, I decided I'd do the next three years standing on my head if necessary.

The next day, at wrestling practice, we did 12 rounds of sparring, changing the opponent every round. One of my opponents was our assistant coach, who gave me good advice for competition. He said: "We Chinese people always look at the center, but we don't look at the legs. So, when you see the opponent's leg is over extended, just grab it, without hesitation." I think this stems from the fact that real shuai jiao wrestlers tend to use the jacket to throw the opponent, whereas wrestlers with freestyle experience will go for the legs. This advice was part of the changing face of this art and another consequence of shuai jiao being in this department, rather than in the Wu Shu Institute, where no one would have known another way.

I loved training at that intensity because it was like MMA training, but a lot of the wrestlers got hurt and a couple had to be helped off the mats because this was so unusual for us. One day, we came in and the coach told us to grab weight plates. He then had us do plate exercises for two and a half hours. I'd only seen about three of my teammates regularly in the weight room. Neither they nor I trained there for two and a half hours at a stretch. Again, people got injured and some were out for days. I finally lied about an important meeting with my adviser and snuck out the back.

The next day, during a training break, one wrestler talked to me about the difference in US and Chinese training. He told me that the university Greco-Roman team trains about six to seven hours per day, six days a week. He said that a Korean wrestling team came to train with them and basically beat them in every scrimmage. When the Chinese asked the Koreans about their training schedule, the Koreans said they were training between two and a half and four hours per day.

The Chinese were and are overtraining. And it wasn't just that they were overdoing it on individual training days, but the entire Chinese system was overkill. The sports school system pushed a handful of athletes to train full time for years to qualify for the national team, but they missed out on a proper education. The US system was much more egalitarian with all public schools fielding sports teams. Kids went to school full time, but had serious training five days a week after school, and then competed on an established circuit in their school district, county, conference, region, state, and at the national level.

According to the National Federation of State High School Associations, in the 2006-07 school year, 257,246 boys (and 5,048 girls) from 9,445 schools participated in wrestling, making scholastic wrestling the sixth most popular sport among high school boys. There were more schools doing wrestling in the US than there were wrestlers in China. And keep in mind that the population of China is almost four times that of the US.

China has seven dedicated sports universities and other universities with significant sports departments. In the US, collegiate wrestling is governed by several bodies. The NCAA (National Collegiate Athletic Association) covers all sports in four-year public universities, while the NCWA (National College Wrestling Association) is just for wrestling at the college level, and the NJCAA (National Junior College Athletic Association) runs wrestling at public, two-year colleges and universities. Combined, there are about 8,400 wrestlers, from 223 teams, competing in collegiate wrestling. The US Olympic wrestling team is composed of twenty wrestlers drawn from the more than a quarter of a million wrestlers in the US collegiate and scholastic systems.

Although its population is greater, the PRC has far fewer universities than the US, so a much smaller proportion of China's population has an opportunity to pursue higher education. And when it comes to the Olympics, in spite of having a population of about 1.3 billion, China draws from a pool of tens of thousands of athletes per sport, rather than the hundreds of thousands or even millions per sport in the US.

On a human level, the US also provides a full education to its athletes. When American athletes fail to make the Olympic team, they fall back on their bachelor's degree and go get a job. In China, athletes could be washed out of the system at any point due to injury or lack of performance, and wind up on the street with nothing.

The next morning I had three homework assignments to do. One, for my Chinese writing class, was an easy presentation on Chinese characters found on campus. I chose *shuāi jiāo shì*, "wrestling room." I then had two assignments for my doctoral classes. This was the first time I had to research and write a short paper in Chinese, for a class where most of the students were Chinese. It was scary, and it took a whole day, but I finished one, a short paper on multidisciplinary coaching, looking at factors like psychology, economics, environment, and talent identification in athletic training. I started on it in the morning, and — except for a two-hour break for training — worked straight through until about 8.30 p.m. I wrote it very slowly, one simple Chinese sentence at a time.

After writing that paper, I pretty much collapsed on my bed. I was wondering if needed to start drinking, or maybe sniffing glue. Or drinking glue.

The third assignment, which I put off till the next day, related to my research proposal for my Ph.D. advisor. I still needed to iron out the requirements with my classmates, then I could start. This was another example of the importance of being able to speak Chinese and of getting along with the classmates. Without their help, I'd have been lost.

One of the ironies of this Chinese-taught program was that, although I had to write and present in Chinese, there was no requirement that the sources be in Chinese. In fact, for modern coaching and sports science, it was assumed that the best sources would be in English.

When I wrote papers about Chinese traditional wrestling, however, I had to read research in Chinese, take notes, and write in Chinese. When I encountered a word I didn't know, I had to write it, using a stylus, on the screen of my electronic dictionary, so as to find the meaning and pronunciation. But I found it very difficult to write or even copy a new Chinese character, because not only do you have to get all of the strokes right, but they also have to be in the right order, or the machine would use its predictive capability and guess, wrongly, which word you were writing. At that point, I'd have to wipe the screen and start again. It could sometimes take ten minutes to look up a single character. Reading a single page of text could therefore take hours. To read a few articles and write a one- or two-page paper could take me more than 12 hours.

On the plus side, I didn't have to sweat about paraphrasing, because my written Chinese was so bad there was no way it'd look anything like the original source.

Listening to presentations in one of my Ph.D. lectures, I found out that the Chinese word for cheerleading squad is *lālāduì*, "la, la team." In many parts of Asia, particularly in Korea, they have competitive cheerleading teams, but they don't have cheerleaders who cheer for sports. It's fascinating when an American concept gets adopted in a foreign country, but takes on a different meaning or serves a different function in its new home.

In Chinese, a sexy but perhaps immoral girl is referred to as a *làmèi* "spicy girl." The *là* in spicy sounds like the *lā* in cheerleader, but it's a different character with a different tone. I think they should have used the spicy one; I wonder if there's someone I can talk to about getting that changed.

Speaking of spicy, eating soup dumplings (*xiǎo lóngbāo*) after morning sanda training, I inhaled some red pepper by accident. It was so painful and horrible. My throat felt like I'd smoked 50 cigarettes. After I finished hawking, coughing, vomiting, and spitting, I sat down to finish my dumplings. If the *Kung Fu Panda* movies taught me any life lessons at all, it was that nothing, nothing can keep you from really good dumplings.

In wrestling, we did no-jacket sparring. In the first fight, I lost two throws because I didn't know the rules. Apparently throwing the guy out of the circle was worth points. After that I had one where the guy threw me, so I stopped fighting, but it turned out they were going for a three-second pin. Once I knew that, I was able to fight off my back, catch wrestling style, where you sit in a V-position, not allowing your shoulder blades to touch, and you keep fighting.

One of my teammates pinned me with a Greco-Roman neck crank sort of submission. That was horrible. I got several takedowns from grabbing a leg and I got one double leg from my knees which I'd never got during sparring before.

It was great to take this break from Chinese wrestling, which is stand-up wrestling, meaning you just wrestle for the throw. There's no pin and no ground fighting. Stand-up wrestling is a lot less taxing than MMA or freestyle wrestling. MMA rounds are five minutes. In Western wrestling they're two to three minutes. In Chinese wrestling they're just two. I was happy with either two- or three-minute rounds. Two-minute rounds were nice on a big team, because you could rotate through more opponents and benefit from different people's styles. One of the huge benefits of training at a university is that per session I had anywhere from 18 to 30 partners to choose from, all of whom were fit and had good technique. In an MMA gym, by contrast, you might walk in and find no one your size or at your level to spar with.

In general, I didn't love Chinese shuai jiao wrestling, preferring freestyle and MMA. From a self-defense standpoint, however, if I or my teammates were ever attacked on the street, and the attacker was wearing a wrestling jacket, I was confident we could take him down.

During a break, my wrestling classmate asked me if I knew his friend who was in my sanda class. He described the guy as tall and black. "Black" in China means anyone whose skin is one-eighth of a shade darker than the speaker. In fact, some of these "black" guys aren't even as dark as me.

I wasn't sure who he meant, then he added, "The one you kicked in the groin."

Build a thousand bridges, kick one undergraduate in the groin, and you'll forever be known as a groin-kicker, not a bridge-builder. The worst part of this story was that I still had to ask, "Which guy that I kicked in the groin?"

At sanda ge do class, Jiang Laoshi was a brilliant and likable coach. We were learning ground fighting for the first time, and he had me teach the class how to go from a sanda throw, follow the opponent to the ground, and do an arm bar. China had changed so much since I'd first studied at Shaolin Temple, a decade earlier. Back then, no one knew what MMA was and they believed China had the best martial arts and the best fighters. People like Jiang Laoshi were staying current and knew that for sanda ge do to truly be ge do, the students should learn the latest techniques for ground fighting.

My roommate always used a translator on his tablet to communicate with me. He'd bought a broom and dustpan, telling me: "We can use together." I think he meant "share," but this is what happens when you use a dictionary. Another time, he came in really late and wrote "Sorry, go to KTV and delay return." I'm sure the word he used in Japanese was "late" as in "Sorry, I came home late." Late can mean delayed but not in this instance.

My Chinese dictionary translated a Chinese character as "a cowrie." That wasn't much of a help, because I'm not the kind of person who'd tell someone he had a cowrie when he didn't know what a cowrie is. I looked up cowrie in an English dictionary and it said that cowrie is a small marine mollusk. And that made no sense, given the context of the sentence. But at least I had learned what cowrie was and hoped one day to use that word in a book.

In sanda class, we worked on two takedowns, throwing from the clinch. Both were repeats of throws we'd learned in other sanda classes and were similar to throws in shuai jiao class. It seemed that between all the classes, the moves would repeat and repeat. In fact, later, when I'd added judo and Greco-Roman wrestling to my training and research, I'd often find a slight variation of the same throw existed across judo, sanda, freestyle, shuai jiao, Greco-Roman, and MMA.

In boxing, you do shadow boxing. Really great wrestlers, like Dan Gable, said they spent hours doing shadow wrestling. In sanda, we did *kōngde* drills, literally "empty" or "air" drills, training alone, imagining an opponent, mimicking the movements of the throws, over and over. In a wushu lecture, the teacher said, "The difference between wushu and sanda is the opponent. In wushu you practice alone and compete alone. In sanda, you're training to fight another person."

We did pad work for the first time, about four rounds each, only working on one combination, *dī biān tī* and *gāo biān tī*, low round house and high round house. I partnered with Ma Pei, the big pro, but we had trouble communicating, because of his thick accent. Jiang Hauiying, the smaller pro sanda fighter, usually had to translate Ma Pei's Chinese into my Chinese and vice versa for us to talk. When I held pads for Ma Pei, his kicks were so powerful, I felt like my forearms were going to snap.

I was so much older than the other international students. Really, I could have been their father. I felt a little protective of them. I sometimes gave them important life advice, like my roommate who was training for the Olympics: I told him, "Run very, very fast." I even made him write it down so he wouldn't forget.

There was a big, strong Shanghai kid hanging around the university who'd graduated high school in Texas. He told me he was planning to go back in 2014 for college. Meanwhile, he was doing independent study and weightlifting at SUS. He told me, "I really want to build up my abs and then walk on the beach. That's a good way to get girls." It was so funny. He was me at 19, and I just had to laugh. But then, because young guys don't have any self-confidence, he asked me, "That's how you get girls, isn't it?"

I laughed again and said, "Yes, that's exactly how you get girls, by concentrating on yourself. Girls love guys that are really into themselves."

Some of our lectures were fascinating. Some were boring. And some were downright offensive. In a wushu lecture, the teacher actually said, "Chinese people use Kung Fu. Black people use guns." I didn't see a statement like that going over in an American classroom.

I looked across the room at my Mongolian classmates and wondered if they thought it was strange to sleep in the same place every night. Did they wake up and start packing up their dorm rooms to move to better grazing ground?

Sometimes, when I'd tuned into the class, I'd suddenly realize that the teacher had said my name, but it would take a few seconds for me to find my way back, because I was a million miles away, fighting aliens or sailing the seas. I always felt embarrassed when that happened. One time, the teacher asked me, "Isn't that right, Āndōngní?" I had no idea what had been said, so I gave my opinion. "If the teacher said it, it must be right."

· · ● · ·

The university notified the doctoral candidates that we needed to fill out a doctoral study and research plan. My classmate gave me a copy of hers to use as a model. Under Training Objectives, it said:

(A) Conscientiously study Marxism-Leninism, Mao Zedong Thought, Deng Xiaoping Theory and Three Represents Important Thought, the Four Cardinal Principles; moral character, rigorous style of study, discipline; have a strong sense of professionalism, dedication and serious scientific attitude.

I hadn't done a Ph.D. in sport in the US, but I suspected that research plans there didn't require any analogous statement.

At wrestling practice, the coach told us that fear and fatigue are the two things that could cost us a fight. Fatigue wasn't a factor, because we trained so hard, but as for fear, he said, "There are only three people you need to fear: someone who doesn't care about face, someone who doesn't care about money, or someone who doesn't care about life." If you meet one of those three, you pretty much have to kill them to stop them.

We played rugby as a warm up. It was full tackle, and obviously no helmets or gear. Unlike American football, whichever team got control of the ball could run for touchdowns, or whichever team stole the ball could run for touchdowns. It was really fast paced. The guys were terrible at passing and throwing, but being a wrestling team, the tackles were hilarious. You had to pretty much kill the guy for the ball to be out of play. We had these huge pileups of guys wrestling each other. We played man-on-man defense like in basketball, and it was my job to tackle the best player on the other team as soon as the whistle blew, whether he had the ball or not. I just tackled him and pinned him to keep him from playing. He was like a one-man army, scoring more than the rest of his team combined. We wrestled six rounds after that. Then I had to present my first research paper in a Ph.D. lecture.

I had two research courses. One was also attended by my Chinese classmates, but the other was for foreign students only, so we could learn how to conduct research using Chinese-language materials. In the latter class, we were told to form teams and present a paper on sports diplomacy. It turned out that who you wanted to work with was largely determined by your ability to communicate with them. Apart from a very few Africans, I was probably the only native speaker of English in the Ph.D. program. There were multiple Vietnamese, Russians, and Japanese, so they tended to form teams together. The Koreans almost never came to class; if they had, they'd have worked together.

The teacher assigned me to a group consisting of two students with a reasonable Chinese level and a Vietnamese who could barely communicate. When he discovered I understood some Vietnamese, he stopped trying to speak Chinese and only talked to me in Vietnamese. Word spread, and suddenly all the Vietnamese students were talking to me in Vietnamese —

which was fine, but most of the time, I only understood about a fifth of what they said. Nonetheless, it made them happy and it made me a lot of friends, so it worked out.

In the end, it turned out that the Vietnamese guy was good at formatting Powerpoint presentations, so he helped us with the visuals, whereas the other students and I did most of the research and I did most of the presentation.

After each group presented, we were required to ask questions. We had legitimate questions for most of the groups, but out of the blue, a Korean group, who'd not been to class even once, walked in and demanded to present, so they wouldn't fail the class. The teacher allowed them to do this, but once they'd finished, no one wanted to ask them anything. Finally, a Vietnamese student asked something that had nothing to do with the presentation: "Why does everyone in Korea get plastic surgery?"

When we had presentations in the other class, which included my Chinese classmates, the teacher accused three different Chinese students of plagiarism. When I heard those students' excuses, I cracked up, because it was exactly the same nonsense I'd heard when teaching at Shanghai University. It often went something like this:

Teacher: "Why did you plagiarize?"

Student: "I felt the author was an expert."

Teacher: "Yes, he is. But why did you plagiarize?"

Student: "I felt this subject was important."

Teacher: "Yes, it is. And why did you plagiarize?"

It just went on and on. I had this conversation many times when I was teaching. I looked at how frustrated the teacher became and I just smiled, thinking, "Better you than me."

At Friday night wrestling practice, the wrestling coach was away. He'd left a note saying the team could play soccer and then go home — but that

I should wrestle six rounds with different opponents. So the guys set up rotations, alternately playing soccer and wrestling me. I wound up wrestling 45 minutes with very few breaks, during which my opponent changed three or four times. It was a great night of training. Afterward, everyone was laughing and fighting. This was the exact reason I wanted to be in this program.

The next morning, as I walked onto the campus, it hit me that SUS didn't have a stadium. Surely a stadium should be a standard feature at a sports university. But I guess it wouldn't be if you never invited the public to watch your competitions. Although it was effectively an open campus, and people could usually just walk in and watch training sessions or competitions, the latter weren't advertised, tickets weren't sold, and if people came to watch, there was no place for them to sit.

On one of the green spaces, I saw a bunch of kids practicing baseball, with uniforms and proper gear. The previous day, I'd seen guys playing American football. Since SUS had intramural baseball and football teams, wouldn't it make sense to recruit the American students? Not me — I meant other Americans who could play those sports. We even had one American guy, majoring in movie kung fu, who'd played professional baseball in the US. But foreign students weren't invited to participate in intramural sports, except on a limited number of foreigner-only teams.

During my second or third year, a group of Germans came for one semester and although they formed their own soccer team and easily defeated the best soccer team in the university, none of them were allowed to play on the university team or represent the university in competition. Later, the Chinese students, wanting revenge, challenging the Germans to basketball. One of the Germans told me, "We're all academic students, not athletes. And we have played soccer our whole lives, but just for fun. When it came to basketball, we really had no clue, but we were much taller than everyone else." The Germans eked out a narrow victory. And that was the last time they were asked to play sports with the Chinese students. Most of them went the rest of the semester having very little contact with the local students. This made me ask, once again, what does Germany or China get out of these exchanges where foreign students are completely segregated and have little or no exposure to local language and culture?

The Foreign Students Department wanted foreign students to learn about Chinese culture, so they organized a Chinese New Year celebration — but only for foreign students, and all of the performances were by foreign students. Other than a few administrators, there were no Chinese in attendance. There was also a dragon-boat team composed entirely of foreigners. One of the Americans told me, "They put the team together at a meeting, gave us SUS uniforms, so they could take photos for advertising, then had us practice once. The next day was the competition, and a Shanghai girls' high school team beat us. It was so humiliating."

There were several foreigners who were athletes and who could have been added to a combined Chinese-foreign team. They would have been willing to train and have a shared experience with Chinese students, but this never happened.

Whenever I discussed this phenomenon with other foreign students, I gave the speech from *Rocky IV*. "When I first walked into the wrestling tournament in China, I saw a lot of people hating me. And, I guess, I didn't like them much neither. During this fight, I've seen a lot of changing, in the way yous feel about me, and in the way I feel about you. In here, there were two guys killing each other, but I guess that's better than twenty million. I guess what I'm trying to say, is that if I can change, and you can change, everybody can change!"

There's an old saying that somewhere in the PRC, there's a foreigner buried beneath a headstone which reads: "Here lies the man who tried to change China."

In general, I found that doing scholarly research on martial arts is a bit dubious. There are so few proper historical records that most of what's been written is theory, conjecture, hearsay, or widely-accepted myth. If you try to verify something you've read, you find the same facts repeated across multiple websites and media. This in no way adds to the credibility. It just means they'd all copied from the same source.

Meanwhile, for MMA, which has only existed, arguably, since 1993, there are reems of statistics, countless thousands of hours of video, articles, interviews, academic papers, analysis, and books, with citations and references, supported by evidence. MMA, which came from the West, is proven and effective, while kung fu, which is mystic and mainly supported by belief and rumors, came from the East.

My doctoral dissertation topic was a cross-cultural comparison of Western and Chinese wrestling, and small observations like this one supported my thesis that culture defines wrestling. All cultures have wrestling. Almost all cultures also have martial arts, and all cultures have language. But the styles vary from place to place. Since humans are biologically very similar everywhere, the differences in wrestling, martial arts, and language must be cultural.

At sanda class, Zhou Laoshi would teach us a takedown, then my wrestling teammate, Zheng Tong and I would practice it a bunch of times and it worked every time. Then he'd ask, "OK if I resist now?" The wrestling guys have incredible balance and takedown defense, so the only way to get him down at that point was to go into wrestling mode and change the technique — and change, and change, and adapt. And he'd counter and counter. And eventually I'd get him down, or not. Then I always started laughing thinking, our sanda class really isn't that different from our wrestling practice.

Zheng Tong was a really nice kid and an accomplished wrestler, but a bit of a meathead. To attend a regular university, Chinese kids normally have to pass an incredibly difficult exam, the multi-day *gāokǎo*. Each year, several kids commit suicide. My teammates were largely spared this exam; to enter SUS, they just needed two or more years of sports school, plus a passing grade in the sports examination, which covered English, Math, and Chinese Culture. They gained extra points if they'd won championships. Zheng Tong, for instance, had once been China's Under-18 Greco-Roman champion. This gave him enough points to win a place at SUS.

He'd been telling me for some time that he wanted to fight MMA and had asked me to hook him up with fights. He was a good grappler, but every time the subject of MMA came up, I remind him that the opponents would be kicking and punching him in the face. He always answered defensively, saying he wasn't scared. To that I replied, "I didn't think you're scared, I just wanted to make sure you knew about the hitting and kicking."

He got in street fights all of the time. He probably wasn't afraid, and was likely a very dangerous fighter, against normal people on the street. But facing a pro fighter, who knew how to kick, move, plan, and win, he'd be at a huge disadvantage.

One night in Zhou Laoshi's sanda class, she asked us all to pick a partner and spar. Zheng Tong and I partnered, and I could see from the get-go that he thought it'd be easy to just move in and take me down, because he had superior wrestling skills. But he wound up learning a lesson about what happens in an MMA fight.

When the round first started, I outpunched him every time he tried to throw a punch. When he kicked, I caught his leg, but instead of even trying to take him down, I punched him in the face while still holding his leg. Eventually, he figured out that his best strategy would be to duck, cover up, and rush in. When he did that, I threw punches in combinations, moving backward. Once, he was inside and grabbed me for a takedown, I just defended, escaped, and punched on my way out. A couple of times, when he came in to grapple, I grabbed his head and tricked him into trying to out Thai-clinch me. That's a battle few wrestlers can win, unless they've trained in Thailand or Cambodia. Because the rules seemed to be a bit lax, I went ahead and threw knees to the chest and head, while we were clinching.

During the second round, he just threw his hands up, stepped out of the fight circle and ran over to the teacher. "I don't understand what to do," he blurted out. "Every time I try and do something, he hits me."

"Yeah, I'm definitely going to help him get some pro MMA fights," I thought to myself. "I'm sorry I ever doubted him."

After class, Zheng Tong and I went to eat. Outside the restaurant they had a small bamboo playpen, built for a Chinese toddler, which looked like those bamboo tiger cages the Viet Cong put American POWs in. In the back of the restaurant, I expected to find them playing Russian roulette for money.

Back in my room, I was struggling to deal with research and communication in a country which tried to have its own versions of software and apps which were incompatible with international standards. In general, I found that Chinese students and professors didn't use email. I often had to call them on the phone, to tell them I'd sent an email. Most people used WeChat, but once in a while I met students still using QQ, an old Chinese version of email which they'd used when I first lived in China in 2003. Additionally, they all had pirated software on their computers. For the students, it was because they were too cheap to buy actual Word, Windows, and Microsoft Office. For the professors, it was because government institutions weren't permitted to use Windows and Microsoft. They were meant to use Chinese equivalents which weren't compatible with the West, but obviously everyone in the world needed to conform to standards if they wished to share information, so the professors had pirated software which was somewhat compatible with Word, Office, Windows, Microsoft, and Powerpoint.

My professor once sent me a bundle of dissertations, but they were in some type of Chinese RAR folder, rather than a Zip File. I had to download a special reader just to be able to open it. In China, to access Google or Chrome, you need to use a VPN. But you had to turn the VPN off to access most Chinese sites and to download from those sites. It was often a juggling act, using the VPN and Google to do a search, then shutting off the VPN to click on and open a Chinese site. Navigating Chinese sites was linguistically difficult, and you had to have the VPN on to use Google Translate. This all required a lot of switching. Meanwhile, the internet speed was even worse at SUS than elsewhere in China. Doing a simple download and install was sometimes an overnight task.

Hours later, after I'd downloaded and installed the Chinese RAR, I opened the bundle and discovered that the dissertations were in CAJ format, the Chinese equivalent of PDF. So, I had to turn on my VPN, do a search, find a download, close the VPN, and install the CAJ reader. About the time the sun was coming up, I was ready to begin the tedious task of reading about thirty doctoral dissertations, in Chinese, one painful character at a time. It was time to go to class.

In the modern coaching class, the professor assigned us a reading about scientific coaching and the chemical and metabolic processes that happen inside the muscles. It also covered how to plan training in cycles of 14 weeks, with heavy strength training and high-speed training on the same day and alternating speed and technique training, with 72-hour recovery. Reading this and applying it to MMA, I was thinking how unusual MMA is. It's the only sport where people competing at the professional level are still taking classes and still learning techniques. In other sports, say tennis, a top pro takes classes or coaching to improve and refine his/her technique. The same is true of wrestling or judo. But MMA guys are already fighting pro and maybe haven't earned a blue belt in jiu-jitsu yet or haven't had even a single day of training with a boxing coach. When you're still learning your sport, you can't use these scientific performance training techniques, because there's no place on the training schedule which reads "Learn how to do your sport."

After Friday night training, I read dissertations till the Chinese characters began whirling and dancing around in the air, making strafing runs at my head, like King Kong on top of the Empire State Building, being attacked by puny biplanes. I tried swatting them away, but then decided it was time to sleep.

On Saturday morning, I woke up and did my review of the week, to monitor my progress in both language and training. I'd had fewer temper tantrums that week, which was probably because my Chinese was getting a little better, so I was less frustrated. Also, I knew I was getting fitter, because instead of sweating about five liters per day, now I was only sweating about three liters. It made recovery a lot easier, leaving me with more time and energy to dedicate to learning Chinese. The other indicator that I was getting fitter was that I normally felt like a train wreck by the end of the week, but this week, I just felt like a fender bender. To be fair, it was one of those accidents you had with your dad's car which you felt was a fender bender, but which he thought was a tragedy.

Things were getting better. But there was still a long way to go. And, remembering Professor Dai's ongoing assignment, I had even less idea about the meaning of Shaolin Kung Fu. Did it have something to do with dedicated and disciplined lonely practice with only yourself as an opponent and no potential extrinsic reward?

Chapter 7
The Bruce Lee Papers

All Communist work, including sport, must obey the requirements of revolutionary war.

—Jim Riordan,
"The Role of Sport in Soviet Foreign Policy,"
***International Journal* (Vol. 43, No. 4, Autumn 1988)**

Injured, I cut back on training a bit, so I could recover and work on a report for one of my classes. The subject was really interesting — I had to write a summary of my advisor's dissertation on kung fu movies — so the only aspect of this course that was difficult was the language. Well, that and the training. If the program was in English, and if I didn't wrestle or do sanda, this would be the easiest school in the world.

For several days, I'd had traditional Chinese medicine strips stuck to my shoulder, neck and deltoid areas. My room now smelled so much like a Chinese herbalist's shop, it put me in the mood to buy a mogwai.

That morning, I came to a horrible realization that I was too old now to play myself in a movie. They'll just have to get a younger guy who can take all the hits and knows how to play the role better than me.

When I got to my 8 a.m. class, I found out it'd been canceled. However, two of my classmates were there. They took me to the library so I could help them select English dissertations for their research, and they did the same for me in Chinese. Then, I went to Professor Dai's office to talk about my dissertation and my wrestling and to turn in my homework. He told me that he was happy with my progress and granted me permission to go back the US for Christmas. It had been a very productive day— and I was home by 9:30 a.m!

It turned out that the three-hour classes only met for eight weeks, so most of the Ph.D. classes had ended for the term. Apart from training and Chinese class and one academic class, therefore, my schedule was relatively open. I could just spend the rest of the semester writing research papers, studying Chinese, and training.

My advisor had me working on a research paper about the cultural impact of the three great kung fu movie stars (Bruce Lee, Jackie Chan, and Jet Li) and how they differed. Unrelated to this, I was working on an English-language article about Bruce Lee for a US magazine. I'd pitched that article by explaining that I was reading Chinese-language academic papers and news articles about Bruce Lee, and so could present a fresh image of the greatest name in martial arts, from a Chinese perspective.

While in the library seeking academic works in Chinese about Bruce Lee, I thought that, while I was there, I would also search for some English-language materials. One of the first I came across was an article about Bruce Lee and Leo Fong. Two years earlier, I'd been in California to do a movie with Leo Fong called *The Mute Executioner*. Afterward, a different magazine had had me write an article on Master Fong's relationship with Bruce Lee. It turned out that Leo Fong had a number of letters that Bruce Lee had written him. Collectors had offered him lots of money for them, but rather than cash in, Master Fong had allowed them to be published, to share Bruce Lee's wisdom with the world.

I checked my name in the dissertation archives, to see if they had my Leo Fong article, and it turned out that the library held 43 of my articles. I was amazed and gratified that the English-language writing I'd been doing had found its way into Chinese academic archives.

I was enjoying my two, parallel assignments. However, I worried that the things I'd write about Bruce Lee in English would upset my Ph.D. advisor. When research Bruce Lee in Chinese sources, you get a mix of legend, theory, conjecture, wishful thinking, pure lies, and nationalism.

In reality, Bruce Lee was born in the US and he was a US citizen. His grandmother was German, so he had Caucasian blood. He was raised in British Hong Kong, spent most of his adulthood in the US, and he married an American woman. These were facts I'd never heard anyone mention at the university. He couldn't speak Mandarin and he never visited the Chinese mainland, even though numerous Chinese-language articles describe his so-called exploits in China.

Most of Lee's life took place in English-speaking environments and is recorded through newspapers, movies, interviews, historians, students, friends, and family outside of China. Also, the PRC government vilified him until a few years ago, when they decided to promote him to build China's image. At that point, they decided to produce a fifty-episode biographical TV serial about him, which they claimed to be the longest "documentary" ever made on a single person.

Professor Dai wanted me to use his papers as a base and expand his dissertation on the impact of Lee, Chan, and Li. The problem I had with the assignment was this: Arguably Bruce Lee had more impact on martial arts than any other single person has ever had on any sport, except maybe Arnold Schwarzenegger on bodybuilding; yet neither Chan nor Li can be compared to Lee in terms of importance.

Jet Li was the first five-time national wushu champion and first person from the PRC to make it in Hollywood movies, but in my opinion he's had close to zero impact on martial arts. Jackie Chan, on the other hand, is notable because he was a contemporary of Bruce Lee. He invented his own genre of comedy martial arts movies, and he has achieved a lot in many fields, including charity work and other forms of entertainment. Also, Chan can be credited with keeping martial arts movies alive after the death of Bruce Lee. Chan's importance stems from his connection to Bruce Lee. We can definitely say more about him than about Jet Li, but still Bruce Lee is by far the most important.

Reading Chinese-language articles about Bruce Lee, I noticed they seemed to lack all of the names I'd instantly associate with Lee, like Dan Inosanto, Taky Kimura, Chuck Norris, Wally Jay, and Ed Parker.

As part of my research, I watched most of the fifty-part series, *The Legend of Bruce Lee*. I loved the campy theme song's lyrics: "All the warriors in this world, join the passion of this master's soul. From China's hills and shores, we still listen to Bruce Lee's battle call!"

Episode 1 starts with Bruce Lee in high school in Hong Kong, with no mention of the fact that he was a US citizen of part Caucasian descent. Hong Kong is depicted as full of racial segregation and hatred toward the British, which I'm not certain was really the case. In the Mandarin version, everyone speaks standard Mandarin, yet they call Lee by his English name; as far as I know, he never went by that name when he lived in Hong Kong.

The series shows Bruce Lee's Wing Chun instructor, Ip Man, living in a temple, which makes no sense for a movie set in mid-20th century Hong Kong. He also looked nothing like the real Ip Man, more like a movie kung fu teacher. In one scene, Lee doesn't want to learn the basic kung fu exercises (*jīběngōng*), but a senior student says to him the same thing I heard from the wrestling shifu in Beijing. "Teacher tells you to practice something. You practice something."

The series blows the whole schoolboy boxing thing way out of proportion. While it's well documented that Bruce Lee won a high school boxing competition, it's not documented that he ever trained in boxing. His teenage boxing opponent tells him that when he lived in the Philippines, he was taught by a great boxing coach named Inosanto. In real life, Dan Inosanto was one of Bruce Lee's best friends in the US. He was only four years older than Bruce, and so probably wasn't a famous martial arts teacher when he was just 19. He was never a boxing instructor, and although he's of Filipino descent, he's never lived in the Philippines.

The opponent informs Lee that Inosanto had studied judo and many other martial arts and now lives in the US; he suggests that Lee look for him if he ever goes to the US. So, according to the serial, Lee wanted to learn from the person who taught the loser in a school boxing tournament.

My teacher's published papers, I found, were riddled with myth, legend, and false information. Some of the citations and references were to movies or even works of fiction. My teacher seemed to believe *The Legend of Bruce Lee* was accurate, citing it more than once. In one paper, he wrote: "In the 2000 *Guinness World Records*, Bruce Lee holds five records." I tried to verify this, but couldn't confirm it. It was most likely a fabrication.

According to a different Chinese-language source, Lee said: "Like other types of arts, fundamentally speaking, martial arts is a kind of intellectual self-awareness. In a fight, it is not just the opponent that is knocked down, but also your selfishness, your fears, that can be knocked out. You can destroy all your mental confusion. Because once you understand this truth, you will achieve real freedom." (My translation).

I found it a little weird, reading Chinese texts which contained Bruce Lee quotes in Chinese which he most likely said in English. For the scholarly papers I was writing in Chinese, I could use them as is, and add a citation. For my English-language articles, at first I thought I could translate them into English and use them with a citation. But then I realized that after two rounds of translation, they were probably nothing like the original. Then another possibility sprung to mind: They may have been made up completely. I finally decided I couldn't use any Bruce Lee "facts" or "quotes" from Chinese-language sources in my English-language magazine article. Of course, this had been my hook, differentiating my article from millions of other pieces written about Lee. I'd told the editor that I would write a Bruce Lee article using Chinese sources, and bring something new to Western readers. But it turned out that those sources may well have been new because they were fake.

Watching *The Legend of Bruce Lee* was good for my Mandarin listening skills. But the funny thing was, watching all this Lee stuff made me want to rewatch the US movie *Dragon: The Bruce Lee Story*. That film, plus the documentaries *I Am Bruce Lee* and *How Bruce Lee Changed the World* are probably my favorite Bruce Lee media ever created.

I eventually managed to finish the paper and presentation about the three big movie heroes. I didn't, however, complete the Bruce Lee story for the US, despite the insane number of hours I'd put into it. If I'd written my conscience, and released it in China, I'd basically be criticizing my teacher, challenging many of the "facts" he'd cited. As I explained, I couldn't write an article in English from the Chinese perspective, because it would have been based on lies. I told the magazine's editor I could do an article saying, "this is what Chinese-language sources claim, but it's not true." While he was somewhat interested, he also didn't like the idea of publishing an article which only attacked commonly held myths and beliefs about Bruce Lee.

Since I couldn't complete the article I'd set out to write, I tried to find an original angle no one had previously explored. Bruce Lee is credited with a lot of firsts, but one I think nobody else had written about appeared in his film, *The Game of Death*. In it, he and his team fight their way up a tower, on each level meeting different kinds of fighters, and advancing to the next level only after winning defeating them. This kind of challenge has since become a very common structure for martial-arts videos games.

It wasn't enough to carry a whole article, however. So the great Bruce Lee article I'd spent so much time on never went anywhere.

When I turned in my paper on Lee, Chan, and Li, I learned I was one of only two students to complete the assignment on time. That sort of made up for all of the energy I'd expended on the Bruce Lee magazine article that I never wrote. And, I thought: Maybe someday I'll get to tell the story of the phantom Bruce Lee article in a book.

In my sanda ge do class, my teacher wanted us to practice wrestling, because ge do includes ground fighting and chin na grappling. I was already much larger and more experienced than the other students, because they were all Ph.D. candidates, not professional fighters. When we changed from sanda to wrestling, the skill gap became laughable. We were supposed to try and take the opponent down and pin him for thirty seconds. Instead, I just stood there, let my opponent attack me, and when I got bored, I did a reversal and took him down. From having taught MMA in Malaysia, I'd become skilled at taking an opponent down slowly, without hurting them. Then I just let him stand up again, because pinning him for thirty seconds would have been mean.

For a very long time, I've been so used to living with pain that I forget it's not normal. When I was with the wrestling team, for example, I just accepted that four times out of five, the person hitting the mat would be me. And I got slammed like that, countless times in each sparring session. But for normal people, I guess it can be very demoralizing to get repeatedly thrown on the ground, regardless of how gently it's done.

My opponent for this exercise was a guy who was getting his Ph.D. in sanda. He did his demo interview the same day as mine, back in April, when we all presented and defended our dissertation research plans. On that day, I'd asked him if we could fight each other as our demo, but he pretended not to hear me.

Since that day, we'd been in class together and we got along really well. But he was simply not a fighter. On this wrestling day, he actually got angry. He started complaining to the teacher that he couldn't get me down. Then we moved on to another exercise, and another, and he was still complaining. In the elevator and on the walk out of the building and across campus, he was still complaining. It was almost surreal. He'd suffered an injury, and he was mentally defeated. But I guess normal people never have to deal with that feeling.

I'd been walking around in immense pain for a few weeks, and complaining I couldn't buy aspirin in China to deal with my shoulder injury. A friend suggested that I check Chinese medicinal-tea shops, because many medicinal teas contain aspirin. I then remembered that, the first time I'd lived at Shaolin Temple, my training brother Miao Hai had fallen ill, and a monk who was also a traditional healer had given him a bag full of special tea, which he drank several times per day. On the second day, he dumped out the bag and began picking through its contents, which looked like the sawdust they put in hamster cages. I asked what he was doing, and he said: "I'm picking out the blue ones, they make me sleep too much." Next to the pile of sawdust was a pile of blue pills. I'd uncovered the secret reason why Chinese medicinal teas killed pain and made you sleep: They're laced with over-the-counter drugs.

So I could have bought Chinese medicinal tea, picked through it and extracted the aspirin. "You know what else contains aspirin?" I fumed. "Aspirin contains aspirin. Just sell me some bloody aspirin."

China, you win, yet again!

My American friend AJ gave me some American-made Aleve, an over-the-counter painkiller and anti-inflammatory. Because I never drink, smoke, or take drugs, an aspirin puts me on the moon. I couldn't believe how much better I felt after a single dose of Aleve. I also slept a lot better because I wasn't in such pain. I only grimaced when I raised my arms to put on a shirt. And then I thought: If two Aleve felt that good, imagine fifty. Or heroin!

I'd fought AJ in an MMA smoker in Shanghai back in April. Then we'd fought each other again in a sanda smoker at Shaolin Temple in July. Then I had my first wrestling tournament. So, since coming to China, I'd had three fights, with AJ being my opponent for two of them. I didn't want to have to tell him this, but I thought we needed to start fighting other people.

One of my Chinese teachers told us that Chinese parents care more about education than parents in the US, because there are too many people in China and competition for jobs is brutal, so there's no choice. She said it in that robotic voice which means, "This is a standard answer, which all Chinese people will give you if you ask them the same question." The answer actually defies basic economic theory. A bigger population should also mean greater demand for goods and services. Greater demand means more jobs. Proving this, the unemployment rate in China isn't dramatically higher than it is in the US.

After class, I bumped into Zheng Tong, who was smoking. Even though he never attended classes (except occasionally his sports classes), he frequently visited the campus to see his friends. He'd grown up in a sports school and wrestled his whole life. He knew a lot about Greco-Roman, freestyle, and Chinese wrestling. Yet he'd lost so easily in the wrestling tournament a few weeks earlier that I wondered what the problem was, and why he wasn't the best on the team.

That day he told me his story. When he was 16, he'd been junior national champion in Greco-Roman wrestling. Afterward, he suffered a spinal injury and was bedridden for two years. He'd just started training again when I met him. There was very little chance that he'd ever get back into shape, regain full use of his spine, and win enough competitions to return to national-level competitions. Accordingly, he was relegated to being a wrestling major and a member of our shuai jiao team. But he hated that sport.

He told me this story with some sadness. But then his face brightened, and he said: "But if I hadn't got injured, we'd never have met."

Because I was spending a lot of time reading and writing research papers, I lacked the time, energy, and motivation to actively study Chinese. Nevertheless, I seemed to be getting a lot better and faster at writing papers in Chinese. Originally, Professor Dai had assigned a classmate to rewrite or translate my papers for me. When she told him that I was writing them myself, in Chinese, he was both surprised and happy. He said that my papers were fine for now, but for the actual dissertation, I'd need an editor/proofreader. This says a lot about the difficulty of the Chinese language, that even after three years of reading and writing papers weekly, I wasn't expected to be able to write an academic paper on my own.

In my modern coaching class, there was me, a Russian girl who couldn't really speak Chinese or English, and five Vietnamese who were a bit better at Chinese, but their level was still low. The other students were all Chinese. I often got the impression that the teacher didn't like foreign students. One day, without warning, he put the whole class — including the Chinese students, on the spot — demanding that we stand at the front and translate our homework reading assignment from English to Chinese. If I'd known, I'd have prepared for it. Yet when the teacher discovered that no one was ready, he got angry at the whole class.

The following week, I prepared both a PPT presentation and a written paper to give him, rather than just standing in the front and awkwardly translating like the Chinese students did. In addition to Chinese characters, I always put Chinese and hanyu pinyin on my PPT slides, to be sure I'd know how to read them. When he saw the pinyin, the teacher asked me, "What language is that?"

In the Chinese writing class, in addition to Chinese characters, pinyin and English, I also wrote in Vietnamese, so my classmates could all understand. So, just joking, I said, "It's Vietnamese." The whole class laughed. I gave my presentation and several times along the way, he stopped me and shouted at the Chinese students, saying they didn't prepare as well as me, and also he was shocked that I used outside sources. This seemed to be a real weakness of Chinese students. They didn't know how to find and use sources. When I was done, he was clearly impressed. When I sat down, he said, "But I have one question: Why did you write in Vietnamese?"

All the Vietnamese students started laughing. The Chinese students were just squirming nervously in their chairs. They all knew it was pinyin, not Vietnamese. But now there was an issue of face. I'd accidentally set the teacher up for public humiliation, which wasn't my intention. As I said, I think he already hated us foreign students. Thinking back, I probably should have lied and said, "I wrote Vietnamese to help my classmates understand." No one would have pointed out the lie, and the teacher could have saved face. But idiot that I am, I came clean. "Sorry, teacher. I was joking. I didn't write Vietnamese. I wrote pinyin, so I could read it easily."

The teacher looked really angry. He said, "Next time *shuō qùlái*." Sometimes, when Chinese people say something cryptic, I'm not sure if they're being clever, underhanded, or if I just failed to understand because I'm not a native speaker. But "Next time *shuō qùlái*" could mean, "Next time I ask you a question, answer truthfully." Or it could mean, "Answer loudly and audibly." I wasn't sure if it was advice, or I just confirmed for him how much he hated us.

The next question he asked me was: "Do you know the name of the world 100-meter sprint champion?"

"No, I don't," I told him.

"Oh, well, you don't know a lot about sport. I guess you just know the material on those PPTs that you made."

That class ended this week. I just needed to write my two final papers and turn them in. I wasn't going to miss that professor.

Since I'd begun training again in April, I'd had four pretty serious injuries. I was trying to figure out why I got hurt so much worse in China than I had back in Malaysia, when I was fighting full time. This is what I came up with: I was older; I'd taken a year off; my average training partner in China was much bigger; and the wrestling level here was much higher. Even though I did more MMA sparring in Malaysia, I was getting slammed more in China, and with a larger opponent crashing down on top of me.

Shanghai University of Sport is arguably the second-best training facility in China, but sports-medicine treatments weren't available. I thought that therapies including massage, electric shock, acupuncture, chiropractic, or hot compress would help the injury heal twice as fast. Convinced neither Aleve nor those pleasant-smelling medicine strips would fix my shoulder, I got a referral from our 17th-century on-campus clinic to go to the city hospital.

Signs in China often include terrible English. Instead of translating, they'd do better to see how things are written in English-speaking countries. In the hospital I went to, the Emergency Room was called "First Aid." There are certain things, warning signs like "Slippery When Wet," which you need to just check, rather than translate or look up in a dictionary.

Once in Taiwan, before taking a group of students to a water park, I talked with a Taiwanese teacher who'd been teaching English for years, and who'd made the same trip with students numerous times. I told her in Chinese: "We're taking the kids to the water park next Wednesday." However, I didn't know how to say "water park" in Mandarin, so I asked her. She thought for a minute, then said, *shuǐ gōngyuán* literally means "water" and "park."

I told her I thought it was unusual that the Chinese language would use a direct translation from English. She gave me a fake smile and a meaningless "Yes." For this response, I knew that she didn't know, she hadn't thought about it, and she wasn't going to start. I later verified that *shuǐ gōngyuán* has no meaning in Chinese. She was employed as an English teacher, and she'd taken these kids to the park several times, and yet it'd never occurred to her to know how to say "water park" in English. *Shuǐ gōngyuán* wasn't going to help me at all if I needed to communicate with a Taiwanese person such as a taxi driver.

At the hospital, there were dozens of queues, but the people waiting in them were unable to tell me what they were waiting for. From past experience, I knew there'd be a series of lines to wait in, people to tell my physical problems to, stamps, tickets, payments… more medicine strips. Suddenly, my arm stopped hurting, so I gave up and headed home.

On the street, I bumped into one of my Chinese classmates. He was excited to tell me that a famous Chinese wushu master was coming to teach a class that Sunday, and he invited me to go meet him. He went on to say that the master was adept at Wushu Taolu (performance forms) and staff forms. I thanked him, and said I was flattered he'd invited me, but I really had no interest in Wushu Taolu or weapons. He then emphasized the fact that the guy was really good and repeated the invitation. I thanked him again, and said that I really couldn't spare the time, especially because Wushu Taolu and weapons had nothing to do with my studies.

He invited me four more times and wouldn't allow me to gracefully decline. I had to walk away, but he followed me down the street, saying, "OK, I will call you Sunday."

I suspect our Ph.D. advisor had decided to make this Wushu Taolu session mandatory, and that this student had been tasked with ensuring I'd attend. If he'd told me that I had to go, and I still didn't want to attend, I could have discussed it with our advisor. But the way my classmate had framed it created an illusion that I was free to say "No." So I did. Now he'd probably be in trouble with our advisor if I didn't attend, which I did not.

Another classmate had been helping me format the final version of my Ph.D. dissertation proposal. When I got back to my room, I checked my email and found she'd sent it over. Of course, it looked much nicer than I could ever have made it look. Also, on my advisor's instructions, she'd added some elements which were mandatory, but which I was clueless about. Apparently, as part of my wrestling research, in addition to wrestling at the Naadam Festival in Mongolia, I was planning to "conscientiously study Marxism-Leninism, Mao Zedong Thought, Deng Xiaoping Theory and 'Three Represents' important thought." I wasn't sure if I could do all of that, but I was willing to try.

In one class, we discussed how much money various countries gave their Olympic champions. In China, a gold medal winner got the equivalent of about half a million US dollars. In Vietnam, Ghana, and some less developed countries, a gold medal is worth tens of thousands of US dollars.

When it came my turn, I had to tell them that the US government gives you nothing for winning an Olympic gold. Medal-winning athletes get some money from the US Olympic Committee, but the committee isn't government-funded and athletes get nothing from the government: "In fact, as an athlete in the US, you find your own coach, and pay him or her out of your own pocket. You pay your own training costs and living costs, and buy your own equipment. Then, after the Olympics, you're broke."

A Japanese girl said, "But in America, they can get a lot from endorsements, after the Olympics." I replied that that was true, but only for a few people, and generally only those who succeed in the most popular sports.

"So what about the others?" my classmates asked.

"They wind up with nothing." I said.

I told them that after the 1984 Olympics, I'd read how gymnast Mary Lou Retton had become one of the era's few athletes to become a millionaire, outside of big-money sports like boxing, basketball, football, baseball, and hockey. A litmus test I often use to determine how famous people from unpopular sports are is to ask people to name current professional basketball players. Even people like me, who don't follow sports, can name several. Then I ask them to name a famous decathlete. If they have any answer, it's usually Bruce Jenner, who won the decathlon in the 1976 Olympics. Three other Americans have won the decathlon gold since then, but few people know their names, which means they most likely didn't make a lot of money.

In the 2012 Olympics, the US won 46 gold medals. In its entire history, Vietnam has only won one gold medal. Thailand has won ten, Philippines one, and Malaysia zero. My point is not to disparage these countries but to explain that when you come from almost any country, other than the US, when you win Olympic gold, you're one of very few, and are much more likely to garner fame and fortune. If you're American, by contrast, you become one of many. The US has won over 1,000 gold medals in the Summer Olympics.

One of my foreign classmates mentioned that he had to go pick up his HSK certificate. I told him that when I received mine, I was really disappointed. I expected it to be on heavy bond paper or cardboard, like a diploma. Instead, it was just my scores, printed on regular paper. "I wanted something I could hang on the wall," I told him.

"Yeah, or something you could wear around your neck and show everyone on campus, like a wrestling medal," he replied. He said it in a neutral tone, but it seemed a bit judgmental. The joke was on him anyway. I hadn't worn my wrestling medal since it came off in the shower.

I ran into the only Italian student at SUS. He walked with me back to the dorm, after sanda, speaking Italian. I wanted to go to my room and shower and eat, but he begged me to stay and talk to him. He explained that he had no one at all to talk to in his native tongue. It was really kind of sad. Also, my Italian is far from fluent. I felt bad for anyone who was depending on me for their Italian language communication partner. I hung out with him for about a half hour. Afterward, he made me promise to visit him, so he could speak Italian. I'd been feeling really lonely, with not many English native speakers around, but I really felt bad for the Italian guy. On a side note, the one and only Thai guy was extremely popular and spoke English well, and was pretty much the center of all social activity among the foreign students. He also told me I was the only person that he could speak Thai with. This program was tough, but very interesting.

As for learning Chinese, my current situation was almost a best-case scenario, and yet I wasn't 100-percent immersed. I spent a lot of time online, doing research in English. I also got so burned out from constant Chinese input that, in my free time, I watched American TV online. My classmates and teammates were friendly to each other, but we didn't spend a lot of time together socially for various cultural reasons. All in all, I estimated that I got about 30 hours of Chinese input per week in my classes and training, plus another 10 or 15 while writing my reports at home. Still not a 100-percent immersion environment.

To come up with these numbers, I didn't count a two-hour training session as two hours of exposure to Chinese, because most of that time we were training, not talking. My class hours, by contrast, were two to three hours of full-on Chinese listening. Although I spent closer to 28 hours doing research each week, some of it was in English and some of it I needed to translate, so I didn't count it as 28 hours of input. In language learning like most things, to achieve accurate results, we have to apply a discount.

In several of my linguistics articles, I talked about the "the myth of immersion." Most people overestimate the value of immersion. For one thing, it only helps you if you already have a high enough language level to comprehend the input. The other thing that's overestimated is the volume of language you're exposed to. The claim that, if you live in a country, you're exposed 24/7, is preposterous. You sleep about eight hours per night, so at best your exposure is 16/7. Also, you generally don't expose yourself to constant chatter during your waking hours. In both Shaolin Temple and SUS, I had more hours of exposure to Chinese language than most people could possibly organize for themselves living under other circumstances, and I still estimated it to be only about 40 hours per week, or roughly 6/7.

After a week of layoff for my shoulder injury, I started back to very light training. I rode the exercise bicycle for an hour, then stretched out. Afterward, I felt much better and did the same for each of the next few days, slowly adding abs and weights to the routine. A week later, I returned to fight training.

The first day back was a two-and-a-half-hour sanda class. It was very challenging, but I got through it OK in spite of the injury. My neck and shoulder were still stiff and painful and I was very concerned about getting body slammed there. On a brighter note, my wrestling skills were starting to transfer over to both sanda takedowns and sanda takedown defense. But nothing, no force on Earth, not even compound interest, could make me kick well.

Back when I selected my sanda courses, I chose the beginner class because my friend AJ — a much better kickboxer than me — was in the pro class, and he told me that everyone there could kill me. Eventually, Jiang Laoshi, my favorite coach, invited me to his high-level class and it was fine. The fighters were better and they pushed me, but no one intentionally bullied me.

By this time, the beginner class with Zhou Laoshi was starting to become too easy for me. I lacked good sparring partners. Zheng Tong was the only one who had the strength and wrestling skills to make sparring interesting, but he rarely came to class and never did anything the teacher said. Nor did he use sanda techniques, so sparring with him didn't really help me learn sanda. The good side of the class was that we learned the throws step by step. But now that I was a few months into both wresting and sanda, and now that I'd adjusted to the high-level sanda class, I was thinking I might drop Zhou Laoshi's course.

When I came back to class after my injury, I actually had the feeling I'd been voted off the island. Zheng Tong was missing and no one else would partner with me. Zhou Laoshi said to me, "Maybe you'd be better off just hitting the bag for an hour and a half, because this class is too easy for you." I figured that could be Chinese for, "Don't come back here anymore."

The next morning, I turned in two important research papers, then attended wrestling practice. I needed to be very careful not to reinjure my shoulder, so we went a little slower than usual. However, I wrestled well, and I think having a break probably helped. I was able to see the angles and get better takedowns. Afterward, we took some photos for my magazine article about Chinese wrestling.

The coach told us that we didn't have training that Friday night. Instead, I went to a sanda class taught by Jiang Laoshi. Ma Pei, the 78 kg (172 lbs) pro who went to all of Jiang Laoshi's classes, was there, so we sparred together. Jiang Laoshi had us do several rounds of boxing sparring, followed by boxing plus takedowns.

A foreign friend at the university who'd fought in China joked: "At the weigh-in, all of the guys, no matter their weight, had the same build. The only difference was the heavyweights had bigger legs." It was true. When I saw sanda guys walking around campus, their thighs seemed to stick out on both sides. And this was how Ma Pei was built: His upper body was toned but much weaker than mine, yet his kicks were devastating. Also, he trained three times every day, and the session he shared with me was always the final workout of the day, when he was tired and just didn't care one way or the other. I couldn't imagine how much better he'd fight in the morning, or if he gave a darn. I was sure he'd have beaten me in a real sanda fight, because of the kicks, but my wrestling was really paying off.

I also boxed with Jiang Huaiying, the 55 kg (121 lbs) pro. He was able to out-point me in boxing much of the time because he was so fast. But I was being very careful to not use force and to not hold and hit, which I suspected was illegal in sanda and which would have been a jerk move against a smaller fighter.

On Saturdays, I ran open wrestling and MMA class at the university. When Kirk — the nationally ranked Greco-Roman wrestler from Canada who I'd met at the tournament — came, I let him run the class. I really enjoy exploring and comparing different styles. We'd take a simple technique, like a front headlock takedown, then discuss how it's done in Chinese wrestling, where you can't touch your knee on the ground, in Greco-Roman, where the guys are strong as Superman, but you're prohibited from using your legs, and in freestyle or MMA where all you want is to get the opponent down at any cost and dominate him.

Walking back to the dorm, I said to a Russian who trained with us that Russia and China had decades of communism, but since 1989, I guess Russians no longer believed government propaganda. "What propaganda?" he asked. Then it hit me. Maybe it was me who'd fallen for government propaganda.

My roommate was Skyping with his family back in Japan. I couldn't understand a single word of Japanese, but I'd seen enough giant monster movies to know he was exaggerating. But I shouldn't complain. Japanese are good friends to confide in. Culturally, they'd never breech your confidence by telling anyone your secret. And if they did, no one would understand what they were saying.

At Monday night's sanda class, we finally did full sparring, kicking, punching, and takedowns — but we still went easy, and the other guys wore chest protectors and headgear. I sparred four rounds with a huge guy. He was much taller than me; he had less skill, but weighed at least as much as me. Even with him I had trouble getting past the side kick. I could get in whenever I wanted to, but I had to eat a side kick. Side kicks differ to roundhouse kicks in that, if you take one in the gut while charging in, the fight might be over.

The most powerful kick in sanda is the side kick. The most powerful kick in Muay Thai is the roundhouse. In many ways, the side kick is better for keeping someone off of you. As a Westerner in China, I tried to use my boxing and wrestling, but that meant getting past that side kick, which sometimes meant walking right into an oncoming locomotive.

Next, I did four rounds with Ma Pei. He wasn't trying to kill me, so that helped. But my boxing and wrestling were definitely working out. On the kicks, he seemed not to be prepared for the constant Muay Thai low kick, combined with boxing. But I was sure he could have just flattened me with a side kick any time he wanted.

Coming out of sanda practice, I bumped into one of the girls from the wrestling team. She asked me, "Did you just finish studying?" Anywhere else in the world, I'd have said, "No, I just finished training." But relative to this university, I answered, "Yes, I just finished studying." I needed to put some ice on my ankle, so I said, "Now, I have to go home and do my homework."

My American friend, Debranna, who was in the third year of the MA program, gave me a lot of good advice. She also recommended one of her classmates, Zhang Chengfeng, to help me edit my Chinese term papers.

Zhang Chengfeng had been an athlete (in badminton or tennis, I think) but had chosen to pursue the academic track. He was much better educated than my teammates, but also far busier. Every time I saw him, he was running across campus at lightspeed, dropping everything whenever his advisor called.

The work he did for me was great, and I needed an ongoing relationship like this, so I wanted to pay him. But no matter how much I tried, he just wouldn't accept any money. The following evening, I invited him and Debranna out to dinner.

We walked into the restaurant and surprised the staff, who were play fighting in the back. An American friend of mine once observed that whenever you walk into a restaurant in China, the staff are often engaged in horseplay. The other amazing thing is that they talk to each other constantly. Usually, they're kids from poorer parts of China. They live, sleep, eat, and work in the restaurant, with the same small group of people every single day, all day, without a moment of privacy. I always wondered what they had to talk about.

Every time I sit down to eat with chopsticks, I think of a Jerry Seinfeld routine: "I don't know how the Chinese missed the spoon and decided to eat with chopsticks. Thousands of years ago, a Chinese farmer woke up, ate his breakfast noodles with sticks, then went out to the field and worked all day with a shovel."

At wrestling practice the next day, the team did a lot of acrobatics, which I hated even when I wasn't injured. Because of my shoulder injury, I couldn't do any acrobatics at all, so the coach had a few of the guys just work with me on techniques. It was extremely useful training because without the competition of sparring, my ego remained in check, and we just concentrated on proper technique.

Because of my Ph.D. research, I was fascinated by how people adept at one fighting code transitioned into other codes, to see how their skills carried over. For example, the judo team trained at the same time as the wrestling team. Watching the judo team sparring and ground fighting, I wanted to jump in with them and see where my wrestling carried over and where they'd do things I'd never think of.

My teammates used a lot of body locks and lifts, which were more common in Greco-Roman wrestling than in shuai jiao, although they weren't illegal. To get a body lock, however, you had to let go of the jacket. So, most shuai jiao purists tended not to use the body locks. Many older shifus saw modern wrestlers and MMA fighters as using strength instead of skill. They preferred the Chinese tripping techniques to lifts, which they felt were the straightforward application of brute force.

In my opinion, we'll see more and more of these lifting techniques, body locking, and leg grabbing as we move forward, because most of the kids at the sports schools in China are learning modern wrestling full time and Chinese wrestling only part time.

In freestyle wrestling or MMA, it's not only legal, but often beneficial to go down with the opponent when you throw him. The goal would be to land in an advantageous position and go for a pin in wrestling or ground and pound for submissions in MMA. In shuai jiao, however, if you fall with your opponent, you lose points. In freestyle or MMA, you can even hit the ground first, but take the opponent over, land on top and have the advantage. In shuai jiao, by contrast, the competitor who hits the ground first loses.

In freestyle, judo, Greco-Roman, MMA, and Chinese wrestling the seoi nage, shoulder throw was possible, but much more common in Chinese wrestling. In Greco and freestyle, the opponent's arm might be too slippery to grip and throw, but in shuai jiao, you could just grip his jacket, similar to how you would in judo. In MMA, you also had the slipperiness issue, but an additional danger was that, by turning your back to your opponent, you risked getting choked.

My teammates and I were discussing these differences when one of my friends, Wang Yechao, said he'd like to try some MMA training. The following night, I took him with me to the MMA gym downtown.

At the MMA gym that night, I taught wrestling while one of the young pro fighters taught BJJ. Afterward, I got to spar three times: with my teammate, with a sambo guy, and then with a huge, scary Frenchman with a decent skill set. I'd forgotten how much I loved MMA sparring.

In the one round I did with him, it didn't seem that any of Wang Yechao's wrestling skills carried over. When he shot or went for takedowns, I was able to defend, or move, or strike, and he didn't seem to like getting hit. We went to the ground a couple of times, but he didn't know what to do.

When you box a wrestler, you want to stay at the maximum length of your jab and strike. If you are a good kicker, use your kicks, move, and avoid being taken down. When he went for takedowns, I was able to resist because I trained on the same team and practiced avoiding takedowns for several hours each week. So, even though his wrestling ability was much better than mine, I was able to to avoid the takedown. The answer to overcoming wrestling or BJJ seems to be that you have to train seriously in wrestling and BJJ — then use wrestling in reverse, to avoid being taken down. When I finally took Wang Yechao down it was through a reversal. I never actively looked for the takedown, I just capitalized in his mistake. On the ground, I was careful to make him land on his belly. Wrestlers can't fight off their bellies.

I'd figured that a Greco-Roman wrestler would be the scariest guy in an MMA context. But it's also likely that Wang Yechao was overwhelmed by the entire experience of walking into a professional MMA gym where there were a lot of foreigners, and training in a foreign martial art. Also, I was so used to grappling with boxing gloves on that I forgot that other people find it unusual. Possibly, after a week of training, he'd be fighting twice as well. But even this lesson had been a good one for both of us.

We took the gloves off and did some pummeling. Wang Yechao taught me an easy trick, to move from over-and-under, to back control. It was so simple, I couldn't believe no one had ever shown me this before. By pulling down on the opponent's head, when you duck under his arm, you avoid getting choked. It was great! So often it's like this — you have a two-hour session on this or that, but the thing you learn and remember is something your friend shows you during a water break, or in the last two minutes before the session ends.

On the subway ride back to the university, Wang Yechao and I were talking about the sparring I did at the MMA school. He wanted to know why I'd boxed so much with him, and I told him it was because I was trying to avoid having such a good Greco-Roman wrestler grab my upper body. He asked me why I fought the sambo guy the way I did, so I explained that I wasn't afraid of him taking me down or outboxing me, but I didn't want to fight him on the ground. Therefore I boxed him and did upper-body wrestling with him till he got tired. In the clinch, I put my ear close to his mouth and listened to his breathing, to see how tired he was. When he was ready, I took him down, careful to land on his back and not in his guard or even inside of his arms.

Finally, he asked about the big French guy. I said the Frenchman had posed a lot of problems. He was too heavy for me to take down, so I tried to outbox him, but he was a better boxer and stronger than me. Next time, I'd try kicking. After I told him all of this, Wang Yechao said, "You're very intelligent." His compliment said a lot about his training and his experience. Although he'd been raised in a wrestling academy and had been fighting his whole life, no one had ever talked to him like that. Chinese coaches don't seem to have these kinds of discussions, about strategy and planning, about assessing your opponent, and adjusting your strategy based on the type of opponent or how he fights.

The next day, I received a call at 1:15 p.m. telling me I was late for a Ph.D. meeting about which I knew nothing. I had to run to the university and watch three doctoral candidates defend their dissertations. This lasted until 5:40 p.m. I realized that getting through this program was as much cultural as linguistic, knowing how to deal with the expectations of Chinese academia. Once again, the Korean Ph.D. candidate couldn't answer any questions during the defense, because he didn't understand. It was awful to watch, and it filled me with dread for my defense, two years down the road.

I was supposed to go to sanda class at 6:30 p.m., and I'd even lined up a videographer to film an episode of *Martial Arts Odyssey*. But I was so tired and hadn't even had lunch yet, so I blew off both training and filming, and went for dinner with an American friend, then spoke English non-stop till late in the evening.

Being a Ph.D. was like being a hospital doctor. I was always on call. I never knew when the university was going to call and tell me I was late for a meeting or some kind of mandatory function. Because they refused to explain things, when I got that call, I didn't know what was expected of me. I didn't know if they were calling me to listen to a presentation, give a presentation, perform martial arts, to ritually murder me, or to make me do math for fabulous prizes. When I left the house each morning, I carried a huge bag of stuff, to be prepared for anything. I packed a shirt and tie, my boxing gloves, food, water, wrestling shoes, desalination tablets, a toothbrush, a notebook, a sextant, and a cylinder that would send a distress signal if I fell in salt water.

I wished my roommate would find a girlfriend, so he wouldn't be in the room so much. I didn't have so many classes now, and when I wasn't training, I was in the room writing reports. It seemed a lot smaller when we were both there.

Lying in bed, slowly sinking into sleep, I wondered, was conscientious study of Marxism-Leninism, Mao Zedong Thought, Deng Xiaoping Theory and the Three Represents important for grasping an understanding of Shaolin Kung Fu?

Shanghai University Students in mandatory military training

Shanghai University of Sport admin building

Foreign student housing

Shanghai University of Sport shuaijiao team

The old weight lifting gym

My shuaijiao teammates were all Greco-Roman wrestlers

Shuaijiao team training

Shuaijiao training

There was girl's shuaijiao and freestyle, but no men's freestyle at the university

Minutes outside of the richest city in China

Amazing how much of China still looks the same as 30 years ago

Greco-Roman wrestling training

Greco-Roman wrestling training

Some of my teammates really tried to transition from Greco-Roman wrestling to shuaijiao

Taking the ankle

Giving a Chinese-language presentation about wushu culture

San da training, kick catching

I liked finding ways to incorporate catch wrestling in my san da training.

The same throw exists in judo, shuaijiao, freestyle, and MMA

Sanda competition

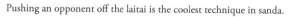

Pushing an opponent off the laitai is the coolest technique in sanda.

Sanda training

Chapter 8
Watching a Defense

*The politicization of sport, during the Cultural Revolution (1966-1976)
led to disastrous results for the development of China's athletic programs, with
party slogans and instructions from leaders as the only available views on
sports.*

**—Fan Hong and Lu Zhouxiang,
"Sport in the Great Proletarian Cultural Revolution (1966–1976)"
(in *The Politicization of Sport in Modern China*)**

My roommate, Natsuki, stopped going to Chinese writing class because he said it was too easy for him. Being Japanese, he already knew how to read and write a number of traditional Chinese characters, but he didn't know their Mandarin pronunciations or the exact Chinese meaning, which sometimes differed from their meaning in Japanese. He generally couldn't read an article, just individual characters and simple sentences. I felt that unless he continued to study, he was never going to learn Chinese. Also, he needed more listening and speaking practice, because it was still painful to communicate with him in Mandarin.

We had to attend the Korean student's latest attempt at passing his Ph.D. dissertation defense. It was obvious to me that much of his difficulty was linguistic and that his Chinese wasn't going to dramatically improve between attempts. So here I was, again watching him fail to understand or answer professors' questions. I understood some things he didn't, but I didn't know if I understood enough yet to get through a Ph.D. defense. This prompted me to memorize the following: "You make a very interesting point. I see you've put a lot of thought into this. This raises other interesting questions, which I'm better prepared to answer. Like this one...."

At the break, someone asked me if I could understand everything said in the dissertation defense. I was often asked this, and I never knew how to answer. The fact was, I intentionally tuned out most of the time. Once, when I tuned back in, I looked around the room at all of the professors, and wondered, "Who started this rumor that Chinese people look young?" It seemed to me that they looked ten years younger than their true age until 27 or so, and then they looked old. Most of the professors my age, except Jiang Laoshi, looked worn out and used up.

In the West, age seems to be less of a factor in attaining expertise. The US has the largest population of university students aged about 40 in the world. Americans tend to believe that, with hard work, you can catch up and overtake younger people in many disciplines, including sports.

In terms of sports, American fighters are athletes, using modern training techniques. In the US, there's an intensity of training which would allow you to step in off the street, begin training, and after four months or a year or two years, fight in a competition. The best guy in the gym could be a 17-year-old or a 25-year-old who's been training intensely for five years. He may be much better than a 30-year-old who's been training three times a week for 20 years. In China, using traditional training, it seems that time, measured in years, determines proficiency. On the traditional wrestling team, the best guys are the ones in their late twenties who began as children, and have trained the most years. They reach a peak at some point, where they have the greatest number of years of training, but their bodies begin to deteriorate. Then they retire from competition. The idea of walking in at age 25 or 35 or 45, with no experience, training harder, and catching up, simply didn't exist. Many coaches I've met, in various Asian countries, had stories about teaching Western students who came to Thailand, China, or Cambodia — often with no background in the sport at all — lived in the gym, trained six hours per day every day, and became one of the best in a year or two.

This isn't to say that youth doesn't have its advantages. One of my young fighter friends told me that he'd just had a baby girl. He was so lucky. He'll be younger than me when she graduates from college. If I had a child now, I'd be lucky to still be alive when she learned to walk.

And all of this was more interesting for me to think about than listening to the dissertation criticism and defense going on in front of me.

During their defense, each candidate is meant to express thanks to their teachers and classmates for getting them through their studies. The date happened to be Thanksgiving Day, and one of the candidates actually said, "Today is the day that Western people celebrate Thanksgiving." While I was flattered that they knew about Thanksgiving, it was one more example of how little they really knew about the outside world. Obviously, Thanksgiving isn't a Western holiday. It's an American holiday. To be more accurate, Canada, Germany and other countries also have some sort of a Thanksgiving on their calendar, but it's not a huge national holiday like American Thanksgiving. And in other countries the holiday is celebrated in August or September, depending on when their growing season ends.

As I sat through four and a half hours of boring Chinese presentations, I thought to myself: "I wish more people would fill entire PPT slides with text, then read in a monotone voice, droning on and on, and never making eye-contact."

At the end of the dissertation, after thanking the audience, the candidate is expected to ask for a critique. But the Chinese term they use is *pīpíng*, which literally means "criticism" or "to find fault with something."

This sounded like the communist struggle sessions where people gathered and publicly criticized a class enemy, a revisionist, or a person with capitalist leanings.

In Chinese meetings, whenever they open the floor to questions, before asking a question each person usually makes an incredibly long and boring speech, confirming the opinion of the most senior person in the room. As a foreigner, I struggled to keep up, or I'd miss the question. I therefore tuned in intensely. But I could only do that for so long before my brain drifted away to a more pleasant and interesting destination. The next thing I knew, I was rescuing the Princess of Alderaan, the person had stopped talking, and I didn't know what the question was.

My professor actually started smoking in the auditorium, but at least he waited until the dissertation defense had ended. When there was a break, my classmates and I went out to the hallway to avoid the cigarette smoke. Duan Limae, a student who often helped me, told me that Jiang Laoshi, my favorite sanda teacher, should have been my advisor, because he knew more about fighting and wrestling. Even though I was inclined to agree with her, it was tantamount to blasphemy to say something like that. And, of course, attempting to switch advisors would have been suicide. Finally, from a strategic standpoint, it was probably more valuable having the department head as my advisor, making it more likely I'd graduate.

After the defense, I went to sanda class, where we did my favorite training: no stretching, no warm up, no exercises, just 25 minutes of sparring against a 92 kg (203 lbs) pro. My wrestling teammate Wang Yechao also came to spar with us.

Normally, when you spar or fight MMA against a grappler, it's dangerous, because they're adept at catching kicks and taking you down. Sanda fighters are extremely good at kick catching, because it's a huge part of their training. But when sparring MMA with pure wrestlers, like my teammates, it wasn't that dangerous to kick because they just weren't used to seeing kicks coming at them and they didn't know how to react. But I still believed that if they went berserker and simply charged in, they could take down nearly anyone. I think one of the reasons American wrestlers have done so well in UFC is that Americans are simply more aggressive and competitive. Also, a large percentage of American wrestlers are the type of people who really like to mix it up, scrap, and fight. No Chinese wrestlers I've met seem to have that personality.

When a fighter moves from one code of fighting to another, certain instincts from his previous sport might be a disadvantage. Here's a clear example: In Western wrestling, the goal is to pin your opponent's back on the mat and win; a last-ditch defense in that sport is to simply roll over on your stomach, as it's very difficult to forcibly move someone on their stomach onto their back and pin them. But in MMA, if wrestler rolls on his belly, he gives up his neck, allowing the opponent to choke him easily. Alternatively, the MMA fighter will back mount him and strike him; the wrestler on his belly will be defenseless.

Most MMA fighters learn to sprawl, to defend the single leg takedown. A mistake I often see non-wrestlers make, however, is that after the sprawl, the fighter on top falsely believes he's safe. He's then slow to move to the next position. A trained wrestler will simply drive through, even after the sprawl, and complete the takedown.

After training, Wang Yechao told me that Chinese students lived four to a room on campus. Because they were only permitted to use the showers between 6 p.m. and 9 p.m., on days when we had morning training, he had to go to class without showering first. He also told me that the night we went to the MMA gym, he got back too late to have a shower.

Shanghai University students had told me similar stories, complaining about filth and the lack of sanitation, heating, and AC in their dorms. Also, the electricity was cut at 11 p.m., so they couldn't study or charge their devices. Back in the days of real communism, when all students were on government scholarships, I guess people had to accept what they got and feel grateful for it. But nowadays tuition is expensive by Chinese standards — and yet students don't get basic comforts or a hygienic environment.

The next morning, I passed the room of a Vietnamese friend who always left his door open. He'd been at SUS for four years and no longer needed to attend classes. He was devoting all his time to his dissertation, which could be a bit lonely, so he moved a coffee table and four chairs into his room, left the door open, and made really good Vietnamese coffee all day for anyone who stopped by. He invited me in for coffee and a chat. It was a civilized way to spend the morning.

There were fifty Vietnamese students in SUS. They cooked together, hung out together, and had parties and celebrations together. When I told Debranna, the American girl, that I thought it unlikely that, in a group of fifty, everyone liked each other, she replied: "They don't, but the social pressure to stay with their compatriots is bigger than their personal tastes or preferences." She went on to say that she knew for a fact that the university's eight Japanese students didn't all like each other, yet they spent a lot of time together.

We then talked about the habits of Americans living overseas. Time and time again, I've found that Americans aren't particularly cliquish. Many might not have local friends, but they'll have international friends, rather than staying with other Americans.

When I lived in Malaysia, I was invited to a barbecue by the Brazilian community, and they had friends in the Italian community. When they asked me if there was an American community, I told them that, Americans simply didn't meet in communities like that. There were seven or eight Americans at SUS. If we bumped into each other, we usually chatted. But I'd only been out socially with two of them, and just the once in both cases. Debranna said she believed it was because Americans are independent by nature, and also that our personal tastes outweigh our nationalism. The fact that you're American and I'm American doesn't mean we're buddies. Also, I believed it had a lot to do with language. Because we speak English, Americans can hang out with any international group. It seemed to me that the Vietnamese and Japanese spent so much time with their compatriots for language reasons. Koreans, on the other hand, hung out together because they were elitist, and wouldn't lower themselves to talk to non-Koreans. That's the impression I got, anyway.

A friend who was considering moving to China sent me an email asking if I'd noticed any health issues since living there. I told him: "Yes, I'm always bruised and bleeding and my muscles and joints hurt. Also, my arm popped out of socket, so you'll need to prepare for that."

I had a paper due in my modern coaching class. The book I was using was in English, but the paper had to be written in Chinese, and I needed additional sources. I had to find the correct Chinese words for such concepts as: lactic acid fermentation; ATP production; action speed; active speed; complex speed; and so on. Neither Google Translate nor electronic dictionaries were much help, as they tended to generate direct, word-for-word translations of these terms, results which had no meaning for a native speaker of Mandarin.

Some observers have said that the PRC is close to surpassing the US in the number of academic or scientific papers published. However, these estimates are based on the sheer number of papers, not their quality. Given what I've witnessed in Chinese universities, I have to believe that these papers don't contain a lot of original research, as most of the papers I saw were just aggregates of research already done elsewhere.

One way China has increased scholarly-paper publication is by increasing graduation requirements. At SUS, Chinese students working toward master's degrees or Ph.D. degrees had to publish six times before graduation.

Most of our courses ended with the professor assigning a paper, which generally represented your entire grade for the course. Consequently, it was extremely important that I knew whether or not my professor had received my paper, since we'd no longer be seeing each other in class.

Most professors stipulated that term papers be emailed to them, rather than printed and delivered. The problem, however, was that some professors were too important to acknowledge receipt of the paper. Not knowing if my teacher had received my assignment or not was maddening. I therefore always sent the email, then tracked them down on campus and asked them if they'd got it or not. When I did that, I always brought a printed copy of the paper, just in case. It normally took about half a day. Every time I did this, I wondered what people did before email, when you needed to track your teachers down and hand them your paper in person.

When buying my breakfast, I saw large clusters of students out on the street, talking with purpose. Something was obviously up. I asked what was going on, and they told me that a national ping pong competition was being held at the university and that all classes had been canceled. National ping pong championships don't just sneak up on you. I believe that someone knew about this at least a day in advance, and could have informed us of any schedule changes. Another student said that only the morning classes had been canceled. A teacher walked over and told us that actually no classes were canceled, but morning classes had been moved to the afternoon. I said: "I have a 1 p.m. class, so I should be fine, right?" She asked, "Who's your teacher?" I told her it was Li Laoshi. Then someone said, "He's in the ping pong association, so he won't be in class today." Someone else said that Li Laoshi had called in sick. I called Li Laoshi and he said we'd have class at 1 p.m. as usual.

Li Laoshi's class was really important to me that day, because I was supposed to give my final presentation. At 12.50 p.m., I received a text message saying: "The mandatory meeting for doctoral candidates in the Wushu Institute has already started. Where are you?" If they wanted me to be on time, they should have told me in advance. I called them and said I had to go to class and do a final presentation. On the way into the classroom building, I bumped into the head of the Chinese department who said, "Āndōngní, glad I found you. Li Laoshi's class was canceled." He then explained to me the incredible planning that had caused the cancellation of the class: "Because morning classes are taking place in the afternoon, there are no empty classrooms, so afternoon classes have to be canceled." I was annoyed, but I ran over to the wushu meeting, where everyone gave me dirty looks for arriving late.

Twenty minutes into this boring meeting, I received a text from my classmate: "Why aren't you in Li Laoshi's class?"

The meeting ended with half an hour left for me to give my final presentation, so long as I could find Li Laoshi's class. I ran over to the classroom building. Sure enough, morning class was in my classroom and Li Laoshi was nowhere to be found. I called him, and he said they were in an empty classroom at the end of the hall.

From a Chinese point of view, everything had worked out for the best. I attended my mandatory wushu meeting and got to do my final presentation. So it was win-win.

The report and PPT for Li Laoshi's class was a source review of five Chinese dissertations relating to Bruce Lee. Luckily, I'd taught source review writing in three of the four semesters I'd worked at Shanghai University. As a result, I'd read about 1,000 source reviews.

After the presentation, I had wrestling practice where we did freestyle and Greco-Roman. I was familiar with some freestyle techniques because they were similar to MMA wrestling, but I didn't know any Greco-Roman techniques. When we did actual Greco matches, I didn't know the rules at all. My opponent got me down and put me on my back a couple of times, so I just fought off my back, like in MMA — but they told me that, because both of my shoulder blades were on the ground, I'd already lost.

In the second round, when I got taken down, I fought off my back, careful to have only one shoulder blade on the ground. But they stopped the fight, explaining, "You can't have both shoulder blades on the ground."

"I didn't!" I protested, but let it go.

In the third round, the opponent grabbed me in a Greco-Roman hold which is a cross arm choke in MMA. He took me down, put me on my back and was trying to either pin me or get me to tap. I did neither. I had one shoulder blade up off the mat, and I was able to breath, sort of. So, I just relaxed and started looking for a way out, like I would in MMA. But again they stopped the match, saying I'd had two shoulder blades on the ground. When I disputed this, they agreed with me — then said: "Yeah, but with one shoulder blade down already, the pin would have been easy, so we stopped the match."

Later, in sanda class we practiced a classic sanda takedown. When the opponent kicks, you catch the leg, trap it firmly against your body, and drive your shoulder into the opponent's hip. But, and this is most important, you must brace the opponent's opposite knee with your hand, so he falls right over. This technique is very common in both Chinese wrestling and sanda. In shuai jiao, however, you do it by attacking the opponent and grabbing his leg, because he won't be kicking you.

There are two basic styles of teaching martial arts and fighting sports and I've never been able to decide which one is better. Traditionally, the teacher taught basic movements, and students drilled those movements. Then they drilled against a willing opponent, then an unwilling opponent, then they did the move in sparring. The other style is the Brazilian or Thai approach. The kid hangs around the gym and watches. When he feels ready, he imitates the movements he sees. Then he starts sparring, and he learns as he goes. I've seen both of these methods work, and they both make sense.

That night at sanda class, Zheng Tong showed up without his boxing gloves, as always. I asked him again why he never brought his gloves, and he gave me the answer he always gives: "I have very expensive gloves, very nice ones, but I forget to bring them." That made no sense. The only reason he'd own gloves would be to use them at sanda practice. So how could he forget them? He hardly ever wore athletic clothes for sanda class, arriving in his jeans or whatever he happened to be wearing.

One night, Zheng Tong walked into Zhou Laoshi's sanda class about thirty minutes late, wearing furry house shoes that looked like bear paws. Zhou Laoshi asked him where his shoes were, and Zheng Tong replied: "I'm wearing them." When Zhou Laoshi said, "Those are house shoes," Zheng Tong looked down, staring at his feet as if seeing them for the first time, and said: "Oh, I must have lost them."

Zheng Tong told me he scored zero in all of his academic classes. While he did well at wrestling practice, he didn't seem to have discipline for anything else. In sports classes, particularly sanda, he seemed to be incredibly unfocused. He was nearly always late or absent. He never did the exercises and drills the rest of the class was doing. And he couldn't remember, week to week, sometimes minute to minute, what we were meant to be practicing. Sometimes Zhou Laoshi would demonstrate a throw several times, then tell us to practice it five times each. Zheng Tong and I'd pair off and he'd ask me, "What are we supposed to do?"

Zhou Laoshi told the class there'd be an exam soon and that they needed to practice the six basic throws. I told Zheng Tong I'd help him practice, but then he just wanted to box or wrestle or let me throw him. On test day, he had no clue what to do, and scored zero points.

After class, Zheng Tong asked me to be his shifu and teach him MMA. I told him he wasn't serious. If I'd seen him hitting the bag regularly, I'd teach him. He looked depressed because I'd not agreed. I also pointed out that most Saturdays we had open training, and although he'd said he'd come he never did.

What I didn't tell him was this: Zheng Tong was now living at a school with one of the best sanda programs in the world. If he actually wanted to learn to fight, he had the perfect opportunity, but was choosing not to.

He told me that, after graduating, he wanted to go back to his home province and open an MMA school, and that he'd invite me to be the instructor. When I asked, "After you graduate? How can you graduate with zero points?" he looked confused, like he'd never linked those two concepts before. I asked him what his parents would say to him when he went home for Lunar New Year and told them he'd scored zero points.

He mimed getting punched in the face. I told him, "You see, that's terrible. You need to work harder at school." But he smiled and said, "It's OK, I'm not afraid to get hit."

Next, he said: "I hate studying. I only like sports classes." But, I pointed out, "Even in sports classes you don't apply yourself. You do nothing in sanda."

He countered: "That's because the teacher only teaches us basics. I want to start fighting."

Back in my room, I complained to Natsuki, my roommate, that my coaches often stopped practice, made us stand at attention, and then talked for 45 minutes. His face turned angry in an instant, and he shouted, "China coach too much talk." I guess he'd had the same experience.

· ● · ·

Since coming to China, I'd been coughing up all kinds of horrible stuff on a daily basis, especially after training. Shanghai was the only city on Earth where teachers got black lung disease. I was wondering if I should start smoking filtered cigarettes to scrub the air before it got into my lungs.

One morning, we woke up to discover that Shanghai's Air Quality Index (AQI) had just surpassed 504. In the US, an AQI of 250 is considered poisonous. New York, on the same day, was 80. The prediction for the next day in New York was 60, and the government of New York State was discouraging elderly and vulnerable people from doing heavy exercise. Natsuki's coach back in Japan called him and urged him not to train. Japanese employees were told to remain indoors with the windows closed. When the AQI is above 300, you can't see to the end of the block. An AQI of 500 is so bad that you can't see the back of the classroom. Making my way from my room to the training hall was like walking through a cold, smoky, and depressing dystopian future, like those portrayed in *Soylent Green, 1984,* or *Blade Runner.* There were very few people outdoors and the ones I saw were red-eyed and coughing.

The coach wasn't at the wrestling hall, but the team was there, playing indoor soccer. The pollution was so bad you couldn't see clearly across the length of the training hall. I'd never seen such horrendous air in my life. I did one hour of conditioning, then a few minutes of wrestling with my friends when they'd finished their soccer game, and then we called it a night. I think that training had been officially canceled, and the soccer was simply because these sports kids really didn't know what else to do with themselves. But, of course, playing soccer is as bad as actual training, in terms of inhaling pollution.

One constructive thing did come out of the evening. The wrestler who'd taken me down the previous day using a Greco-Roman neck choke submission was there. I asked him to teach me the move. I really liked it, because it could be done from a clinch, even if you had zero underhooks.

Later, I showed him and some others how I'd fight out of it, MMA style, by throwing my foot over the guy's head and reversing him. The biggest guy on our team — Yang Wenbin at 110 kg (243 lbs) and 185 cm (6'1") — wanted to see if he could submit me from that position. He had my head and neck really tight, but he was a wrestler, not an MMA or BJJ fighter. So all I had to do was relax, and I was able to breathe at about 60 percent normal. He was too tall for me to get my leg over his head, so I just let him drag me around in circles, while I slowly worked my arm free. Once it was free, I pressed his face with my elbow, sat up, and reversed him. I got him in the MMA version of the same hold, and he tapped.

I told my teammates: "Put yourself in the worst position, and fight out of it. Then do that again and again, every day in training. When the fight comes, there'll be nothing they can throw at you that you aren't ready for."

Because of the air quality, schools were closed and people were urged to stay home. The streets were noticeably empty, and visibility was down to maybe 25 meters (82 ft). At the university, neither classes nor practice sessions were officially canceled, but the campus was like a ghost town. When I did my morning conditioning and strength training, the gym was nearly empty.

One of my professors sent me a copy of a ninth-century Chinese wrestling book titled *Wrestling Mind.* I struggled reading modern texts, and this book — written in classical Chinese — was even less comprehensible to me. Even some of my classmates had trouble reading some of the classical martial arts texts we'd found. Checking on Amazon, I found just one Chinese wrestling book translated into English, *The Method of Chinese Wrestling*, written by Tong Zhongyi and translated by Tim Cartmell. Tim and I later became Facebook friends, and he gave me some helpful advice during my studies.

I turned in the final two papers of the semester and then crashed. After a day and a half of sleep, I felt absolutely bored, depressed, fat, and lazy. The air quality was still horrendous, and I got permission from my Ph.D. advisor to leave China for a bit. I wanted to head to Cambodia for training, and then home for the holidays. At SUS, there was no men's freestyle wrestling, but in Cambodia, I could train with one of the national freestyle wrestling team's coaches. I felt it would help both my wrestling and my research.

On the morning of my flight, someone called me down to the street in front of the dorm. The wrestling team captain was waiting for me there. He handed me a beautiful notebook, where every single member of the team had written a message for me. Many of them wrote "Merry Christmas" in English or Chinese. Most of the longer messages were in Chinese, saying how much they'd enjoyed training together. It was incredibly sweet. The biggest guy on my team, and one of my best friends, Yang Wenbin, had written in English, "Ideal Fighting."

I couldn't agree more. I was deeply touched.

In the taxi, it occurred to me that you have to admire the tenacity of the Chinese motorist. He doesn't allow red lights or pedestrians to stop him from doing whatever the hell he wants.

At the airport, I saw a North American woman blabbering on endlessly to a Chinese stranger about her trip to South Africa. The Chinese guy never said anything. It wasn't even clear if he spoke English. The story was long and boring, and he just stared dead ahead, glassy eyed. But it was OK, because when she finished, she laughed, to show what a great story it'd been.

The flight was an opportunity to think. Was Shaolin Kung Fu the ability to present and defend your dissertation in Chinese? Was it the willingness to drop everything and run to a dissertation defense at the last minute? In Chinese culture, the student is basically on-the-clock and should do what his master says, not caring if the schedule changes multiple times an hour, since you're committed to following him that hour anyway. But this is true across Chinese culture, not just in Shaolin Kung Fu. So that probably couldn't be the answer. Maybe, by going through the motions and doing everything you're told to do, you're meant to discover the meaning of Shaolin Kung Fu. And maybe that realization was the answer.

The plane descended over rice paddies, and approached Phnom Penh.

Chapter 9
Cambodia, Home, and Back to SUS

The traditional revolutionary spirit of struggle was espoused by the Chinese Communist Party's policy on sport.

— **Fan Hong,**
"'Iron Bodies': Women, War, and Sport in the Early Communist Movement in Modern China,"
***Journal of Sport History* (Vol. 24, No. 1, Spring 1997)**

I woke up in Phnom Penh, and went down to the street for my favorite Cambodian breakfast: grilled pork, fried eggs, fish sauce, a baguet, and two huge cups of the best iced coffee in the world, sweetened with condensed milk.

After breakfast, I walked over to the Olympic Stadium to meet my wrestling coach, Japleun. We'd known each other for a number of years, having worked together on some TV documentaries and having wrestled each other in a traditional competition. He'd been a champion wrestler. Now in his thirties, he still competed, while making the transition to coaching. As a Cambodian national athlete he received a salary of about US$50 per month, paid nine months of the year. Luckily, his wife and his younger brother were also celebrated national wrestlers, so the family was able to get by financially. They had a bamboo house about thirty minutes outside the city, where they also had some rice fields and animals. Back in the village, Japleun was raising his young son to be a great wrestler. The money I paid him for a single wrestling lesson was equivalent to about a week's salary, and we were doing lessons every day.

The training hall was dark, dusty, and very hot, but it was great to be training with Japleun. The national wrestlers trained twice a day. When they were supposed to be resting, several of them came to partner with me, out of respect for Japleun.

I'd had some kind of disgustingly swollen infected growth on my knee for weeks. I couldn't decide if it would be safer to see a doctor in China, a doctor in Cambodia, or lance it myself. I kept wishing I could just buy medicinal leeches, as it seemed like the sort of infection that could be sucked out. I'd have done it myself, but I'd have needed to buy a bunch of breath mints for afterward.

Japleun differed to other Khmer fighters I'd trained with, in that he was always thinking of ways to apply wrestling to MMA. He watched a highlight reel of my MMA fights, identified where I had weaknesses, and taught me techniques to overcome those situations. He showed me how to use a neck crank, combined with neck crank sit-through takedown, in lieu of a guillotine.

A retired American, named Bill Nelson, who'd been an Arizona State wrestler and a high school wrestling coach came to train with us a couple times while I was in the Penh. It was impressive how much technique he still had, even at his age. The Khmer wrestlers all joked about me and Bill, saying: "Old but still strong."

During wrestling, Japleun had me tossing the wrestling dummy. I was having trouble getting the throw right and about the tenth time I did it wrong, I kicked the dummy out of frustration. When I did, the thing on my knee just exploded and blood ran all down my leg. I looked like a shark attack victim in a horror movie. My Khmer friends were worried, but I told them, "It's OK. The decision was made for me." On the way home, I bought some Betadine, cleaned it out, and put a plaster on it. It's always nice to have one less thing to worry about.

Just as we were finishing training, I saw a girl who was riding through the Olympic Stadium grounds fall off her motorcycle and smack her head. She hadn't been wearing a helmet. I went running over to see if I could help. When I got there, she was breathing and she wasn't bleeding. That's pretty much where my first-aid knowledge ends — I only know how to stop the bleeding or restore breathing. She probably had a concussion, because she seemed completely out of it. A Khmer guy, stopped his motorcycle, ran over, and began aggressively rubbing Tiger Balm all over her face and head, raising and twisting her head and neck while doing so. A crowd had gathered, including a friend of the injured girl. And no one objected to what he was doing.

Japleun pulled up on his motorcycle. I hopped on and rode back to my hotel.

Apart from wrestling, I was working on a paper for Professor Dai, comparing Khmer martial arts with Chinese martial arts. Back in 2004, I'd been the first foreigner to train in the Khmer martial art of bokator. In 2007, another American, Derek Morris, and I became the first foreigners promoted to black krama (black belt). His promotion was for black krama in the full style, whereas mine was only for bokator fighting.

Although bokator looked nothing like Shaolin Kung Fu, there were a number of cultural commonalities, like the existence of animal forms, use of weapons, katas, and of course kicks, punches, knees, elbows, and other kinds of strikes. Bokator also included jap bap, or Khmer traditional wrestling which was not exactly part of my dissertation research, but again, somewhat related.

It was significant that bokator included both striking and wrestling. According to Tong Zhongyi's *The Method of Chinese Wrestling*, in ancient China wrestlers learned both pugilism and shuai jiao. And, of course, Jiang Laoshi had taught us sanda ge do, which included wrestling, kicking, punching, throwing, and ground fighting. Ancient Greece had pankration, a combination of wrestling and boxing. We could almost say that MMA used to exist, in both Asia and Europe, in ancient times. Then it disappeared for centuries, eventually coming back to life in the early 1990s. In Japan and Brazil, mixed-style and Luta Livre type competitions had been held prior to the emergence of UFC, but the modern rebirth of mixed-style fighting — the pivotal event that popularized and brought it to living rooms and dojos across the world — was UFC 1 in 1993.

Another commonality between bokator and Shaolin Kung Fu is that both featured body hardening and conditioning. I wasn't much into body conditioning. Paddy Carso, my boxing coach in Cambodia, always said that your body would harden naturally from working the pads and the bag, and from sparring, and I'd always agreed with that. But most of the bokator guys invested hundreds of hours in punching boards and pounding their shins with bamboo, to toughen their skin and deaden the nerves.

The first time I was at Shaolin Temple, the students all knew about body hardening. Many of them were trying to do it, but only a small minority were succeeding. It seemed 100 percent of bokator students were practicing some kind of body hardening.

The animal styles in bokator include: monkey, dragon, tiger, horse, duck, garuda (a mythical animal with a human body and bird's head), snake, and others. Shaolin Kung Fu had the dragon, the snake, the tiger, the leopard, and the crane. Although not an original Shaolin animal, the monkey was also a popular kung fu form in China. Several of the animals were the same in both styles, while some of the bokator animals were unique to Southeast Asia.

Shaolin Kung Fu weapons include the Shaolin fork, sword, spade, whip, and long staff. Bokator has a sword and a long staff, but also two short swords, two short sticks, a small stick which fits inside of your fist, and the krama (a traditional Khmer scarf). The krama could be used for pulling, tying, wrestling, choking, joint locking, or as a whip or a sling, to throw stones.

Although bokator practitioners can fight, fighting isn't their main focus. Students who wish to focus on fighting can learn pradal serey (kickboxing) or MMA. In the same way, students in China's Shaolin schools have usually divided into two groups: wushu form practitioners or sanda fighters.

Apart from my own observations and musings, I needed to do solid, academic research on martial arts and wrestling, in order to write my papers. In the West, including the Arab world, wrestling records go back thousands of years. According to the International Federation of Associated Wrestling Styles (FILA), the oldest written mention of wrestling dates from 5,000 years ago. The first illustrated wrestling textbook was printed in 1512, in color, by German artist Albrecht Dürer.

Doing academic research on martial arts is difficult because, prior to the 19th or 20th centuries, most Asian countries — with the exceptions of Japan, China, and maybe Korea — didn't have good written records of their martial arts. Additionally, not many Ph.D.-level scholars have researched martial arts. Consequently, much of what's published is the work of amateur researchers who push a particular bias, and aren't always skilled at separating verified information from conjecture, myth, or legend. They often make the mistake of believing something just because it's been widely believed and repeated. The fact that something has been said many times, or that many believe it, doesn't make it true.

When I did Google searches, I kept landing on articles, published on martial arts websites, which blatantly plagiarized articles I'd written about bokator and other martial arts. I don't mind the copyright infringement, but this meant that only a small fraction of the articles in existence were the result of original research.

In the Khmer language, the only mention of bokator in print, prior to my 2004 articles, was an entry in a Cambodian dictionary from in the 1960s. It referred to bokator as a traditional weapon, made of sharpened bamboo, attached to the forearms. Older evidence exists in the form of bas-reliefs carved on temple walls. These depict Khmer warriors employing a martial art, but as there's no writing, the word bokator doesn't appear. Contrary to claims made by Khmer martial artists, these carvings don't prove that bokator existed back then. The debate between Thailand and Cambodia over who invented bokator has never been settled, due to the lack of evidence.

Professor Dai liked to see very clear, side-by-side comparison and contrast in academic papers. For that reason, I included this lack of verified information as a contrast between bokator and the long, well-documented history of Shaolin Kung Fu.

I trained twice a day while in Phnom Penh — with Japleun in the mornings, and with the bokator guys, the MMA team, or the Khmer pradal serey kickboxers (an art very similar to Muay Thai, but don't tell the Khmers that, or they get angry) in the afternoons.

Eh Phuthong, the country's all-time greatest kickboxer, had been a good friend ever since killing me in an action movie in 2004. Since then, whenever I visited Cambodia, he'd welcomed me to train with him. An American accountant who had an MBA and had founded an international-level accounting university in Cambodia, he was a former wrestler and a patron of Cambodian sports, financing numerous sports teams and competitions. When he was free, he'd come to the Olympic Stadium, where everyone knew him, and train with Japleun and me. Both men were excellent at breaking down the techniques, step-by-step and drilling them with me.

Most of the training in freestyle wrestling can carry over to MMA. Some things do not, however. In freestyle, to avoid the pin, a guy will often lay flat on his belly. In MMA, that would be the kiss of death, because you'd get choked from behind. In freestyle, a lot of training goes into ways of forcibly rolling your opponent, from his belly, to his back. I didn't think I needed that part for MMA. Accordingly, we concentrated on things that Japleun and I felt I needed. One modification Japleun made for me was teaching me to shoot, without having to set my knee on the ground, which was hard for me to do because of injuries. My shots were therefore slightly higher than other people's, but it was OK, because if I got caught, I could upper-body wrestle.

On weekends, the wrestling team offered training for prospective wrestlers, and Japleun invited me to that because they always worked on basics in a very methodical way. It was so much easier learning techniques in this environment than in MMA, because here no one was kicking me in the face.

Japleun invited me a few times to train with the actual national team, but the head coach was a scary North Korean who just screamed at people all of the time, making me miss being kicked and punched in the face.

The training was great, but toward the end, I was missing having the variety of sparring partners I had back in China. After we had our final session, there was one more thing I needed to do before leaving Phnom Penh.

A friend from the MMA team took me to visit a man I called, "The Pain Doctor." This unlicensed traditional chiropractor fixed all of my injuries whenever I was in Phnom Penh, using incredibly painful deep-tissue pressure point massage and joint manipulation. Allegedly, he could cure anything. He was also an ex-fighter who really understood fighting injuries, so all of the fighters swore by him. When we walked in, he was setting a woman's broken leg, which he then wrapped in newspaper and copious amount of packing tape.

When it was my turn, he inspected my shoulder and neck injury and determined that I'd been training too hard. He then asked me if I'd been submitted on the right side. Next, he asked if my knee was also giving me problems. Finally, he touched a very painful part of my shin and said that all of my pain and all of my injuries were caused by my shoulder injury. According to him, my shoulder had come slightly out of socket when I was injured in the wrestling tournament.

He had me lie on the table, and called my friends over to compare my two shoulders from behind. They confirmed that a bone was sticking out on one side and not the other. He shifted the shoulder back into place, realigned my spine, worked through some scar tissue or a mass of jangled nerves on my knees, and drove his elbows into my shins and feet. I was screaming the whole time. His fingers were like steel knives, digging deep into my flesh. The pain was blinding, and for the first time in my life, I passed out from pain. After the invasive part, he did some sort of massage on my neck and head, and I fell into a very deep sleep.

When I woke up, he said that everything should work properly again, and that I'd regain full strength and motion of my right arm, which I hadn't had in years. A few days later, although I was still a little sore and painful from the treatment, I definitely had much better range of motion on the injured shoulder, and it no longer felt like it was out of joint. Soon I was lifting weights and doing pushups again.

Phnom Penh had been a huge success. I learned a lot of wrestling, finished my paper for my advisor, and got my shoulder fixed. I also ate dramatically better and more healthily in Cambodia than in China. The variety of restaurants and ethnic foods available in Phnom Penh is incredible. Not only did a lot of restaurants in Phnom Penh have root beer, but I even found one that had chocolate Yoo-Hoo. In addition to the great and affordable restaurants, the grocery stores all carried American products. Deodorant, which I sometimes had trouble finding in China, was sold everywhere, as were breakfast cereal, peanut butter, chocolate, cake mix, and other products that in Shanghai you could only find in specialty shops.

••●••

My next stop was home, for Christmas. In New York, there's a jiu-jitsu center near my house, but I sort of hate jiu-jitsu. It's too intelligent and technical. I just feel that boxing and wrestling go so much better with my personal brand of blind rage.

Many of the Chinese-language shuai jiao texts I'd read claimed that judo had been based on shuai jiao. After three years of research, I'd find no evidence, outside of Chinese sources, to support this claim. However, as the two arts look somewhat similar, and practitioners wear a similar kimono-style top, I thought it'd be important to expand my research and my practice, and gain at least a baseline understanding of judo. While I was home, I sought out a judo master, and took formal judo lessons for the first time in my life.

I asked Grand Master Gary Rasanen about judo's applicability in MMA, and he said, "95 percent of all judo throws could be done without a judogi [karate uniform]. With a judogi, you grab the sleeve. Without the judogi, when a guy throws a punch, he's giving you his body the same as when he grabs you with the judogi."

The same is true of MMA and sanda. Throws often come from catching the opponent's kick, or timing your shot for when he really loads up on that right hand and throws a huge punch. And actually, one of the things I like about the gi vs. no gi discussion is that the throws in sanda come from Chinese wrestling. So, on any given day at the university, I could walk into two practice sessions and notice they were doing the exact same throw in both, one with jackets and one without.

I also went to Manhattan to train in catch wrestling and sambo with Sambo Steve Koepfer. When I asked him the difference between catch wrestling and jiu-jitsu, he said, "Catch wrestling is wrestling. You can win by pin." You still need to get position before submission, just like in jiu-jitsu, but the biggest difference is that you can win by pin. You can even pull guard, but you cannot be flat on your back, your shoulder blades need to be up. Another big difference between catch and jiu-jitsu is that catch has no points. You have to win by pin or submission. A lot of people like that better, because they feel that winning on points isn't domination.

The significance of catch wrestling in my doctoral dissertation research was that catch wrestling or "catch as catch can wrestling" had once been a big-money professional sport in the US and Europe. Catch was so big that President Theodore Roosevelt once said, about catch wrestling champion Georg Hackenschmidt, "If I wasn't president of the United States, I would like to be Georg Hackenschmidt."

Catch was added to the modern Olympics, appearing in the games of 1904, 1908, and 1920. Eventually, both the American Athletic Union (AAU), which governs amateur sports in the US, and the International Olympic Committee, said they'd sanction catch if it were made safer. The submissions and chokes were removed, but the rest was left pretty much intact and called freestyle wrestling. The sanctioning bodies for US high schools demanded that further changes be made, to make the sport even safer and more suitable for children, and this resulted in the invention of American folk-style wrestling.

Consequently, catch was the father of both Olympic freestyle and US scholastic folk-style and collegiate-style wrestling. It was also the father of modern pro wrestling, which, over time, replaced holds and chokes with flying acrobatics and stunts. Much later, catch became integral to MMA, when Karl Gotch and Billy Robinson taught the art to Japanese and Americans fighting out of Japan. Sadly, most young athletes are unaware of this important piece of history. What's more, it was a chunk of research that was more interesting and better documented than the Chinese wrestling history I was meant to be comparing it to.

At home with my Italian-American family, we ate huge, incredible meals that somehow lasted into the next meal and the next, until it was time to go out and eat again. Although I'd have loved to have stayed with my family longer, I needed to get back to China and work off the weight I'd gained.

··●··

Landing in Shanghai, I was faced with a choice. The subway from the airport to my university would take two hours but cost almost nothing. A taxi would be RMB 180 to 200 (about US$26). I was so tired I opted for the taxi. I got in and told the driver to go to Shanghai University of Sport. As he pulled onto the highway, he said he didn't know where the university was.

"Wait, how will we get there if you don't know where it is?" I asked. He said that we could look for it, but without much confidence. Not on my dime! I thought. Out of frustration, I said, "Take me to People's Square, and I'll take the subway from there." People's Square was halfway home, in subway terms, but about as far from the airport as the university. After paying the driver RMB 170 to get to People's Square, I still had a 45-minute subway ride home. The experience was both awful and expensive. Later, I'd learn to better deal with taxi culture, which is to simply say "OK." Then the driver would eventually find the destination. Also, most taxi drivers, while lost, would shut off the meter. So I should have just remained in the taxi — but I didn't know that in Year One of my studies.

The dorm was cold because not many students had come back yet. I woke up in the morning, made my breakfast coffee with Shanghai tap water — instead of the bottled water I usually used — then set my alarm clock and waited to see if it'd make me sick. Most of the food shops near the university were closed for New Year. The only place I could find to buy food was the university cafeteria, where the food was still gross, but gratefully the portions were small. Seeing no other option, I bought multiple portions of meat and vegetable which only cost about RMB 3 (less than US$ 0.50) each. The other place that was open was McDonalds. I definitely needed to find a way to cook healthy meals for myself.

There was no training at the university, because of Chinese New Year, so I went to the MMA gym, paid my fees, and then taught class. I thought to myself, if I wanted to teach so badly, maybe I should open a gym. It'd be cheaper.

After teaching class, I found an excellent grappler to go with for four rounds. And although I've been choked into submission a number of times, this was the first time I ever went completely unconscious. He had me in a grip which I wasn't sure was going to be a neck crank or a choke. He did a gator roll and I went out. When I came to, the first thing I thought was: "I hope I didn't poop my pants like Steven Seagal." Legend has it that Steven Seagal pooped his pants after being choked out by Gene Lebell. Luckily, that didn't happen to me, but it was still exhausting. But you know what they say (actually, it's what I say): "If you're not getting submitted ten times a night, you're training with the wrong people."

My studies were in the Wu Shu Institute, but what I was doing was different than most of my classmates. The philosophy and culture of wrestling were dramatically different than those of Chinese martial arts. Unlike Wushu Taolu, wrestling is a fighting competition between two opponents. A wrestler doesn't know what his opponent will do. He can't plan all of his moves in advance because the art of wrestling requires him to adjust his strategy and movement according to the strategy and movement of his opponent. When an opponent attacks, a wrestler can defend and escape, or he can counterattack. Some wrestlers are defensive fighters. They wait until the opponent attacks, then they use the opponent's mistakes against him. They counterattack, tripping the opponent to the ground.

Riding the subway back to the university, I saw a lot of horse decorations and a semi-depressing thought struck me. It was the Year of the Horse, my second in Asia. I'd looped the Chinese calendar since coming to Asia. Twelve years had somehow slipped by.

It was time for me to make the joke I make every year about this time: "Three days into the Year of the Horse, and I'm still drawing snakes on my checks."

Even though I had difficulty reading and writing Chinese, I spoke Chinese a lot, listened to Chinese, trained with Chinese classmates, and was forced to eat Chinese food, so in the end I decided that I was half Chinese and 100-percent Italian. And 1,000-percent American. Add those together and you get 1,150 percent, which explained why I was so overweight.

Natsuki was in Japan, so the room was extremely quiet, not that he ever made noise. I opened my email and found good news from home: My stories about Chinese wrestling were running in magazines in the US, along with pictures of my teammates. This just goes to show that you can be born in Jiangsu and still become a media star in America. Isn't that the Chinese dream?

After a shower, I lay in bed, translating into English an old wrestling text a teacher had given me. I then realized it was *The Method of Chinese Wrestling* by Tong Zhongyi. I'd already read Tim Cartmell's translation of it, and when I pulled that book off my shelf, and compared it to my translation, I noticed sadly that his translation made so much more sense than mine.

The next morning, I saw some of the foreign students, in servers' uniforms, heading off toward the mall. A lot of the foreign students couldn't afford to go home during vacations, so they stayed in the dorms and looked for holiday jobs. An African guy and several of the Mongolians found jobs in a restaurant, earning RMB 100 (US$ 16) per day plus food. As a teacher, I was getting over RMB 200 (US$ 32) per hour. In a single hour, I earned what to them is two days' salary. Gross that up for New York minimum wage and they'd be getting US$ 10 per hour, or about US$ 80 a day, in a restaurant. Keeping the ratio the same, that should mean that I'd be getting US$ 160 an hour as an adjunct professor in New York — which, of course, is many times more than what I'd actually be earning. Adjuncts get about US$ 50 an hour in most American colleges. This shows that income disparity in China is probably a lot higher than it is in US. My hourly rate kept creeping up, and by the time I left China in 2019, my rate was RMB 750 (US$ 120) an hour, which was slightly more than the weekly salary of a restaurant worker.

It's funny that, as a child, you dread the start of school. But as an adult, I was so happy when everyone finally came back and classes and training resumed.

I asked my classmate Duan Limae to help me register for classes, but she just told me to go to the building with the green roof. I went there, walked into a random office, asking about registration, and they sent me to the Office of Doctoral Affairs. The guy there told me to go to some other office in some other building, and that was where I put the brakes on. I contacted Duan Limae and insisted that I needed her help. The next morning, she took me to the same office I'd been in the previous day. We spoke to the same guy, who told us about 26 times, over a period of a half hour, that it was impossible to register me for classes, and that we'd need to go somewhere else. Then he registered me for my classes, and printed out my schedule for me.

This term, I had three Chinese classes and two doctoral classes, plus training.

When I got back to the dorm, I stopped in the office downstairs and asked if they had my grades from last term. While the woman was printing my grades, she said, "Here, let me print your schedule for you, so you know what classes to go to this term." She handed me a list with the exact set of classes that Duan Limae had registered me for at the Office of Doctoral Affairs. At no point had anyone told me just to go to the office in the very building where I lived to get my schedule, but apparently that was the procedure. In the end, as was always the case in China, everything just worked out. In future semesters, all I had to do was stop by the office downstairs and get my new schedule

Checking the grade report they'd just given me, I could see that of my four doctoral courses, I'd scored 86, 87, and 87 in the three academic courses, and 95 in sanda ge do. Grades for my Chinese classes hadn't been posted yet, but I thought I'd done well.

In the first sanda session of the new semester, I found that my fighting style had changed a lot because of my shoulder injury and the training I'd done in Cambodia. My shoulder injury meant I'd lost nearly all punching power in my right arm. Even before going to Cambodia, I found that Ma Pei had figured me out and every time I threw the left jab, he was timing it and hitting me with a straight sidekick to the body. So the whole time I was training in Cambodia, I experimented with using a right-hand lead. After I returned, I found I was boxing out of a southpaw stance, with my right hand in front, but I was still jabbing with the left hand. Technically, it was now a left cross, but I was using it as my job.

The cool thing about southpaw stance is that it left my opponent open to body kicks, which he kept circling into. Also, he couldn't take me down easily because he didn't know how to adjust his takedowns to fight a lefty. Another advantage was that in wrestling, you're supposed to wrestle right-hand forward, so this put me in a much stronger wrestling stance. The only disadvantage was that he once swept me by kicking my right leg, which was way out in front. I could see that I needed to work on that.

After sanda, I had to attend a wushu lecture. I wasn't surprised anymore when my professors, particularly the martial arts professors, spoke in *chéngyǔ* phrases, it was still tedious to listen to. The teacher said, "Ideal fighting includes coordination of the internal and the external," then asked, "Does anyone know what that means?" But it was a rhetorical question; no answer was expected. He waited a second or two, as if providing us the opportunity to answer, and gave a sly smile, to show how stupid everyone else in the room was. Then he explained: "Coordination of the external and internal means *shǒu, yǎn, shēn, fǎ, bu, qi, li,* and *gōng.*"

He gave that a moment to sink in and then he asked a second rhetorical question. "Does anyone know what that means?"

We weren't expected to answer, only to stare blankly, and we obliged. He then shook his head, as if to say, "How can people be so dumb?" On those occasions, when there was another professor in the room, he'd have looked over at that professor and said something disparaging about us like, "Have you ever seen such ignorant doctoral candidates?"

Then he explained that *shǒu* referred to hand techniques, *yǎn* to eyes, *shēn* to body, *fǎ* to method, and *gōng* to kung fu. He went on to explain each element separately, using additional *chéngyǔ* and more rhetorical questions, followed by further explanation.

One time, when he asked "Does anyone know what those are?" I wrote in my notebook: No, but I bet you're about to tell us. By the time he was done explaining, I'd forgotten the larger context of the original set of characters, and how that related to whatever the lecture was about.

While three-hour doctoral lectures were extremely tedious, when Jiang Laoshi once shared a *chéngyǔ* with us after sparring, I not only understood it, but loved it and remembered it. Appreciation of *chéngyǔ* likely depends on motivation and context.

Jiang Laoshi said, "The essence of fighting is *tī, dǎ, shuāi, ná*." He then explained that *tī* means kicking, *dǎ* means punching, *shuāi* refers to shuai jiao (wrestling), while *ná* alludes to *qínná* (chin na, grabbing and joint locking).

So, hundreds or maybe even thousands of years ago, Chinese masters knew about MMA.

Another interesting parallel between the ancients and modern MMA appears in *The Method of Chinese Wrestling*, in which Tong Zhongyi told of a strength exercise called "barrel running." Basically, it involved a huge clay pot, about chest height, that the wrestler had to roll, upright, walking it back and forth, across the training yard. Modern MMA fighters do exactly the same exercise, but rolling and flipping a truck tire.

At wrestling practice, the wresting training I'd done in Cambodia really paid off. In sparring, my usual big sparring partner couldn't get me down, and I was able to get a body lock and under hooks on him repeatedly. He then worked with me on neck drag and ankle-pick which I'd started learning in Cambodia. I just couldn't say enough good things about Japleun.

The MMA gym was sponsoring a smoker in March and I'd been arguing with an internet troll from the US named Bred Schroed (not his real name), a pilot living in China. He was convinced that being a vegan and a traditional martial artist made him a better fighter (although he'd never fought), and that he could "destroy" me. I invited him to Shanghai to be my opponent. He agreed, but as the fight drew closer, he issued a new threat, something like, "I will destroy you, not on that day, but at some undisclosed time in the distant future." Tough words from a tough man.

When you're preparing for a fight, you get your sparring partners to emulate the person you'll be up against. I joked with all of my friends that I'd hired a 40-year-old, vegan sparring partner, 10 kg (22 lbs) smaller than me, who had no training or experience, and, asked him to come to training and act like Bred Schroed. So, instead of showing up for training, he called me on the phone, telling me he'd destroy me and then hanging up. And now I had to pay him his sparring fee, as he'd acted like Bred Schroed.

It was a new semester, and that meant trying out new classes. Jiang Laoshi invited me to his Monday night sanda class, but I wound up hating it. It wasn't his fault. It was because it was a beginners' class. There were no professional fighters in the group. Also, the students were all small and scared of me. No one was willing to partner with me, even after Jiang Laoshi told them to. Andrea, the Italian, was in that class, so he volunteered to be my partner. I was grateful, but he was really small, no more than 60 kg (132 lbs), and he was a Wushu Taolu guy. The first drill was a man-carry, where we had to take turns carrying each other. That just didn't seem fair, as I outweighed him by 50 percent. Next, we had to kick each other — also unfair. After about an hour, I made an excuse to Jiang Laoshi and just left. I think he knew what the problem was. He made sure I'd come to his other class with the two pros, Ma Pei and Jiang Huaying, but never asked me to come back to the beginners' class.

I tried another class which had some bigger guys who were willing to work with me. They didn't know much sanda, but they all had some kind of fighting kung fu or karate background, so it was interesting trying to get around their long kicks.

During a meeting in Professor Dai's office, we got on to the subject of food. In China, people from the various regions seem to really like their regional cuisines. There's a saying: "South, sweet; North, salty; East, spicy; and West, sour." In my experience 100 percent of the people from the South like sweet foods, while 100 percent of those from the East like spicy dishes. In the US, you can be from anywhere and like or dislike anything you want.

The other graduate students were talking about regional foods from their hometowns, when Professor Dai looked at me and said that I was lucky to be in China, rather than the US, so I could enjoy good food. Of course, I agreed with him.

Some of my classmates asked me about the regional foods in my hometown. Brooklyn? I could say Italian is our regional food, but other neighborhoods in Brooklyn are Russian, Polish, Latino, Black, or Jewish, and each has its own cuisine. With the exception of dishes like Boston clam chowder, Cajun food, or Tex-Mex, the US doesn't have regional dishes the way many other countries do. For example, in China, many regional dishes and fruits can only be found in their original province. But you can eat Boston clam chowder in Tennessee, Tex-Mex in New York, and Cajun food in Portland. Also, you could probably make the case that Cajun food is sort of from France. And Tex-Mex comes originally from the independent Republic of Texas. So it too is an import. When I tried to explain this to my classmates, they showed signs of pity, surmising that without regional cuisine, people in the regions must be starving.

Chinese people often observed something about me and then ask if it was true of all Americans. A woman actually stopped me on the street once, asked me where I was from. When I told her, she asked: "Do all Americans have big noses?" Another time, the same thing happened, but the person said, "I know an English guy. His nose is even bigger than yours." And then she concluded that English people have bigger noses than Americans.

What I could never get people to understand is that being American isn't an ethnicity. One can't "look" American. When I began teaching in Asia, and I told people that my name was Antonio, I'd often be asked: "Yes, but what's your American name?" Obviously, I'd answer "Antonio." More than once, a school boss asked: "The parents are expecting an American teacher. Would it be OK if we gave you an American name?" To that I answered, "I have an American name. It's Antonio."

Back to food: The first time I lived in China, in 2003, I got used to eating certain foods in the vicinity of Shaolin Temple in Henan. When I later worked in Guangdong, and complained that I couldn't find any of those foods, my Chinese friends would always say: "But Henan is far away." We'd be standing in front of McDonald's and I'd be thinking: America is even further away, yet you have American food. New York is too cold to grow tropical fruits, yet there you can get tropical fruits and foods from around the world. Being American means you can eat food from almost any culture or any location, in any season.

The following day we had a rough sanda class. The teacher had us do about an hour of kicking drills. This was good for me, because kicking was the weakest aspect of my fighting, but my partner, Ma Pei, could kick hard enough to bruise my arm through the pad. He kept asking me if I understood what was going on. "The coach said 'kick hard.' You're not kicking hard. Did you understand his Chinese?" he asked. "Yes, I understood," I confirmed, "but this is the hardest I can kick."

Apart from kicking drills and sparring, we spent a lot of time catching kicks and throwing. Ma Pei's kicking was so powerful that I'd stand no chance against him in a sanda fight. In an MMA fight, I could probably throw him, pin him, and win on ground and pound or submission. But in sanda, even if I did manage to throw him, he'd just stand up and we'd start fighting again.

After several days of cold, wet, and overcast weather, I didn't feel like going to training or going outside. I didn't even want to brush my teeth. I just sat in my room writing reports, but then that started to drive me crazy, so I dragged myself to my off-campus gym for a workout

Just as I was finishing my workout, I smelled wood burning, but didn't think anything of it. When I walked into the locker room, I found it filled with smoke. I'm such a New Yorker that, in spite of the fact that I could neither breath, nor see, I considered taking a shower before going home. When the firefighters came in, I decided it would have been awkward to be naked, while they were doing their job, so I grabbed my stuff from my locker and started toward the door. That's when I realized you can only go so long without breathing, and I began breathing the smoky air.

I made it to the front desk, where everyone had congregated. I overheard someone saying the elevator was shut down. That made sense, but I didn't know how to get out of the building. Then it hit me that I didn't see anyone leaving. This being China, I could imagine there were no emergency exits. A worker came with a flashlight to help me get dressed. When I was done, I asked him how to get out. "You want to get out?" he asked in Chinese, as if he expected I might say, "No."

"Yes, I'd like to leave the burning building," I confirmed. By this time, smoke was filling the reception area. He led me out a backdoor, past a fire wall, to an emergency elevator. As I got in the elevator, I realized I was the only person leaving. I can't imagine that in Chinese culture you just remain in a burning building.

•·•·•·•

In class, I always put my recording device on the desk, where the teacher could see it. But I knew I'd never listen to the playback, so it was seldom even turned on. In China, however, it was important to make a good show of things. That day, the lecture was uncharacteristically interesting. The teacher spent about an hour breaking down the characters in the Chinese words "sports education," making a story about each character, and each component of the words. It was a real eye-opener into how the Chinese perceive their language, and why I believed that almost no foreigner had ever become truly fluent.

In the rest of the lecture, the word *fāzhǎn* ("development") featured prominently. Chinese love this word, and any time they talked about the United States, they inevitably said that the US was *fēicháng fāzhǎn de* ("very developed"). *Fāzhǎn* was also one of the government buzzwords driving the economy and the population. A billboard near the highway entrance read *gèng duō jīhuì duō hǎo fāzhǎn*, "With more opportunity comes more development." If China had a Spider-Man, I bet that would have been his catchphrase.

Professor Dai sent word via a classmate that I needed to start preparing my dissertation defense. The Korean student I'd watched squirming in front of the committee last term, unable to answer their questions, had failed. I was a little scared.

Several of my classmates told me that they wanted me to organize English speaking classes for them. They were all doing research in English, so I told them to bring their research and we could discuss their research or I'd help them translate it. They immediately counter-argued: "No research! We only want conversation."

Since coming to Asia, I'd fought the same battle again and again. Students, and often their parents, would say: "We don't need grammar and exercises, just conversation." But there's no such thing as just doing conversation. You have to have a book or an article or something to work from. Just sitting there and having a conversation doesn't work. Also, there were eight of them. How do you make a conversation with eight people? And one more thing, they were asking me to teach them English because they didn't speak English. If they didn't speak English, how could we just have a conversation for two hours? Fortunately, for me, they never brought up the subject again. I found out later that Professor Dai had told them to ask me to teach them English. And now they had. And I'd said, more or less, "Yes." So we'd all done our duty and were off the hook now.

At wrestling practice, every day, while my teammates were playing ball or some type of warmup game, I did my *jīběngōng*. The benefits of these basic wrestling exercises were becoming apparent when I found myself able to resist leg sweeps more easily. In addition to *jīběngōng*, I also arranged some additional wrestling sessions with my teammates He Yi and Wang Yechao, both of whom refused money for their tutelage. Both said that they had to test for the police soon and welcomed the opportunity to get in better shape. And so, we started training together twice a week.

I told He Yi that, while I was getting better and better at defending takedowns, most of my takedowns came from reversals. I explained to him that I hoped I'd be able to be more aggressive and proactive, strike first, and go in and take the opponent down. He told me that this was normal. He said that when they'd learned wrestling, they first learned to defend takedowns, then reversals, and finally how to attack.

After wrestling, I gathered up the courage to go talk with one of the guys from the judo team. He told me they trained six hours per day, and he put me in side control and I absolutely couldn't move or escape. In judo, he only needed to hold me there for 25 seconds to win. In a way, that was easier than a pin because the opponent could still be fighting, and not have both shoulder blades down, but if he's unable to stand or escape, it's a win.

A new *Star Wars* movie had just come out and I organized a group of international students to go see it. Cultures are different everywhere, and apparently, in some countries, it was normal to just talk all through the movie. This African girl, sitting next to me was just talking and talking, as if the movie wasn't even playing. But when Harrison Ford walked out on screen, she immediately shouted excitedly, "I know that actor!" She just looked so happy to see him, as was I, so I gave her a pass for talking through the first part of the movie. But then she said, "I know him. He's Indiana Jones." And I started cracking up. First, it was flattering and somehow endearing that a young woman from Africa knew the *Indiana Jones* movie franchise that had meant so much to me thirty years earlier, before she was even born. On the other hand, she hadn't mentioned *Star Wars*, and seemed genuinely surprised that Harrison Ford was in this film. I guess she didn't know about *Star Wars* and that this was the first *Star Wars* movie she'd seen, which made me wonder how someone would interpret it without prior knowledge. I couldn't see how the movie would make sense on its own.

The next day, I needed to go downtown and get some videos. Shanghai's subway is far more modern than New York's, but the behavior of the people riding it often made traveling a terrible experience. There were platform doors which only opened when the train arrived. I was standing in front of the door, waiting for the train to come, but I'd mistakenly left a few inches between me and the door. Consequently, a man and his wife, and all their bags and boxes, squeezed between me and the door, getting in front of me. It didn't really matter who got on the train first, but I just wondered, had they not seen me waiting for the train? Did they think I was standing there for some other reason? Or did they just not care about anyone else? And another question: Why did so many people on Shanghai's subway have fifty bags, crates, and boxes?

In Shanghai, people hawk and spit in the subway. In Taiwan, by contrast, you aren't allowed to eat, drink, or even chew gum. I was always amazed when I saw cops writing someone a ticket in Shanghai's subway, because I couldn't imagine what type of bad behavior was actually illegal. Pushing people aside so you could take their seat, blocking the entrance or exit, shouting, screaming, talking loudly on a cellphone, eating, carrying live chickens or crates of fruit, watching movies or playing videos games without headphones, and letting infants pee and poop, all seemed acceptable. So what exactly had these people done that was against the law?

Waiting to get on the subway one time, I had to step out of line and wait somewhere else because the woman next to me kept hawking and spitting. I was afraid I'd vomit, and I wasn't sure if that was a ticketable offense.

When I got back to the dorm, a Vietnamese classmate asked me to edit a letter of recommendation letter, written by her professor of Marxist Thought in Vietnam, so she could get a scholarship to study in China for a Ph.D. in Marxist Thought. As I read it, I wondered if she actually believed in Marxism, or if she was just seizing on an opportunity. Part of the letter talked about socialist economics, which I feel is an oxymoron. It was also riddled with communist buzzwords like "benefit the society… zealous… deeper understanding of socialist imparities… perpetual revolution."

Vietnam is somewhat repressive politically, but even poor Vietnamese people can afford to take a bus to Cambodia, Laos, or even Thailand and see another way of life. Also, internet censorship isn't as extreme in Vietnam as in China. So I wonder if the average Vietnamese citizen believes less of the socialist rhetoric he's fed compared to the average Chinese person.

Every time we presented a paper at school, other students were called upon to criticize the presenter. The word they used in Chinese doesn't translate as "critique," but actually as "criticize." And when you were called on to criticize someone, you had to do it. Usually, someone was grading your criticism of the other student. And if he was told to criticize your criticism, then he'd find fault with it. This may sound crazy to Western ears, but actually it helped students see if they'd betrayed the ideals of the revolution, and were in danger of becoming revisionists or enemies of the people.

In one class, I had to present a source review of technical analysis of Chinese wrestling, and my professor required us to bring a Chinese friend to class to criticize our presentation. I got one of my friends, Zhang Chengfeng, who wasn't an athlete, to come and criticize me. Just as a joke, the final slide of my Powerpoint had a picture of me choking my teammate, Zheng Tong. The caption read: "Thank you for listening. If you criticize me, I'll wrestle you."

Ignoring the warning, my otherwise very meek and kind friend became some sort of demon. He ripped into me and tore me apart in front of the class. Afterward, when I sat down next to him, he said, "You were the best one."

In the entire university, only three classrooms — the ones used for first-year Chinese language students — had heating. Once you'd begun your major, you sat through boring lectures in the freezing cold. I always felt like Bob Cratchit in those classes, sitting on my hands, trying to keep them warm. Once in a while, I'd brave the cold to write a few notes, then quickly sit on my hands again. But they say that hypothermia builds character.

After sitting in class, wearing four layers of clothing and a hat and a coat, I'd walk over to the unheated training hall, and it'd take forever to warm up. I had to be careful to get there early so I wouldn't be tempted to jump in and begin wrestling before my body was ready. There were days where the temperature inside the training hall was only ten degrees Celsius (50 degrees Fahrenheit).

I always started a warmup wearing all of my clothes. Then I'd slowly strip off, layer by layer, as my body got warmer. Finally, I'd be down to my shorts and a T-shirt, and sweating. At that point, I was ready to wrestle. The whole process could take as long as 45 minutes.

Once I started sweating, I couldn't slow down again, or my sweat would make me freeze. After training, I had to put all my clothes back on my soaking wet, sweaty, stinking body, just to walk the 300 meters (less than a fifth of a mile) back to the dorm. And my sweatshirts had to be washed every day, because they soaked up the icy sweat from my body.

I was doing almost all my strength and conditioning training at my off-campus gym, because it was heated and there were showers. As bad as this was, the Chinese students had it worse. Their dorms had neither heating, nor AC, nor showers. Wow! *Hěn fāzhǎn de* (Very developed!)

·•●•·

Michael, the American student, told me that both AJ and his friend, who I'll refer to as "Dave," were on the verge of dropping out. AJ was complaining that he couldn't get good martial arts training at SUS. Dave, by contrast, just didn't seem serious. Although he'd been in China for several years before beginning the program, Dave didn't speak any Mandarin. He also stopped going to Chinese classes in the second week of the semester. Ironically, Dave's major was Sports Journalism, which required him to pass the HSK-6, the highest-level Chinese language exam, by the time he graduated, and to write at the level of a native speaker of Chinese. I told Michael, "It takes native speakers about 22 years to get to that level."

At that point, I'd written about eight papers in Chinese and done six presentations. The two papers I'd submitted for publication had both been rejected. And if it hadn't been for Google Translate, I wouldn't have got as far as I had. Even then, my papers had to be edited, not only for grammar and vocabulary, but also for syntax, because there Chinese people express certain concepts in very specific ways that foreigners — even those who know a lot about the language — aren't likely to know. I admitted to Michael, "I'm confident I'll continue to improve, but I'll never be able to just sit down and write a finished paper in Chinese."

I just didn't see how Dave was going to pass a journalism exam which about 40 percent of Chinese native speakers failed. Dave's story reaffirmed how skewed the average person's perception of language learning is. Most likely, when Dave called home, his family believed that his proposed program was completely doable, and that in two years of studying at SUS, he'd become fluent because he was immersed — "the myth of immersion" once again.

My Mongolian friend, Zolar, was a successful language learner. When school first started, I wanted so much to be friends with the Mongolian students, because I was fascinated by their country and wanted to live there some day. (I didn't know it then, of course, but about six years later, I'd be happily living and wrestling in the land of Genghis Khan.) The big Mongolian wrestler, Bata and I became friends, because we wrestled together, and he spoke Mongolian. The others, particularly Zolar, were super nice, and wanted to be friends, but they couldn't speak Chinese.

Usually, the Mongolian students would try to room together. Zolar, by luck of the draw, was assigned to one of the few three-person rooms along with a Thai and a Vietnamese. Because they had no common language, they were all forced to learn Mandarin and to use it every day. It also helped that they were all friendly individuals who wanted to converse with one another, rather than just keeping to themselves when they were in their room. Consequently, about eight months into the academic year, all three of them were at least conversant in Chinese. They'd definitely learned it faster and better than any of the others who'd started back in September.

Once, I stopped by to visit Zolar we had a normal conversation in Mandarin for about thirty minutes. He then looked over at the clock and excused himself, saying it was his study time. He and his roommates all kept to a strict schedule for studying Chinese.

Another foreigner who spoke amazing Mandarin was a second-year master's degree student from Ghana called Eric. He'd already passed HSK-5. I told him about how disciplined Zolar and his roommates were and about the hours I'd put in and the private tutors I'd hired. He got very excited and nearly yelled: "You have to do that. The university's Chinese classes are useless. You have to do it on your own." He said it took hundreds of hours of efforts. Similarly, a Czech student, told me that to pass HSK-5, he'd done roughly eight hours per day of self-study.

·•●··

I ran over to the on-campus weight room, to squeeze in a workout before it closed. While I was working out, a kid walked up to me, called me by name, and then, in Tarzan English, began asking me about MMA. I answered him in Mandarin, hoping he'd speak to me normally, but he kept talking to me like Ruprecht The Monkey Boy. I asked how he knew I was involved with MMA and if we'd met before. He replied that he'd seen me on Weixin (Chinese social media). On his phone, he showed me a photo my teammate Zheng Tong had posted of me choking him out. It'd been seen all over the campus.

On Tuesday, I went to wrestling practice and found my teammates playing soccer. A friend tried to convince me that soccer could benefit my wrestling. He said: "You get a lot out of incorporating other sports into your training." I told him, "I incorporate sanda, traditional wrestling, freestyle wrestling, and MMA. That's enough." Truth be told, I hated non-fighting sports. I can neither throw nor catch a ball. I'm the only American unable to play baseball, American football, or basketball, who's never watched a full game of any of those on TV, has never played a game, has never cared to play a game, and would be reticent to play a game if it meant saving the lives of orphans being held hostage. I started boxing and kickboxing at the age of 12 and those were the only sports I did for most of my life, except for a brief foray into swimming and triathlon when I was young. So I just did my *jībĕngōng* exercises by myself. Normally, at some point, my three best friends from the team — Yang Wenbin, Zheng Tong, and Wang Yechao — would come over and wrestle with me for 45 minutes.

Unfortunately, Yang Wenbin and Zheng Tong were absent. Wang Ye-chao was there, but because he had a date after practice, he said he didn't want to break a sweat. Chinese students were only allowed to shower at certain times, and he wouldn't have been able to shower after practice. He even apologized to me. He was an excellent friend.

Checking my email after class, I found another of these maddening messages from a random Chinese person who wanted to get to know some foreigners. Someone named Li had written me via QQ, a Chinese instant messaging app.

Li: Where do you come from?

Me: Have we met?

Li: No.

Li: I am Chinese

Li: I am a student

Me: How did you get my QQ ID?

Li: Sorry my English is not good.

Me: Then why would you write to me?

Li: Yes, I write to you.

Me: No, I mean, if I don't know you, and you don't speak English, why would you want to write to me?

Li: You help me better my English

Me: Sorry, I really don't see what's in it for me.

Li: Yes, you.

Me: No, I mean, I don't see why I would want to talk to you.

Li: Help me, my English

Me: Sorry, I don't have time for this.

Li: I don't waste your time

Me: Yes, you do. Messaging me wastes my time.

I closed QQ and watched a documentary about Judd Reid, the first foreigner to complete the 1,000-day-long "Young Lions" karate training program in Japan. The kyokushin episode of *Martial Arts Odyssey* was the most painful one we ever shot, and I left with tremendous respect for kyokushin black belts. What Reid endured, all day, every day, seven days a week for three years, was an inspiration. He'd promised his teacher that he'd complete the program, win the world championship — which he did in 2010 — and then fight a 100-man kumite, which he wound up doing a few years later. This inspired me to try and arrange a kumite. I called the MMA coach and asked him, since Bred Schroed had pulled out of my fight, if he could set me up with a whole bunch of opponents on the same evening instead. A date was set and tickets were sold. So now I was preparing to fight again.

Professor Dai's question — is Shaolin Kung Fu only at Shaolin Temple? — led me to believe that it was not. Was it also in Cambodia? Was bokator somehow related? What about Judd Reid? He'd done a Japanese martial art and had dedicated himself entirely to the perfection of it. Was that Shaolin Kung Fu? Writing papers, MMA, wrestling, studying Chinese, watching *Star Wars*, getting ready for a fight... I had no idea if any of this was leading toward an understanding of what Shaolin Kung Fu is, or if it was all distracting me from finding the answer to the question.

Chapter 10
The Fight

The party and Chinese government will continue to attach great importance to politics and ideology, so the political function of sports in China will not suddenly disappear.

—Bi Shiming,
"Academic Propositions Lacking Science and Rationality,"
Journal of Tianjin Institute of Sport **(Vol. 3, 2007)**

I was late to wrestling practice. Just as I walked in, the team was heading out the door, to play basketball against the tai chi majors. Luckily, the coach had left two guys behind with orders to wrestle me. One was Zheng Tong; the other was Jing Pusu, the only member of the team I'd never spoken to. We wrestled for about forty minutes, then rested and hung out. Both of them expressed some regrets at having grown up in sports schools, as they might not qualify for a good job after graduation.

I was thinking about Kirk, my Canadian wrestling friend. He was 42 and hadn't wrestled in twenty years, and yet none of my teammates could take him down. On top of that, he had a bachelor's degree and a teaching license. In Shanghai, he had a great job at an international school, earning much more than I made as a university lecturer. This reaffirmed my belief that North America led the world in striking a balance between sports performance and education, producing top athletes who also had brains and job skills.

My teammates described their classes to me. They seemed to get very little in the way of academics, but had a lot of sports classes. While I had to write multiple reports per course, they would be expected to write one very minimal undergraduate thesis just before graduating. I jokingly said: "I write more Chinese reports than you guys." They both laughed, but then Zheng Tong said, with a note of sadness in his voice, "I can't write a report."

A few times Zheng Tong had stopped by my room, and I'd asked him to help proofread some presentations I was working on. He'd told me that he didn't know all of the Chinese words on my slides. This was particularly alarming since the slides were about wrestling, the one thing he was really good at.

I told Zheng Tong that when I first met him, in sanda class, I thought his name was Zhengtong Gama, because the sanda teacher was constantly shouting "Zheng Tong, *gànma*?" Gànma means "What are you doing?" I sort of stole this joke from an old Richard Pryor routine where he said that, while he was growing up, he thought his name was Richard-damnit, because his father was always yelling "Richard, damn it!"

The team finished their basketball and a few of them came to sit and talk with us. I'd just started back at work and they were asking about my job. Sparing them all of the details, I was teaching weekends in a Japanese school in downtown Shanghai. Meanwhile, Shanghai University had also called me back to my old job, for which I was paid at a part-time rate, which came close to what I'd earned on my full-time contract, but without paid leave and holidays.

As soon as you tell Chinese people you're working, they want to know how much money you're making. If I said something like, "I'd rather not say," they'd insist, "But we're all friends." When I first came to China, I tried lying and saying I earned a typical Chinese salary, but then they'd get angry at me, "You should be making much more than that." Also, they'd lose respect for me, because they thought I was a low-earner. But telling them my actual wage wasn't be good either, as what I earned per hour usually exceeded their daily wage. So I often weaseled out of telling my teammates my salary, and asked them if they were working.

One of my teammates was bouncer in a bar. He worked from 6 p.m. to 3 a.m. and earned RMB 200 (US$ 32) — pretty good money for a student. Another teammate was working at McDonald's, where he got RMB 12 an hour, so less than RMB 100 for a full shift. The bouncer told me that the manager of the bouncers got RMB 800 for each bouncer he hired. The manager kept RMB 600 of this, paying the bouncers the remaining RMB 200. I'd see this employment model repeated time and time again in China, but I could never figure out how to become the guy who hires and pays everyone else.

I ran back to the dorm, took a shower, grabbed my folder and headed over to a Ph.D. class where I had to give a presentation titled "A Comparison of Shaolin Kung Fu and Cambodian Traditional Martial Art: Bokator." Watching students from various countries present, it hit me that Americans are taught to give presentations, but people from most other countries don't seem to be for some reason. Regardless of where they came from, most students just droned on, making no attempt to be interesting, to attract the viewers' attention, or to interact with the audience. In the US, we're taught that you have to win the audience over. You talk to, not at, the audience. You have to be entertaining or people won't listen. In Asia, the audience is required to sit there. And no one cares if they enjoy themselves or even if they pay attention.

After my presentation, the teacher concluded "We Chinese people are not good at presentations."

Talking to my classmates, professors, and others, it was amazing how often, in casual conversation, Chinese people began their sentence with

Wǒmen zhōngguó rén ("We Chinese people…"), as if all 1.3 billion of them had the same abilities or the same opinions. Sometimes they even followed this with a basic statement of preference like, "We Chinese people like vanilla more than chocolate." I could never decide if people were authorized to speak for the whole country or if they all attended meetings where they were told: "If someone asks you which flavor of ice cream you like, tell them 'We all like vanilla.'"

While my Mongolian classmate was walking back to the dorm with me, I asked him to comment on the insane but true story I'd read about Taiwan's government — which for decades had regarded Mongolia as part of the Nationalist Republic of China — accepting Mongolia's independence in 2002. He flipped a double bird and shouted in English, "F---them!" I imagine that, before 2002, most Mongolians didn't even know they were part of Taiwan.

On the way to eat, I was wondering if I could get a list of new students who'd started this semester. Some of them probably hadn't seen my wrestling medal yet.

·•●•·

Food had been a problem ever since I arrived at SUS. The lack of green vegetables and fruit made me worry I'd develop scurvy. Luckily, two Family Mart convenience stores near the university sold salads. I'd been eating salads and hot bento-box lunches with vegetables every day. Most fruit vendors sold fruit that was horrible yet very expensive; I'd get it home and have to discard about 40 percent of it right away. Finally, I found a vendor I could trust, and for a short while I had both salad and fruit.

Sadly, nothing in China ever lasts. During my time at SUS, the Family Marts often went days at a time without getting salad deliveries. Shops in China had an incredibly high turnover rate. My fruit vendor closed down, and it was a few months before another one opened. That one wasn't good, and it also closed. Over the course of a year, maybe 70 percent of shops on any given street would go out of business. In the second year of my studies, the university supermarket closed, taking with it the only ATM machine on campus. It was ten months until it reopened. Finding healthy food in China was a challenge which I never fully overcame. If you're done with your pork grease, do you mind if I dip my bread in it?

The next morning, traveling downtown to teach at the Japanese school, the subway was packed beyond belief, as it was every Saturday morning. I almost never got a seat. When I complained that they should have more trains on weekends, people told me: "They can't have more trains, because there aren't enough passengers on weekends." I countered that with: "Well, if there aren't enough passengers, why can't I get a seat?"

That evening, I had wrestling with Wang Yechao. The Greco-Roman team was training on the other side of the mats, and amazingly, their coach was sitting there smoking. I started wrestling, and I was gasping for breath. I wondered if I should stop, drop, and roll.

In MMA and BJJ the first two takedowns you generally learn are the low single-leg on one knee and the low double-leg on two knees. I'd never liked either of these takedowns, because they're too easy to stuff, and if you get caught, you're at a serious disadvantage on your knees. When I wrestled with my team, I hardly ever saw the guys shoot a low single on one knee and had never seen them shoot a double on two knees. I asked Wang Yechao about it, and he told me that almost the whole team came from a Greco background, so none of them were as good at those techniques as a freestyle wrestling team would be. In Greco, touching the legs is illegal.

Over a period of months, Wang Yechao told me repeatedly that Zheng Tong was the most knowledgeable and best wrestler on our team. Zheng Tong was one of the few who'd been in sports schools his entire education, starting with elementary school. Most of the others, it turned out, didn't switch to sports school until they were in junior high or high school. Zheng Tong had more than 12 years of wrestling under his belt. And, sadly, Wang

Yechao also told me, Zheng Tong was about to get kicked out of the university because he had a GPA of zero.

My big fight night was coming soon. Every time, counting down to the days and hours till the fight, I always got oddly nostalgic, thinking back to my most important coaches and teachers, all of the way back to my first martial arts teacher, H. David Collins in Tennessee. On fight day, I always went through my pre-fight ritual, watching the documentary *Facing Ali*. He was The Greatest of All Time, and will be remembered across the ages

On fight night, several of the international students and a few of my Chinese classmates went with me. Greg turned up, as did Li Laoshi, my HSK teacher.

Originally, I'd wanted a kumite-style fight with an insane number of opponents, fighting a fresh one each round. Instead, I wound up with four opponents: Three of them were professional fighters, and if you added any two of their ages together, I was still older. It wasn't the epic event I'd hoped for, but it was a great experience. I learned a lot and, if nothing else, I learned that doing a 100-man kumite would take at least a year of solid prep.

I fought two pro Chinese sanda guys under sanda rules. The only time I'd ever fought sanda was the one time at Shaolin Temple. To fight real pros was exciting. I couldn't believe how hard they could kick with their straight kicks and sidekicks. I thanked God that ever since I'd started doing MMA, I'd carried my guard extremely high and even braced my hands on my forehead. As a result, I was able to absorb kicks that would have killed me if they'd hit my head.

Obviously, I couldn't beat them at sanda, but I was able to get past most of their deadly powerful kicks and take them down. This meant, if I'd been facing a sanda guy in MMA, I should be able to get him to the ground. Also, I was able to close the distance and completely smother them with my clinch, which would have resulted in a takedown, except that in sanda the referee breaks you after three seconds. So, if it'd been MMA, I'd have completed most of these takedowns. Even with the three-second rule, I took both opponents down, but they never took me down.

Next, I fought a Westerner in MMA. When the referee yelled, "Fight!" I charged across the ring, and instantly got a body lock on my opponent, without taking any damage. The only reason it took a bit of time to get him to the ground was because he was holding on to the ropes, which is illegal. This is another reason I hate fighting in a boxing ring, rather than in a cage. It seemed like a long time to me, but I got him down pretty quickly to ground and pound him.

Because this was a relaxed-rules kumite, the ref asked me if I wanted to just let him up and restart in standing, giving the audience something to watch, rather than just laying on top, pounding him till he tapped. I agreed. We stood up, and the second takedown went even faster than the first. One of my strikes had clearly broken his nose and I didn't wish to continue, because it wasn't a professional fight. I'd taken him down twice, pinned him, and pounded him, without getting hit even once, and I saw no way that he was going to escape, particularly with a broken nose. Reading the situation the same way, the ref asked if we should stop, I said "Yes," and the opponent said something like, "Well, if you want to stop, we can."

In the final match, I fought against one of the pro sanda guys in Western boxing — and I have to admit it: I'd forgotten how to box. Dirty boxing is an important component of MMA, but it's illegal in boxing. For the previous nine months, I'd concentrated almost exclusively on wrestling and the wrestling component of sanda. And it showed. I felt really confident about my wrestling, but I thought I should go train with a boxing coach for a while if I planned to do any professional MMA fights.

In the end, these "fights" were more like hard sparring than actual fights. Also, I only fought four opponents. It wasn't the level of personal challenge I'd envisioned, but it was a start. A lot of people at the event, and online, said that I was representing old guys everywhere. That was one of the reasons I chose to wear a Captain America T-shirt, because he's the oldest mortal Avenger. Randy

Couture, one of my wrestling/MMA heroes, who was still winning world titles at my age, also had the secondary nickname of Captain America.

As much as it felt good to wear my Captain America T-shirt while fighting, I couldn't but help noticing how much the emblem on the chest looked like a bull's eye. As I'd also worn Khmer shorts, out of respect for my Cambodian bokator teacher, I came up with the name Captain Khmerican.

Each time I completed a takedown, my HSK Chinese teacher, Li Laoshi, yelled *Hěn lihai!* which basically means "Very fierce!" Afterward, she told me she'd loved the sanda — which I'd done just OK at — but she didn't like the MMA which I dominated. She said, "I guess you were tired during the MMA, so you just laid on top of your opponent."

Greg was covering the fight for a magazine. Afterward, he asked me, "What was that thing the other coach kept yelling while you were fighting?"

I thought a minute. "Was it *fànguī*? They yell that a lot when I fight. It means 'You broke the rules.'" He wrote that in his notebook and then asked the meaning of *sǎotǐ*. I began laughing, "It means sweep the leg." All I could think of was *The Karate Kid*: "Sweep the leg, Johnny."

One Chinese classmate paid me the best compliment. After the fight, he sent me a text in English which read, "You really are the Captain of America."

That night in bed, reflecting on my fights, I was thinking about a friend of mine, Will "The Kill" Chope, fighting bare-knuckle in Burma and Japan, and wondering what that must be like. With my style of dirty-boxing and MMA, the smaller MMA gloves definitely worked better for me than the larger boxing gloves. But I thought bare-knuckle would work even better, since I didn't usually have to take too many hits, and of course, I could wrestle better with bare hands. If you think about transitioning to a street fight, in a street fight you don't wear gloves but you wear shoes. This is exactly how I wrestled. And being able to wear shoes would really make my kicks that much more painful. And close-in dirty boxing would work better bare-fisted, because bare knuckles slip through an opponent's guard much more easily.

The next morning, I arrived at my 9:45 a.m. class early to set up my recorder, because I was supposed to give a presentation. No one else was there. Finally, at about 9:45 a.m. my Singaporean classmate showed up. He checked his phone: At 9:01 a.m., he'd received a message telling him class had been changed to 9 a.m. and to a different building, so we went there. I'd not been notified at all, and as none of the other foreign students attended, I guess they also didn't receive any word of the change.

The teacher scolded us for being late, but allowed me to give my presentation, which I thankfully received a good mark on. Afterward, I had to stop by and see my advisor. He'd just read a paper I'd written. When I came in his office, he handed me an article and said, "Try to write more like this one next time."

"I wish I could," I thought to myself.

Next was a horribly boring three-hour graduate lecture. The classroom wasn't heated, so each Thursday morning I sat there wearing everything I owned. The lecturer stressed how important it was to go into the field and do research. This was a bit ironic, as about thirty percent of the students in the class were foreign. Technically, we were already in the field doing research.

After that lecture I had wrestling class, where my teammates had to practice being referees, judges, scorer, and timekeepers for an upcoming high-school wrestling tournament. Because this was a sports university, and not just a training facility, my teammates were actually graded on their wrestling class, and had to pass exams. As it was assumed they'd go on to be coaches, one thing they had to do was learn to run tournaments for their students.

Each morning, the first half hour or so of practice was a sort of classroom setting where my teammates learned the details of running a wrestling event. I usually showed up late and did my *jīběngōng* exercises till they'd finished.

In the second half of class, some of us had to wrestle tournament-style, while the rest practiced running the tournament. It was awesome. I wrestled two full, official freestyle matches, back-to-back, with no rest. The first one was against one of my largest and strongest teammates, who'd done Greco-Roman for years at sports school. He beat me, but it was a good match. My second match was against a 19-year-old freshman who'd lived in sports schools throughout his education. I'm not sure if he'd learned Greco or freestyle. Not only did I win, but I won by a lot.

Yang Wenbin, one of my best friends on the team, had worked with me for one very long day, on ground fighting, and how to get the reversals and earn points on the ground. He also taught me to roll the opponent over when he was laying on his belly. In wrestling, guys lay on their belly to avoid the pin. In MMA, this is exactly where you want them. But in wrestling, you need to learn to roll them over to get the win. It all paid off that day.

The funny thing about my experiences at SUS is how significant they felt to me at the time, and how interesting or unusual they'd sound to others years later, but how normal this all was for my teammates. They'd had countless mock tournaments over the years, but didn't remember the outcomes, or even the events themselves, because it was just a very small and ordinary part of their lives. Once again, I was reminded that this was their world, and as much as I wanted to feel I was one of them, I was just a tourist. Like with linguistics, it was the myth of immersion.

Later, I was supposed to be working on a source review for my dissertation, but when I went to get a Coke from my freezer, I realized the freezer wasn't closing right. After several minutes' inspection, I discovered there was ice buildup. This kept the freezer open, letting air in, causing condensation, which then froze and added to the problem.

I began chopping ice with a knife, but that wasn't getting me anywhere, so I boiled pot after pot of water to melt the ice. Then I had to clean the wet floor... At some point, I must have been abducted by aliens, because several hours passed without me knowing. When I realized that it was dark outside, it occurred to me that I'd made no progress on my dissertation.

Determined to catch up, I sat down, wrote for about ten minutes, then realized I hadn't eaten. I went down to the street to buy some barbecue. Just as the vendor handed me my skewers of meat, I heard a little kid yelling "*Tāmen láile! Tāmen láile!*" (They're coming! They're coming!). The street vendors ran for cover as two police vans rolled up. I was going to stay around and see what happened to the vendors, but decided to escape, lest my dinner be impounded as evidence.

Back in my room, dinner eaten, I received an email from my Ph.D. advisor: "That must take great efforts to listen to criticism, and strive to achieve great progress." Even if you didn't agree, you certainly couldn't disagree.

The next day, one of my graduate lectures was supposed to end at 11:15 a.m., but the teacher always talked way past the bell. It sounded like he was winding down and I thought today might be the day we finished on time. He hit a logical place to stop for the day. It was 11:14 a.m. and he made a short joke. We all chuckled obediently, and I thought: "Hey, this guy isn't so bad. He's going to let us go." Then he turned to the class leader and said, "Please refill my tea." It took him another twenty minutes to drink that tea and finish lecturing.

In the next class, we had a visiting lecturer who'd done part of her studies in the US. When she saw that I was the only foreigner, she asked, in English "How good is your Chinese?" This was such a common way that people had of evaluating my Chinese, by asking me in English. Oddly, in the many years that I'd been teaching, we were never told to evaluate a student's English by asking them in some other language how well they spoke English. Wouldn't it have made more sense to ask me in Chinese? Or better, just to talk to me in Chinese and see if I understood? Or, and I know this is a long shot, make an assumption that, since I was already there, in the Ph.D. program, and she was just a guest who'd never be coming again, she could just assume that I belonged there and she could just go about her business and lecture as usual.

Not only was this an irrational way to evaluate my Chinese level, but regardless of how I answered, how would she have used this information? If I'd said that I don't speak Mandarin well, or that my Chinese is excellent, would she have altered her lecture?

My American friend texted me from inside his class saying, "The teacher just gave us a 15-minute lecture on why the people in Tibet and Xinjiang are bad, because they broke from the greater Chinese family."

In another class, one of our professors told us that his total compensation at the university, counting allowances and salary was RMB 9,000 (US$ 1,430) per month, which wasn't too bad for China, where the average annual income was about US$ 10,000 per year. But it had taken him years to arrive at that income. Beginning monthly salaries for junior professors in China were US$ 300 to 500. The more senior a professor became, the better chance he or she had of earning additional money by sitting on boards and committees, sometimes at other universities. They also received cash bonuses for publishing papers; this created an entire industry of paid journals. Professors paid to have their papers published, then received a bonus from the university which exceeded the cost of publishing.

These cash bonuses were one of the many reasons why China was leading the world in the number of papers published, but not quality academic papers or in innovation. Professors and students were motivated to publish anything, even terrible rehashes or plagiarized papers which had been done countless times before. The cost of publishing depended on the prestige of the journal, and the bonus paid to the professor depended on his or her prestige. More senior professors could afford to publish in the better journals, paying higher fees but also receiving larger bonuses.

My classmates were always amazed when I told them that I was paid for my articles. One of them said, "It doesn't work like that here. You have to be rich to publish in China."

· · ● · ·

Once, I was heading to the main shopping street when it began to rain. I ducked down a back alley I'd never been down before. It turned out to lead past the SUS faculty dorms.

The junior professors were living in the most disgusting conditions I'd seen since leaving Shaolin Temple in 2003. There was a communal kitchen with a smashed door, so it didn't lock and I could see inside. It looked as though animals had been nesting in there, with fur, feathers, and filth covering every inch of counter space. I just couldn't see how humans could cook or eat in there. Next, I was overwhelmed by the smell of urine and realized I was walking past the communal toilet. One of the junior professors had told me that they lived two or three to a room. Of course, they didn't have AC or heating.

The junior professors lived marginally better than their Chinese students, but much worse than foreign students. And the monthly stipend paid to foreign doctoral students was on par with a junior professor's salary.

Obviously, no one would have chosen to live in these dorms unless it was absolutely necessary. Real-estate prices in Shanghai, however, meant that those on a junior professor's salary had no other choice. And, of course, in China you're expected to own an apartment before getting married. This was becoming a problem, because fewer young men could afford apartments and it was getting harder for people to·marry.

To move up the social ladder and to achieve a reasonable quality of life, professors worked hard to increase their income. Senior professors could turn in receipts and claim for expenses; this created another industry of providing receipts. It was not uncommon for a professor who did you a favor to call and ask if you could bring him or her all your receipts, so they could claim them. Often, people who helped me with research or editing asked me to bring them receipts. One professor hired me to proofread a dissertation. He then asked me to bring him my receipts; after claiming them as his own expenses, he used the money to pay me.

It seemed that the wushu professors were luckier than many others, because they could earn money as members of the Wu Shu Federation. They got paid to judge or referee at tournaments, or as organizers and executives of the federation. And, of course, they could earn money teaching martial arts. Several of the professors had teaching contracts with public high schools or elementary schools. They'd select their leading students, pay them a small amount of money, and send them to do the actual teaching. The professors would then make a big show of visiting the school a few times each year. On those occasions, they'd teach special classes and monitor training, but the key work was maintaining the relationship and renewing the contract.

There were rumors that some professors accepted bribes from students, and that when graduate students received research money, they were expected to turn it over to their professor. However, I never saw this with my own eyes.

Once, in my first semester, I thought that I needed to do what I'd heard other students did: Stop by my advisor's office and give him a bottle of liquor. Fortunately, I bumped into an upper classmate, Han Hongyu, who worked for my advisor. When I told him I was going to give Professor Dai a gift, Han Hongyu became animated: "No! Don't do that. He doesn't accept bribes." I didn't feel good about giving a gift in the first place, and I was so glad to have dodged a bullet on this, but now I also felt embarrassed.

After I graduated SUS, I immediately entered the Ph.D. program at the School of Economics, Shanghai University. My professors there told me similar stories about what was referred to as fractional salary. Even after twenty years on the job, a professor's actual salary may still have been under US$ 1,000 a month, but they received other payments, bonuses, and allowances which combined gave them a livable wage. One of the new doctoral candidates in the School of Economics listed her job as economics professor, and all of the classmates were amazed. When they asked her how she could be an economics professor without a Ph.D. in the field, she explained that there was a shortage of economics professors and that the standard at the university had been lowered in order to fill every position. Our advisor, Dong Laoshi seconded this. He explained that, in Shanghai, some economics Ph.D. holders earned US$ 10,000 per month working for banks: "Who'd choose to be a professor and be poor for the rest of their life?"

Dong Laoshi told us that he'd become a professor before the economic reforms. At that time, his stipend as a Ph.D. candidate was several times what his friends earned in full-time jobs. At SUS, Professor Dai had told us similar stories about how bad things were before the economy was opened up. Everyone was so poor that being a professor was much better. Professors earned more than workers and didn't have to toil in a factory or on a farm. But eventually private-sector jobs, particularly in IT and finance, began paying dramatically more. And so all of my professors had developed multiple side-hustles in order to survive.

Having said all of this, at the end of my seven years in China, having myself been a professor who studied in two Ph.D. programs at two different universities, I don't think I got the whole picture. The faculty parking lot at SUS was full of American and German cars. These cars cost dramatically more in China than they did in the US. Another time, I was at a faculty lunch with Professor Dai and several high-ranking professors from other universities. Dai told me, "My daughter is studying at Hunter College, New York City." I told him that my mother and grandmother had both graduated from there. Then the professor sitting next to him told me his daughter was studying in Alabama. Next thing I knew, every professor at the table told me that one — and, in some cases, two — of their children were studying in the US. During the rest of my tenure in the PRC, whenever a professor found out that I was American, they'd tell me about their children who were studying overseas.

Those foreign-brand cars cost US$ 25,000 or more in China. The professors all owned off-campus apartments. In Shanghai, the average apartment costs over US$ 700,000. And finally, sending a son or daughter to the

US for a four-year degree needs well over US$ 120,000. Given retirement ages in China (55 for women, 60 for men), and that the average Ph.D. graduate is about 29 years old, few professors are likely to work for more than thirty years. Even if they earn a top annual salary of US$ 17,000 for a large part of their career, I really couldn't see how they'd afford the lifestyle they were living. There had to be more to the story.

·· ● ··

On the wrestling team, we were wrestling for the pin. This was a new experience for me, but one I liked, because unlike in Chinese wrestling, which ends when you hit the ground, freestyle wrestling kept me sharp in terms of reacting and trying to get dominant position on the ground. We had a new guy on the team who came from a sports high school known for its high level of training. His Greco-Roman skills were incredible, with all of those classic movements, like lifting his opponent in the air, twisting his body into a corkscrew, and tossing him behind.

Some of the wrestlers were asking me how MMA and wrestling compared, and I told them that a leg has longer travel than a punch. Also, a lot of kickers had some kind of a "tell," a particular movement they did prior to kicking, which could alert you that a kick is coming. A wrestler could capitalize on that tell and take the kicker down. But a good kicker is fast and you won't see it. Also, although I'd been in Asia for 13 years by then, I'd been a boxer for 20 of the years before. My eyes still weren't fully conditioned to seeing kicks and punches coming in at the weird angles that sometimes happen in MMA or sanda. Consequently, my strategy was just to always keep my guard high, and protect my head.

In training, I worked by sense of touch. My MMA coach in Malaysia, for example, would kick me in the head (true story) and when I felt the pain, I just ducked and grabbed his base leg out from under him. We did similar drills on my thighs: When I felt the pain, I ducked, moved in, and took a double leg takedown. So even in cases where they'd seen me catch an opponent's kick, I usually didn't see it coming. I just reacted to the pain. I concluded by telling them, "As we get older, we lose speed, reflexes, and reactions. We have to fight and train much smarter, finding ways to compensate."

In one of my academic classes, I was working on a paper about the correlation between poverty and sports in the US. A Japanese student asked about obesity in North America, and suggested that it was perhaps the result of American genes. I told her: "American isn't a race. There's no American gene. Americans are fat because they eat too much and move too little." Asians often have trouble separating ethnicity from legal citizenship. I heard stories of adopted Chinese babies, coming back to visit China, and no one in China understanding why they couldn't speak Chinese. By the same token, Americans don't understand that they need to eat less and move more. We all have our shortcomings.

Researching differences between poor states and rich states in terms of income and the percentage of obese or overweight people, I discovered that the wealthiest state in 2013 was Maryland, with an average annual income of over US$ 70,000. The poorest state was Mississippi, where income averaged just under US$ 38,000. In Maryland, 27 percent of the population was obese or overweight, while in Mississippi it was 40 percent. This was something my classmates just couldn't accept. In most countries, poor people can't afford to overeat. In the US, poor people tend to be fatter than rich people.

In many foreign countries, sports are a means for poor kids to work their way out of poverty. In the US, however, the best places for training in Olympic sports, such as wrestling, are universities. Consequently, our athletes tend to be from middle-class families. When I was growing up, junior high school athletes graduated up to competing for spots on the high school team, and high school team members graduated up to competing for spots on college teams. Since training at junior high and high school is free, the selection process is relatively egalitarian across socio-economics backgrounds, although still favoring athletes from middle-class families who have supportive home environments and access to better nutrition.

Today, numerous sports are dominated by paid leagues, outside of school. Travel-Soccer and gymnastics are extremely expensive to compete in, so not everyone can participate. Kids from these leagues have much better training, so they generally win the spots on the school teams. This skews the pool of athletes toward the wealthy.

MMA in the US is a complete anomaly among fight sports, as it's extremely expensive to take jiu-jitsu lessons and there's no scholastic jiu-jitsu or MMA option. Consequently, MMA fighters tend to be from middle-class families. My classmates were always asking me how much I was paid for my fights and I'd tell them, "About the same as I spend on a week's worth of training." Most of the Asian classmates, particularly from less developed countries, just couldn't understand why rich, skinny Americans, paid money to play professional sports and get beat up.

I had to admit, they had a point.

Jaka connected me with a master's degree student at SUS who'd trained his whole life at one of the best traditional wrestling schools in China. Jaka said the guy was complaining about how he had no one to practice with. I sent him a text, asking if he'd like to train with me, and he agreed. Next, I asked if he could do freestyle with me, but he said that he only knew Chinese wrestling. So I said, "OK, I'll bring my jacket." Then he asked if I had two jackets, because he didn't have one. I told him I didn't. Then he asked where to meet. I told him we'd meet at the wrestling hall, but he then asked me where it was. I hadn't even met him yet, but I already disliked him.

Next, he asked if I'd teach him English. I told him, "If you teach me wrestling, I'll teach you English. Just bring your English textbook, and I'll teach you after or before the wrestling lesson."

He agreed to bring his textbook. On the day of training, he showed up, not even wearing exercise clothing. When I asked why, he said "I don't have a wrestling jacket, so I don't see how we can train."

"We could just wrestle without the jackets." I suggested. But he didn't seem to want to do that. In the end, I convinced him to at least teach me *jīběngōng*. When we finished, I asked, "Did you bring your English book?"

"No, I thought we could just talk," he answered in Chinese. It was the same argument over again. He couldn't speak English at all, but wanted to do a one-hour conversation.

"I asked you to bring your book, because it'd be impossible for you learn English, without it," I told him. The whole time, I was picturing how awful it would be to listen to tortured, one-word-at-a-time English for an hour, with him not understanding any of my responses. He tried to protest, but I stood my ground: "Without a book, there's nothing I can do for you. But if you come tomorrow and wrestle with me for one hour, I'll work with you, from your English textbook, for an hour."

He agreed. But a few hours later, he texted me, saying: "I think you need a more professional wrestling teacher. Like this will help no one. I think better we don't train together."

Later, when I talked to Jaka, I got the rest of the story. It turned out that the way Jaka had met this guy was that he'd approached Jaka about teaching him English. Jaka's Chinese wasn't that good yet, so all of their discussion and negotiation was in English. When Jaka told him that he charged RMB 200 (US$ 32) an hour for English lessons, the wrestler said he couldn't afford it. Jaka then told him about me, and connected us. When I met the wrestler, he seemed disappointed that I spoke Mandarin. I guess he thought he could practice English by teaching me wrestling in English, or he could make me forget that I wanted to wrestle, and just practice English.

I had lunch with Daniel from Kazakhstan. His Chinese and English were both excellent. A phenomenon I observed was that, while master's and doctoral students varied widely in their Chinese levels, bachelor's degree students all seemed to be at a consistently high level. I attributed this to the fact that the bachelor's degree students had an intense regime of course work, all day, every day, for the entire 16 weeks of the semester, including homework, exams, and group projects. Additionally, there were far more bachelor's degree students with a much smaller percentage of foreign students, so many of the bachelor's degree students were the only foreigners on their courses, which meant they had to work with Chinese classmates. Being younger, they probably found it easier to be friends with their classmates. Moreover, being both younger and bachelor's degree students, the professors most likely didn't accommodate them as much as they did the graduate students. Consequently, a second-year bachelor's degree student often had better Chinese than a graduating Ph.D. or master's degree student.

The exception seemed to be the Koreans, who had no interest in China or school, and very little interest in non-Koreans. Daniel introduced me to a Korean student who was in the third year of his bachelor's degree, but he couldn't even string a grammatically correct sentence together in Chinese. It was nearly impossible to communicate with him.

I asked him: "How are you in your third year [meaning his fourth year in China, because incoming students took full-time Chinese language classes for a year before beginning their degrees] and yet you can't speak Chinese?"

He mumbled something about serving in the army, which Daniel then confirmed.

I thought to myself: "Really? A Korean guy was in the army? In a country with mandatory conscription? Wow! How unique!"

"But that doesn't answer the question," I pointed out. "Why can't he speak Chinese?" They again repeated the army excuse. To which I answered, "I was in the army, but I speak Chinese. So the two aren't mutually exclusive." If being in the army precludes one from speaking Mandarin, what does the Chinese army do? They've one of the biggest armies in the world, and if this guy was right, they couldn't speak to one another.

My advisor emailed me to tell me that my research "wasn't theoretical enough." I wanted to tell him: "At my age, I don't have time for theories anymore. I have to start dealing only in sure things."

I put on some salsa music, got my plastic tub full of detergent and water, and did a dance on my laundry. I then hung it up with more misgivings than usual. It was that time of year when you wouldn't normally use the AC or the heater, and my laundry simply didn't dry. Shanghai's humidity is around 70 percent all the time. After washing by hand, my clothes were extremely wet, and it could take three days or more for them to dry, by which time they were often mildewed and had to be washed again.

Eventually, I figured out a strategy for spring laundry. I did it in the morning, just before going to class. I closed the windows and doors, and turned the heating on, full blast. It was nice to come home to a tropical house, reminiscent of my life in Thailand or Cambodia. It was remarkable how much money the university had saved by not providing us with clothes dryers. It was similar to the water they saved with the low-flow toilets that I had to flush eight times, using about four times as much water as a normal toilet.

AJ and his coach invited me to train with them and some other sanda fighters. We did eight rounds of round-robin sparring on the raised fighting platform, which I'd never done before. It was the most striking sparring I'd done since coming to China. I promised them I wouldn't just take them down, but instead, try to fight them standing, to give us both a chance to work on our kicks and punches. It was good practice to spar with guys who were so much younger and faster, and at such a high level.

The platform worked well for me, I think largely because my first martial arts school, when I was a kid, didn't have a ring. It was a martial arts school Monday through Saturday, but on Sunday it was a church. We sparred on the floor, but we always had to be careful not to fall on the piano. As a result, to this day, I have uncanny situational awareness when I'm fighting and can always steer myself clear of the edge, or a piano.

I had a bit of a bloody nose at the end, but was absolutely elated. Their coach said he'd keep up this level of intensity until after the national championships. If they invited me to train with them, I figured I'd either become deadly — or die in the process.

Later the same day, I had the hardest day of wrestling training I'd ever had. I came in and did *jībĕngōng* while the team played soccer. Then we started wrestling, back to traditional wrestling with jackets to prepare for the national championships in June. We did four three-minute rounds of wrestling techniques; then four five-minute rounds of sparring; then four three-minute rounds of sparring; then another four three-minute rounds of techniques. By the end, we were all exhausted. Most of the guys were injured, and I just couldn't believe how in China the coach would think nothing of suddenly quadrupling the training like that. Afterward, we stood at attention and the coach yelled at us for twenty minutes about how lazy we were. Welcome to Chinese training methodology.

As I limped back to my room, bloody, tired, and sore, I thought to myself: Eight rounds of wrestling laughs at eight rounds of sanda.

The next morning, the alarm went off at 5 a.m., because I had to get ready for work. Shanghai University managed to get all of my week's work crammed into a single day, when I had no doctoral classes. This meant leaving for work at 6 a.m. and getting home at about 8 p.m. But the money I earned from that one day of work was close to the monthly salary of most of my classmates.

A taxi picked me up in front of the dorm, and took me to the Shanghai University campus where I used to live, to catch a teachers' bus to the other campus. It was about a two-hour commute, door to door. The moment the bus pulled onto the Shanghai University campus, I had to laugh. The first think I noticed was how much smaller the students were. Also, none of the students looked injured.

At SUS, I was only in the upper 30 percent in terms of height and weight. I was a Ph.D. student and a wrestling team member. Everyone called me Āndōngní and spoke to me in Mandarin. At Shanghai University, everyone was small. They called me Antonio, talked to me in English, and I was a teacher.

Another immediately evident difference was that undergraduates at SUS seemed so much happier than Shanghai University students. SUS students were always laughing, smiling, and playing. A lot of Shanghai University students, by contrast, had dead eyes and an air of resignation. Of course, the Shanghai University students were light-years ahead of those at SUS in academic achievement. But the SUS students wrestled better. Life has its tradeoffs, I guess.

Making my way to the teachers' room, it was nice to see all my old colleagues and a few of my students who'd failed to graduate. When interacting with students, one thing I had to keep reminding myself of was that at SUS, I hit students on a daily basis. At Shanghai University, that would probably get me fired.

After that incredibly long work day, I got on the bus for the beginning of my two-hour commute home. The whole way, the only thing that kept me going was imagining the huge quantity of barbecue I was going to eat for dinner. Just minutes before I arrived, however, the police raided the street vendors again, and there was nothing to eat. I went to the fruit shop, cursing my luck, when the barbecue guy turned up. He was hiding behind the kiwis, whispering "Psst! Psst!" When he had my attention, he looked around, suspiciously, and asked, "You want barbecue?" I nodded. "Follow me," he said.

He led me down some backstreets to where he'd stashed his barbecue cart. While he cooked, he told me the story. He said the police came three times a week and took RMB 500 (US$ 79) from him. If he paid, he could keep selling. If he ran away, as he had that night, he didn't have to pay anything, but then he couldn't sell. Of course, in order to set up his cart each night, he had to first buy a great deal of perishable meat and vegetables. If the police came, it seemed to me that it'd be cheaper to pay the RMB 500, then try to sell his wares and recoup the money. I bet the police saw it that way too.

Ever since I'd got back from Cambodia, there were three things I'd been working on at wrestling practice. One was an arm drag. The second was a lateral drop throw, where — when your opponent has one under-hook — you trap his arm and simply fall to that side, take him down, and land on top, in side-control. And the third one was completing the single-leg, even if the opponent either sprawled or pushed down on your head. When learning new techniques, you drill and drill, but when you find yourself doing them in sparring, then you've actually learned them. That week I finally pulled off completing the single-leg, in spite of the opponent sprawling and pushing down on my head.

I was wrestling the strongest guy on our team and saw a chance to grab his leg and go for a high single-leg takedown. He defended by putting his entire body weight, with all of his muscle, on my head, and driving my face into the mat. But I persisted. I drove through and completed the takedown with his entire strength pushing the back of my head. I think neither of us could believe it.

I was so elated that I must have had a huge smile on my face when I was walking back to the dorm, because one of my friends said, "You look great today, not like you usually look after practice." A left-handed compliment is still a compliment.

Luo Yuanzhou was a master's degree student of my Ph.D. advisor. He'd studied Chinese classics for his bachelor's degree. Although he loved wushu and was an avid practitioner and researcher, he was always slightly different than the other advisees, who'd all studied wushu for their bachelors. He and I hit it off immediately when we met at our first advisement meeting. It soon became clear to me that he was much smarter and more introspective than the other students. I also suspected that he was a Buddhist, but professed not to have a religion, so he'd be seen as a good communist. He always wore his prayer beads, and I often saw him in prayer, which he claimed was meditation. Another unique aspect of Luo Yuanzhou was that, because he'd studied classics, he could read and write traditional Chinese characters.

When he heard that I'd originally learned Chinese in Taiwan, he was so excited that I had first learned traditional characters. And it was good that I had, because he had his phone set up so he texted everyone in traditional characters. I always wondered if this was something the others held against him, either because they thought he was a traditionalist or maybe that they thought he supported Taiwan. But he was an excellent friend to me, helping me with my research and even coming to watch me fight.

By text, I asked Luo Yuanzhou if he was going home for Qingming Festival (Tomb Sweeping Day), a traditional holiday during which Chinese people return to their hometowns and tend to the graves of their ancestors. While classes were canceled, and bachelor's degree students would go home, master's and doctoral-level students actually had to obtain permission from their advisor to go home, even during periods when school was closed. The advisors often denied permission, and those graduate students had to stay on the campus, in spite of the cafeteria and other amenities being closed.

Luo Yuanzhou told me that he wasn't going home, so I suggested we meet for coffee during the holiday. He replied: "What time? I'm busy doing research. Not tomorrow afternoon, because I have to write."

I honestly didn't intend to make specific plans. I was just being polite. I texted back, "I don't know. But when I'm free, I'll call you. And if you can, you can. If you can't, you can't."

He immediately wrote back, and we agreed on 2 p.m. the next day — even though he said he'd be busy. The following day, he called or texted me three or four times after 1 p.m. At 1:45 p.m., he knocked on my door. I was ready to take a break from writing anyway, so it was fine. Down on the street, we picked up another graduate student, Zhang Chengfeng, who'd helped me with some editing and research, and we went to this horrible coffee shop near campus, one of only two horrible coffee shops.

I told the boys to order anything they wanted. They said they didn't want anything, as is the custom in China, so I insisted, "Please, I brought you here. Please order something." They both said, "The same as you." I couldn't possibly make them drink coffee for the first time in their lives, so I ordered them some sort of a fruit-flavored tea drink and a pastry.

Luo Yuanzhou and I immediately started talking about wushu, and Zhang Chengfeng commented about how he knew nothing about martial arts. "I bet you're getting an education from editing my papers, though," I joked. He said that he was, and that he saw it as a learning opportunity. "I am Chinese. I should know about my own culture."

I appreciated him saying that, although I suspected it was a burden for him to help me, and I was trying to find some other solution. The problem was that the academic-track students were a small minority at the university. Furthermore, I had no way of meeting them, because I mainly made friends through training. Additionally, a lot of the academic students couldn't be trusted to edit or research anything related to martial arts, because they had no baseline knowledge. So I until I found a better option, I kept looking for ways to pay Zhang Chengfeng.

I said to Luo Yuanzhou, "You and I both do martial arts, but what we do is very different."

He nodded, and explained that Western martial arts are external: "When you punch, you use muscle power. And muscle power, muscle mass, is the perception of strength in the West. In China, strength is perceived differently." Chinese martial arts, on the other hand, are both internal and external. "In Chinese martial arts, the entire body is mobilized. The breath and mind work together. There's no other thought in your mind, only this punch. Your entire consciousness, your entire self, and the power of your entire body is focused on a single punch."

Luo Yuanzhou went on to explain: "Strength in China and in the West comes from different places. In China, we use *zhěngjìn* or *húnyuán lì* [literally meaning 'wholehearted or full-circle force'], and we say, *yǐ qì cù lì* ["with breath exert energy," or a force that's exerted with the breath]. Chinese people think that in wushu ge do, strength can be amplified with breath, exceeding your normal strength. This is why wushu practitioners shout 'he, hu, ha' and similar sounds, because they discovered that shouting these sounds increased their strength."

He confirmed that this was the difference between Chinese and Western martial arts, but then went deeper: "Western martial arts include boxing and wrestling. But China also has wrestling. And Chinese shuai jiao wrestling is different from Western wrestling. In shuai jiao, the power comes from breath, and the technique, combined with the breath, amplifies your strength. I've watched you wrestling, and you often get behind the opponent, lift him, and throw him down. But in Chinese wrestling they focus all their energy on a single point of balance and throw."

He was a deep thinker. I predicted that when Luo Yuanzhou was really old, he'd have a long white beard and live in a temple or a cave, dispensing martial-arts wisdom. Once, I walked into the office and he was standing at attention while the professor screamed at him, like a drill sergeant. It was embarrassing. I backed out of the room and waited for him outside. When he came out, I felt awkward, trying not to broach the subject. He, however, seemed fine with what had just happened. His program was a full four years and I just couldn't imagine being subjected to that type of abuse for that long. But maybe in his Buddhism or in his reading of ancient texts, he found peace.

It seemed that within minutes of us sitting down and starting to talk, my two Chinese friends had both finished their pastries and were about half way done with their drinks, and were already eyeing the door. When they figured out that I'd meant for us to sit for a while, Zhang Chengfeng said, "You really enjoy your life." It was such a funny comment, but the concept of just relaxing with a cup of coffee wasn't common in China. They definitely had tea culture, but the behavior and expectations while drinking tea were very different than just hanging out, drinking coffee and talking. We wound up compromising on the time and leaving after about thirty minutes, less than what I'd have thought, but longer than they'd expected.

AJ's coach had connected me with a businessman who wanted private MMA lesson. I had never liked teaching private lessons, but I wasn't sure what my financial situation would be like in the future, so I accepted. Having no idea what to charge, I just said "RMB 200 [US$ 32] hour," because it was the first number that popped into my head. Actually, I'd dramatically undercut myself. A Chinese coach would have charged between RMB 200 and 400 and a foreign coach could have asked for RMB 500 (US$ 79). And since I really didn't want to do it, I should have asked for RMB 500. That way, if the guy had balked at the price, I was off the hook; if he'd accepted that hourly rate, I could suffer through it for a good chunk of money. Instead, I had to suffer through the hour for peanuts.

The real problem with teaching one-on-one MMA is that you have to demonstrate on the student himself, so he never gets to watch you do the techniques. Also, once you teach the technique, the student does it on you, over and over and over. I had to just keep letting him throw me.

When it came to ground fighting, it was nearly impossible to teach, one-on-one, because I was lying on the bottom, teaching him how to tie me up like a pretzel, and I had no way of showing him.

He paid for five lessons up front. After the fourth lesson I quit, but he refused to take the money back. That was kind of him. Also, the experience of quitting wasn't as bad as I had anticipated. In Chinese culture, one nice thing is that if you say, "I'm busy with school and work and cannot teach you anymore," it's considered polite to just accept your word for it and not challenge you. Had I been in his shoes, I'd have said, "But you had school and work when you agreed to do this. What's changed?"

After my final lesson with him, I needed to work on a very important report. But first I was dying for a sandwich. I got back to my room, and realized I'd run out of peanut butter. I therefore smeared raspberry jelly on bread and covered it with crushed up Reese's Cups. It was the most amazing sandwich anyone has ever made and I hope to patent it.

Along with my sandwich I had coffee, which I always made insanely, ridiculously strong. I started with two heaping tablespoons of instant coffee, added the same quantity of sugar, and one heaping tablespoon of creamer. Then I dumped in one or two packets of three-in-one instant coffee. This coffee was integral to my writing process. I'd write for a while, then walk over to my coffee desk. Yes, I had a separate desk in the room with an electric kettle for making coffee. I'd fill my coffee cup about half way with the above-mentioned powders, pour in half a cup of hot water and carefully stir the mud till it sunk down enough that I could add a little more hot water. Then I sat back down, drank my coffee, and wrote. Every twenty minutes or so, I'd add a bit of hot water and refill the cup. Every few hours, I added more coffee powder. When I had to leave for school or training, I left my half-empty cup on my desk and resumed adding water and coffee and writing when I returned.

At night, after I finished my second training session of the day, there was usually about a quarter of a cup of incredibly strong, cold coffee sitting on my desk that had been there all day. Because it was night time, I added hot coco and water and finished it off. I washed the cup, brushed my teeth, watched *Archer*, and went to bed. And this insane, *Rain Man*-esque routine is how I produced all of those Chinese language reports.

After my sandwich, I started working on my research paper, but hit a snag. Normally I needed to use a combination of my own Chinese-language knowledge and Google Translate to read lengthy Chinese texts. But I had some texts which I couldn't copy and paste into Translate. Fortunately, Zhang Chengfeng was able to do some voodoo computer magic and convert them to a format that allowed me to run them through Translate. It was a huge help, because this current report was the first step toward my research-proposal defense, the final approval of my research question and proposal, before entering the research phase of the Ph.D. program.

At SUS, we were expected to spend the first one to two years doing coursework and preliminary research and writing, as I had done. During that time, we were meant to develop our research question and write a formal report, explaining why it was a good question and how we would answer it. My adviser had to sign off on my research-proposal defense, then I'd be permitted to submit it for review. Afterward, there'd be a formal panel of professors, very much like a dissertation defense, where I'd present my report and report question. If it was approved, I could move ahead and begin writing the dissertation. If it was rejected, I'd have to wait a year, and try again. Obviously, I wanted to make sure I passed first time.

The sun was down now, and — like flipping a switch — loud music and drunken laughter began coming from the room next door.

About a month earlier, some Spanish people had moved in beside me, coming to SUS for an eight-week Chinese-language course. But they weren't the fun kind of Spanish, like we had in America, the kind who brought us Santana, masked wrestling, *Sabado Gigante*, and car air-shock competitions. No, these people were the other kind of Spanish, from that old kingdom in Europe, which leads the world in unemployment, and yet feels superior. Because they were just language students, they weren't serious. While the rest of us were under constant deadlines, they were having the time of their lives.

For the first several weeks, they were up all night, laughing and joking, playing music and talking at the top of their lungs. In addition to keeping me awake with their parties, they were smoking so much I was coughing in my bed. I really wanted to go over and cause them to have an accident, but then they moved the party to another floor, where I subsequently heard the Koreans threatening to call the police on them. I found it insane that language students, who largely didn't give a darn, lived beside graduate students who were under serious pressure to write their dissertations... and, in many cases, also happened to be very dangerous individuals.

From what I understood from other foreign students, the Spanish invaders partied all night, slept all day, and didn't go to class. One of the guys looked to be about 40 years old and very creepy, like if he hadn't been here, he'd have been lurking around a juvenile cemetery. He was constantly smoking in the hallway, which was against the rules. A lot of us were athletes; coming back from training, the last thing we wanted was to breathe cigarette smoke.

This was a sports university, but he seemed to be neither studying nor doing sport. I passed him in the stairwell one morning and he blew smoke in my face. I exploded in Spanish and yelled, "No smoking in here." He stood there defiantly, gave me the stink-eye, and asked, "Is that a rule?" I was so flabbergasted, I couldn't even answer. My *Terminator* dropdown menu appeared next to my left eye, and the choices were:

A. Attack!

B. F-you a—hole!

C. No, it's not a rule. It's human courtesy.

Instead, in Spanish, I just said, "Go ahead and smoke." And walked away. I think the reason so many Spanish smoke is because they don't have jobs. Smoking helps to fill the day.

A few days later, he got a haircut that made him look like a mental patient, or a medieval page, or like a medieval page who'd gone crazy and became a mental patient. As he was up all night, when you saw him in the daytime, he didn't look all that alert, like he'd been medicated. He shuffled, completing the image of a mental patient. I once came out of my room around 2 p.m. and he was shuffling down the hallway in his pajamas and slippers. I think it was because they'd taken away his belt and shoelaces when they checked him in.

Since Bred Schroed refused to fight me, I still needed a nemesis, and this guy made the short list.

Heading to my advisor's office, I was trying to decide how much trouble I'd get into if I injured the Spaniard, and whether or not I could use his smoking as an excuse. I walked in, and found my advisor, surrounded by all of his advisees and smoking. I now wondered if I owed the Spaniard an apology.

Professor Dai talked to us about the research-proposal defense scheduled for the end of the term. This week and next week I had to turn in a report and do a presentation, sort of a first step toward preparing for the defense. After the meeting, Duan Limae sent me the requirements and I wrote non-stop for about four days. Then I sent the report to a friend in Taiwan to be edited. I actually wrote myself stupid, slurring my speech, bouncing off the walls…

The edited paper came back the next day, and I spent the whole day preparing the presentation. The following day, Luo Yuanzhou showed me how to format and print the paper, telling me how many copies I needed and which professors and departments I had to send them to. We finished just in time for my sanda class. The next morning, I had to get up at 5 a.m. and teach at Shanghai University, only getting home in the evening. I was feeling a lot of pressure and feeling very old.

What any of this had to do with understanding the meaning of Shaolin Kung Fu, I just couldn't see. On the other hand, I was confident that if Luo Yuanzhou didn't have the answer already, he was closer to finding it than I was.

Sanda training

My wrestling teammates messing around, demonstrating amazing technique and power technique

Chinese-language presentation on Cambodian and Chinese martial arts compared

Sanda training

My wrestling teammates messing around, demonstrating amazing technique and power technique

Sanda training

Wushu exam, my classmates looked awesome. I looked like Rocky.

Wushu exam, my classmates all did traditional martial arts form

I often went on photo trips around Shanghai and nearby cities

Telling fortunes on the street

Traditional Popcorn

The state-approved Catholic church was not allowed to recognize His holiness the Pope.

At a Chinese MMA gym, they had no wrestling coach and no one trained in muay Thai, just sanda

Little kids fighting in Sanda demo

MMA fight night in Shanghai

MMA fight nigh

MMA fight night

MMA fight night

All of the fighters from MMA fight night

SUS graduate Yuan Zumou, the shou bo master

Shou bo

Shuaijiao guys on shou bo day

My best teammate and most loyal friend, Zhengtong

AJ the American studying Sanda at SUS

Chapter 11
Shuai Jiao Time

The training of the body for the strength of the nation.

—**Mao Zedong**

The pressure and exhaustion of preparing for both my dissertation research proposal defense and the Chinese national wrestling championships — plus working — had me questioning if it wasn't time to just give up on my fighting. I dragged myself to morning practice, although I absolutely didn't want to go, and as is always the case, I had an incredible practice, and figured out some things I'd been thinking about. The takeaway was: When you don't feel like training, go anyway.

Talking to Professor Dai after practice, I wanted to say "United Nations," but I didn't know the organization's Chinese name. I tried both "United Nations" and "UN" in English, but he'd never heard of it. I tried describing it, but when you describe something like the UN in another language, it becomes very cumbersome. Without context, it's possible that even a native speaker wouldn't guess your meaning. I'd have thought that the abbreviation "UN" would have gotten through, because there would have been banners or logos visible, even in Chinese government news reports. But, it seemed to me, if a person doesn't speak a foreign language, his/her mind would just reject Latin letters. In every American town, you'll see a Chinese restaurant with the word "restaurant" written in Chinese characters. However, the people who drive past every day would never learn to recognize the word "restaurant" if given a Chinese vocabulary list.

The "Great Firewall of China" — the draconian internet barrier which prevents Chinese people from accessing foreign media — is one reason why Chinese people aren't very aware of what happens outside their country. The language barrier is another huge issue. Even if these sites were unblocked, only a small percentage of people would have the English-language skills necessary to read foreign news and gain insights from abroad.

The nature of pictographic writing makes it nearly impossible for the Chinese language to adopt loanwords. The majority of European languages have Germanic, Romance, or Slavic roots. Hungarian shares no common origin with other European languages, yet in Hungarian you could easily guess all but one of these common, international words: telefon, Olimpia, Televízió, banán, Taxi, and Egyesült Nemzetek. And in the Bantu language of the Shona people of Zimbabwe, all but one of these words are easily recognizable: runhare, Olimpiki, Terevhizheni, bhanana, tekisi, and United Nations. In Chinese, however, all of these relatively universal words are unrecognizable: *diànhuà*, *àoyùnhuì*, *diànshì*, *xiāngjiāo*, *chūzū chē*, and *Liánhéguó*.

The fact that these nearly universal words are different in Chinese must have significant psycholinguistic implications, reaffirming the widespread Chinese belief that China is unique and separate from all other countries of the world.

In my next Ph.D. class, the teacher singled me out and asked about American perceptions of the Olympic Games. I said something about peace and building relationships with different countries. She smiled, nodded her head, then translated my statement into better Chinese for the class, checking with me to make sure I agreed with what she said I'd said. I nodded.

Then she said, "This is very different than the Chinese perception. The Chinese perception of the Olympics is: bigger, stronger, faster." I had to laugh, because this was the US perception of the Chinese perception of the Olympics. So I said, "The Chinese goal in the Olympics is winning medals." She gave me one of those, "Now you get it" smiles, and the class laughed along with her. It was one of the many moments I'd had in China where I saw that the average Chinese person had exactly the same perception of China that we foreigners or foreign media had. Often, they identify the exact same problems as we do. Nonetheless, I had trouble squaring this revelation with my experience of Chinese giving pre-programmed defensive answers to questions which they saw as critical of the PRC.

The teacher went on to ask me how an athlete got on Team USA. I said you needed to win at high school, then district, then state, then region, then nationals… then college…

She said that in China, they did a lottery. "Everyone fills in the application and puts it in an envelope with money and drops it into the lottery box."

The following morning, I did strength and conditioning, then an intense sanda session with eight rounds of sparring to help AJ prepare for US national sanda competition. He'd previously spent a lot of time and money to register for a championship in Hong Kong, only to be told, after he arrived, that he was too old and that no foreigners were allowed. Consequently, he was planning to fly back to the US, where he knew he'd be permitted to compete.

Afterward, I was hating life and dreading wrestling training. It'd become decidedly less fun since we'd begun training for the national championships. I'd get to the training room, and rather than play soccer, the team did really intense running exercises, while I did *jībĕngōng*. Then we wrestled. We sparred eight rounds. I wrestled one of the best guys on the team and, in three minutes, not only did I not give up a single point, but I reversed him and got a two-point throw. With most of my other teammates, we were back and forth as always. But I did manage to pull off two throws that I'd been working on. One was a sanda throw where you sort of slide into your opponent in standing, sliding your knee behind him and your forearm so close to his face, that he leans back to avoid it, and he falls over your knee. This was the first time in my life I did that one in sparring. My MMA coach in Shanghai had had a lot of sanda fights and he was able to use that throw in MMA, and now I'd finally done it.

Another throw I used was from the clinch. You use your knee to push the side of your opponent's knee and lift his arm while pushing his head, and he falls over. This was about the third or fourth time I'd used this one. I got a lot of points for counters and reversals. Many times I got thrown, I managed to take the other guy down and convert his two-point throw into a one-point throw. Another thing was that the *jībĕngōng* was really paying off. At least two or three times, I wound up in a comical ballet, where I lifted my opponent's leg off the ground with my leg, but he didn't go down. So we battled, each with one leg off the ground, until one person eventually outmuscled the other and completed the take down.

One of the teammates I wrestled with was a lot shorter than me, but built like a bull from a lifetime doing Greco-Roman. He was one of the few guys who was shorter than me and I realized it was a whole different game, wrestling someone that small. When a Chinese traditional wrestling match starts, generally the first thing the opponents do is grab each other's jackets. Normally, with taller guys, I stay at the length of their arms, so they don't have leverage to throw me. But with a short guy, there was literally nowhere to go. His arms were so short, it was like I was instantly inside of his zone of control.

After sparring, we did strength training. When we'd finished, the coach cut me loose, but he kept the rest of the team there for another half hour, yelling at them.

That night, at a dinner for Shanghai University teachers, sponsored by the University of Technology, Sydney, I found myself at a table full of people with doctoral degrees. Wanting to compare our Ph.D. experiences and get some advice, I asked: "In your Ph.D., did most of your points come from takedowns or reversals?" Surprisingly, the answer was neither.

After dinner, I was in my room, alternating between work on my dissertation, watching the International Vale Tudo Championship, and taking in the movie *The Outlaw Josey Wales*. It occurred to me that MMA deserved a chapter in my dissertation, as one of the modern evolutions of wrestling. I had a lot of wrestling documentation dating back thousands of years to Persia, Iraq, and later Greece and Rome. Since Greek pankration was part of my research, I felt including MMA and WWE would be valid.

According to a report on mixedmartialarts.com, of ten current UFC champions or contenders, seven were former All State or All-American wrestlers, while only two were BJJ black belts. The influence of wrestling on MMA is undeniable.

Martial arts are permitted in MMA, but the standard mix is wrestling, BJJ, Muay Thai and boxing. People have often asked me if I think the MMA mix will change in the future. And, while I can't predict the future, I just don't see any other martial arts coming up. One of the reasons why wrestling dominates and excellent arts like sambo or sanda do not is simply because wrestling and BJJ are the only two grappling arts practiced by millions of people around the globe. In the US alone, nearly a quarter of a million kids are on competitive wrestling teams, and many graduate high school with over 100 matches behind them. In Brazil, I was told that nearly all BJJ clubs have regular fights and fight nights. Those guys gain a ton of experience. Sambo guys and sanda fighters, on the other hand, may be good in MMA — but those arts will never take over, because they lack the exposure and experience that wrestling has.

I've begun documenting the prevalence of Chinese wushu techniques in MMA. In the 1990s, there were almost none. After 2010, however, side kicks and spinning back kicks had become commonplace. Listening to the commentary on a lot of MMA fights, I noticed that the phrase "spinning back fist" was usually followed by the phrase "almost connected." Even though people weren't often having success with the spinning back fist, it was becoming a commonplace technique. And when it did connect, it often resulted in a knockout, or a broken arm.

Another change I saw in the first few years of the 21st century was that, when you took someone down, you forced them against the cage, so you could tie them up and ground and pound them. Today, if you forced them against the cage, they would wall-walk and escape. In the old days, if you were on top, you tried to push the opponent against the cage. Today, the person on the bottom often tries to drag the two of you closer to the cage, so he can use his legs to push off and stand up. This observation isn't exactly related to Chinese martial arts, but it's another piece of evidence that MMA is constantly evolving, becoming more technical and adding techniques, while traditional martial arts, by definition, remain largely stagnant.

In early vale tudo and MMA, there were no weight categories, no rounds, and no time limits, because that was felt to be more realistic. Weight categories, rounds, and time limits in Chinese wrestling are also a fairly new development. In countries like Mongolia and India, traditional wrestling still lacks time limits or weight categories. As different as Western wrestling and Chinese wrestling are, there have been some similarities in the way they've developed.

Thinking about the influence of BJJ on MMA, I decided that I should include a small section on jiu-jitsu, and because jiu-jitsu originated from judo, I had to cover judo. The decision to include at least some judo in my dissertation had already been made, however, because so many Chinese sources claimed that Japanese judo had stolen from Chinese shuai jiao.

The next evening, the wrestling coach didn't show up, so the team relaxed and played soccer. He could have just goofed off, but instead Zheng Tong trained with me because he was one of the most solid friends I've ever met. He reminded me of a loyal Rottweiler or a devoted wolfdog in that, if anyone ever even looked like they'd hurt me, he'd rip out their throat with his teeth. I hope I never say anything self-deprecating, or he might attack me.

A wrestler since the age of nine, Zheng Tong told me that he was getting bored. He kept pushing me to get him some MMA fights. In the meantime, he'd obtained permission to train with the university's professional sanda team. He was now training sanda twice a day, and still coming to all of the wrestling practices. I worked with him on his sanda throws. Although his wrestling was much better than mine, I was still had more experienced at integrating wrestling into sanda or MMA. Zheng Tong actually said to me, "Your sanda ge do is excellent." I laughed and said, "Well, I did score 95 on a Ph.D.-level sanda ge do class."

My Canadian friend Kirk came to train with us. He and Zheng Tong started wrestling, and everyone stopped what they were doing so they could watch. Kirk's techniques were really amazing. My teammates were thrilled and inspired by this 45-year-old man who had such great wrestling skills. I was also amazed at how Zheng Tong was wrestling with Kirk. After a lifetime, he had nothing to prove. When he wrestled me or our teammates, he wrestled at a certain level. But the level I saw him wrestling with Kirk was much higher. I also noted just how well Zheng Tong could wrestle when he wanted to. Wang Yechao had told me that, in his opinion, Zheng Tong was the best wrestler on the team. Now I saw why, and this gave me hope that if he decided he really wanted to fight MMA, maybe he could.

After the two of them took a break, the team left. Kirk stayed, to teach Zheng Tong and I. Kirk worked with us on completing a single or double when the opponent has you in a choke. This was something I'd started learning in Cambodia, and Kirk now took it a bit further. We also worked on the throw I'd learned from my accountant friend in Cambodia, where your opponent has one underhook, and you more or less fall in the direction of his underhook and it takes him to the ground, and you land in side control. Then Kirk showed me how to refine the technique by popping your hips. Both he and Zheng Tong said it was a difficult throw to get against a good wrestler. But both agreed that from the clinch, most MMA guys wouldn't even know about it and couldn't defend against it.

Zheng Tong and I repaid Kirk by showing him some of our sanda ge do, which he said he hadn't seen much of before. Afterward, Kirk went home and Zheng Tong and I went to the weight room and completed our strength training.

The next day was a Saturday, and I was teaching at the Japanese school all day. I walked into the office and one of the corporate guys, who was Chinese, approached me. He was speaking English, even though everyone else there spoke to me in Chinese. He was babbling on in terrible, agrammatical, mispronounced English, and I couldn't make head or tails of what he was saying. Finally, I sort of understood that he meant: "If the computer in your classroom dies in the middle of a lesson, please let me know."

The computer in question had been acting up for over a year. It would work fine for about half a lesson, then shut down for no reason. I'd have to restart it, and then it was fine again. It was annoying, but not a huge problem. I assumed that, since I wasn't the only teacher to use that room, the school must have known for the last year or so that it didn't work, but they simply didn't want to spend the money to repair it. Since this was the first time he'd asked me to tell him if the computer shut down, I assumed they'd finally had it repaired.

I thank him and assured him I'd let him know. I'd started to walk away, happy that the computer had finally been fixed, when he said: "Because all your students have been complaining to me that the computer has this problem." Now he was admitting that he'd known about the problem, but that the school hadn't fixed it.

In Chinese, I asked, "All my students told you? And what, you didn't believe them?"

"No, I believe them," he stammered.

"Then why did you ask me to check? This problem has been continuing for a year. Did you think they were tricking you?"

"No, no, I just today, thinking about this problem…"

"Well, you need to do more than think. How about solving the problem?"

"Yes, but I don't know what to do."

I thought to myself: "Fix it, repair it, buy a new one. There, I just gave you three possible solutions." As I walked away, he said, "Can you please check it?"

Why did he want me to check to see if the computer was having a problem for the 366th day? Was it because of the old adage, "Fool me 365 times, shame on you. Fool me 366 or more times, shame on me."

I got to my classroom, and of course the computer hadn't been repaired. It still had the same problem, but I never broached the subject again. Problem solved!

Aside from that corporate guy and the computer debacle, teaching at the Japanese school was a great experience. The Japanese students were businesspeople, many of them close to my age, who were working in Shanghai. We discovered that we had much more in common with each other than we did with most Chinese people our age. For one thing, my students had all grown up watching the same TV shows as I had: *Star Trek*, *The Rockford Files*, and *The Six Million Dollar Man*.

Just that week, China's state-run Xinhua News Agency had reported that four US television shows, *The Big Bang Theory*, *The Practice*, *The Good Wife*, and *NCIS*, were being banned. I couldn't see how these shows posed a direct threat to public order, but the government didn't want people watching them for some reason. Censorship continues to separate China from the world and prevent people from making connections.

My Japanese students, by contrast, hadn't just grown up with US TV shows. They also loved baseball and enjoyed talking about sumo. The common ground we could talk about included the shared experience of being foreigners in China and having to pass the HSK exam.

I asked one of my Japanese students, who was close to my age, how they wrote Chinese script before there were computers. He said that he'd worked in the China department of his company, in Yokohama, in the 1980s. Every morning, his boss would receive a situation report from the Shanghai office by telex. Because there weren't any Chinese keyboards, they used a four-digit cipher code, by which, each Chinese character was assigned a four-digit code number. The telex would arrive in numbers, then someone in the Yokohama office had to decode it. While he was telling me this, I was thinking of every World War II movie I'd ever seen. I pictured my student, in a naval uniform, receiving a secret message via telex, then telling the captain where to attack the US fleet.

For writing, he said they had typewriters with keyboards for the two phonetic alphabets used in Japanese. However, certain documents needed to be written in Chinese script. To do this, they needed a special typewriter, which sounded like an ancient moveable type printer. There were boxes and boxes of Chinese characters, made of metal, and a specialist would search them out and place them in the typewriter in reverse order. The student told me that this was a highly skilled job. This operator earned double what anyone else in the company earned, but once the first computers arrived, he was let go.

Teaching Japanese students was fun, but it was still teaching and could be very frustrating. In one business classes, an intermediate-level Japanese student read the sentence, "This is how the concept of 'market segmentation' works." I asked, "Do you know what that means?"

She suddenly became flustered and started blurting out "Segmentation works? Segmentation works? Segmentation works?" She was frantically flipping through her dictionary, mumbling "Segmentation works" when I stopped her. "No, the sentence says "This is how the concept of 'market segmentation'" ...(pause) "works." To which, she instantly replied, "Segmentation works?" I took a deep breath and said, "Now, listen again. "This is how the concept of 'market segmentation'....pause. Wait for it, p-a-u-s-e.....works." And her reply — which made me look for a window to jump from — was "Segmentation works?" I just told her to look it up for homework. We moved on to the rest of the article.

After work, I went to the mall to buy a camera. I know nothing about electronics or cameras, and hate shopping in general, so buying a camera in China was a trauma I may never recover from.

My brother, who's much smarter than me, told me that I needed a certain Nikon. I walked into the shop and they had one with a telephoto lens for RMB 4,100 (US$ 651). I haggled a bit and they dropped the price to RMB 3,900 (US$ 619). Once I'd agreed and paid, they told me to sit while they went to get me a new camera in a box. While I was sitting, the woman kept showing me this other, much more expensive, non-brand camera, with electronic zoom, rather than a detachable zoom lens. I thanked her for showing it to me, but said that I'd just prefer the camera I'd already paid for.

She came closer, held out the camera and pressed the zoom button, extending and retracting the zoom, to show me how great it was. I stared away disinterestedly, while politely saying, "Yes, that's lovely, but no thanks." Originally, they'd told me to wait three minutes. Ten minutes had passed, but my camera hadn't materialized. So, I asked "Where's my camera?" The woman held up the model she'd been showing me and said, "You want this one, right?"

"No, I told you several times I don't want that one." I insisted.

She looked disappointed. "Which one do you want?"

"I want the one that I chose when I came in here. The one I paid for. The one you claimed you were getting from the warehouse, while I waited."

The boss jumped in, saying, "Calm down, calm down. It's just that this camera is better."

"Get me my bloody camera, now!" I growled.

"OK" said the boss. He pulled out his phone and asked someone to deliver the Nikon. I couldn't believe it. They hadn't even ordered it, and now I was waiting again.

"This camera is much better," said the woman, holding it out to me. The look on my face surely conveyed that no means no.

When my camera finally arrived, 15 minutes later, they set the box on the table in front of me, and walked away. I stared at the box and I stared at the boss. Finally, he asked me, "Open?"

"Yes, open it." I confirmed, "And show me all of the components that it comes with. And make sure everything is there."

As he was going through the accessories, he snatched the lens that came with the camera and put it in the display case.

"What are you doing?" I asked.

"We will give you the zoom lens. You don't want this one."

My Spidey sense was tingling. Why didn't he want me to have the factory lens? Part of my issue and frustration in this whole situation was that I really didn't know much about cameras or what to look for. I had no way of knowing if I was being ripped off. I picked up my camera with the zoom lens and did what I imagine all customers in China do, I checked the furthest zoom and said, "Wow! That sure can shoot stuff far away."

"You, see? This lens is good. Much better than the factory one."

I thought about that for a minute, then I told him: "It's not necessarily better, just zoom, right?"

"No, you don't understand, this lens can take pictures far away."

"Yes, I understand the concept of a zoom lens. But it isn't necessarily better, just further away, right?"

The guy rolled his eyes at how ignorant I was. "This other lens is smaller. It can't take pictures far away."

That's when it hit me, that I hadn't checked my zoom lens on the closest setting. It turned out, on the closest setting, I couldn't even take a picture across the room. Even from a distance of several meters I was getting images of noses and skin pores, rather than faces.

I tried the factory lens, and although it only had a zoom of 50, it seemed more practical for everyday use. It turned out that the big lens was a 50–220, which meant I absolutely couldn't have used it for anything but telephoto.

"I want the small one," I said.

"But this one is bigger," The guy insisted.

In the end, I made him give me the smaller lens and refund RMB 300 (US$ 48) of my money. As for why he didn't want me to take the small lens, it turned out that the smaller lens was a real Nikon lens, but the telephoto item wasn't. This experience was a window into Chinese culture, where the bigger lens is always better, simply because it's bigger.

The following morning, I arrived at the wrestling hall, expecting a horribly intensive training session ahead of the national championships. However, the session was easy, because we received a visit from the fencing team. During the semester, various teams would go and train with other teams, so the kids could get exposure to different sports. Our sanda class had previously been visited by the tai chi team, for example. Wrestlers versus fencers: It's a good thing the fencers didn't bring their épées or my teammates would have lost. Well, not Zheng Tong — it'd take more than a few stab wounds to kill him. I picture his severed hand crawling across the floor and continuing the fight.

We played a lot of games and practiced basic break falls with the fencers, while I did *jīběngōng*. Afterward, the coach assigned two wrestlers to wrestle against me, and I got about 45 minutes of sparring and private lessons. Zheng Tong's signature move was the seio nagi shoulder throw. He could do it in standing or from his knees, and seemed to be able to get it from almost any position in wrestling. He tried teaching me how to do it, but I just wasn't very good at it.

Another teammate came over to spar with me. He caught me with a side hip-throw that was textbook perfect. While I was up in the air, I was thinking: "I really hope he pulls my arm and completes the spin, or I'll land on my head and probably be paralyzed for the rest of my life. I tucked my chin, and at the last second, my partner pulled the arm, and I crashed down harmlessly on my shoulder blades. But it scared me. The kid who did that to me only weighed about 72 kg (159 lbs). This was the amazing power of Greco-Roman wrestling, and one more reason why I was tired of internet arguments about whether a traditional martial artist or a street fighter could beat a trained fighter or wrestler.

I asked my teammate Lu Kaijie what he planned to do. He told me he wanted to be a wrestler. He said he'd once been rated no. 5 in China in Greco-Roman, but was now considered a second-tier athlete. He wanted to compete his way to first-tier. I thought that was strange; he was the only one of my teammates who said he wanted to be a wrestler. He and Zheng Tong were both aiming to join the Greco championships in July, but I didn't see how they'd stand a chance against guys who trained with top-tier partners six or seven hours per day.

Lu Kaijie and I wrestled. He and all of my teammates were cutting insane amounts of weight and none of them had the power they'd had a month earlier. Yang Wenbin, the biggest guy on the team, had cut 18 kg (40 lbs) so far. I was now able to outmuscle him. Lu Kaijie was a good opponent, but he tired out very quickly because of the weight cut.

After wrestling, I went straight to the weight room, downstairs from the wrestling hall, did my strength training, and then did my cardio. After eating, showering, and sleeping, I worked to finish a paper that compared sports education in the US to sports education in China.

One of the first things I saw when I turned on my computer was an advert which read "Preparing for Pre-school." And it made perfect sense. Obviously, if you don't go to the right pre-K you'll never be accepted into a good kindergarten. And without the right kindergarten, how could you expect to go to a top-tier elementary school... I've seen some of the coloring that goes on in these substandard pre-K schools... outside of the lines, wrong colors! Children as old as two don't know how to cut with scissors in some of those so-called-schools.

The children featured in the ad were all wearing ties and vests, like tiny businesspeople. The fact there was a market for academic pre-K said a lot about the Chinese education system. I'd read that Chinese families spend up to 30 percent of their income on their children's education, even if they have only one child. In the West, the media often implies that the Chinese education system is superior to those in North America and Europe. A point they miss, however, is that the *gāokǎo* (the National College Entrance Examination) is a state exam. In theory (at least) public schools should prepare kids to pass the *gāokǎo* and meet the standards for entry into public universities. In reality they don't, so parents are forced to pay for private education. Unfortunately, the Western media has got that one wrong again and again, so now many Westerners are convinced that China's education system is better than the system in the US.

In 2013, Shanghai schools reached the top of the Programme for International Student Assessment (PISA) rankings, which compares the quality of education across countries. The self-loathing Western media cited this as further proof that Chinese education is better than US education. However, the results weren't representative of the whole of China. The data was gathered from the best schools in Shanghai, so all it meant is that the best schools in China are better than average schools in the US. But the best schools in the US would also be better than average schools in the US. The PISA said nothing about average schools in China.

According to US census data, the average US adult has 13 years of education. Some 88 percent of American adults hold a high school diploma and 33 percent have graduated university. Nationmaster.com shows the average adult in China as having just 6.4 years of formal education, while 17.45 million children in China aren't attending school. Female literacy in

China is 87.6 percent, while in the US it's 99 percent. Also, the difference between urban and rural schools in China is staggering. The website China-Mike.com points out that the literacy test for urban dwellers consists of 2,000 Chinese characters, while rural dwellers are considered literate if they can read 1,500 Chinese characters. You need to know about 2,000 characters to read a newspaper, so rural people may be considered literate even if they're unable to read a newspaper.

Relevant to my sports education research, one of the many advantages of the US system is that scholastic sports are available at almost all public schools. In China, child athletes attend sports schools, where they receive very little academic education. Around 250,000 children in China attend sports schools. That means 250,000 kids who, like my teammate Zheng Tong, would lack basic education and even reading skills when they reach adulthood. Even with this gold-medal production line, the US still had more athletes than China. According to a report from USA Swimming, in 2012 there were 300,884 amateur competitive swimmers in the United States, including high school, university, and other competitive teams. Swimmers alone in the US outnumber Chinese athletes across all sports.

Track and field in the US is even bigger. According to the National Federation of State High School Associations, nearly a million students participate in track and field at the high school level. To put this in perspective, China's population is quadruple that of the US, yet American track and field athletes outnumber all athletes in China by a ratio of four to one.

·•●••

A shuai jiao master from France, Yuan Laoshi (a 1963 SUS wrestling graduate) had come to SUS to give some lectures and workshops about shuai jiao and shou bo. He'd founded France's shou bo association. Shou bo literally means "hand fight," and it's a form of Chinese ge do, wrestling which includes kicking and punching. Some Korean sources claim that shou bo is an ancient Korean art, which happened to have a Chinese name and was written with Chinese characters. (Until the 19th century, Korean was usually written in Chinese script.)

Critics have claimed that shou bo isn't a real martial art because the rules and syllabus were written by Yuan Laoshi in modern times. My counter argument is this: Like sanda ge do, we know that in ancient times, Chinese wrestlers could kick and punch, and possibly grapple and ground fight, but we don't know the details or the rules. There are records, dating back to the Han Dynasty, of a style of unarmed, no-holds-barred fighting, called *shǒubó*, which was similar to modern shou bo. While modern shou bo may not be identical to a corresponding art from the third century, some type of very similar kicking/punching/throwing art existed.

Critics of sanda ge do, shou bo, and even sanda, argue that they're synthetic arts, since their existence in ancient times can't be properly verified. Proponents of these arts say that, although the rules are new, the techniques are original. I tend to stand with the latter.

I went to hear Yuan Laoshi's lecture. It was so odd to see my wrestling teammates sitting in class, wearing regular clothes. They looked as out of place as I did on the wrestling mats. Yuan Laoshi said that in his art, shuo bo, the goal is non-violence and non-force. He said, "Look for the elegance." So I was pretty much out.

When Jiang Laoshi, my favorite sanda teacher heard that Yuan Laoshi was coming, he commented, "Shuo bo is sanda with a jacket." But after hearing Yuan Laoshi go over the rules, it sounded more like a Chinese version of savat, with technical, well-placed kicks, rather than destroying your opponent's thighs, kicking them over and over, until he collapses. The rules prohibited shin kicks, knee strikes, and punches to the face. But the rule that completely shut me out was, "No holding while hitting."

When I first heard there was a Chinese MMA-style art called shuo bo where people wore wrestling jackets, all I kept thinking was: 'When the bell rings, I'm going to grab the jacket, wrap it around their head, and punch them in the face until the round ends, like a hockey player.' But sadly, Yuan Laoshi said that you weren't allowed to hold and hit. Now they'd taken away my best weapon.

Later, Yuan Laoshi worked with our wrestling team, teaching us shou bo. When he began showing us a little bit of chin na (Chinese submission locks), Zheng Tong immediately said to me, "It doesn't work. Chinese martial arts don't work at all, except sanda and shuai jiao." I tried to be open-minded, but I'd also decided that shou bo just wasn't going to work for me. It was too limiting compared to MMA or even sanda.

Yuan Laoshi next moved on to teaching us some refined techniques of Chinese wrestling. His tutelage helped a lot. Afterward, in sparring, I did my famous lateral drop which I'd been working on. The coach saw me do that takedown and at almost the same instant, a French wrestler slammed Zheng Tong. The coach yelled to the Chinese students: "Look at all these foreigners using our Chinese wrestling techniques. You guys better work hard to catch up."

After training, I had a Ph.D. class. For these three-hour graduate lectures, I'd often bring water, soda, and a chocolate bar. If I'd just finished training, I'd need more food. I'd have preferred a hot meal, but the smell of my Sterno stove would disturb the other students.

That day, I couldn't do any eating in class, because I had a final report and presentation, to prepare for my dissertation research proposal defense, which would occur in June. I did just OK, but not great. The teacher told me what I needed to improve ahead of the real event. Truth be told, I was scared about the actual panel presentation. I was the only foreigner, and the panel of professors could ask anything they wanted.

I was considering hiring a Chinese tutor again, because I didn't think my language was making any progress. I was nearly done with lectures for the year, so my exposure to the Chinese language was limited to my interactions with the wrestling team. In an academic context, I often found myself stammering in Mandarin. But as soon as they asked something about martial arts, I became the John Houseman of the Chinese language.

The next day, at the end of practicing sanda with AJ and our Chinese classmates, a group of sanda fighters came in the sanda room and began warming up and running laps. They didn't look like our pro team, so I asked AJ's coach if they were from outside the university. Before he could answer, AJ said: "Of course they're from outside, don't you see how they're staring at us? Like they've never seen a foreigner before." It was true, their eyes were glued to us, which was hilarious, because they were running laps, but their eyes remained fixed on us. I was worried someone would sustain a neck injury or suffer a collision.

I was so used to speaking Chinese all of the time, being called by my Chinese name, and being surrounded by Chinese classmates, that I forgot I looked different. I'd also forgotten that many Chinese people had never seen a foreigner, or had had very little contact with foreigners, and might stare at us like this.

That night, at wrestling training with Kirk, Zheng Tong brought along his best friend from his sports school in Shandong. He called him *Dìdì* ("little brother"). *Dìdì* only knew Greco-Roman, so, for the first time in my life, I sparred Greco rules. He was a lot smaller than me, but had been training for about ten years. It was a puzzle, thinking how to throw him without grabbing or tripping his legs.

While Zheng Tong and Kirk were still wrestling, I chatted with *Dìdì*. He was 20 years old and wasn't attending a sports university, so I asked what he'd been doing since graduating sports high school, two years earlier. He replied, "Nothing." I asked him if he'd like to study at a sports university, but he told me that he hated studying. I wondered what he'd do now. There are about 250,000 kids in sports schools across China. In the 2012 Summer Olympics in London, the PRC team comprised 396 athletes. What will the other 249,604 do with their lives?

Kirk and Zheng Tong came over to join us and Kirk and I began talking. At that point, *Dìdi* started walking away. Zheng Tong asked him, "Where are you going?" He answered, "I don't understand what they're saying." It was another example of my forgetting that it wasn't normal for the average Chinese athlete to be wrestling with two foreigners, or to hear us speaking English.

Zheng Tong scolded his friend, "I don't understand them either. But we can still wrestle with them and learn something."

Teaching at Shanghai University the next day was rough. I was teaching two courses where all of the students had failed at least once, and some were repeating the course for the third time. I honestly didn't believe that most of the kids were incapable, They were just unmotivated and undisciplined.

A student with the English name Randy arrived twenty minutes late for a timed assessment which counted for 30 percent of the semester's grade. When the time was up, and I was collecting the students' papers, he demanded to keep writing. I tried to take his paper away, but he fought with me, until I had to raise my voice, and snatch the paper out of his hands. He cried and pleaded while I packed my bag. Things almost got ugly when he blocked the door and wouldn't let me leave the classroom, begging to be allowed more time. Once again, I had to shout, to get him to step aside. He followed me down the hall, begging, pleading, and crying, all of the way into the teacher's lounge. It was all I could do to make him leave, shouting, "Get out!" He simply didn't seem to understand that the rules applied to him, too, and that every student had the same time limit. I filed a report about the incident, just in case he claimed I'd treated him unfairly. The administration stood by me 100 percent, telling me that this particular student had developmental issues, as well as trouble communicating and learning.

Later, I felt bad, because he should have been in a special class. This is another issue with China's educational system. They don't seem to have special education programs for students who need help. If the family is wealthy enough, they send their kids to international programs like the one I taught in. If the family was poor, however, the students would just fail and be denied an education.

The following day, Professor Dai told us to attend a training session in the wushu performance hall, where we'd had our admissions exam. Yuan Laoshi was teaching a shuai jiao/shou bo session for the wushu students. We all came in, stood at attention, and a heavyweight professor told us that, to help promote Chinese culture, SUS was now forming an official shuai jiao club within the Wu Shu Institute. The team would be open to all wushu students, including foreigners, and would be competing all over China. This was amazing news for me. I figured that with my MMA and wrestling background, I'd have a huge advantage over wushu students in a shuai jiao competition. I'd hoped to compete in sports while training at SUS; it would be so cool to have a collection of medals and memories by the time I graduated.

The professor then told us that jackets had been ordered for all of us, and they'd be arriving soon. In the meantime, we should start practicing.

At wushu events and exams, I'd always felt like the odd man out, but now, my shuai jiao and shuai jiao research would be given a degree of legitimacy.

·•●•·

Han Hongyu — who'd previously assumed I couldn't speak Chinese, and asked Professor Dai how I could do a Ph.D. — didn't seem to like me very much. When I bumped into him outside the Wu Shu Institute, dressed for training, he asked, "Where are you going?"

"Wrestling practice," I answered.

"But we have a lecture at 2:30 p.m.," he admonished.

"Yes, but it's 10 a.m. now. I'll be done in time."

Han Hongyu mumbled something about how nice it must be to be foreigner, living a carefree life at SUS, while Chinese students slaved to complete their research.

During the shou bo practice, all of the wushu classmates kept making a big deal about my presence and kept asking me to comment on shou bo and shuai jiao, based on modern wrestling and MMA. Half of them knew me from the sanda classes that we had together. Some of them had come to the free open wrestling classes that I'd been teaching on weekends. Others had come to watch me fight. The doctoral students had seen my fight videos on Chinese social media. Everyone knew I was a fighter and a wrestler — and, of course, I was the only foreigner. Also, among wushu students, I was the biggest and the strongest, so there were constant jokes about who was going to have to partner with me. During practice, they all kept wanting to take photos with me. Yuan Laoshi and his assistant talked to me in French quite a bit.

Han Hongyu seemed really jealous. He jumped in and said, apropos of nothing, "Āndōngní and I have the same adviser." Everyone nodded, then continued talking to me.

Yuan Laoshi asked if I'd brought my wrestling jacket. I almost hadn't, since I knew most people wouldn't have one. He told me to put it on, so now classmates were asking about the jacket and where I'd trained… I could see Han Hongyu getting angry that no one was paying attention to him.

Throughout the training, the master kept talking to me and watching my technique. The master's assistant couldn't speak Chinese, so he'd talk to me in French and I'd translate for my classmates.

This visibly upset Han Hongyu. My graduating depended in part on him, so I had to keep up a good relationship with him. But part of me felt like saying: "Han Hongyu, I invited you to open wrestling, but you chose not to come. You told me you had Chinese wrestling experience, so I asked you if you wanted to join the wrestling team, but you declined... instead of training and fighting, you chose to drink and smoke. Every person on the planet has the option of learning French or English, but you chose to learn neither." Of course, I said none of this to him. Instead, I tried to find ways to include him or ask his opinion on training and techniques.

After training, a leading professor from the Wu Shu Institute told us to select a team captain and co-captain. I was the first, and the loudest, to suggest Han Hongyu. He politely refused, by saying, "But you're our *lǎodà* [informal leader]." In the end, he accepted the position of captain.

The professors and the master chose me as co-captain, which the students supported. I really didn't think this was a good idea. Even though they said they wanted the team to be inclusive, the club probably stood the best chance of survival if the officers were Chinese. I nominated one of my doctoral classmates who was specializing in sanda. He nominated me. The professor and the master from France both said it should be me.

Then the professors and the master took me to lunch, but not Han Hongyu. At that lunch, they told me I'd be going to France in December to represent SUS in a wrestling competition. I made a mental note to take Han Hongyu out and get him drunk to ensure a good relationship.

Yuan Laoshi told me he'd graduated from Shanghai University of Sport in 1963. One of the professors at the lunch had been his student back then. He still had nice wrestling ears. Yuan Laoshi recognized Wang Wenyong's name on my jacket. He said that they used to be together in the same club, but he'd moved on and modernized, and that's why his club was doing well in France. The Wang Wenyong Club, however, was still old fashioned. Yuan Laoshi switched between French and Chinese when he spoke to me. He said that at the Wang Wenyong Club they were still kowtowing, and actually used the word "kowtow." One of the things he'd done to modernize the sport in France, he told me, was to cut out the Beijing-style drinking and smoking.

That night, it hit me that the wrestling jackets had never been delivered. Over the next three years, I'd be called in for numerous meetings relating to the formation of the Wu Shu Institute's shuai jiao club, but it never materialized. That was the only time that Yuan Laoshi came to visit, and no one sent me to France.

The next morning, I had a good sanda training session with AJ and some pros. The pros worked with me on kick catching and traditional throws. I taught them some modern wrestling and MMA techniques that might give them a bit of an edge. A French kid from Fudan University came to train with us. As I taught him some boxing, we conducted the whole class in Chinese, because we both spoke Mandarin better than we spoke each other's language. And that was fine, because I was used to always speaking Chinese when teaching MMA. But it was kind of funny to see two Caucasians speaking Mandarin to one another. My Chinese training mates had a good laugh over it.

I think one of the reasons why boxers peak at a younger age than MMA fighters is that, once you fight at a pro-level in boxing, it's more or less assumed that you already know all of the techniques. While these techniques can always be honed, the real peak in boxing is your personal, physical fitness peak. But in MMA you're always learning more techniques. An older fighter, one who's been in the game longer, may therefore know more techniques or have better techniques. Physical fitness is also important, of course, but I think technique can compensate for declining physical abilities in MMA more than it can in boxing.

Later, I bumped into my wrestling teammates at the weight room. They seemed to be going there more often as we got closer to the national championships.

When I went back to my room, I found that my roommate Natsuki had slept all day. I asked him how he was. He said that recently he'd grown very tired of China and was considering quitting. "This is not sport university!" he shouted in English.

I had to agree with him that the training was hit or miss. For him, as an Olympic hopeful, this university had likely ended his career. For me, I was just a part-time pro, but if were a full-time pro, SUS would still sort of work out for me because of the great sparring partners I'd found. Anytime I wanted a training session, but had nothing planned, I'd just stop by the sanda hall and see who else was there. Inevitably, some other excellent pros or fighters turned up who I could train with. Theoretically, I could train here and then find and register for fights on my own. But for amateur athletes, hoping to go to the Olympics, it was different. They needed to be part of a team in order to participate in regional and international competitions. And being Japanese, SUS had already told Natsuki he wasn't permitted to compete.

I needed to eat a nutritious snack and take a break before going back to the university. In China, to get some extra protein, I used to eat these tubed meat sticks which the label claimed were "made from meat-flavored byproducts." They were utterly disgusting, but they were animal protein. Sort of.

My obsession with the concept of the 100-man kumite hadn't abated. Watching the video for the millionth time, I wondered if when Judd Reid was fighting the 94th opponent, he was thinking, "Oh good, only six guys to go." I couldn't imagine having already fought 188 minutes and still having six fresh opponents left. Kyokushin was certainly the toughest style I'd ever encountered.

On the day all new master's degree students had to go for an admissions interview, Jaka texted me and asked if I'd had to pay RMB 200 (about US$ 32) in cash at my admissions interview. I told him that I hadn't. He texted me again: "A couple of high-ranking university guys I've never seen before, running a mandatory interview, and collecting RMB 200 from each interviewee. Seems kind of shady to me." Several other students told me they'd had the same experience.

I went over to the sanda room and found some shuai jiao guys to train with. Afterward, I bumped into a couple of undergrads I knew who were in the academic track. While we were talking, my wrestling master, Meng Shifu, called from Beijing. I talked to him for a bit, but was really struggling with his dialect. I turned to my classmate and asked, in Chinese, "This is my traditional Chinese wrestling master from Beijing. I'm having trouble understanding him. Can you please find out what he wants and tell me in normal Chinese?"

He froze when I handed him the phone, and protested, in Chinese: "But my English is terrible."

"Why would you need to speak English?" I asked.

"Isn't your wrestling master a foreigner?" he asked.

This was one of those moments where I felt like Charlton Heston in *Planet of the Apes*: "It's a mad house!" Why would my traditional Chinese wrestling master from Beijing be a foreigner? Why would I be speaking to him in Chinese? Why would I need my Chinese friend to talk to him in English and translate what he says into better Chinese for me?

It turned out that Meng Shifu was inviting me to come to Beijing for a competition, but I respectfully told him I couldn't get away.

As Wang Yechao and I walked back to the dorms, I saw three guys walking toward us with incredibly expensive sport clothing, and their trousers tucked into fancy spats. They all wore baseball hats and expensive sunglasses, and they had fashionable bags full of gear. I said to Wang Yechao, "I bet they're Korean."

He instantly agreed. "Most likely! Koreans always have expensive clothes and fancy hats and travel in groups," he said. It amazed me that even the Chinese students, who had very little contact with the Koreans, had the same opinions about them as we foreign students did.

Rumor had it that the university administration was now taking steps to force the Koreans to attend classes and learn Chinese. Korean students were now required to attend an extra two hours of Chinese classes every day. But whenever I walked past the class, they were all speaking Korean. From what I understood, they hadn't learned any Chinese at all.

There was a public holiday, and I took a full day off from training for the first time in a very long time. One of my Shaolin friends, Hugo from Mexico, came to visit Jaka, and we three Shaolin alumni went out for lunch. We ate huge legs of goat, then sat in a spa hotel's beautiful courtyard drinking coffee. I felt more relaxed than I had in months. When I got back to my room, I made huge progress on my dissertation proposal, writing for four straight hours.

When I took a break, I checked my email. My advisor had sent me another of his classic demotivating emails that I didn't understand. I'd learned to scan his messages for the word *zuòyè* (homework). If it appeared, I knew I needed to write something. If not, I just assumed the email said that my research was crap.

The next day, on the way to the weight room, I saw my teammate He Yi and asked how his police exam had gone. He said that he'd passed every part except the interview. "What happened in the interview?" I asked, unable to imagine that they wouldn't want him. He told me he'd failed because he hadn't paid a bribe. Every other applicant had handed the interviewer an envelope when they walked in, he said.

I later asked Zheng Tong and some of my other friends about this. They told me that anytime you had an interview for work, you had to pay a bribe. One friend went so far as to say "If my parents weren't here in China, I'd leave."

In the weight room, a sanda fighter kept starring at my Shaolin Temple T-shirt. He finally got up the courage to talk to me and ask about the shirt. It turned out that he'd spent seven or eight years at Tagou, the largest school at Shaolin, and also one of the most famous schools for sanda in China. He'd come to the university to fight on the pro sanda team, but then he got injured and couldn't fight anymore. He still hung around the sanda team, and seemed really bitter about the way things had turned out, saying: "China's sports system just uses you and throws you away." That's true, in my opinion, but now he was better off. He'd moved out of the athletic dorms and lived in the normal Chinese dorms. He trained part time and went to classes full time. His fighting career was over, but at least now he was getting an education.

Some sanda guys were working out with their shirts off, as usual. They'd lift weights for about two minutes, then go stare at themselves in the mirror. I'd been in the weight room with the track team, the boxing team, the wrestling team, and wushu students. Of all sports, the sanda teams had the highest percentage of guys who worked out shirtless and spent the most time in front of the mirror, talking about their bodies. Wrestlers almost never did that. In fact, I think wrestlers did it less than your average 20-year-old in a gym does.

Later I sent an email to Matthew Polly, author of *American Shaolin*. He spent over a year training in sanda at Tagou, so I told him about my observation, writing: "It reminded me of what you said in your Shaolin book about how the sanda guys were jocks and had jock mentality compared to the Shaolin guys." His response was priceless: "Good to hear the sanda guys haven't changed. Wrestlers are grinders. Strikers are pretty boys who all imagine they'll be the next Bruce Lee."

Prancing around with no shirt on didn't seem like the right path to discovering the meaning of Shaolin Kung Fu. Grinding — meaning the extreme discipline and pain that wrestlers endure — while good for the soul, also probably wasn't going to lead to the answer. And this left me still wondering: What exactly is Shaolin Kung Fu?

Chapter 12
Hospital Days and End of Year One

Sport for defense services and sports defend the socialist motherland.

— **Xiao Mouwen,**
"Historical Evolution of New China's Mass Sports Policy,"
Sports Science **(Vol. 29, No. 4, 2009)**

Being a university teacher who was teaching in a foreign-language environment, and simultaneously a student who studied in a foreign-language environment, was an excellent opportunity to explore language learning from two different perspectives.

Some students are smart and have a fairly large vocabulary, but cultural barriers prevent them from learning. For example, because many Asian students are forced from an early age to memorize long lists of words, it's very common for them to be married to the concept that each English word has exactly one translation in their mother tongue. This belief is often so ingrained that, in spite of my education and being a native speaker, I can't dissuade them from it.

It was 2014, long before COVID-19, and I didn't think many Chinese students would know the English word "pandemic." I had a very high-level group of students read a text about the threat of a pandemic wiping out most of Europe. They knew the word "epidemic," and I explained that both words related to a disease outbreak, a fact which should have been clear from the context of the article they were reading.

Next, I asked if they knew the word "pan." Instantly, they all said "frying pan." I commended them on knowing frying pan, but pointed out that, in this context, "pan" had a different meaning. To which they responded, "frying pan." I told them that "pan" meant all, and that a pandemic was an epidemic that crossed national borders.

I asked a student to read aloud a section about the pandemic sweeping across a country and killing people. Then I asked: "Does this sound like they're talking about a disease or a frying pan?" But here I hit two barriers to learning. The first was that in the West, we're taught the Socratic method. It's normal for teachers to ask us questions as a means of eliminating possible solutions until only the correct answer remains. In China, students often thought I was just changing the subject and complicating the discussion by asking unrelated questions.

The other issue is that during their first 12 years of education, students are forced to read texts, but they don't need to actually understand them. They read texts, because they're commanded to do so. Then they answer questions, and every question has just one correct answer. If they fail the first time, the correct answers are given to them. They memorize the correct answers and regurgitate them on the exam — and this can all be done without understanding a text.

I showed the students that substituting the word "frying pan" for "pandemic" in the sentence made no sense. "The frying pan swept across Europe, killing hundreds of thousands. Doctors hoped to develop a vaccine to fight the frying pan."

The fact that switching "pandemic" with "frying pan" in the sentence made no sense didn't dissuade them from their belief that pan meant frying pan. "Yes, because the frying pans are dirty," explained one student. He immediately rethought the word "dirty" and said, "unsanitary." The fact he knew the latter word clearly supports my belief that the students' difficulty with the word "pandemic" wasn't linguistic.

I complimented him on the use of his vocabulary, but reiterated that pandemics have nothing to do with frying pans.

"Out of the frying pan and into the fire," blurted out one student. "In China, our frying pans are much larger and better than those in the US," said another. "A broad, shallow, metal container used in various forms of frying, baking, and washing," said a third, clearly reading from his smartphone. It seemed the students were looking for, or possibly needed, each English word to have exactly one meaning and one translation.

Parallel to my interest in spoken languages, I've always had a fascination with sign language and how deaf people interpret language. At SUS, we were required to take a course on Adaptive Physical Education, for which I wrote a report about the hearing-impaired MMA fighter, Matt "The Hammer" Hamill. His parents were down-to-earth farmers who didn't regard their son as being different. They simply raised him the same as any other farm kid. He grew up doing chores and playing sports. The parents didn't know how to sign, so they simply talked to him, constantly, as any parent would with a child who could hear. As a result, Matt reads lips exceptionally well and speaks well enough to give interviews. He became a decorated world-class wrestler as well as a UFC fighter. He also earned a bachelor's degree in electrical engineering, married, and raised a family.

Hammill's story was inspirational on so many levels. I also believe that his success and the success of other deaf people could give us greater insight into how languages are learned and processed by the brain.

For my final report, I wrote about disabled people who competed in wrestling. When I googled the phrase "wrestlers with disabilities," I was amazed how many news stories and videos came up. Several covered high school kids in the US who overcame incredible odds and excelled or at least participated in the sport of wrestling. These stories were all so inspiring, but I kept leaking tears on my keyboard. There were kids with severe birth defects, Down's Syndrome, or missing limbs — or even suffering from blindness — who still competed in wrestling. I'd never have done this research or heard these stories had I not been in this class. I felt very lucky.

The irony was that the only handicapped-accessible or barrier-free building on the SUS campus was the training hall, where disabled people were unlikely to go. Obvious places, like classrooms, lacked ramps or elevators. This was a particular problem at a university where many of us, myself included, wound up horribly injured or on crutches several times during our years of study. Each morning, on the way to lectures, I'd see students with training injuries being helped up the steps by their classmates.

After I realized that SUS wasn't handicapped-accessible, I began to think about Shanghai University, where I taught. It occurred to me that I'd never seen a disabled student at either university. I never saw anyone using a wheelchair or a walker, except for students who'd been injured in accidents or when playing sports. I never saw a blind student or a deaf student. I never saw someone with obvious physical differences. This led to some secondary research in which I found out that these students wouldn't generally have a chance to lead a "normal" life, the way they would in the US. In China, they might have access to some type of special education, but they wouldn't be permitted to attend most public universities or take most majors.

The lecture class on disabled athletes was taught by a professor who'd done extensive research in the United States. She told us the US had the best programs for disabled athletes, but Beijing had decided that — on top of winning more Olympic gold medals than any other country — they also want to dominate the Paralympics. Accordingly, China had begun developing teams of disabled athletes.

I decided to add a chapter in my dissertation about disabled wrestlers. I found precisely zero examples in China, but in the US there were countless heartwarming and inspiring stories about disabled wrestlers. Then I had another revelation: The disabled wrestlers I was writing about had all attended public school and competed in scholastic wrestling against non-disabled opponents. Many of them went on to attend public universities and some competed in collegiate sports against non-disabled opponents. No part of that story would have been possible in China.

This was another example of the country's public face versus the reality of its government's actions. Beijing claimed to want to promote sports for disabled people, but the authorities didn't allow — or at least they discouraged — disabled people from attending public schools and universities or from joining regular sports teams.

My original intent, in my dissertation, was to compare Chinese and Western wrestling, giving the two equal coverage. I'd expected that they'd be equally interesting. Instead, toward the end of my first year, I was beginning to realize that the story of Western wrestling, after about 1850, takes place almost exclusively in the US. Greco-Roman wrestling was invented in France in the mid-19th century, and catch wrestling was invented in England. They both spread to the United States, and from that point on wrestling developed mostly in the US. Catch wrestling became one of the highest-paid professional sports in the US. Freestyle wrestling was invented there, as were folk-style and collegiate-style wrestling. Professional wrestling has always existed, but the US took it to a new level with World Wrestling Entertainment (WWE). Similarly, mixed-style fighting events were held in other countries, but the US brought mixed martial arts (MMA) to the world with the Ultimate Fighting Championship (UFC).

When I started, I thought I'd find that, although China hadn't participated in these developments, they'd have their own fascinating history of wrestling development. But that didn't seem to be the case. Also, documentation on the Chinese side was a real issue. There was more documented wrestling history from the past 150 years in the US than there was for the complete history of wrestling in China. In the case of disabled wrestlers, for example, I had a whole chapter on disabled American wrestlers but just two sentences explaining that China had none. The professional wrestling chapter was similar. It mentions that wrestlers entertained the imperial court in ancient China, but on the US side, I could go into great detail about Hulkamania, Rock 'n' Wrestling, and André the Giant. But, of course, some ancient paintings and a few lines of text prove that wrestling entertainment existed in China long before the American nation was even born.

My professors suggested I look into the economics of wrestling, such as how wrestlers make money and where they make the most. In China and much of Asia, athletes are paid large amounts of money if they win Olympic medals. In the US, this isn't the case, but American athletes have other options, such as going into MMA or professional wrestling. I'd already decided to devote chapters to both of these. Again, information on the Chinese side was minimal, whereas the story of how pro wrestling migrated from Europe to the US, eventually culminating in the WWE, was fascinating. While China had some professional wrestling, it was never a big money event, and didn't really penetrate public consciousness. There are businessmen in Shanghai who pay top dollar to watch WWE, but few of them had ever seen or shown any interest in Chinese professional wrestling shows.

At every turn, it just became more and more difficult to give equal space to Chinese and Western wrestling in my dissertation.

·•●··

At wrestling practice, while the team worked on techniques for the national championships, I did freestyle wrestling with Chen Zhengxin, a 22-year-old who'd been training and competing in Greco-Roman since the age of four. He told me the reason he'd only just recently joined our team was that he'd just retired from competing in Greco at the highest levels.

I learned a lot from him. He could take me down at will, but I did manage to pull him down with me once or twice. Nonetheless, he could have literally killed me with his Greco skills at any moment. A few times, I was able to get his leg, because he wasn't used to defending his legs, but his balance was so incredible, that even when I had 100-percent control of his leg, I still couldn't get him down.

Over the weeks, as my team trained with ferocity, I realized I had no place in the national championships. In every session where I was given a choice of what to work on, I opted for freestyle. My freestyle was really coming along, but even then I only learned freestyle for the purpose of becoming a better MMA fighter, not to seriously compete in freestyle wrestling. I was beginning to think I should tell the coach that I'd pull out of nationals.

The next day, we did eight rounds of traditional shuai jiao sparring, which I filmed. Later, reviewing the video, I saw that it was incredibly rare that I even grabbed my opponent's jacket, which is the whole point of Chinese wrestling. Instead, all of my throws were from body locks and taking a leg. My teammates fought that way, too, using a combination of Greco and freestyle. It had become our team's normal culture — but with the nationals just weeks away, the guys were all trying to strictly adhere to traditional rules. In fact, Wang Yechao, one of my best friends, actually refused to partner with me, saying, "I want to train for nationals."

The coach had already told Chen Zhengxin that he couldn't wrestle in the nationals because he'd only been with our team for a few weeks and had literally zero Chinese wrestling skills, even though he could still win by using Greco techniques. A guest coach who was helping us prepare for nationals scolded Chen Zhengxin because his techniques all came from Greco. He kept yelling, "Grab the jacket! That's what it's there for."

An example of a technique I often used which was not technically illegal, but very frowned upon in shuai jiao, was the standing kimura lock, in which you grip one of your opponent's arms with two hands, one on the wrist and the other wrapped around his elbow. In MMA, it could be used as a submission, to hyperextend an opponent's arm, but in wrestling, it was legal to use it as a hold, a control position, as long as you didn't push it to the point that it became painful. I usually used this technique if someone took my back in standing, which is exactly how one of my favorite catch wrestlers, Kazushi Sakuraba, used it in MMA.

The wrestlers on our team were so good that, if one of them got your back, you were going up in the air and landing on your head. A common defense, in both freestyle and Greco, was to drop to your knees. This is something I didn't want to get used to doing, in case it ever came up in an MMA fight. In MMA, dropping to your knees, when an opponent has your back, would be an invitation for him to choke you. So instead I took a Kimura grip and used it to wrestle my way out. With the Kimura on, your opponent can't suplex you.

The guest coach seemed really surprised to see a non-Chinese in the training hall. He asked my team what I studied. They all said, "*Ziyóu bójí*," Chinese for MMA. But not everyone has heard of it, and the coach asked, "What's that?" Before I could answer, literally every one of my teammates began grabbing their own throats, making choking motions. I had to laugh.

The guest coach went over the rules for nationals. You could only clinch or grab a leg for three seconds before completing the takedown. He also said it was possible to be penalized for throwing from body lock or from sacrifice throws. It sounded like the nationals would just be a terrible experience for me of getting beat up and demoralized. Also, the event was around the same time as my dissertation proposal defense. I probably couldn't do both. We only had about five weeks of school left; then the proposal defense; then off to Cambodia and Vietnam to train in wrestling and sanda. In the end, I told the coach I was going to pull out of the nationals.

Even though I'd pulled out of wrestling nationals, I thought I could do some sanda competitions. But later, when I talked to Jiang Huaying, he told me that sanda was moving to a ten-point must system, similar to boxing and MMA. They also changed the rules, so that you got zero points for a throw if you went down with your opponent. That essentially meant I couldn't fight sanda at all. Now, with a ten-point must system, guys wouldn't even be doing throws anymore, because they cost a lot of energy and they wouldn't help you gain points and win. With the new rules, sanda would just become Muay Thai with no clinch, knees, or elbows. And without points for throws, I'd get decimated.

I stayed in the rest of the day, writing and marking my students' midterms. One nice thing about teaching the repeat remedial classes was that fewer students turned in their work. I had less marking to do. Instead of paying me extra, Shanghai University should have paid me less than they did for regular classes!

After marking, I finished writing my proposal defense. Next, I finished writing an article on wrestling history for a foreign magazine. Having ten minutes to kill, I watched five Mike Tyson fights.

Later, Kirk called me from the wrestling room, asking if I wanted to practice. He worked with me on several throws I'd been having difficulty with. I weighed myself after this, my third workout of the day, and saw I was 97 kg (214 lbs). If I'd been trying to bulk up, I'd have been a success. At the beginning of the semester, I weighed 94 kg (207 lbs). I had to believe that I was gaining weight due to the combination of a horrible diet, weight training, wrestling, and *jīběngōng*. The thing about *jīběngōng* is that it works the leg muscles. If you want to put on weight, just build up your leg muscles. They're really heavy.

Food was a persistent problem. Most of the food in and around SUS was very low-quality, high in carbs and oil, and low in protein and nutrition. The meat dishes in the cafeteria were oily and drenched in sugar-laden sauces. The cafeteria served some vegetables, but they were overcooked and swimming in sauce. Unfortunately. I couldn't always get salads from convenience stores.

To get my fill of protein, I was eating probably twice as many calories as I needed for the day. Chinese houses and restaurants seldom have ovens, so most dishes are fried in oil. In fact, all of the food sold near the university was fried in oil, except for the barbecued meat, and that was doused and basted in oil. Barbecued meat was still about the cleanest source of protein I could find, even if, when carrying it home, I'd leave a trail of oil in the hallway. I just didn't understand why they couldn't just let meat be meat and vegetables be vegetables.

One morning, I was riding the subway to the Japanese school. My stop was approaching, so I got up and stood by the door. A woman forced her way in front of me, so she could stand between me and the door, ostensibly so she could get off the train first and get home one person faster. But when the doors opened, she took about half a step out the door, and froze mid-stride so she could read something on her phone. Of course, she was completely blocking the way and no one could get off the train. I yelled, "Excuse me!" in Mandarin. She ignored me, so I shouldered into her a bit harder than I meant to and she spun around. I was going to apologize, but she was so focused on her phone that she hadn't even noticed. I thought it might have been rude to interrupt her to apologize, so I just went on.

Preparing my lesson in the teacher's room, looking at the materials, I wondered how anyone ever managed to learn English. ESL books always contained so many useless concepts and vocabulary words like "radio." And they always had some radio-type broadcasts in the listening exercises. Ten years earlier, my young students had known what a radio was. But I wondered if they ever listened to it. Now, I wondered if my current students had ever seen or listened to a radio even once.

Although the books weren't great, my high-level Japanese students were always interesting to talk to. When they told me about their lives, growing up in Japan, it was similar to growing up in the US. They'd had part-time jobs and played sports. One manager told me he'd gone to college on a football scholarship. They told me that Chinese children were always picked up by their parents or grandparents at school and that they never walked or traveled to and from school alone. They all felt that Chinese kids were missing out on one of the developmental experiences of childhood. As we shared funny stories about how we got into all sorts of adventures and mischief when walking home from school, I felt I had more in common with these Japanese than I did with Chinese people.

Heading home on the subway, I grimaced at the pain in my shoulder each time the train hit a bump. I'd regained most of my range of motion, but clearly still hadn't recovered. I was finally desperate enough to go back to the university clinic to try and get a referral for a major hospital. Without even stopping at my room, I went straight to the campus clinic and paid my RMB 1 (US$ 0.16). I told the doctor my shoulder had been painful for months and I was suffering from a lack of strength and limited mobility. He nodded and said, "It's probably injured. You may want to go to a real hospital."

He wrote a referral for me, and I got a teammate to go with me. We made it through the first step, shouting at the woman through bulletproof glass. I made it to the second step, paying money. On the way to the department selected by the bulletproof-glass lady — which was the wrong department — I noticed the Chinese traditional medicine and acupuncture department. Abandoning the diagnosis made by the cashier, I decided to see if I could just go get the problem fixed myself.

I went back downstairs, got my payment receipt transferred over to the traditional medicine, then described my symptoms to someone who wasn't a doctor. She prescribed three treatments of acupuncture. I then had to wait in line and pay for the treatments. Then I had to wait in line to see a doctor.

The doctor was asking me about my injury, so I told her I was a member of the wrestling team. It was a hot day, and I was wearing a T-shirt. I thought it was pretty evident from my build that I was on a wrestling team. She then asked what I did for a living, and I said I was a university lecturer. She asked: "And is this injury work-related?" No, as a university lecturer, I tend not to get a lot of serious work-related injuries. "It's wrestling related." I told her, for the second time. "Don't exercise so much." she advised me.

So much as what? I wondered. She had no idea how much I exercised now, neither had she told me by how much to reduce it. Also, the injury was clearly an impact injury, trauma, not just a joint that had slowly worn down through overuse.

She sent me to another station, where I told the doctor that I belonged to a wrestling team. He said, "Oh, you got hurt when you fell down?" In Chinese, the word for "fall down" and the word "to be wrestled down" is the same. So I agreed, thinking he meant that I'd been injured when I was taken down. I still thought it was a strange question, though, because I imagine most wrestling injuries happen from takedowns and not from the weigh-ins. But then my Chinese classmate jumped in and repeated to the doctor: "He's on the wrestling team. He got hurt wrestling."

Even if the doctor hadn't heard or understood me, I obviously had said something other than "I fell down." Then my teammate, who's a native speaker, told him two more times, that I was on the wrestling team and had been injured wrestling. The doctor, however, rejected the information, because it was unusual. "Yes, he fell down," the doctor repeated. "People often get hurt when they fall down." The only good that came out of this was that it confirmed to me that it wasn't just me. Chinese people did this to each other as well.

Another odd thing about doctors in China is that most of them are very unhealthy and know nothing about sports. In New York, when you go to a chiropractor or physiotherapist, they ask you what sport you do and they instantly know what injuries to look for. Occasionally, Chinese doctors would ask me if I exercised, and I was tempted to answer, "No, these muscles are the result of an allergic reaction."

The doctor gave me a prescription for "selective non-steroidal anti-inflammatory drug." I thought, that's good. I'd been so on-edge lately, that if I took the steroid kind, I might kill someone.

He then sent me to the acupuncture treatment room. I thanked my teammate and told him he could go home. The treatment room was a large open ward with about twenty beds, halfway hidden by curtains to give an illusion of privacy. As every bed was full, I had to wait my turn, out in the hallway. Most of the patients were elderly people, which reminded me why acupuncturists and physiotherapists in Asia never seem to know anything about sports injuries. I guess most of the people they treat are suffering from arthritis and other complications of aging. Some of the patients were wearing hospital pajamas, meaning they were staying in the hospital, and likely had other things wrong with them. They were the ones I wanted to avoid, in case it was something contagious.

When my turn finally came, they called me into the treatment room. Inside the air was smoky, because the doctors burned herbs on the skin of some patients. They asked me to lie on a table which had blood on the pillow and shoeprints on the sheets. Rather than using disposables, the acupuncture needles were the reusable kind. (For obvious reasons, this is illegal in most developed countries). When they told me to take off my shoes, I noticed there were discarded needles all over the floor, so it reminded me of a crack house. I made a mental note not to touch the floor with my bare feet.

The treatment consisted of a lot of needles and some electric shocks, followed by bamboo cups and burning incense on my skin. While I lay there, all pinned and wired up, a patient in another bed began shouting for the doctor, but no one came for at least 15 minutes.

Eventually, the doctor did return to see to the patient. He then removed my needles and told me I could go. I guess I was the last patient of the morning, because a woman came in to change the sheets on all the beds. She wore neither gloves nor a mask, and she simply threw the used sheets in a pile on the dirty floor. On the way out, I saw a metal tray full of used needles, so I guessed they washed them and reused them.

Hygiene and the risk of hepatitis aside, my shoulder did feel better.

After I got home, one of my wrestling teammates stopped by see me. It was his first time in the foreign dorms. Reading the names on the doors, he asked me: "Are all Vietnamese people named Nguyen?"

He came in my room, looked around and told me, "It's a pity that you foreigners only have one roommate. It's very boring, living alone." Chinese people never seemed to need alone time or even quiet time to work or think.

He'd come by to tell me that the team had pulled out of the nationals for the same reasons I had. They knew that while they could take opponents down and get points, they weren't really using traditional techniques. Accordingly, they canceled and decided that our training would concentrate on improving our traditional wrestling skills for the remaining four weeks of the semester. That part made sense. But he also said they were now planning to compete in September, which made no sense because the team takes the entire summer off. I saw how out of shape they all were after Chinese New Year, but after three months of summer holidays... Anyway, at least it wasn't just me who wanted to pull out.

The next day, at wrestling, the coach set up a tournament-style practice, complete with referees and scorekeepers. Those jobs were given to team members who were still injured from a previous day, when the coach had decided we should do two-and-a-half hours of weightlifting.

There were no eliminations in our tournament. Even if you lost, you stayed in and wrestled the next round. Essentially, this was round-robin sparring. We changed partners each five-minute round until we'd each wrestled eight different people. It was grueling; a lot of wrestlers limped off injured or wrestled terribly because of exhaustion.

By the end, no one seemed to be wrestling anymore. When the coach asked, four times, if everyone had wrestled their last match, no one answered. This was exactly what happened when I taught English. He asked yet again, and still no one answered. He looked really frustrated, so he ordered us to line up with our match partners. Whoever hadn't wrestled, he reckoned, wouldn't have a partner.

Most days, after we finished training, the coach had us stand at attention, while he yelled at the team for a half hour or so. Normally he told me I could go, so I didn't have to listen. This day, he forgot to send me out. And if I'd left, I would have left my match partner standing alone. So I stayed. There were three students who didn't have match partners: Zheng Tong, a girl, and a huge heavyweight. He asked them again if they'd wrestled the last match. Finally, they answered that they hadn't.

The coach went nuts, screaming, "Didn't you hear me ask 'Who didn't wrestle?' Do you not understand me when I talk? I asked many times, but you didn't answer." Up to this point, I felt he was more than right. This was the exact frustration I felt when I was teaching and it took ten minutes of anger and yelling, to get an answer to a question the students could have answered the first eight times I asked it. But then he punched the three of them in the face, with a closed fist, including the girl. He was a huge heavyweight, with powerful shoulders and back, I just couldn't imagine how he could punch a girl. Then he kicked them in the thigh and the belly. Next, he slapped Zheng Tong and kicked him a couple of extra times.

I'd been taking photos that day, and had my camera in my hand. Wang Yechao gently reached out, and held my camera arm down, signaling that I shouldn't take photos of this beating. His action was unnecessary, though — I was too traumatized to do anything but stand and stare, open-mouthed.

After the beating, the coach screamed at the team for another half hour. I was looking for a way out when a cellphone began ringing in someone's bag. The coach got really angry. "Whose phone is that?" I just started walking over to the bags. He asked if it was mine. I said, "Maybe." It absolutely wasn't mine, but it gave me an out. I grabbed my gear, and without even considering changing clothes, I walked right out the door on shaky legs.

That night, I went for dinner at a street eatery, and the guy cooking my dinner was smoking a cigarette. It was a barbecue restaurant. I guess the cigarette added a smoky flavor and nicotine goodness.

Luckily, Han Hongyu, my advisor's assistant, was there. I'd been trying all semester to engage with him socially. He was sitting with three ex-classmates from his master's program. They were fairly drunk already, but I told the waitress to send four bottles of beer to their table. When they called me over to sit with them, they thought it was strange that I'd ordered four beers but refused to drink one of them. "I don't drink alcohol." I explained. "But I figured you guys could use four more." The table was already covered in empty bottles.

One of Han Hongyu's friends said to me: "You foreigners have such big noses and eyes. I don't see how you can be a boxer. It seems really easy to hit your nose and eyes and break them." I stood up from the table and asked if he'd like to try. It turned out he didn't. It seems everyone is a philosopher, but very few people like to test the theories they dream up.

I sat back down and Han Hongyu gave me some advice about my research and my dissertation proposal. I hoped that we'd made some kind of a breakthrough in our friendship. He even told me again that he had a Chinese wrestling background and that we should start training together. Over the next two weeks, I called him three more times for wrestling, but finally gave up. We never became friends.

•••••

Zheng Tong had been training with the sanda team for a few weeks now, hoping to become an MMA fighter. Actually, he'd told me that he'd been training with them. I hadn't verified it, and given how lax he was about everything else, I wondered if he was actually going every day and what he was doing when he was there. We sparred, and his boxing was still incredibly bad. I invited him and two of other friends to train at the MMA gym: Jiang Huaying, my sanda friend, and Ren Zhiying, a would-be sanda fighter from the university golf team.

Zheng Tong was always hanging around the martial arts classes and training sessions, because he desperately wanted to be a fighter, but for some reason, everyone hated him, except me. Rumor had it that his family was super wealthy. He had a brand-new expensive car at least once per semester, but he never had any cash in his pocket. One time, he offered to drive me somewhere in his Mercedes, but on the appointed day, he couldn't buy gas. So the car just sat, parked on a street near the university, and we had to take a bus. It turned out that his father was a real-estate developer who periodically came into huge sums of money, when he'd complete or sell a project, but in between sales, the family had no cash. Zheng Tong's allowance was RMB 2,000 (US$ 317) a month, but he couldn't get any other cash from his parents, even if he asked. However, on this occasion, he must have just received his allowance, because he had money for gas. He drove us; along the way we stopped off, so he could introduce us to a retired sanda fighter he was friends with.

The former champion was an interesting guy, with a lot of opinions and a lot to say about fighting, strategy, and mindset. He reminded me of one of those old kung fu masters in the movies, except that he was only 32 years old. He poured tea and told us the facts of life, sanda style. He had an amazing way of reading people. When I sat down, he said to me: "Your legs are very powerful, but have no flexibility, so your kicking must be very bad. But your entire body is proportionate, shoulders, arms, and back are all as large as your legs, so you're probably good at wrestling and boxing."

He'd apparently watched Zheng Tong learning sanda at the university and said, "Zheng Tong is very powerful, but he lacks movement, flexibility, techniques, and the mindset to learn sanda. He can never do it." While I thought that was a bit harsh, I agreed. My guess, however, was that Zheng Tong could learn MMA, if he could change his attitude and embrace discipline and hard work. Ultimately, however, I guess the sanda fighter was right. A fundamental change of personality was extremely unlikely.

The sanda fighter decided to go to the MMA gym with us, and coach us during sparring. We got to spar a lot of rounds with each other and also with the trainers and students at the MMA gym. I always forgot that I look different, and the way my friends treated me, it seemed I was just Āndōngní, not "some white guy." But when we got to the MMA gym, my teammates were acting a little unusual. I then realized it was because they'd never been surrounded by so many foreigners before. Most of the staff and some of the students were Chinese, but nearly all of the trainers and pro fighters were foreign. Also, there were foreign women there, exercising in revealing clothing; the look of animal lust on Zheng Tong's face made me worry that we'd have an incident. Afterward, I heard him bragging to some Chinese friends: "I sparred with foreigners tonight. There was even a black guy."

Zheng Tong and I did both MMA sparring and boxing. Whichever we did, his boxing was unbelievably bad. He just ducked his head and ran at me swinging wildly. Then he'd crash into me and try to take me down. In MMA, he'd get the takedown, but from the ground I'd always take him down and get the win. In boxing, when he crashed into me, we'd have to break. Each time we broke and reset, I'd land one or two really solid, clean punches to his face. Then he'd crash into me, and we'd break and reset. Eventually, those two solid punches, every thirty seconds or so, added up. I could see the sanda champ shaking his head, like, "This is never going to happen."

Next, Zheng Tong did submission wrestling with the MMA coach. Most of the foreign students stopped training to come and watch my teammate wrestle. Everyone was impressed that Zheng Tong, with no jiu-jitsu experience at all, was able to get the takedown and stay in dominant position, holding off the submissions for a long time. All of the Greco-Roman guys on the wrestling team had a handful of power submissions which come from Greco wrestling. The most common ones are a kind of arm triangle and a couple of neck cranks which cut off your breathing. But the Greco chokes, while scary to normal people, usually won't tap out someone with BJJ or MMA experience, because they just relax and the choke isn't tight enough to completely stop the breathing. Zheng Tong got one of these chokes on the coach, but obviously the coach was able to wait it out and escape. At one point, Zheng Tong wrapped his arms around both of coach's legs, lifted him off the ground and slammed him. In the end, the coach won each of the submission rounds, usually with a neck crank.

Jiang Huaying and Ren Zhiying had both heard of Muay Thai, but had never seen it up close or experienced it. Ren Zhiying really enjoyed learning some techniques from the Muay Thai coach. Nowadays, some sanda tournaments allow knees. But the Thais are the real masters of the knee. The Muay Thai coach was showing him how to step off at a 45-degree angle with the back foot, before throwing a front knee. This takes you out of the way of any answering punches, and puts you right in your opponent' blind side, for your follow up punches and kicks.

A hugely powerful hardcore Muay Thai coach named Karl was willing to get in the ring and spar with Jiang Huaying, who only weighed about 65 kg (143 lbs). One of the big differences between Muay Thai and sanda, which the coach was able to teach Jiang Huaying, was to catch and kick. In sanda, when you catch the kick, you throw the opponent to the ground. In Muay Thai, when you catch the kick, you kick the opponent.

Walking through the subway station, on the way back to the university, my friends and I were talking about fighting, but it seemed every other passenger was staring at his or her phone. The only reason we didn't have more collisions was because I remained alert, dodging through this mass of zombies. I felt like a character in *The Walking Dead*, worried what might happen if I also got addicted to cellphone games. I guessed we'd all just crash into each other until someone died.

The internet in the dorm was out again, so I went to McDonalds to get coffee and do some work. Looking around, I felt genuinely worried about where humanity was headed. I saw couples out to dinner, each person staring at his or her own phone, not talking to the other. There were parents spending quality time with their children at McDonalds, because of the free WiFi. The kid sat there bored, while the parent played on a tablet.

The next day, the manager at my fitness gym called me in, saying they wanted me to teach an MMA class. To build interest in my MMA class, he asked if every time I came to work out, I could get in the ring and work pads. I asked who'd hold pads for me, and the manager said, "All our instructors are from the sports university. They know how to hold pads."

Being from a sports university doesn't mean you know how to hold pads. The only one with a combat sport background was the girl who they'd tried to set me up with for private wrestling lessons, and she wouldn't know how to hold pads. Additionally, the instructors all sort of said they were too small to hold pads for me, which I agreed with. In the end, they chose this huge bodybuilder guy, because of his size and because we'd look better on social media. When they told him he had to hold pads for me, he literally screamed and backed out of the room, terrified. This guy had biceps the size of thighs and was twenty years younger than me, but he was frightened to merely hold pads for me. I couldn't imagine what would happen if they told him he had to spar with me.

We did a demo, in the ring in the middle of the gym, with this guy holding pads and me kicking and punching, but he was so scared, he kept backing up. He even jumped out of the ring a few times. In the end, I told the manager I'd just demo by hitting the bag.

I went home to take a shower and check the pain in my chest. A few days earlier, I was washing my chest and I suddenly cried out in excruciating pain. It turned out that I had two huge and painful lumps on my chest. I tried to ignore them, but they hurt when I slept. At sanda, AJ had kicked me in the chest and my legs buckled from the pain. I knew that I needed to get to a proper hospital and find out if it was anything serious. WebMD said men could get breast cancer, and the symptoms matched.

After work on Saturday, I returned to the on-campus clinic, paid, got a ticket, went upstairs, and found a bent little man alone in a dirty room, sitting in the dark. "Are you a doctor?" I had to ask. He looked like a troll, something that lived in a cave, gnawing on old rotting bones. He nodded, and asked me what was wrong. After I told him, he said the clinic couldn't do an MRI or ultrasound. He handed me a referral to a big hospital, but it didn't say anything about my symptoms or the tests I needed. So I asked him: "Could you just write on that paper that I need an MRI or an ultrasound? So I won't have trouble with the vocabulary when I get to the hospital?" He replied that I should get a friend to go with me. However, I insisted, and in the end Gollum finally gave in. He wrote two characters on a piece of paper for me. When I pay one-sixth of a dollar, I expect a little service.

I walked into the big hospital, vowing to be braver than I'd been the first time. This time, I made it to the second floor before I gave up.

In spite of my DIY note that may or may not have said "MRI and X-ray" in Chinese, I finally had to break down and call a Chinese friend for help. Being that this was potentially a lot more serious than a dislocated shoulder, I called Zhang Chengfeng, an academic graduate student, as opposed to calling one of my teammates. It was a lot easier having my friend negotiate with the various gatekeepers who protect the people from accessing the people's healthcare system. After numerous lines, forms, and fees, we made it to a doctor who after examining me, said I had to get more imaging done and then come back.

We went to the cashier to pay for the imaging, but the window was closed. We went to the main cashier, and the lady screamed at us like naughty children saying the window was closed and we'd have to wait until Monday. It was Friday, and I was about have the longest weakened of my life.

As I knew that this could be cancer, I was naturally quite upset to begin with. Add to that the stress of the constant run-around, being sent here and there, and forms and payments, and then to not only be refused service, but to be shouted at, just broke me.

Since there was nothing else we could do, I wanted to take Zhang Chengfeng out to eat at the KFC across the street.

I ordered my food, in Mandarin, pointed at it on the picture menu, then said: "The chicken sandwich meal. The RMB 30 [US$ 4.75] one." The KFC kid asked, "Just the sandwich?" And I said, "No, the meal." I pointed at it again, stabbing my finger on the menu laying in front of him. "The RMB 30 one, " I repeated. He rang it up and said, "RMB 15." I handed him a RMB 100 bill and then it hit me. "Why is it RMB 15? It should be RMB 30!"

The manager came over and asked, "Do you want just a sandwich or the meal?" I was shouting now: "I want the meal. The RMB 30 meal. The one I pointed at. The one I told him three times already." At this point, I saw the employee giving me the stink-eye. He really looked like he wanted to fight, so I gave him the crook-eye back. Then, switching to Brooklyn English, I asked "You wanna throw hands?" At that point, the kid said in English, "F—k your head."

F—k your head? That gave me something to think about for the rest of the day. Clearly an insult, but what exactly did it mean?

Through all of this, the manager did nothing, Not even when the kid said "F—k your head." I think somehow that, when I said "throw hands," the kid heard something like "blah-blah your head," so he was like "Two can play at that game. Blah-blah your head, too!"

After I ate and had time to calm down, I felt bad about what had happened. I also felt a little sick. I thought it was from the emotional dump. But maybe he'd put rat poison in my food. And that upset me, because he hadn't asked if I wanted rat poison.

Heading back to the dorm, my body felt heavy and my brain felt thick, like I was looking at the world through gelatin. I ducked into a convenience store and bought a bunch of candy bars. Zhang Chengfeng warned me that candy isn't healthy. I thought: "Well, if you're so smart, you tell me how to deal with my emotions without eating chocolate."

Laying on my bed, I reviewed my options. I thought I had a cancerous tumor. I hated the hospital. And the kid at KFC may want to kill me. I was wondering if it'd be possible to get a sharp knife and a wide-bore straw and just extract the tumor myself. Ironically, the best place to get a wide-bore straw was KFC. I'd therefore just have to go with Plan A: Wait until Monday and go back to the hospital. Afterward, we could eat somewhere else.

I don't know what happened to Saturday. On Sunday, I received a call at 8:15 a.m., telling me I had a meeting with my advisor at 9:30 a.m. Typical Chinese academic scheduling. You often didn't find out about a meeting until it was already in progress. Normally, I might have protested, or claimed I was busy, but technically, I was supposed to meet with my advisor once a week, and this term, I'd only met with him three times. The way I saw it, one inconvenient, unscheduled meeting was better than 12 scheduled ones.

Fortunately, the meeting turned out to be surprisingly productive. We talked about the writing of my dissertation and my proposal defense. Originally, I'd been told that my proposal presentation and defense would be in June. As recently as a few days earlier, I'd been told again that it would happen in June. Today, when I asked my advisor if he knew the exact date, he said, "October." I was so shocked that I repeated, "October?" Occasionally, when I'm shocked and just repeating things, Chinese people think I haven't understood, so they try to convey the information again using English. But this being the Wu Shu Institute, no one could speak English. Han Hongyu did the best he could. "Octember" he said.

Ah yes, now it was all so clear. Beware the dreaded Ides of Octember. Of course, there was no mention of — and no one had any memory of — having told me multiple times, over the past months, that the proposal would be in June. By Chinese logic, however, you shouldn't care. You have to be here for three years anyway. No matter what schedules are made or changed during the three years, it actually changes nothing about the outcome. If the presentation is June or October, as long as you're prepared and you present, that's all that matters. And there's some logic in that.

While it was all a bit frustrating, it also meant I was already prepared, and wouldn't need to do anything before October. It also meant I could leave for the summer, as soon as my few remaining courses had their finals.

Early Monday morning, Zhang Chengfeng accompanied me back to the hospital, so we could take a number. The admissions had just opened, yet we still wound up being number 89. Within minutes, there were literally hundreds of people staring up at the board, waiting for their number. It was like Las Vegas. I half expected that people would be betting money and shouting, "Come on 45! Come on 45!" and "Ooooo! 29! Crapped out again."

I wondered how safe it was to be packed in with so many sick people. But then, every time I saw something dirty, crowded, or less than perfect in the hospital, I'd just remind myself, "To see a doctor costs RMB 15 [US$ 2.40]. If this was the States, I couldn't afford to be here. Of course, neither could most of these other people. So at least the line would be shorter."

When you're waiting for hours on end in a hospital, you've nothing to do but stare at the faces in the crowd and make up supervillain names for them. I saw a cute girl and started flirting. But then it hit me: "This is a hospital. You don't know why she's here." I went back to my supervillain name game, dubbing her, "Siren Malady."

When my number finally came up, I was called into a room to see a doctor. Before he touched my chest, he put on the used rubber glove that he had laying on the table. I didn't think it would do either of us any good. The doctor looked at my chart and handed it to the nurse. She exclaimed "Aaaaah!" I wasn't sure what to make of that, but I thought she needed to work on her poker face.

The doctor told me the nurse would take me to do a test that he'd interpret, and then he'd let me know if it was cancer or not. She led me to a room on another floor, told me to take off my shirt and lay on the bed. Next, she pulled out a syringe the size of a turkey baster. It looked like the syringe from the overdose scene in *Pulp Fiction*.

"You must lay very still, because I'll stick this needle into the lump on your chest and it'll hurt," she said.

It was already so tender that just taking a shower hurt. I couldn't imagine what it was going to feel like, having that huge needle digging into it. Also, I didn't know a lot about biology, but I assumed the lump was buried deep under my skin. I guess that's why the needle was so long. She also explained to me that they weren't taking fluid, but rather tissue, and this is why the needle had to be so broad, and why the pain would be so intense.

I lay down, with my body rigid as a board. She told me to relax, but obviously that never works. I looked away and she began to stab the needle into my chest. It was like one of those vampire movies. I kept expecting her to drive it in with a stone. I shouted and cried and squirmed, and she warned me: "You have to stop moving or you could get hurt."

I looked down at the sides and the foot of the bed, half expecting to see Frankenstein-type restraints, because that was the only way I could imagine I was going to be able to remain still. She tried again, but the pain was blinding, so — although I'm 100-percent against drugs or alcohol — I asked for drugs. When she said she had none, I asked for alcohol. But once again, I was out of luck.

I asked if she had someone who could hold me down, but the only other person on duty was a nurse who weighed about half my bodyweight. Zhang Chengfeng wasn't bigger, so I saw no other option than to man-up and take it. I clenched down, told her she could proceed, and I screamed, but managed to lay reasonably still while this needle inched into my chest, then extracted some tissue. When it was over, I was dripping with sweat.

The lab results took another day. I had to go to the lab myself, pay for results, collect them, and bring them to the doctor. Coincidentally, I bumped into him in the elevator. He held the results up to the light and said. "It's nothing. Probably a fatty deposit. It should go away in about a month." Elevator diagnoses are always the best.

It turned out that he was right. In fact, it was gone within days, which confirmed my normal way of dealing with medical problems, which was to ignore them.

From start to finish, for everything — acupuncture treatments, imaging on my shoulder and on my chest, drawing and analyzing blood, prescription medicine, and elevator analysis — my total expenses were about RMB 510 (US$ 81). And I actually got part of that back through some sort of student health insurance plan. They also told me I had used up my deductible for the year, which I took as a license to live more recklessly and let the state pay the bills.

· • ● • ·

It was the first brutally hot day of the year in Shanghai. The Chinese student dorms didn't have AC, but the foreign dorms did. I used up all my phone minutes sending texts to my Chinese classmates, complaining that the AC in my room was too powerful and I was freezing.

The next day was Saturday, so I had to teach at the Japanese school. While I really enjoyed talking to my high-level students, they were an anomaly. When I checked the schedule, I saw that I'd have beginners and intermediate students for the whole six hours. I referred to those days as "dumb down my English till it hurts days." While Japanese students seemed to be better and more disciplined than Chinese students, on average they weren't nearly as good at communicating. In the intermediate classes, I had adult students who'd not only studied English for countless years, but who'd lived and worked in English-speaking countries, and yet they still often gave me one-word non-answers. The best ones were the agrammatical questions, where I had to be a combination of Sherlock Holmes and Mr. Spock to figure out what they wanted to say. For example, one of my students asked me, "Late mean dead?" It took me a while, but then I realized, "Yes, in the context, late means dead." Then, to her credit, she tried to make her own example, to check her understanding. "Late to work…die…*karoshi* mean overwork?"

"Yes, it does," I agreed, supportively.

After class, I discovered that Burger King in Shanghai finally had a sandwich that was right for me: Three layers of beef and two of pork, like a little eight-dollar slice of Heaven.

That night, my training mates Jiang Huaying and Ma Pei went with me to try a local MMA gym. It was a bit of a disappointment. When we arrived, I asked the coach if their grappling instructors taught wrestling or BJJ. He said they didn't do grappling, so I asked what they had. His reply was, "Sanda and Muay Thai."

"Are your Muay Thai teachers from Thailand?"

"No, they're from China," he told me.

"Did they fight or train in Thailand?"

"No," he answered.

It was typical in China to offer Muay Thai at MMA clubs, but the trainers actually knew nothing about Muay Thai. They were usually sanda majors who may or may not have ever watched a Muay Thai fight.

Thinking we could salvage the evening by getting some good sanda takedown training, I asked. However, the coach said, "When we do sanda, we don't do takedowns."

I began to wonder: How exactly was this MMA?

The workout consisted largely of Shaolin kick drills. These are very good for fighters everywhere, I think, but also suggested to me that the owners and coaches were wushu practitioners who knew nothing about Muay Thai or MMA. When the teacher scolded me, because my back wasn't straight enough and my hands weren't pointing at the ceiling, I felt like I was back at Shaolin Temple. During some of the combination drills, they asked me but not the other students to do knees. This is also typical, claiming it's Muay Thai but not using knees or elbows. There was no sparring at the end. One of the reasons I went there was to meet some new people, but after training, they all just went home.

After practice, I ate several Snickers bars. Looking at the quantity of sugar I ate in a day, I wondered if I was actually an elf who'd been adopted by a human family.

On the subway ride home, I was grossed out. It's not just that Chinese people eat on the subway, but they tend to eat high-involvement foods which don't necessarily stay in their mouths, such as fruits and seeds where you need to bite off the skin or suck out the pits and spit them on the floor. You know how dirty your hands get on a subway? The last thing you'd want to do is handle food, then suck on it.

The next morning, in sanda training, a teammate tried to practice his English. The Chinese word for sparring is *shízhàn*, and he asked me, in English, "Do you want to do realistic combat?" — that being the literal translation of *shízhàn*. They were all mired in dictionary, and it was usually very difficult to convince them that the literal translation wasn't always correct.

After sanda, I stayed in my room, finishing a paper and a presentation I was writing about ancient wrestling. Looking at old pictures painted on vases and murals, from China, Greece, and the Middle East, I saw the same techniques. Even the *jīběngōng* was obvious in some of the pictures. Not only were the techniques the same, across continents in ancient times, but we were still doing the same techniques in training today.

Greek pankration is of great historical importance. In the original Greek Olympic Games, mixed-style fighting was already a codified event. We know that mix style fights, or ge do, existed in China, but we have no documentation about the details. In the West, however, there are ancient records, showing that Eurybatus of Laconia won the Olympic wrestling in 708 BC and Lygdamis of Syracuse won Pancratium in 648 BC. It fascinated me that the entire world had come full circle, and that this sport — codified in Greece, but probably also happening in some limited way in China — eventually became a global phenomenon which brought together the wrestling and fighting styles of every nation and every people.

It was also incredible to look at these pankration pictures and see throws used in Chinese wrestling and submissions used in BJJ and catch wrestling.

The theory I was working on was that wrestling styles and fighting styles around the world had similar techniques because the humans practicing them weren't that different. A technique that makes a Korean man fall down will also make an Argentinian fall down. But there were differences across arts. One of the fundamental differences between MMA and wrestling is that in wrestling, rolling to your stomach is a defensive position, to avoid the pin. Accordingly, wrestlers practice rolling the opponent to obtain points and to go for the pin, whereas in MMA, you practice back mounting him and choking him. And, in shuai jiao, there is no ground fighting, so you'd practice neither of these. If the rules prevent you from doing a certain technique, then generally that art won't teach those techniques, and you'll not practice them. For example, boxers don't practice kicking or wrestling. Over time, this means that certain techniques are lost to certain arts and even to whole countries. China, today, unlike Japan or the West, doesn't have a ground-fighting art.

Rules cause techniques to be lost to various arts and countries. So the question is, why do rules differ from country to country, from art to art? The answer must be culture. It must be that culture defines the rules and rules wind up defining the art. This is what I came up with and this idea would remain in the back of my mind during my research for the remaining two years.

I went down to the street, found my favorite barbecue guy, and put in my order. While he was cooking my dinner, I remembered I needed milk, so I ducked into the convenience store. When I came out, he was gone. Heading down into the alleys behind the university, I found him, just finishing my dinner.

"The police came," he said, to explain his disappearance.

We'd been through this drill before, or so I thought. Suddenly, he said something he'd never said before: "Go back to the main road, stand by the fruit vendor, and someone will bring your dinner to you." It was exactly like a drug deal. He couldn't even be seen accepting money. But I guess if the police saw him cooking, he could claim it was for personal use. Eventually, he passed my food through a hole in the back of the fruit vendor, and the fruit vendor lady sold me my dinner. Very entertaining, but also very cloak and dagger. Is this what they call dinner theater?

I snuck my secret barbecue back to my room. While I was eating, Michael, one of the Americans, stopped by because he wanted to teach my Japanese roommate, Natsuki, and some other students, Danyar from Kazakhstan and Zolar from Mongolia, about water balloons. They went up on the roof, and I went back to work.

Hours later, I heard a commotion in the hallway. I opened my door to see some angry Koreans kicking the door of the African girl who lived across the hall. I assumed this had something to do with my friends who were up on the roof, throwing water balloons. I hung around, to make sure things didn't escalate, or that they wouldn't threaten the African girl. The Koreans found the ladder to the roof and began yelling at my friends, who refused to come down. They said they'd tell the house superintendent what happened. After the Koreans disappeared, Michael and the others came down from the roof, laughing hysterically.

On Monday morning, as I was heading to class, I saw my four friends standing more or less at attention, being told off by the head of the Foreign Students Department. Apparently the police had been there, following up on a complaint about someone throwing objects off the roof over the weekend. SUS had told the police that my friends were wild, drunken foreign students and it had all been a huge misunderstanding. The students avoided actually having to face the police themselves, but there could still be disciplinary action on the part of the university.

Zolar spoke decent Chinese, but almost no English, so he didn't know what was being said in the meeting. Michael later told me that at one point, Zolar stood up and began protesting, "We didn't even hit the Koreans. The balloons just landed next to them." Michael immediately shouted, "Be quiet, dude!" The university officials asked: "What Koreans?"

It later turned out that it wasn't the Koreans who'd ratted them out. The four had also thrown a balloon near a Chinese girl, and she'd called the police.

According to placards hanging all over the dorms, after an infraction of the rules, there was meant to be a public criticism session. If that actually happened, I wanted in. I even began writing up my criticism based on criticisms I'd seen Chinese students write about each other: "You are bad men. You have no culture, no manners. And you did something against society!" That would set them straight.

Luckily, my friends got off with a warning. The Koreans didn't follow up on their threats of revenge. And, sadly, I never got to participate in a criticism session.

I brought my teammates and training mates to the MMA gym again, and was thinking about how, when I joined the wrestling team, I'd had no formal wrestling training at all. I only had my MMA background, but yet — even on the first day, even when I was losing every sparring match — I was still difficult to take down and occasionally got takedowns and reversals. My teammates were still much better than me, but with an MMA background, which focused mostly on grappling, I was no pushover.

My Kazakh friend, Jack, who had a bit of wrestling skill, but was really an MMA fighter, wrestled Zheng Tong. The latter won, but he'd had to work really hard for the win, and Jack stuffed a lot of his takedowns. Similarly, there were guys in the MMA gym who I found it very hard to wrestle, even though they had no wrestling background. I think MMA people and maybe BJJ people do things that wrestlers don't expect, and unless a wrestler specifically trains in MMA, all of his skills won't immediately transfer.

After several rounds of sparring, my teammates took off their shirts. I suddenly remembered how hard it was to wrestle someone who's all sweaty.

During this year of learning Chinese traditional wrestling, I'd kept saying what an advantage it was, because we learned to throw from the upper body, which suited MMA. Also, because everyone else would be trying to take the legs, it was good to do something no one expected. The disadvantage, however, is that in a pro MMA fight, the fighters don't wear shirts. They get very slippery, making upper-body throws a lot harder.

The MMA coach kept encouraging me to bring my teammates to the MMA gym, to help his fighters. Every time I was in the gym, I'd only see between zero and three fighters, but he always claimed that he had ten or more, and that they'd left just before I arrived. Each time he told me to bring my friends, I reminded him to tell his ten fighters to be there, so my guys would have someone to partner with. Somehow, the ten fighters were never there, and several of the times that we went, he wasn't even there. When he was there, he always had some excuse about how the ten fighters were gone for one reason or another.

Every time we went, the lady at reception kept asking why we hadn't paid. Each night, I told her that the coach had invited us to spar with his ten fighters. She never seemed happy about this response. And, of course, we never actually met the ten fighters, or sparred with them.

That night, she finally demanded money. I called the coach and explained the situation to him. He'd always claimed to be the owner of the gym, although I'd suspected he wasn't. I put him on the phone with the receptionist — allegedly his employee — and assumed he'd just tell her we could train for free. Instead, when she handed the phone back to me, he said: "I don't want to get in the middle of this. You probably need to just give her a few hundred RMB to calm her down."

I had no intention of paying anyone anything. If they'd told us from the start that we had to pay, we wouldn't have come. Instead, they invited us, or I should say, the coach invited us, and we came on the understanding that we wouldn't have to pay. I, of course, was the only one with any money, and I wasn't going to be extorted this way. To be fair, the receptionist wasn't extorting me. The coach had probably invited us without telling her, then lacked the fortitude to tell her. This also confirmed to me that he was a huge liar and that he wasn't the gym's owner. The guy had a terrible reputation throughout China. He was known for taking photos of himself at big fight events, claiming he'd organized them. He'd take pictures of himself with famous fighters or movie stars, claiming he'd brought them to China. He'd also sold out numerous fighters, telling them they were getting an easy fight for low money or no money. But later, those fighters discovered they'd be fighting a champion and that the coach was making a lot of money from the event.

That would be the last time I'd bring my friends to his gym or set foot there alone. This came after two years of me paying membership fees, but teaching MMA/wrestling classes most of the time. Quitting that gym would save me some money and aggravation, but it also meant I wouldn't be able to use it to fill gaps in my training routine on the countless days that the on-campus gyms and training halls were inexplicably locked, or when the wrestling coach disappeared or told the team to just play soccer.

Training in China felt like constantly swimming upstream. Two months earlier, training on the wrestling team was so weak that the coach would, on a daily basis, assign someone to wrestle with me while the team goofed off. Then about six weeks earlier, when the coach announced we were training for nationals, he pushed us so hard that people were vomiting, collapsing, and getting injured, and I almost quit. But that only lasted two weeks. Then he was gone for a week on a business trip. Then the team trained with the fencing team for a week. Somewhere in there, a tai chi team came, and a high school team of some sort… Then there was one day of intense-match sparring, so important that the coach punched several wrestlers in the face, including a girl. Then I pulled out of nationals. Then the team pulled out of nationals. Then coach went on a business trip. And training evaporated again.

Then we had a guest coach and the team was only doing warm-ups and playing ball. One day, the best Greco-Roman guy on the team volunteered to wrestle with me, rather than play ball. The next day, after I did *jīběngōng*, it didn't look like anyone was going to volunteer to wrestle. The new coach didn't know me well, so he probably didn't think of choosing someone. I was too embarrassed to ask, so I just went to the weight room.

Somewhere in there, I started taking my friends to the MMA gym to get consistent training in, but now that option was out. Eighty percent of all of the wrestling I knew, I had learned on this team. I had to be grateful, but I couldn't help imagining how much more I could have learned if they'd trained consistently.

My immediate problem, however, was the reception lady who demanded money. I should have told her that I had paid the coach, so the two of them would get in a fight. But, instead, I just made it clear that I wasn't going to pay, and I wouldn't be coming back. While she probably would have been happier getting some money, she also realized that coach had caused all of this, and I suspected their relationship was about to change.

The semester was winding down, so I didn't expect training to get any better. At work, I was trying to figure out why some of my students had given me their final paper, worth 55 percent of their grade, with a cover page which was torn, ripped, jagged, on low quality paper, not A4, and printed on both sides. Then, I realized, there was a sample cover page in the book. Rather than photocopy it, some students simply tore it out and stapled it to the front of their report. This was like academic Darwinism. These students would probably fail my class, and several of their other classes, till they dropped out or were cut from the university, preventing them from similarly influencing future generations of students.

Trying to do research in the dorms was becoming impossible. Google was blocked, even using a VPN. Then I realized it was the 25th anniversary of the Tiananmen Square massacre. Whenever the government had a big meeting or some sensitive political issue arose, the Great Firewall of China would be fortified, and even with a VPN, work became nearly impossible. Each year, leading up to the Tiananmen anniversary, activists would be rounded up and arrested, and internet censorship would increase. The university offered a free sightseeing trip for foreign students on that day, presumably to prevent them from posting about Tiananmen Square, or maybe even to keep them from talking about it.

Since it was taking up to an hour to open an email, I decided to stop working and just watch some Cung Le videos. His sanda fights were epic, and it was easy to see why he was completely undefeated, even in China. He'd wrested at high school in the US, and used his wrestling to completely dominate his opponents in sanda. By the end of the first minute or so, he'd usually thrown his opponent several times. By the third round, most of them were too defeated mentally to continue fighting. I was always a little self-conscious about using too many throws. But after watching Cung Le, I hoped I could copy his style.

I needed a workout. I wanted to go to the off-campus gym, lift weights, then eat, then sleep, then work some more. It was almost 11 a.m., but I hated walking out my door at that time, because every Chinese person I met would ask me, "Have you eaten yet?" To which I'd respond, "I've eaten breakfast, but not lunch. I'll eat lunch after my workout." Often, this caused people to worry about my health. How can a human who doesn't eat lunch at 12 noon exactly survive?

Before walking out, I went and stuck my head under my roommate's desk, to test my theory that he never cleaned anything. I'd dropped a sandwich back there, three months earlier. It was still there.

The next day, at wrestling practice, we did a bit of stand up wrestling. My teammate He Yi, who was pretty tall, kept catching me in a headlock. He told me the reason wasn't just because I ducked my head on entry, which he advised against, but also because he was taller. He said it was easier for a taller guy to catch me that way. Growing up as a boxer, I always wanted to crouch down and get low. But in wrestling, I had to learn how to lower my body, without ducking my head.

After that, we practiced ground work, rolling the opponent from his belly to his back for the pin. We'd reached a point where we could do up to eight rounds of standing sparring, without collapsing. But three five-minute rounds of ground fighting left us all exhausted. Ground fighting is so much more taxing than stand up, and something we never did in Chinese wrestling.

I asked my teammates when the last day of wrestling would be. They actually said "July," which made no sense, since the official end of the semester was June 15. The following day, I went to practice and everyone was wearing normal clothes, taking photos. Apparently, the previous day had been the last day of wrestling.

A Chinese classmate asked me to go to the library with him and help him download dissertations related to the biomechanics of taekwondo. The first dissertation I found which looked likely was titled "Joint and Muscle Coordination in Taekwondo." But he shook his head. "No, I want biomechanics." The next one was something like "Ligament and Bone Alignment in Taekwondo Kicking."

"No," he said. "I want biomechanics."

I'd always wondered why my Chinese classmates needed to spend every minute of every day in the library and yet never finished writing their research. Now I knew why. They rejected every source that didn't have the exact word combination they wanted.

On the way back to the dorm, I bumped into some foreign students who asked me if I wanted to be part of a dragon boat team. They said that if I didn't want to row, I could be the drum guy. But I was thinking about the movie *Ben Hur*, and how I might be a lot happier as the whip guy.

We went out for large quantities of low-quality Chinese/Italian food. I took one look at the menu and said, "You can't get that in a restaurant in New York." They had corn and mayo pizza, tuna and mayo pizza, fruit pizza, and two ingredients that I'd never seen together in a single dish, roast beef and tuna sauce.

Back in my room, I was wondering where "polite, quiet, shy and introverted" ends and *hikikomori* begins. Apart from training and the very occasional class, my roommate hadn't left the room in weeks. There were days when he didn't even go out to eat. He just lay on his bed, alternately sleeping and looking at his tablet. It's so hard to tell if Japanese people are depressed, because at their happiest they just look calm and emotionless. The previous night, he'd lodged a protest with me about the AC. I guess that, when you never leave the room, the internal environment becomes incredibly important to you. It seemed really important to him to just lie around sweating.

Trying to buy me some alone time, the one time Michael convinced Natsuki to leave the room, he nearly got our Japanese friend arrested and kicked out of school. It now seemed Natsuki was determined not to leave the room until he flew back to Tokyo. Naturally, he planned to do that after I'd already left for the summer.

We had our last Ph.D. class for the semester and I turned in my final report. Now, I had nothing on until September, except working on my dissertation. That's what I thought, anyway. The Wu Shu Institute was still telling me that the research-proposal defense was coming up in the next few days or weeks, and that I shouldn't leave. But I was having my doubts. Originally, they'd told me that it'd be in October (or possibly "Octmember"). But then they changed it to a certain date in June. A week later, they changed it to a different date in June.

After it'd been postponed five or six times, I decided it wasn't happening until the fall semester. This hypothesis was further supported by every other student I knew, in other departments, telling me that the whole university did the proposal defense at the same time and that it was scheduled for October. I tried asking again and explaining that to the faculty and upperclassmen in the Wu Shu Institute, but they all said I was wrong. Even my advisor was insisting that it would be this term, although none of them seemed to know the exact date. And given the size of the event, forming multiple panels of professors, to hear the presentations of all of the doctoral candidates from the department, it didn't seem like the sort of thing that would sneak up on you. A lot of planning had to go into it, since some professors would be coming from elsewhere. Additionally, other universities were already winding down, and the professors were going off on holiday.

Han Hongyu called on June 9, to tell me I'd better prepare well because the proposal would be held on June 5. He didn't seem to know that that was four days earlier.

I bumped into a couple of classmates running frantically around campus, making copies of their proposal, saying the event would be the next day. The next day, some of them told me it would be the following week. Even the department officials and professors were giving me various dates that were a week out or two weeks out. Meanwhile, I was having trouble tracking most of the professors down because they'd already left for summer vacation. My classmates, somehow, were fine with this nonsense and were really stressing, trying to prepare for the proposal on these various dates. None even set a date to leave for the summer.

Since I had nothing else to do in Shanghai, I was planning to head to Cambodia for freestyle wrestling training, then Vietnam for sanda, then home for more judo.

I left the room and headed to my final sanda practice with Jiang Huaying and Ma Pei. On the wrestling team we had weight divisions, although everyone wrestled with everyone, regardless of size. Because of the weight divisions, I had several guys about my size to train with. But in sanda, the biggest guys I trained with were only about 75 to 78 kg (165 to 172 lbs). I just didn't have access to sanda guys my size. My guess is that they wouldn't kick as well or move as well as the smaller guys, but maybe they could outbox me or defend my takedowns better. One problem with finding guys my size to spar with was that, apart from real pros, a lot of guys my size were just not that tough. They were big and never got picked on or never had to defend themselves growing up. In the gym, maybe they relied on strength rather than technique, so they often weren't very good. My sanda mate, Jiang Huaying, for example, only weighed 65 kg (143 lbs), but all he ever wanted to do was spar. And he didn't care how many rounds or how big or how good the opponent was. He just loved to fight.

At the fitness gym, however, they were trying to get their biggest, most heavily-muscled trainer to spar with me, but he was terrified. I'd have liked to have seen that guy spar Jiang Huaying. I predicted Jiang Huaying would kill him, by a jumping spinning back kick to the abdomen, followed by sidekicks to the face.

One of my teammates stopped by the sanda room to talk to me. When I told him I was planning to go training in Cambodia and Vietnam. He asked "Vietnam? You mean, near Korea?" I told him, "Nothing is near Korea."

I went to the library to get a bunch of dissertations to take with me, so I could work on my research over the summer. Along the way, I bumped into Han Hongyu, who told me that I had to attend a meeting which would run from 1 p.m. to 5:30 p.m. I glanced at my phone, and the time was already 1:15 p.m. I got really upset because I was leaving the next day. I was busy, and hadn't built a four-and-a-half-hour meeting into my schedule.

Han Hongyu noticed that I was distressed and asked me what was wrong. I had to restrain myself from shouting, but I said: "If it's so important why didn't you tell me in advance? If you want me to attend meetings and functions, you just need to tell me beforehand."

His response was: "I told several people last night."

I think I broke a filling, gritting my teeth. "Yes, you told other people. But if you want me to go to a meeting, you have to tell me."

He simply couldn't understand why I couldn't drop everything to go with him to the meeting. He began negotiating: "You go to the library, and just come for the end of the meeting, from 3:30 p.m."

I agreed, but I knew it was a lie. I went to the library, shut off my phone, and did my research. Then I ate lunch, did more prep work for my trip, and went to the gym. But I went to the off-campus gym so no one would see me. I couldn't wait to get out of Shanghai and not have the specter of surprise meetings jumping out at me.

The next morning, I woke up early, grabbed my bags and bought a breakfast wrap sandwich at a convenience store. It was just awful! The wrap part tasted exactly like wax paper that had been in the microwave. On the way to the train station, I wondered why Chinese people clip their nails on the subway. It was extremely common to see people clipping away and letting the pieces fall on the floor. Once — and this is the truth — when the guy had finished with his fingernails, he took off his shoes and did his toes.

Entering the train station, I put my luggage on the X-ray conveyor, then walked to the other end and waited for it to come out. A woman behind me put her luggage in the conveyor after me. Then she walked to the other end and bumped me out of the way, so she could wait for her bag. I was tired and didn't feel like fighting, so I just waited behind her. My luggage came out first, of course, but because she'd bumped me, I couldn't get it. This gummed up the conveyor belt and she couldn't get her luggage either. Then the people waiting in line couldn't put their luggage in and they all started pushing one another. Eventually, I faked right, and when the woman went to block, I jumped left, got around her, grabbed my luggage and escaped the madness.

In China, people always wanted to get on an elevator before letting others off. The same was true for subways and trains. The best one I saw was on a flight to Cambodia. A woman tried to get into the airplane's bathroom before the occupant came out. They both got stuck in the collapsible door, and three flight attendants had to pry them out.

Subway to the train station, train to the airport, plane to Hong Kong, plane to Phnom Penh... start to finish the trip took more than ten hours. After I'd checked into my hotel in Cambodia, I checked my email, and saw an angry message from my doctoral adviser, saying: "I don't agree with your trip to Cambodia and Vietnam."

He said he was worried I wouldn't be ready for my research proposal defense in October. That at least confirmed it'd be in October, and not three weeks ago or tomorrow, as I'd been told. Actually, I'd already written it and had it edited. My proposal was about double the standard length. My advisor had told me to add a history of wrestling in Rome and Greece, so I decided to include a huge section on pankration. Those were some of the most fun sections to research and to write.

The real issue with my trip wasn't that he was worried about my proposal. It was because I was planning to go to Vietnam after Cambodia. Beijing and Hanoi had just had a major political falling-out. Anti-PRC riots in Vietnam had left at least 21 Chinese people dead. I was going to explain to my advisor that, while the US had fought a protracted war in Vietnam, leaving well over a million dead, most Vietnamese people were very pro-US and couldn't possibly hate us as much as they hated China. But something told me he'd get angry if I said that. Instead, I assured him my report was ready and that I'd added all of the parts he'd told me to. Additionally, I said that I needed more first-hand experience with freestyle wrestling and sanda, which I could only get in Cambodia and Vietnam. Finally, appealing to his sense of nationalism, I mentioned that my coaches in Vietnam had all studied in China and we were practicing and promoting Chinese martial arts.

His response was something like: "Do what you want, but if you fail your mock proposal in September, I won't admit you to the actual proposal in October, and your graduation will be delayed by one year."

I went down to the street for grilled pork and iced coffee, sat back and reflected. I had just completed the first full year of a Ph.D. program taught in Chinese. This had been a dream of mine since the first day I set foot in a foreign-language class in high school. I'd learned some shuai jiao, an art which I'd only had a very vague awareness of a year earlier. The same was true for sanda, which I'd learned even more of. I'd made a ton of friends, competed on a wrestling team, had my shoulder popped out of joint, written and presented research in Chinese, had my shoulder popped back into joint by an unlicensed chiropractor, got my job back at the university, been back to Shaolin Temple, trained in a wrestling school in Beijing, trained in Cambodia and Vietnam, learned some judo, written, spoken, been published… and experienced a Chinese university from the inside. And this was not just any university: It was a Chinese sports university.

When I was doing comparative research on American and Chinese sports training and education, I found a few articles in Western media about China's sports schools, but not a single article about the country's sports universities. And here I was, the first American Ph.D. student in that system. At work, at Shanghai University, none of my Chinese colleagues really knew what went on in a sports university. Also, not only was I in a sports university, but I was in the Wu Shu Institute, the most traditional and "most Chinese" department on campus. In many ways, this was right up there with training at Shaolin Temple as an experience that Westerners would see a truly Chinese experience, yet also one that most Chinese people had no knowledge of.

Even so, my Chinese was still broken. I couldn't just curl up in bed with a cup of hot cocoa and read a Chinese novel, like I could in German or Spanish. When I spoke, explained, presented, or taught, I frequently hit linguistic roadblocks. Sometimes, I just didn't know how to express my thoughts at a level appropriate for my age and education.

My senior, Han Hongyu, hated me, and I saw no way to remedy that. My teammates were all nice to me. My training mates, Zheng Tong, Jiang Huaying, and Ma Pei, as well as my wushu classmate Luo Yuanzhou and the academic-track student Zhang Chengfeng, had become excellent friends.

I'd experienced communism and learned propaganda slogans like, "Sport serves the work of the revolution." I'd also survived some of the most frustrating and schizophrenic scheduling known to man. The food in China was killing me, and I'd overcome what I'd feared could be a malignant tumor. And I'd learned an incredible amount about the history of Chinese and Western wrestling.

I felt lucky and blessed — but at the same time like a fraud who'd be discovered at any moment and then crash and burn. I remembered my Spanish lecturer, during my undergraduate years, telling me that, as his doctoral defense approached, he kept questioning whether he was good enough to be a Ph.D. I now understood his position. Meanwhile, this being a Ph.D. in a sports university in China, there were so many unusual hurdles to clear, some physical, some linguistic, some mental, and some intellectual. Also, I still had to get passed by my advisor, Professor Dai, which meant answering the question he'd asked me at our first meeting.

Now I had the whole summer to think about the meaning of Shaolin Kung Fu. Ironically, I'd spent the previous summer in Shaolin Temple, but hadn't come up with an answer.

Two years to go.

A Note on Names and Spelling

lmost everyone mentioned in this book is referred to by his or her real name. In a few instances, I've changed people's names, just in case they feel I've defamed or embarrassed them.

Spoken Mandarin is rendered in hanyu pinyin, as are place names, people's names, and some hard-to-translate nouns. The only exceptions are a few types of martial arts widely known in the West by another spelling, such as kung fu (hanyu pinyin: *gōngfu*).

Made in the USA
Columbia, SC
17 November 2022

71162566R00235